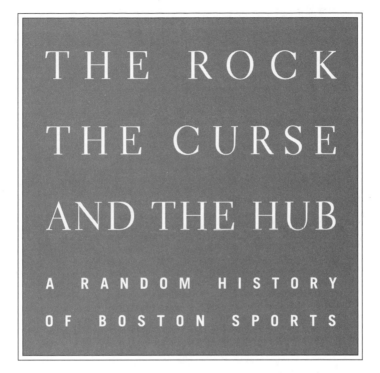

THE ROCK
THE CURSE
AND THE HUB

A RANDOM HISTORY
OF BOSTON SPORTS

Edited by Randy Roberts

HARVARD UNIVERSITY PRESS

Cambridge, Massachusetts, and London, England

2005

Publication of this book has been supported through
the generous provisions of the Maurice and
Lula Bradley Smith Memorial Fund.

Library of Congress Cataloging-in-Publication Data

The rock, the curse, and the hub : a random history of Boston sports /
edited by Randy Roberts.
p. cm.
Includes bibliographical references and index.
ISBN 0-674-01504-5 (cloth : alk. paper)
1. Sports—Massachusetts—Boston—History.
2. Sports—Social aspects—Massachusetts—Boston.
I. Roberts, Randy, 1951–

GV584.5.B6R63 2005
796'.09744'61—dc22   2004057655

To Marjie, for everything
and in memory of Mary and Ferris

CONTENTS

THE ROCK

THE CURSE

AND THE HUB

INTRODUCTION

Just fancy what mingled emotions
Would fill the Puritan heart
To learn what renown was won for his town
By the means of the manly art!
Imagine a Winthrop or Adams
In front of the bulletin board,
Each flinging his hat at the statement that
The first blood was by Sullivan scored.

This poem, written before the turn of the twentieth century by an unremembered member of the fancy, captured Boston's complex
attitude toward sports. Almost from the first there were two Bostons. There
was the official Boston, the town of cold Puritan hearts and the Brahmins in
the shadow of the State House, where sports along with any other frivolous
amusement drew grim frowns. Boston worthies passed laws against some of
these nefarious activities, trying to keep alive a special heritage, fighting

against the dying of the Puritan light. Then there was the unofficial Boston, the Boston of crowded wharves and muddy, congested streets, a bustling city of migrants and immigrants, people who arrived with their own religions, own amusements, own ideas. In John L. Sullivan, Boston's great heavyweight champion, the town discovered a force capable, at least momentarily, of upending the social order. Sullivan's popularity demonstrated Boston's love of sports, and during the next century Bostonians, high and low, developed a passionate love-hate affair with their teams and heroes, a cheering, back-slapping, damning, clothes-rending obsession.

As in every other aspect of American history, the Puritans played—perhaps assumed would be a better word—a central role. To some degree, who they were became what we as Americans are. And this fact is certainly true as regards our attitudes toward sports. Simply mentioning Puritans and sports together raises thorny questions. Maybe the whole difficulty with Puritan historiography is that their critics were on the whole much better writers than their defenders. In the mid-nineteenth century Thomas Babington Macaulay, that sober representative of Victorianism, feared that the Puritan "hated bearbaiting, not because it gave pain to the bear, but because it gave pleasure to the spectators." Two generations later, the less Victorian but equally judgmental H. L. Mencken defined Puritanism as "the haunting fear that some one, some where, may be happy." They set the tone. The Puritans have come down to us as perpetually dour killjoys, more likely than not to make a quick stop at the local magistrate's office to accuse a neighbor of practicing witchcraft before trudging off to church. That vestigial image is faintly palpable in the forbidding shadow of the Boston State House.

Defenders have labored for decades to lighten this image, with little success. But in fact the first Bostonians did not oppose sports if they served some higher purpose, applying to them much the same standard they used to evaluate everything else in their lives. The strange case of John Winthrop's hunting illustrates the point. Winthrop's problem, as historian Edmund S. Morgan so concisely captured it, was "living in this world without taking his mind off God." Walking the Puritan line was a challenging task. Winthrop was a man with "simple tastes who liked good food, good drink, and good company. He liked his wife. He liked to stroll by the river with a fouling [sic] piece and have a go at the birds . . . He liked all the things that God had given him, and he knew it was right to like them, because they were God-given. But how was one to keep from liking them too much? How love the world with moderation and God without?" After long reflection, Winthrop decided to give up hunting, for a number of reasons: it was illegal, it consumed too much time and energy, it was too dangerous and expensive, and, most telling of all, too often he got "nothinge at all towards my cost and laboure." Winthrop probably thought that if God really wanted him to shoot he would have made him a better marksman.

In the early decades of the Massachusetts Bay Colony, sports had their place only in relation to work. Sports provided relaxation, exercise, and relief from the pressing concerns of life. They served as a brief respite, a moment of regeneration that ultimately created more healthy and contented workers. Englishmen in Massachusetts Bay transplanted most of their culture, but they did not replicate the rich English traditions of play and leisure. Attitudes toward sabbath activities and the intense labor demands of life on the edge of a "wilderness" doomed many of the Old World festivals and fairs. Some forms of leisure would eventually be recreated in America, but they differed dramatically from the patterns in England. In America leisure was more suspect, requiring a more elaborate ideological justification. Sports and games had to be justified by some higher ends. In this sense play and work were similar: both identified the nature and status of the person who engaged in them. Who one was was a product of what one did and how one played. In a land and eventually a country without rigid class lines, where individuals could create and re-create themselves, work and play became tools to construct identities and fates.

With so much at stake, how one played—and mastered—the game was no trivial matter. Over the ensuing centuries, success in sports has been as crucial as success in work. It has spawned such expressions as "Winning is the only thing," "Losing is worse than death," "playing for keeps," "Nice guys finish last," and "Second place is another name for the first loser." The effect of such an ideology is to rob sports of its dimension of play. Gliding over a green field in the afternoon sun chasing a descending white ball, a joy beyond comprehension, becomes work. The purity and innocence of ballgames is lost in a sea of statistics, salary disputes, lawsuits, and the other detritus of the sports world. Illustrating this point is the title of George F. Will's 1990 bestseller on baseball: *Men at Work*. Where once professional baseball players were described as "the boys of summer," now they can only be appreciated as hard-working, clear-thinking, constantly calculating men, the sort who would be successful in any endeavor because they know the value of practice, planning, and execution. For Will, as for the founders and developers of Massachusetts Bay and America, sport is serious business. It is work.

Perhaps no term better captures America's complex attitude toward sports than "blue-collar player." The notion that "blue-collar worker" and the play principle have anything in common seems incongruous. The drudgery of hard manual labor and the fun of play occupy opposite ends of the pleasure spectrum. But are they any more incompatible than the idea behind the phrase "the game of life"? Work and play serve the same ends. And the blue-collar player scrapping for a rebound in an NBA regular-season game is not very different from a white-collar player maneuvering a leveraged buyout of a Fortune 500 corporation. As boxing promoter Don King has reminded us so often in the last three decades: "Only in America." Life may be a game, but games are serious work. Therefore, basketball players "work on their games," football players "work in the trenches," and hockey players "work the boards."

Nowhere in America have sports been taken more seriously than in Boston, where they have always been seen as serving some higher purpose. From the earliest Puritan hand-wringing about the morality of play, to the late-nineteenth- and early-twentieth-century debates about the nature of amateurism, to the mid-twentieth-century struggles for racial equality, and to the late-twentieth- and early-twenty-first-century controversies about stadium relocations and franchise shifts, Boston has been at the center of the action. And there have been so many different worlds of Boston sports. There is the ethnic Boston of boxing—Irish John L. Sullivan, Italian Rocky Marciano, and black, blind Sam Langford. There is the WASP Boston—aristocratic Eleonora Randolph Sears, innocent Francis Ouimet, and a century of Harvard-Yale games. Then there is the landscape of Boston—the twenty-six miles of the Marathon, the layout of The Country Club in Brookline, and the scullers on the Charles River. Finally, there are the structures of Boston—Harvard Stadium, Boston Garden, and Fenway Park. But above all there are the names and the legends—Speaker, Ruth, Williams, Yastrzemski, Fisk, Clemens, and Martinez; Pesky, Henry, Shore, and

Orr; Cousy, Russell, Havlicek, and Bird; "Tarzan" Brown, "Snooks" Kelley, "Killer" Kowalski, and "Spaceman" Lee.

This sports heritage is so rich that one could argue that it has defined what Boston is and, with all apologies to Henry James, what it means to be a Bostonian. In a city with traditionally deep ethnic, racial, and class divisions, sports have provided Boston with a common ground, joining people from diverse backgrounds. Celtic Pride and the Curse of the Bambino transcend skin color, ancestry, and bank accounts. They unite lifelong residents of Boston and Bostonians who have relocated to another section of the country. In fact they bind people whose only affinity to Boston is a love of the Celtics, Bruins, or Red Sox.

The essays collected here are for the Red Sox family—and anyone who is passionate about the other sports played in Boston. They are about the pain and joy associated with following and loving Boston's teams and players. All the contributors have an appreciation of Boston sports, but they are not uncritical fans. As historians they are concerned with the meaning of the games, the relationships between the sports and the city, and how sports expose class, racial, ethnic, gender, and other social concerns. They demonstrate that although we can love our teams and be passionate about our games, we can also learn from them. Their essays are like snapshots from the last century: if the players are in the foreground, Boston itself is always part of the background.

The first four pieces range over a half-century of Red Sox history. Aram Goudsouzian examines the origins of the eighty-six-year-long Curse of the Bambino, the Boston of World Series triumphs, influenza outbreaks, and labor conflicts, a time of joy and panic. William E. Leuchtenburg takes up the story of the Red Sox after Ruth's departure for the vast territory to the south of Boston. Although he finds much to grieve over during the next few decades, he ultimately challenges the conventional wisdom by mining the valuable nuggets of the period. And no nugget was more priceless than Ted Williams. Here's a devil's choice: Who in Boston would have traded the career of Ted Williams for another pennant or two? Traded the memory of that swing for a piece of fading cloth? John Demos evaluates the importance of Williams, for baseball, Boston, and himself. And then John M. Carroll reconsiders the year that Carl Yastrzemski saved the Red Sox. In 1967, while America seemed to lose itself, Yaz kept the faith.

The next three essays are united by themes of amateurism, individual excellence, and landscape. But they are separated by the threshold of pain. No events bring together the exhilaration of athletic accomplishment and the painful drudgery of hard work like long-distance running and rowing. The willingness to endure the pain and exhaustion and the ability to achieve a mind-over-matter state are prerequisites for success. David and Matthew Oshinsky review the history of the Boston Marathon, the springtime ritual that rewards the ability to put one foot in front of the other faster than all others for just over twenty-six miles. They show that almost from the first the Marathon underscored social tensions in Boston and America. David Zang focuses on the Harvard crew teams that represented America in the 1968 Olympic Games in Mexico City. The team's successes and failures similarly illuminated the social and political landscape of America. A world away from the searing pain of Marathon running and rowing is golf, a sport in which a player walks and a hired servant carries his bag. For a century country clubs were barriers that separated the haves from the have-nots, hardwood-paneled, leather-chaired places ruled by men who dedicated high-priced urban real estate to a pastoral game because they could. As James T. Campbell shows, however, Francis Ouimet's 1913 United States Open victory at The Country Club in Brookline demonstrated that class and status in Boston and America were more complex than they seemed. And that what happened on a golf course reverberated through American culture.

Most of the physical contact in these sports is incidental. And except for a clash at home plate or an aggressive slide it is not violent. In contrast, with its emphasis on marching into opponents' territory, blitzing linebackers, and throwing bombs, football's violence is planned and necessary. War metaphors aside, the history of football illuminates other aspects of America. Ronald A. Smith traces the conflict between playing like gentlemen and winning the game at turn-of-the-century Harvard. David Welky examines what it costs cities and politicians to keep the games going in turn-of-another-century Boston. In 1900 no one proposed moving Harvard to New Haven. In 2000 the same could not be said about the Patriots. If violence is intended in football, it is the sine qua non of boxing. Elliott J. Gorn suggests that the career of "the champion of all champions," John L. Sullivan, throws light on the Irish in Boston. And Russell Sullivan suggests why the only undefeated heavyweight champion, Rocky Marciano, from Brockton, never became the Italian John L. Sullivan in Boston.

The book concludes with two essays on hockey, one on basketball, and another that looks at an entire year. Stephen Hardy describes a Canadian game that captured the hearts of Bostonians and led to the construction of the Boston Garden, and Randy Roberts looks at the emergence of Bobby Orr. In time the Bruins shared the Garden with the Celtics, whose string of championships remains unmatched in professional sports. Randy Roberts tells the story of one basketball playoff series that featured the two finest big men of the 1960s. Finally, Raymond Arsenault takes us back to that *annus mirabilis* of 1986, the year when almost—*almost*—all the dreams of the Boston faithful came true.

1

All Gods Dead:
Babe Ruth and Boston, 1918–1920

Aram Goudsouzian

"The mighty shadow of Babe Ruth falls athwart Chicago tonight like a menace," proclaimed a reporter before the first game of the 1918 World Series. "He is the difference between defeat and victory." That season the star of the Boston Red Sox became a phenomenon. Besides attaining a 13–7 record and a 2.22 ERA as a starting pitcher, Ruth spent off days playing first base and the outfield. He led the league with eleven home runs and a .555 slugging percentage. Crowds marveled at his herculean drives. He broke the top-story window of a building in Cleveland, cleared stadium walls in St. Louis and Washington, and once hit four home runs in four days. "The more I see of Babe and his heroic hitting the more he seems a figure out of mythology," admired another Boston writer. "He hits like no man ever has, truly the master man of maulers." From the taverns of Boston to the trenches of France, most people figured that Ruth's bat would dominate the Chicago Cubs and the World Series.[1]

But Ruth batted only in the games that he pitched. In the series opener, he batted ninth and outdueled Jim Vaughn for a 1–0 victory. In game four he pitched a shutout into the seventh inning, setting a World Series record with 28⅓ consecutive scoreless innings, a streak he began against Brooklyn in 1916; in game four he also recorded his only hit of the series, a two-run triple that propelled the Red Sox to a 3–2 victory. In games two, three, and five, Ruth sat on the bench.[2]

The Red Sox entered game six with a chance to clinch the series. By then George Whiteman, a stocky, weatherbeaten career minor-leaguer from Texas, had already emerged as the Red Sox's unlikely hero. The left fielder had snared a variety of difficult catches and had figured in almost every Boston run. In game six, his third-inning line drive fooled Cubs right fielder Max Flack, allowing two runs to score. Then, in the eighth inning, with the Red Sox holding onto a 2–1 lead, Whiteman charged a sharp, sinking drive, never breaking stride. He lunged down with both hands, plucked the ball off his shoestrings, flipped over, landed on his head, and emerged from a somersault with the ball in his glove. It was the most spectacular play of the series, and the Fenway Park fans erupted from their pained hush with shrieks and cheers, giving Whiteman a three-minute ovation. One batter later, Whiteman left the game with a sore neck, inspiring another round of huzzahs.[3]

Ruth entered game six to replace Whiteman, but he did not get to hit. The amazing catch had broken Chicago's spirit. The Cubs never reached base again, and when Les Mann grounded out to end the ninth inning, the Red Sox won their fourth championship in seven years.[4]

The threat of Babe Ruth had shaped the series as much as Babe Ruth himself had. Chicago manager Fred Mitchell so feared Ruth that he used two left-handed pitchers for all but two innings of the series. Boston manager Ed Barrow, clinging to conventional wisdom, kept his left-handed slugger off the field. Ironically, Mitchell's strategy and Barrow's conservatism allowed the right-handed Whiteman more playing time. Thus the journeyman—not the phenomenon—became the hero.[5]

It was the last World Series without a home run. The low-scoring, bitterly contested games were hallmarks of "scientific baseball": hit-and-runs, stolen bases, dust-off pitches, drag bunts, double plays. Neither the Cubs nor the Red Sox scored more than three runs in a game, and all four Red Sox victories were achieved by one-run margins, in large part thanks to the scrappy Whiteman. "It was by far the best played series I have ever seen," a sportswriter soon reflected, and a bevy of baseball insiders echoed him.[6]

At the time, no one anticipated that this World Series marked the end of an era. Ruth, cheered by the throngs in Boston and beyond, would soon snap the fetters of scientific baseball and launch a new era in baseball history. He would captivate a sport and a city, and he would do it in a context of social and political unrest that surfaced even before the last out of the World Series.

The 1918 World Series inspired little of its usual passion or pageantry. Attendance declined from previous championships. Only 15,238 people watched game six. Most left Fenway Park without festivity or a verse of "Tessie," the trademark song of the team's unofficial fan club, known as the "Royal Rooters." Instead the fans filed out quietly to battle a gray, chilly mid-September afternoon. Bostonians seemed hesitant, reserved, unwilling to fully embrace their baseball dynasty.[7]

"Is there anyone in Boston who cannot put his finger on the reason for this?" asked Bob Dunbar, a sports columnist for the *Boston Herald and Journal*. "The one 'Go through guy,' the one 'Real, red-hot, red-blooded fan,' was not in the bleachers this year. He's over there in Picardy, down in Lorraine, in front of the Aisne, fighting the battles for our little children, for our wives, our sweethearts and for us. The real man, forever and anon, is the soul of any enterprise, of any audience. When he is absent, then things fall flat and there is no twang to what we formerly thought were our manly national sports and pastimes."[8]

Dunbar was referring, of course, to the Great War. The United States had declared war in April 1917, but not until 1918 did over one million "doughboys" pour into France, giving the Allies a crucial boost in morale and manpower. That summer the American Expeditionary Forces made their first important contributions, and on September 12—one day after the Red Sox won the World Series—General John Pershing led the first all-American offensive of the war, driving the Germans back to the Hindenburg Line, their final line of resistance.[9]

As Dunbar's observations illustrated, the Great War had also affected the American spirit. In fact it had reoriented American society. By September 1918 the federal government was shaping the lives of its citizens as never before. Almost three million men entered the armed forces under the Selective Service Act. As the Food Administration pleaded for "Meatless Mondays" and "Wheatless Wednesdays," the Committee of Public Information produced unceasing streams of propaganda. The war also exposed an ugly underbelly of xenophobia and vigilantism: the Espionage and Sedition Acts violated individual liberties, and the American Protective League launched government-sanctioned "slacker raids," rounding up draft-age men from restaurants, street corners, nickelodeons, and ballparks.[10]

War mobilization altered professional baseball, too. Playing on the sport's mythology as a seedbed of democracy—and desperate to avoid the "slacker" label—baseball officials and owners encouraged enlistment at their parks, bought Liberty Bonds, and sent baseball equipment to soldiers. Players joined the military both before and during the 1918 season, and others joined teams representing war industries. In July Secretary of War Newton Baker ruled that baseball players were subject to the "Work or Fight" order, which required men aged twenty-one to thirty-one either to enlist or to find a war-related occupation. American League president Ban Johnson announced the immediate closing of all parks until war's end. Yet a coterie of owners, including Harry Frazee of the Red Sox, defied Johnson and negotiated to extend the regular season through Labor Day weekend. Thus the Red Sox won the championship about one month before the season's usual end.[11]

Even during the World Series, "the effect of the war was everywhere," as the Boston Globe reported after game one in Chicago. "There was no cheering during the contest, nor was there anything like the usual umpire baiting." The day's loudest roars came after the band played the "Star Spangled Banner." (From this episode sprang the tradition of playing the national anthem at American sporting events.) Game four, the first one at Fenway Park, featured eighty-seven soldiers recently arrived from France. Clad in crisp blue or khaki uniforms—some hobbling on crutches, others missing arms—the wounded soldiers embodied the sacrifices of war.[12]

By September 1918 almost all Boston embraced the war effort. As the headquarters for the huge 26th Division (the "Yankee Division," composed of New England's National Guard units), the city was an epicenter of patriotic fervor. Early in the month a "Win the War for Freedom" parade made its way through city streets, a huge crowd supported the French during a Faneuil Hall ceremony honoring Lafayette, and 25,000 well-wishers cheered a day of competition between soldiers and sailors at Harvard Stadium. On September 12, in response to a national proclamation by President Woodrow Wilson, more than 100,000 Bostonians registered for the draft.[13]

Yet the Great War had also cleaved a rift on the home front. With wartime labor at a premium, workers realized their growing power, and the number of strikes escalated along with American intervention. When the World Series came to Boston, for example, Mayor Andrew Peters was facing a strike threat by the city's firemen.[14]

Baseball suffered from kindred conflicts between capital and labor. At the World Series, before game four, players from both squads arranged a meeting with baseball's three-man National Commission, to take place before game five. The players had expected World Series shares of $2,000 for the winners and $1,400 for the losers. In fact the winners received about $1,100—not only because of low attendance and reduced admission prices, which were results of the Great War, but also because the National Commission had paid shares to the second-, third-, and fourth-place teams in each league. Game five was scheduled to begin at 2:30. By game time, however, the only ones in uniform were Red Sox first baseman Stuffy McInnis and the batboy.[15]

Everyone else awaited negotiations with the National Commission, which had dismissed previous overtures from the players. Ban Johnson, who dominated the commission, did not arrive for the meeting until 2:25, following a long session at a Copley Square bar. After Johnson blubbered through a drunken, maudlin, self-serving plea to player representative Harry Hooper, the players abandoned any hope of negotiation. They retreated into a locker room to discuss their options.[16]

Outside, the fans waited. As mounted police patrolled the field, the band played "Over There," "Keep the Home Fires Burning," and "Tessie." Again the wounded soldiers arrived, and again the fans roared their approval. But the crowd grew restless. Led by Hooper, the players realized the damage that they might inflict upon their sport, and they voted to play under protest. As they dressed, John "Honey Fitz" Fitzgerald, a Royal Rooter and former Boston mayor, read a statement through a megaphone. The teams did not wish "to disappoint the fans, particularly those wounded boys who have been fighting over there." After the band played "Sweet Adeline" in honor of the Irish politician, the players emerged. Many cheered. Others booed. Some cried, "Bolsheviki!"[17]

These political rifts only widened in the next months. That autumn, an era ended—for baseball, for Boston, for the world. The Great War ended, and Americans looked inward. They saw a society in disarray, especially in Boston. The city soon suffered an onslaught of calamities that crumbled the foundation of order, a bruising train of pestilence, strikes, riots, and raids.

First came the pestilence. On August 27, 1918, 8 cases of "Spanish influenza" were reported on Commonwealth Pier, Boston's overcrowded way station for war-bound sailors. The next day 58 more cases arose. Within two weeks about 2,000 sailors had contracted the disease. By then Boston City Hospital had reported the first civilian casualty, and influenza was decimating the overcrowded Fort Devens in nearby Ayer. Five to 10 percent of those who contracted this virulent strain died, either from influenza or from pneumonia. Death was grotesque: victims turned the color of eggplant, suffocating as gelatinous fluid filled their lungs and frothed out their noses.[18]

In Boston, 35 people died on September 16, and another 152 over the next four days. The fatalities peaked at 206 on October 1. The large public gatherings of early September—the sundry war parades and rallies, the draft registration drive of September 12, the three World Series games at Fenway Park—had opened the floodgates for infection. From the last week of September through mid-October the city closed all schools, theaters, dance halls, and saloons. Churches canceled services. Retailers restricted hours. Had the Great War not forced professional baseball to finish early, the World Series might have been canceled, too.[19]

The virus was part of a worldwide epidemic that simultaneously wreaked havoc in Brest, France, and Freetown, Sierra Leone. By early October, influenza waned in Boston but persisted in Lawrence, New Bedford, and Worcester. It also leapt across the United States, devastating some cities and bypassing others, reaching as far as Georgia and California. In Europe, influenza exacerbated the miseries of the front. An American soldier or sailor was almost as likely to die from the flu as from a German bullet. The cure was a mystery, despite a November experiment at the Navy's training station on Deer Island in Boston Harbor, where scientists tested theories of disease transmission on sixty-two prisoners, who risked their lives in exchange for pardons.[20]

Harry Frazee contracted influenza, but he recovered after two days of bed rest and soon returned to his favorite pastime: making himself rich and famous. This consummate entrepreneur of entertainment had won his fortune in the theater, producing popular farces for Broadway and the tent circuit. He had also helped promote the 1915 title bout between Jack Johnson and Jess Willard. Convivial, fast-talking, and handsome in a well-fed sort of way, the thirty-eight-year-old Frazee reveled in publicity. He considered baseball just another form of popular spectacle, and when he bought the Red Sox in 1916, he adhered to the same headline-grabbing tactics that had made him a millionaire. Before the 1918 season, while other owners were worrying about the war, Frazee signed Joe Bush, Wally Schang, Amos Strunk, Dave Shean, and Stuffy McInnis, all key contributors for the World Series champions.[21]

But the shortened season and mediocre gate receipts ensured that Frazee lost money in 1918. After the World Series he proposed taking the clubs to the European front for exhibitions, but Ban Johnson nixed the idea. Most figured, as one newspaper did, that baseball was dead "until universal peace shall have been imposed upon the world and the unspeakable Hun put down where he belongs." Fenway Park locked its gates. Both the American and National Leagues planned to cease operations after their winter meetings. Red Sox ace Carl Mays and World Series hero George Whiteman looked into joining the aviation corps. Babe Ruth took an offer from Bethlehem Steel, but not before boosting his income as a celebrity starter for a motorcycle race, a referee for a boxing match, and a pitcher for exhibition games in Connecticut.[22]

Joe Bush, Wally Schang, Wally Mayer, and Amos Strunk played on a barnstorming squad that advertised itself as the "Red Sox," a sin for which the National Commission disciplined them in early October. The commission further deprived the entire team of the emblems traditionally awarded baseball's champions, as National League president John Heydler later explained, "owing to the disgraceful actions of the players in the strike during the Series."[23]

From the perspective of the National Committee, the players' quests for some economic leverage stank of "slackerism." Baseball's leaders much preferred publicity trumpeting baseball as a bulwark of American values, such as the paeans from the magazine *Baseball*. "Baseball will win the war!" exclaimed one scribe. The sport taught decisiveness, teamwork, and fair play—virtues absent in the kaiser, who was a "bum sport." Reports reached stateside that baseball cured the soldiers' boredom, fostered fraternity among Allied troops, and even taught French soldiers to throw grenades farther. Stars such as Ty Cobb and Christy Mathewson traded in team uniforms for blue or khaki. The accounts suggested that baseball would endure through the struggle.[24]

Then came the Armistice of November 11, precipitating an awe-inspiring display in Boston. By 4:30 A.M., a throng of Italian immigrants had marched from the North End to City Hall, bearing flags and clanging tin pans. Fire alarms, church bells, and whistles greeted dawn. Masses choked the city streets as war industry workers declared an impromptu holiday. Some pranksters raided a stock of talcum powder and showered Tremont Street with white dust, lending downtown a surreal ambience and a faint aroma of lilacs. Every available policeman was on duty, and liquor stores and bars were ordered closed, so the celebration on the eleventh, as well as the following day's parade, remained orderly. "The city is yours," proclaimed Mayor Peters to the people. "Celebrate and let Berlin know of your admiration for democracy."[25]

The surprising armistice meant that baseball would return in 1919. Before a single pitch, however, the game's chief rivalry had thickened. Harry Frazee unilaterally asked William Howard Taft to become a "one-man national commission" who outranked the league presidents. The Red Sox owner had no authority to make the request, which openly challenged Ban Johnson's power. Frazee disingenuously professed that "if William Howard Taft is big enough man to be President of the United States, a judge of the Supreme Court and all that," then "I can't understand why every man who has a nickel in baseball is not sitting up nights figuring how to get Mr. Taft into the national game."[26]

When the American League meetings began on December 12, the enmity between Frazee and Johnson swelled. In closed-door sessions, with New York's Jacob Ruppert and Chicago's Charles Comiskey as his allies, Frazee lambasted Johnson's handling of the war-shortened season, his embarrassing response to the World Series strike threat, and his proposal to shorten the 1919 season to 140 games. Johnson countered by accusing Frazee of permitting gambling at Fenway Park. Though a spurious charge, the defense-by-attack worked. Johnson still had the loyalty of the other five

American League owners, and his resolution for the abbreviated season passed. But Frazee was chiseling away at Johnson's reputation.[27]

Frazee continued his flamboyant machinations by negotiating a controversial trade. He was still in debt to Joe Lannin, the previous Red Sox owner, and the club had a glut of talent as players returned from France. Moreover, all owners had agreed to cut rosters from twenty-five to twenty-one players. So Frazee traded Duffy Lewis, Ernie Shore, and Dutch Leonard to the New York Yankees for lesser players and some money. He then dumped more players in a three-way trade that obtained Detroit infielder Oscar Vitt. He even announced his willingness the sell the Red Sox, albeit at an outrageous price.[28]

Still, Frazee kept finagling for players and headlines. In two separate negotiations, he unsuccessfully sought a left-handed pitcher and a slugging outfielder. He further dealt with the contracts of his own players, whose only leverage was unpaid holdouts. Many players stared down Frazee through the winter, refusing to sign contracts. But almost all had blinked by March 18, when the team's steamer departed New York for spring training in Florida. Babe Ruth kept staring.[29]

Season or off-season, Ruth inspired fascination. He had amassed sterling pitching credentials since joining the Red Sox in 1914. By September 1918 the southpaw was 80–41, and he owned a reputation for clutch pitching in the World Series. But his bat won him greater fame. Early in his career, he batted infrequently and at the bottom of the order. Unshackled of pressure or responsibility, he developed a long, violent, uppercut swing designed to hit home runs, a rarity in the "dead ball" era. The swing matched his personality. A massive libertine with a dark rounded face and puffed-out torso, Ruth emerged from a poor, unstructured childhood with an appetite for drinking binges, epicurean gorges, sexual romps, and high-arcing, crowd-pleasing home runs.[30]

Throughout the winter, the press had debated his greatest worth to the Red Sox. As the *Boston Post* argued that Ruth was a more valuable pitcher, the *Sporting News* called the not-yet-twenty-five-year-old "the greatest slugger who ever lived." Throughout February the *Boston Herald* ran an almost-daily feature called "Where I'd Play Babe Ruth." Managers, owners, players, and even the Middlesex County district attorney weighed in. The series "set the fans talking," according to Bob Dunbar, and even "started many a good-natured argument." Ruth, who wrote the penultimate installment, wanted to play left field every game. Manager Ed Barrow, who wrote the final one, declared that Ruth would be a starting pitcher and pinch hitter.[31]

Meanwhile, using an obvious bargaining chip, Ruth was threatening to become a professional boxer. He even punched a bag a few times. Ruth took his case to reporters, chumming around with them on the golf course or in the *Herald* offices, and the press reported every detail of his saga. Into early February, neither Ruth nor Frazee appeared anxious about the stand-off. Frazee popped into town only during breaks from his road shows, and Ruth and Barrow missed each other by minutes one day at Fenway Park. By late February, however, Red Sox management seemed worried. Ruth demanded $15,000 for one year or $30,000 for three. Frazee offered $8,500 for one year or $25,000 for three. Neither side budged. The *Herald* urged Frazee to "get his wiggle on."[32]

On March 15 Frazee "wiggled" by announcing that he would trade Ruth. The proclamation may have been typical Frazee bluster, but one rumor had Ruth exchanged for Washington pitcher Walter Johnson. One fan professed disbelief, citing the star's skills and versatility. "Is he not," the man added, "the greatest attraction now in the baseball world, as popular abroad as at home? Does anyone leave the ballpark, no matter what the score, if there is a chance of Babe busting up the game?" When the Red Sox sailed for Florida, absent Ruth, reporters fretted. Cartoonists mocked the impasse, picturing Ruth both as a barrister and as a baby. Ruth himself took to print, defending himself on the pages of the *Herald*. Finally Ruth met Frazee in New York. They compromised on a three-year, $27,000 contract, and Ruth rushed to Tampa to meet his teammates.[33]

Ruth's holdout was just one high-profile instance of New England's labor trouble in early 1919. The cost of living had doubled since 1914, and after the armistice, the reins on labor agitation had further slackened. In January more than 100 laid-off truck drivers and freight handlers marched upon the State House and demanded an audience with Governor Calvin Coolidge. In February tens of thousands of textile workers in Lawrence disavowed their union and demanded an eight-hour day without pay reduction. Their strike spread to New Bedford, Fall River, and other mill cities. On April 7 strikers detonated a crude bomb in Lawrence's "lower end," precipitating a firefight with the police. The workers won their demands after ten weeks.

Just as the textile strike ended, however, New England's telephone operators walked off the job, crippling the economy. Before they returned to
work one week later, Boston mayor Andrew Peters had reported to Congress
on unrest among the citizenry, who could make emergency calls only
through volunteer operators.[34]

The middle class feared a crumbling of social order. The Bolshevik Revolution of 1917 had overthrown capitalism in Russia and weakened the Allied
war effort. Abhorring a similar upheaval on their own shores, management
and political authorities smeared "Red" over any labor agitation. "The trouble in Lawrence is not a strike," said U.S. Commissioner of Immigration
Henry Skeffington. "It's a mob." A citizens' committee labeled the textile
strike "a movement founded in Bolshevism."[35]

The committee's anxiety reflected not only the genuine disaffection of
many workers, but also the changing complexion of Boston and its neighbors. Most of the Lawrence strikers were eastern European immigrants.
Seventy-three percent of Bostonians were either first- or second-generation
Americans, and about one-third of the city's population lived below the poverty line. Native-born Yankees fretted that this foreign influx, carrying the
germs of radicalism, would infect their civilization. "Bolshevism Is Really
Anti-Christ," read an *Evening Transcript* headline. A *Boston Herald* cartoon
titled "When the Bolsheviki Invade Baseball" depicted heavily bearded
men in baseball uniforms shooting each other and tossing bombs.[36]

But idealism survived. On February 24 President Woodrow Wilson
landed in Boston upon his return from the first stage of the Paris Peace
Conference. The city saluted him. One thousand soldiers, bayonets fixed,
lined the procession route from Commonwealth Pier to Copley Square.
National emblems and Allied flags decorated the streets. Twenty thousand
people, waving hats and handkerchiefs, cheered Wilson as he waved from
an open car and entered his hotel. That afternoon at Mechanics Hall the
president celebrated a new age, when the nations of the world would "understand one another" and "unite every moral fiber and physical strength to
see that right shall prevail." He touted "peace without victory" and a League
of Nations.[37]

Alas, soon after returning to Paris in March, Wilson suffered a physical
breakdown, and the Allies eventually levied stiff reparations upon the Germans. At home, Republican criticisms of Wilson's precious League of Nations were intensifying. The liberal American optimism for a new world

order was eroding just as the country's labor force was rumbling with disenchantment.[38]

Bostonians had two consolations: their soldiers were coming home, and Babe Ruth was reinventing baseball right before their eyes.

Ruth strutted into the team's Tampa hotel on March 21, smiling around a big black cigar. His teammates cheered him, and heads swiveled wherever Ruth passed. He owned center stage. On the first day of batting practice, he took only huge, from-the-hips swings and splintered two bats. He then captained to victory a squad of reserves (nicknamed "Babe's Busters") in a three-game series against the Red Sox regulars. In the first exhibition, against the New York Giants on April 4, Ruth hit a nearly unfathomable 579-foot home run.[39]

The Red Sox and Giants scrimmaged through early April, touring from Florida to South Carolina to Virginia, annoying each other with brushbacks, beanballs, and brawls. The Red Sox then relaxed by tromping some college and semipro teams around Richmond before heading to Baltimore for an exhibition. Everywhere he went, Ruth attracted crowds. In Charleston Ruth swung so hard that he turned his ankle. In Baltimore he hit four home runs and walked twice in six at-bats. He boasted that he would shatter all existing home-run records, even as Ed Barrow continued to insist that during the season Ruth would pitch and pinch-hit. The manager did, however, play Ruth in left field on opening day against the New York Yankees. Ruth hit a first-inning home run. The Red Sox won four of their first five games in New York and Washington. In Boston, anticipation mounted for the return of the world champions and their massive slugger.[40]

But the real triumphant homecoming belonged to the 26th Division. On April 25, in the largest public gathering in Boston history, 20,000 doughboys marched past the State House, reviewed by New England's six governors and assorted dignitaries. The soldiers then marched down Park Street, circled Boston Common, and paraded up Commonwealth Avenue. The deafening roars of nearly a million people greeted the heroes of Aisne-Marne, St. Mihiel, and Meuse-Argonne. The aristocrats along the elite thoroughfare shared their front stoops, windows, and patriotism with the masses. The *Evening Transcript* noted that "Boston, at least, seems to be safe for democracy."[41]

Six days later, Boston seemed neither safe nor democratic. The morning of May Day, the newspapers reported a thwarted anarchist plot to mail bombs to twenty-two representatives of American capitalism, including J. P. Morgan, Oliver Wendell Holmes, and Boston industrialist William Wood. With the city already on edge, the Lettish Socialist Workmen's Society staged a "Red Flag" parade in Roxbury despite lacking a permit. After a rally at the Dudley Street Opera House, about 1,500 radicals—most from eastern Europe, and half of them women—marched to the corner of War- ren and Waverly Streets, where police confronted them. A melee erupted. Stones flew through the air, and ice picks and clubs swung above the crowds. The police scattered the mob with gunshots. Meanwhile officers poured into the Dudley Square and Roxbury Crossing stations, welcoming help from vigilante soldiers and sailors. They destroyed the socialist head- quarters on Winona Street. The day's casualties included two shot police- man, one shot civilian, a stabbed officer, and dozens more injured. Police arrested 113 radicals.[42]

That same day, the Red Sox opened at Fenway Park against the New York Yankees. With Governor Coolidge throwing out the first ball, wounded sol- diers cheering, and the 101st Infantry band playing, the pregame ceremony was far removed from Roxbury's grisly struggle between reactionaries and radicals. Baseball forged unique myths: individual glory through team coop- eration, timeless play framed by scientific order, rural space within urban contexts. These values offered some normalcy after the Great War. "It is characteristic, perhaps, of the American spirit," noted the *Evening Tran- script* upon interviewing doughboys on Boston Common, "that the chief topic of conversation among this group of veterans was baseball and the chances of the various 'big league' teams this year." As Coolidge hoisted Old Glory atop Fenway, baseball symbolized an exceptional, enduring de- mocracy.[43]

When the game began, Ruth jogged out to left field—a notable event, since Barrow had suspended him for the previous game. In Washington, the manager, suspicious of Ruth's overindulgent lifestyle, had entered his star's hotel room at 6:00 A.M. and found him underneath his covers, holding a lit pipe. Barrow pulled off the covers, found Ruth fully dressed, and stormed out of the room. In the locker room the next day, Ruth challenged his manager: "If you ever come into my room like that again, you son of a bitch, I'll punch you right in the nose." Barrow—an intense, pugnacious, sternly moralistic man—sent everyone else outside the room. Now Ruth sulked away. The incident illustrated Ruth's tendencies toward indulgences of pleasure and emotions of the moment, traits of a man-child reared with little adult supervision. Ruth had returned to Barrow's good graces by the home opener. For the rest of the season, when he arrived at the hotel, he left notes for Barrow. Many began, "Dear Eddie," which no one else called him.[44]

The Red Sox lost that first game in Fenway, and they dropped three of four against the Yankees. They kept slumping through May, and even Ruth was faltering at bat. In a 1–0 loss to Chicago on May 14, Ruth struck out twice, and both times boos filled Fenway. In late May, Boston fell below .500. The Sox lost ten times on a twelve-game road trip; the *Sporting News* likened the excursion to Napoleon's invasion of Russia. After one month, the world champions were in sixth place.[45]

Ruth pitched well, going 4–0 in May, and he batted inconsistently, averaging well below .300 with only three home runs. But his hitting generated more glamor. The single consolation from the disastrous road trip was a grand slam by Ruth against St. Louis. In June, as Ruth improved at the plate, press attention grew. The *Herald* devoted three paragraphs of flowery prose to a June 18 blast. A *Globe* columnist suggested marking Ruth's home runs with white crosses in the bleachers. Fenway gamblers set odds on his clearing the fences for each at-bat. Through June those odds got shorter, from 50:1 to 40:1 to 35:1. On June 23 he hit his seventh home run. By then his batting average had climbed among the league leaders, and he was playing left field more frequently. Yet the Red Sox remained mired in sixth place, with a record of 22–27.[46]

The team's decline surprised its supporters. The media first expected the Red Sox to reverse their slump, but injuries to Joe Bush, Herb Pennock, and Sam Jones devastated the pitching staff, and the hitting was feeble. In 1918 they had possessed a solid pitching rotation, excellent defense, timely hitting, and a resolve to edge out close games. In 1919 they lacked all that. Moreover, Ruth was exhausted. After a June 25 doubleheader against Washington, during which he pitched a complete-game loss in the opener and played left field in the nightcap, Ruth rendered an ultimatum: he would pitch or play left field, but not both. Barrow removed him from the rotation. The decision was about business as much as about baseball. With no hope for a pennant, the team's only attraction was a Babe Ruth home run.[47]

The Red Sox hit the nadir when Carl Mays quit. The ornery submarine pitcher had been chafing at his lack of run support; by early July he had the league's fourth-best ERA, but he was only 5–11. He had already fired a baseball at a jeering spectator and refused to pay the fine. On July 13 in Chicago, catcher Wally Schang tried to throw out a base stealer, and the ball hit Mays in the head. Mays stalked off, left the stadium, left Chicago, and demanded a trade. It was a brazen, petulant display. Yet the Red Sox did not suspend him. With every pennant contender besieging him with trade offers, Frazee decided to relieve some more debts. He sold Mays to the Yankees for two average players and $40,000.[48]

Frazee not only helped the Yankees, but also resumed his challenge to Ban Johnson's authority. Johnson refused to sanction the trade, since Boston should have upheld the game's integrity by punishing Mays. Instead Johnson personally suspended Mays. In response, Yankee owners Jacob Ruppert and Tillinghast Huston obtained an injunction, and by August 9 Mays was pitching for New York. The Yankee owners again allied with owners of the Red Sox and White Sox. At an August 14 meeting of the American League Board of Directors, Ruppert, Frazee, and Charles Comiskey passed a resolution impugning Johnson. Eventually the New York State Supreme Court overturned the suspension and further damaged Johnson's reputation. The rift between the longtime czar of the American League and the cabal of defiant owners widened even further.[49]

Meanwhile the Red Sox stayed below .500. By rewarding Mays for his cheekiness, Frazee had diminished his players' morale and sullied his team's reputation. "As champions last year, they were the pride and joy of the community," wrote the *Evening Transcript* in late July. "But as near tail-enders in this year's pennant race, they have no friends."[50]

Actually, Fenway Park was just starting to fill up again. The trend had nothing to do with wins and losses, and everything to do with Babe Ruth. From late June until season's end—with just a brief return to pitching purgatory after the Mays trade—Ruth concentrated on hitting. And as his home runs surged, so too did public fascination.

Ruth hit a grand slam against the Yankees on June 30, and a newspaper called him "the mighty smiter." After two home runs on July 5 against Philadelphia, he was "the gifted weaver of homeric whangs." A July 24 home run gave the Red Sox a 4–3 win over the Yankees and inspired "yelling and cheering with an abandon that would have made a band of Indians doing a war dance look like pantomime performers." He hit two home runs in one game against Cleveland on July 18; the second was a ninth-inning grand slam that won the game 8–7, a feat so spectacular that the Cleveland fans cheered. In Detroit on July 21 his blast cleared a distant right-field wall, a first-time occasion at Navin Field. Back in Detroit on August 23, he cleared the bleachers with another grand slam. The next day he hit two more home runs. He hit another the following day. Each blast merited headlines, often in larger type than that describing who won the game. In mid-August he surpassed Socks Seybold's American League record with his seventeenth home run. Red Sox fans giddily eyed Buck Freeman's major-league record of twenty-five home runs.[51]

"The Colossus of Clouters" was Boston's main sports story even when he hit no home runs. Ruth's long foul balls, or his towering fly balls that confused fielders and landed fair, earned detailed descriptions in the newspapers. On August 11, with the bases loaded in the seventh inning of a scoreless game, St. Louis intentionally walked him; the Red Sox won 1–0. In Cleveland on July 19, he struck out in the ninth inning with men on base, and the *Boston Globe* alluded to the poem "Casey at the Bat." More often, journalists incorporated references to the popular song "Along Came Ruth." Bob Dunbar called him "far and away the greatest of all drawing cards in the game today"—even greater than Detroit's Ty Cobb, the game's avatar of scientific baseball.[52]

A Babe Ruth home run offered the direct, emotional satisfaction of a spectacular deed, a visceral pleasure untainted by intellect or repression. It was baseball's equivalent to boxing's knockout. (When Ruth hit two home runs the day after a Jack Dempsey title bout, a *Herald* headline likened the heavyweight heroes: "Ruth Dempseys Twice.") Twenty-two thousand watched the Red Sox play in Chicago on July 13. On July 30, 21,000 attended a Fenway Park doubleheader against Detroit—a duel between Cobb (baseball's past) and Ruth (baseball's future). On the first Saturday of August, 31,500 watched the Red Sox and White Sox split two games. It was the largest Fenway crowd since 1914, and a remarkable turnout for a sixth-place team.[53]

Ruth had tapped a vein of American popular culture. Baseball's traditional heroes—men as different as the upright Christy Mathewson and the ornery Ty Cobb—had been celebrated for their intelligence, discipline, and adherence to the team ethic. These were key qualities in the era of scientific baseball, when runs were at a premium. Ruth instead personified an emergent trend, the twentieth-century renunciation of Victorian values for consumerism, entertainment, and pleasures of the moment. He had more in common with Hollywood heroes such as the swashbuckling Douglas Fairbanks—who, not coincidentally, won fame as Hollywood started promoting its actors as "stars." No less than Fairbanks, Ruth was becoming a celebrity, an outsized personality who performed remarkable deeds.[54]

Ruth's celebrity, moreover, came wrapped in civic pride. In the July 1919 issue of *The Dial*, Morris Cohen likened baseball to a religion. Like a church service, the game freed its devotees from worldly concerns and united them with a transcendent spirit. "Is there any other experience in modern life in which multitudes of men so completely and intensely lose their individual selves in the larger life which they call their city?" asked Cohen. In Boston, the fans united not over the team's wins and losses, but over the home runs and strikeouts of Babe Ruth.[55]

Baseball was providing a security blanket of popular culture and patriotism, smothering anxieties about social disintegration. That summer, labor disputes were ravaging the American ideal of a classless society. Boston suffered an inordinate number of strikes. Fishermen and dockworkers struck throughout July. The Cigarmakers Union halted production at numerous Boston factories. The Allied Shoe Workers forced the closing of a Jamaica Plain factory. Building trades employees won a pay increase after a two-month work hiatus. Boston's elevated railway workers struck in mid-July, causing four days of transportation snafus. By year's end, hundreds of Boston occupations had struck, including photograph engravers, actors, meat cutters, fashion models, and the scrubwomen at the State House.[56]

National and international crises heightened the sense of anarchy. Seattle had already had a general strike that winter. Railroad, coal, and steel strikes plagued the country that summer. Race riots devastated Chicago in late July and early August. Communists maintained power in Russia, and Americans feared Bolshevik masterminds behind their own upheavals. Boston had a particularly bizarre display of anticommunism at, of all things, a Chamber of Commerce picnic. In a parody of a Bolshevik deportation, 300 "bewhiskered" Chamber employees marched to Rowe's Wharf, escorted by armed "Finnish White Guards." On the ferry, they threatened to throw capitalist travelers overboard. Upon landing in Nantasket, they maintained their farce by playing a baseball game between the "Lenines" and the "Trotzkies." Both teams won prizes, so as to avoid "anarchistic methods of reprisal."[57]

Adding yet another strain upon the social fabric, the Eighteenth Amendment, ratified that winter, prohibited the "manufacture, sale, or transportation of intoxicating liquors." In Boston, police forced all bars to close on July 1. After one week, however, authorities did allow the temporary sale of 2¾ percent beer and ale. Prohibition exacerbated the resentment of the blue-collar workers who populated most of the city's saloons.[58]

These tensions of class warfare and tribal hostility heated Boston politics, finally boiling over during the Boston Police Strike. The rivalry between Yankee business interests and ethnic working classes defined the city's political life; recent mayors John "Honey Fitz" Fitzgerald and James Curley had won elections after bombastic declarations of Brahmin prejudice and Irish pride. But in Massachusetts, the governor appointed the city's police commissioner. The mayor, who had no control over police patronage, typically appropriated paltry budgets for law enforcement. Boston police thus endured low pay, long hours, and dilapidated stations. In August 1919 they voted to affiliate with the American Federation of Labor.[59]

A triumvirate of Yankee authorities responded, each with his own particular brand of mismanagement. Police Commissioner Edwin Curtis was a gruff autocrat wholly unsuited to negotiation. He insisted upon discharging those who affiliated with the union. Mayor Andrew Peters kept vacationing in Maine, even as Curtis brought the leading policemen to trial in late August. (The mayor preferred golf, yachting, and ether-induced sexual hijinks with a thirteen-year-old cousin named Starr Faithfull.) When Peters finally returned, he only appointed a committee headed by James Jackson Storrow. Meanwhile, Governor Calvin Coolidge held to cautious and reticent form, refusing to intervene even after Curtis requested help. Thus on September 8 Curtis ignored the compromise proposals of the Storrow Committee, adhered to his misguided principles, and suspended nineteen officers. The next morning, most Boston policemen walked off the job.[60]

The first inkling of anarchy arrived early, when a South Boston mob pelted striking officers with mud, stones, eggs, and tomatoes. Police, though part of the Irish working class, represented authority; the strike gave the destitute and disenchanted a chance to flout that authority. Craps games broke out all over Boston Common. Tires were stolen, wallets taken, women debauched. On Tremont and Washington Streets, mobs smashed plate glass windows and stole shoes, hardware, jewelry, and sporting goods. The looting spread to the West End, South End, Back Bay, South Boston, Brighton, and Roxbury. City Hospital treated wounds from gunshots, stabbings, and broken glass. "This Is Not Nevsky Prospect, Petrograd, but Tremont Street, Opposite Boston Common," ran an incredulous headline above reports of ravaged city streets patrolled by violent mobs.[61]

After a night of mayhem, Mayor Peters usurped command. State Guard units finally started arriving in the city. Until then, a volunteer force of mostly middle-class Protestants strove to keep order, arousing particular acrimony. On September 10 a mob of 5,000 blocked up Scollay Square, the downtown district of bordellos, tattoo parlors, and saloons. They attacked a guard unit of Harvard students. A National Guard cavalry outfit saved the college boys just in time, and guard units regulated the city by evening. Some dice games persisted on the Common, but by September 11 the mayhem had dwindled. At least eight had died, twenty-one had been wounded, and the damage ran to hundreds of thousands of dollars.[62]

The Boston Police Strike earned national attention. Although the police sought to join the AFL—an established organization that renounced radicalism—many people feared an ensuing general strike. The court of public opinion rendered a judgment against the officers. Ironically, the chief beneficiary was Governor Coolidge, who had refused to intervene throughout the crisis. On September 12, just as the national media focused on Boston, he restored Curtis's authority over the peacekeeping forces. The striking officers never regained their jobs, and Coolidge famously declared, "There is no right to strike against the public safety by anybody, anywhere, any time." The social fabric seemed in tatters, but Coolidge represented law and order. He won the 1920 Republican nomination for vice-president, and when Warren G. Harding died in 1923, he became president.[63]

Coolidge was not the only Bostonian with a rising profile; Babe Ruth was gathering admirers, too. In fact, during the two worst days of the Police Strike, thousands of fans had milled about Kenmore Square despite the city's turmoil, and despite the probability that heavy rains would cancel the games. Amid the class warfare then pulling the city apart, Bostonians shared a passion for Ruth, and that passion only swelled by the time of the Police Strike, for Ruth had become their home run king.[64]

Ruth's last Boston appearance had been a Labor Day doubleheader against Washington. That day had been an unmitigated triumph. In the first game he drew a rare start as pitcher. He hurled a complete-game 2–1 victory and drove in the winning run with a triple. In the second game, with the score tied 1–1 in the seventh inning, Ruth whipped a line drive into right field that cleared the fence on a line. The crowd roared from the crack of the bat; it kept roaring for ten minutes, until the next inning, when Ruth jogged out to left field. A straw hat floated onto the grass. More men tossed their hats, creating a fountain of straw bubbling through the grandstand. Hats rained onto the field, a magnificent homage to Ruth. A boy in knicker-bockers scampered into left field, where Ruth gave him a warm grin and handshake. The roars continued. "No conquering hero was ever tendered wilder or more enthusiastic acclaim," marveled the *Boston Globe*.[65]

That was Ruth's twenty-fourth home run, one shy of Buck Freeman's re-cord (set during an era of shorter fences and over the course of a full 154-game season). When the Red Sox went to Philadelphia's Shibe Park on September 5, Ruth tied the record with a shot that landed on Twentieth Street. He almost broke the record in his next at-bat, when his fly ball landed two feet from the top of the fence. Back in Boston, he was front-page news, and all his exploits received great attention. He hit two home runs in an exhibition against a semipro team from Baltimore; Buck Freeman praised Ruth as a superior slugger; Hollywood signed Ruth to a $10,000 contract for a six-reel feature film. He was Boston's chief celebrity.[66]

On September 8, at the Polo Grounds, against the Yankees, in the eighth inning, during the front end of a doubleheader, Ruth surpassed Freeman's record with his twenty-sixth home run. The ball was still rising as it ca-reened into the right-field grandstand, clearing space as spectators dodged out of the way. The achievement captivated Boston. Photo spreads and il-lustrations in local newspapers demonstrated Ruth's batting technique and herculean strength. Female admirers sent so much mail that Ruth's team-mates helped him sift through it. When Ruth attended a revue at the Colo-nial Theater during the Police Strike, the audience cheered until the show's star called Ruth to the stage. "Boston's pretty proud of your 26th, Babe," saluted the *Boston Post*. "As proud as it was of its own 26th last spring, when it came back from war."[67]

As guard units restored order on September 11, the rains ceased and baseball resumed. That morning the Back Bay police station received a tip that gunmen were about to rob the Fenway box office. Two state guard companies, 100 volunteers, and some loyal policemen rushed to intercept them. No robbers ever came, and that afternoon the Red Sox swept a double-header against St. Louis. But Ruth failed to hit a home run. Against Cleveland, Detroit, and Chicago, his brief drought continued. At the same time, the sporting press was pointing at another home-run record. Baseball historians had unearthed that in 1884, Ned Williamson of the Chicago Colts had hit twenty-seven home runs. But he had played in Chicago at the Lake Front Park, which featured an absurd 215-foot fence in right field. Nevertheless, the press now recognized his record, so Ruth's home runs remained a premier diversion.[68]

Boston's last chance to see Ruth challenge this record arrived on September 20: "Babe Ruth Day." For the Saturday doubleheader against the White Sox, the Knights of Columbus arranged a tribute. Thirty-one thousand admirers crammed Fenway Park, with State Guardsmen regulating the crowd in lieu of police. (Frazee had milked Ruth's drawing power by selling extra standing-room-only tickets and charging more for grandstand seats.) Ruth took the mound one last time in the opener. He pitched six innings, allowed three runs, and then played left field. In the ninth inning, Ruth came to bat with one out and the score tied 3–3. Chicago pitcher Lefty Williams served a fastball low and off the plate, and Ruth golfed it over the left-field scoreboard, through a window across Lansdowne Street. He won the game and tied Williamson's record. As the mighty "Colossus" strode the base paths, Boston celebrated its dramatic, charismatic hero, unlike any in the history of baseball.[69]

The cheers continued for minutes. The crowd seemed to tire, and then it recovered and cheered some more. Finally, as the thunder softened, the Knights of Columbus held a ceremony for Ruth at home plate. They gave Ruth and his wife a traveling bag and $600 in United States savings certificates. Ruth donated his bat for auction to war-related charities. He also hammed it up for the cameras by delivering a long, wet kiss to his wife.

Then he took the field again. To the crowd's continued delight, he led off the fifth inning with a ground-rule double into the overflow section in right-center field. After a sacrifice and an error, Ruth scored to give his team a 5–4 edge. The lead held up, and the Red Sox won both games from the White Sox, who had already clinched the American League pennant. "'Babe' is a good-natured, unaffected giant of a hero," beamed the *Boston Globe*. "The thousands of us who saw him at his best on his 'day' enjoyed ourselves immensely. It was the greatest windup of a season on a Boston ground we have ever seen."[70]

Boston never again saw Babe Ruth in a Red Sox uniform.

As the Red Sox closed with five games in New York and Washington, Ruth's heroics continued. In New York he broke Williamson's record with the longest home run in the history of the Polo Grounds; the ball soared over the right-field grandstand and into a weedy lot. In Washington he cleared Griffith Stadium's 50-foot right-field wall with room to spare. The Washington blast gave him 29 home runs for the season, with at least one in every American League park. Rival fans cheered both feats. No player had ever inspired such warmth, such awe, such ecstasy.[71]

In the season finale, however, Ruth inspired outrage. He ditched the game in favor of a lucrative exhibition in Baltimore. Washington fans had come only to see Ruth hit his thirtieth home run, and they bellowed at the star's absence. The Red Sox dropped the anticlimactic epilogue 8–7. They finished 66–71, in sixth place.[72]

Ruth had lent the Red Sox season its sole excitement. He led the league with 112 RBI and 103 runs scored. Despite 111 games at left field and four at first base, he also notched a 9–5 pitching record with a 2.97 ERA. But the home runs mattered most. Ruth hit more home runs than ten major-league teams. Gavvy Cravath finished second with only 12 home runs. Most expected Ruth's record to last for ages. "It will be a superman indeed who will improve on it," presumed the *Sporting News*. "Ruth has proved himself to be the mightiest swatter that ever went to bat."[73]

His slugging presaged a new era for baseball. Owners realized that home runs drew fans, and in the next decade they banned pitchers from defacing the ball, restricted spitballs, and rotated more fresh white balls into play. Many stadiums added seats in their outfields, further boosting home-run totals. By 1930, when major-league baseball players hit 1,565 home runs, the skills associated with scientific baseball—bunts, sacrifices, stolen bases— had shriveled in consequence. But in September 1919 baseball's revolution seemed far from inevitable. Ruth's own manager predicted that in 1920 Ruth would shorten his swing and punch the ball to left field. "No, he will not be trying to knock the ball out of the lot next season," said Ed Barrow. He still modeled good hitting on the Ty Cobb gold standard.[74]

Baseball turned upon the hinge of the 1919 season, and Boston participated in another of the sport's upheavals. After the Carl Mays fiasco hardened the existing battle lines, Yankees owner Jacob Ruppert declared that "Ban Johnson will be put out of baseball," and he announced a formal alliance with Frazee and Comiskey. During the winter meetings that December, they threatened to form a new league with National League owners. Johnson had to dissolve the National Commission, and the next year Kenesaw Mountain Landis became baseball's first commissioner.[75]

Landis took power after another shock to baseball's system: the Black Sox scandal, when eight members of the Chicago White Sox conspired to lose the 1919 World Series to the Cincinnati Reds. (This time Boston played only a bit part. While in town for the series that climaxed with "Babe Ruth Day," White Sox first baseman Chick Gandil had hatched the plan with professional gamblers at the Buckminster Hotel in Kenmore Square.) The public learned of the fix in September 1920, and the subsequent trial violated the faith that Americans had placed in the national pastime. That a jury exonerated the eight players meant little to Landis. If baseball were to continue marketing itself as the harbor of American values, he needed to purge such toxins. He banished the Black Sox. The commissioner's image of moral purity helped the game recover from the scandal, and baseball began an era of unprecedented commercial growth.[76]

Babe Ruth ignited that explosion. He did not just excel at baseball in the 1920s; he *embodied* the 1920s. The decade's mass culture loosened the bonds of Victorian restraint, flaunted material abundance, and celebrated the individual. Ruth represented those values on and off the field. His towering moon shots, gregarious personality, and raunchy exploits delighted baseball's burgeoning audience. He hit 54 home runs in 1920, shattering his own record. He hit 59 in 1921, and he set the record again with 60 in 1927. He retired with 714 home runs, and he won four more World Series after 1919. But he won them playing for the Yankees.[77]

How did Harry Frazee let the world's most popular baseball player leave Boston? After the season ended, Ruth played exhibition games throughout New England until departing for California in late October. He hired a personal manager, a publicity agent named Johnny Igoe. He earned $500 a game headlining a West Coast barnstorming team, trained with the former boxer Kid McCoy, explored acting in movies, and entertained reporters with batting-practice home runs and good-natured braggadocio. He also announced a potential barnstorming tour through Hawaii and Australia, even if it meant missing half of the 1920 season.[78]

These side projects expanded Ruth's profile and fattened his wallet. More important, they lent him leverage against Frazee. In mid-October, Ruth demanded a raise to $15,000. On the platform before his train departed for California, he changed the figure to $20,000. He was the game's premier entertainer, and by that standard he was underpaid. But by rejecting his own signed contract, he defied a business propriety. When Ty Cobb labeled him a "contract violator," these two ethics clashed. "A player is worth just as much as he can get," bristled Ruth. "Cobb must be jealous of me because the newspapers have played me up as the biggest attraction in baseball."[79]

Returning to Boston before Christmas, Ruth stuck to his demand. Frazee refused to pay the unprecedented salary. Instead he announced that he might trade Ruth, or any other Red Sox player besides the venerated Harry Hooper. Frazee then traded Bobby Roth and Maurice Shannon for three players from Washington, and he intimated that more deals would follow. A public relations campaign against Ruth began. Red Sox management floated the notion that Ruth was a "disturbing element," a "one-man team" who damaged morale. Never before had such concerns surfaced. As the new decade dawned, Frazee was plotting to oust Ruth.[80]

It had been a most turbulent year. Labor traumas had exposed divisions between the Yankee middle class and the ethnic working class. After the 1918 upheavals of the Great War and the flu epidemic, such debacles shook the city. Additionally, by 1920 President Wilson's plan for a new world order had disintegrated. In November 1919 he had stubbornly refused to modify the League of Nations, and the U.S. Senate would not ratify the peace treaty. Instead of making the world safe for democracy, Americans resigned themselves to rooting out radicals. On January 2, 1920, the Department of Justice rounded up more than 4,000 "Communists, Communist Labor

Party adherents, and certain types of Socialists." The government held almost 1,000 Boston-area suspected radicals on Deer Island under brutal conditions. The authorities eventually freed the American citizens and deported the illegal aliens, but not before one prisoner went insane, two died of pneumonia, and another committed suicide.[81]

On January 5 Frazee announced the sale of Babe Ruth to the New York Yankees. Newspapers reported a range of prices; the correct one was $125,000. The owner outlined his reasons: Ruth had outrageous demands, Ruth was out of shape, Ruth set a bad example for his teammates. Frazee claimed that he would now replenish the team. He failed to mention his persistent debts to previous Red Sox owner Joe Lannin, or that Lannin had obtained an injunction preventing him from selling the team, or that a judge had set a date to auction off the club. Frazee staved off financial injury by selling Ruth. Since he knew how to manipulate publicity, most journalists accepted his empty justifications.[82]

Front-page headlines announced the trade. Articles recalled Ruth's great Boston moments, speculated upon his impact on New York, and culled reactions from baseball experts. Sportswriters created new copy by recirculating Frazee's charges, and they believed that Frazee would rebuild a pennant contender. At first Ruth rejected the trade and insisted that he would play only in Boston. Then, after signing with the Yankees, he criticized Frazee, claiming that the owner had acknowledged his drawing power with a "nickel cigar." In an open letter to Boston fans, Ruth particularly objected to the charge that he was a "disturbing element": "I am friendly with all of the fellows and I firmly believe that they all would go to the limit for me and regret my leaving the club as much I do going."[83]

The fans mourned his loss. "For the love of Mike!" exclaimed one upon hearing of Ruth's sale. Even as sportswriters debated the wisdom of Frazee's action, they acknowledged its unpopularity among the people of Boston. One cartoon pictured Frazee driving a steamroller over a flattened fan. Another showed Frazee admiring an advertisement for his play "My Lady Friends," with disgruntled observers sneering, "That's the only kind he's got left." A third depicted such Boston institutions as the Public Library and Boston Common. In front of them were signs reading "For Sale."[84]

Given the city's recent history, Ruth's departure seemed particularly cruel. The Yankee Division had united Boston for one day; Ruth had captured the city's imagination for months, providing an exciting diversion from a snarl of disease, politics, social discord, and violence. If city residents could connect on nothing else, they could still celebrate Ruth together. So Bostonians could be forgiven some disillusionment. Most shared nothing with Amory Blaine, the Princeton-bred protagonist of *This Side of Paradise*, F. Scott Fitzgerald's debut novel of 1920, but they could identify with his disenchantment: "all Gods dead, all wars fought, all faiths in man shaken."[85]

In the next decade the Yankees dominated baseball, and the Red Sox placed last in the American League in 1923, 1925, 1926, 1927, 1928, 1929, and 1930. They finished a half-game ahead of last-place Chicago in 1924. Ruth was neither the first nor the last star sold by Frazee; even Harry Hooper left the next year. But as the years of futility mounted, Bostonians read karmic implications into Ruth's sale. They blamed Frazee, especially as the Yankees piled World Series upon World Series. "I remember where I was standing the day they sold Babe Ruth," recalled Boston author Cleveland Amory. "I said to my father, 'Dad, you and I will never live to see it, but we will regret it to the day anybody dies.'" Amory defined Boston through its self-flagellant faith in perennial losers, and over eighty-six years, until the Series victory in 2004, Red Sox fans embraced this sacrificial woe. Losing Babe Ruth became part of Boston's identity. It somehow embodied both the Puritan shame of Old Boston and the Catholic guilt of New Boston. "Being a Red Sox fan means a life of sackcloth and ashes, a life of perpetual excuses, a life of misery, of sadness, of want, of penury, all of which Bostonians, underneath, really pray for. A true Bostonian craves it."[86]

But in January 1920, a true Bostonian just wanted Babe Ruth back.

2

The Boston Red Sox, 1901–1946

William E. Leuchtenburg

The saga of the Boston Red Sox is the stuff not of history but of soap opera. It takes only a few minutes to cue someone who is tuning in for the first time to that maudlin afternoon serial "The Curse of the Bambino" on what has transpired in past episodes: the infamous sale of Babe Ruth to the villainous Yankees, Johnny Pesky's hesitation, Bucky Dent's pop-fly homer, the ball dribbling through aging Bill Buckner's gimpy legs, Grady Little's tardy hook. "A team of tragedy, if ever there was one," writes John Demos in an elegant little essay. "And masters, above all else, of the art of Noble Defeat." One longtime Boston fan vowed that he would not permit his young daughter to become a Sox rooter because he did not want her to know a lifetime of heartbreak.

For the Red Sox Nation the "day that will live in infamy" is not December 7, 1941, when Pearl Harbor was bombed, but January 5, 1920, when soulless Harry Frazee sold George Herman Ruth, the Babe, the greatest player of the age, and thereby, according to legend, put a curse on the club. Over the right-field grandstand the Red Sox display five digits, 9–4–1–8–27, to honor their Hall of Fame stars whose numbers have been retired: Ted Williams, Joe Cronin, Bobby Doerr, Carl Yastrzemski, and Carlton Fisk. But, as sportswriter Dan Shaughnessy pointed out, 9–4–1–8 also stands for the long-ago day, September 4, 1918, when Boston won its last world championship prior to 2004. On visits to Yankee Stadium, Red Sox fans were often subjected to the chant "Nine-teen-Eight-een . . . Nine-teen-Eight-een," a taunting reminder of how long it had been since Boston had celebrated, in contrast to the many times Yankee players doused one another with champagne.

After Frazee made his Faustian bargain, the Red Sox were again and again about to taste the cup of victory, only to spill it at the last moment. Over the course of the rest of the twentieth century, Boston was to win four pennants, and each time would go down to defeat in the World Series—each time in the seventh game. In 1986 they came within one pitch of becoming world champions. That was not the only instance of oh-so-close. In 1948 the season ended in a tie, and Boston lost the one-game playoff. The very next season they had a one-game lead over New York with just two games left, and the Yankees denied them by taking both contests.

For Red Sox fans, "the curse of the Bambino" was not an overwrought image, but a palpable reality. A Boston writer commented, "'Disappointments' . . . are like stations of the cross to Red Sox fans, renditions hanging invisibly on the green walls of Fenway Park as the Catholic stations of Jesus' suffering and death hang affixed to church walls . . . Ted Williams and Carl Yastrzemski died for the sins of Harry Frazee . . . They died for us, for Red Sox fans, so we could be reborn each spring." Similarly, a Unitarian minister likened Fenway Park to Nathaniel Hawthorne's *The House of Seven Gables*. "In both cases you have a cursed family because of evil that had been done and it's passed down several generations later," he explained. "I think of the selling of Ruth as the sin that cannot be atoned for." To exorcise the curse, one Sox fan scaled Mount Everest in 2003 and, allegedly on the advice of a Tibetan Buddhist holy man, deposited a photo of the Babe from 1918, *annus mirabilis*, on the summit. In vain. Redemption took one more year.

But melancholia is not the only way to contemplate the Boston experience. There is also a countervailing theme—a tale not of failure but of success. Everything hinges on what benchmark is used. If Red Sox followers insisted on the glory years that reached a climacteric in 1918 as their measuring rod, they were doomed to misery. But if one gauges the Red Sox by contrasting their plight when they were the worst team in baseball, in the dark decade after they lost Ruth, with their achievements in the generations that followed, a very different, and brighter, image emerges.

The abyss of the Ruthless 1920s would have seemed dreadful under any circumstances, but the memory of what had gone before made it all the more bitter, for rarely has any organization descended to such ignominy from such heights. From 1901 through 1918 the Boston club, known first as the Pilgrims and after 1907 as the Red Sox, captured the world championship five times. No other team in the majors was nearly so dominant. Boston won six pennants, and all five of the World Series in which the team played. (On a sixth occasion the New York Giants shied away from a postseason matchup.) In 1912, their first season after the opening of Fenway Park, the Sox registered a winning percentage of .691, highest of the decade. They won an unprecedented 105 games, a mark that would not be surpassed by any team until the illustrious 1927 Yankees. The approach of the 1912 World Series against the formidable New York Giants kindled intense excitement, for in a city badly fragmented by class, religion, and ethnicity, pride in the Red Sox united Beacon Hill Brahmins and Irish Catholic Southies. John F. Kennedy's grandfather, Boston mayor John "Honey Fitz" Fitzgerald, headed a caravan of four trainloads of Royal Rooters to Manhattan to cheer the Sox. The thrilling Series went eight games (one of them called by darkness), with Boston beating New York four games to three.

The Red Sox in these years had what may have been the greatest ball-hawking outfield ever: Tris Speaker, so swift that he could play a shallow center field, even to the point of taking part in infield rundowns; Duffy Lewis, who coped so well with the treacherous, steeply sloping Fenway left field that it was called Duffy's Cliff; and Harry Hooper, who in the 1912 World Series robbed a Giant hitter of a home run by snatching the ball with his bare hand as he tumbled into the bleachers. They could also hit. The inimitable Speaker, with a lifetime average of .344, batted over .300 for eighteen seasons.

In a beguiling vignette published in 1937, the leftwing columnist Heywood Broun revealed the long-lasting impact of seeing Speaker in action. Asked by a young woman, "Mr. Broun, how did you happen to become a Red?" he recounted that, when an undergraduate at Harvard in 1907, he had registered for a course taught by Thomas Nixon Carver on "radical panaceas and their underlying fallacies." Carver devoted the fall and winter to inviting agitators into his classroom to expound upon their theories; in the spring, he tore their arguments to shreds. Broun found the guest speakers compelling, but he missed almost all of Carter's rebuttal because it coincided with the debut of a Red Sox rookie just up from the Texas League. On one memorable spring afternoon, the newcomer, Tris Speaker, hit a double, two triples, and a homer. Furthermore, Broun recalled, Speaker "went all the way back to the flagpole in center field and speared a drive with his gloved hand while still on the dead run. Two innings later he charged in for a low liner and made the catch by sliding the last twenty feet on his stomach. Professor Carver couldn't do that." Broun spent the rest of that glorious spring of 1908 not in Carver's classroom, but at the ballpark, and he never did hear what was wrong with radicalism. And so, he concluded, "I went out into the world the fervent follower of all things red, including the Boston Red Sox."

The pitching corps, too, had some remarkable characters. The man who in 1901 was the first Red Sox pitcher to toss a shutout is less known for his baseball prowess than for his intellectual attainments. Edward Morgan Lewis earned an M.A. at Williams, taught at Columbia, served as president of both the University of Massachusetts and the University of New Hampshire, and was a close friend of Robert Frost, who read at his memorial service in 1936. Other pitchers became legendary. Denton "Cy" Young did not become a Boston player until he was thirty-four, his best years presumably behind him. But in his first season with the club he won thirty-three games, and he went on to ring up 193 of his 511 victories with them. That record of 511, still intact in the twenty-first century, accounts for why the best pitcher each year is designated the winner of the Cy Young Award. In 1904 Young, no longer a kid, hurled a perfect game, and in 1908, at the age of forty, racked up his third no-hitter. Smoky Joe Wood, who, improbably, once played for the Bloomer Girls, had an even more ardent following. It is improbable that anyone in the period threw a ball faster. In 1912, only twenty-two, he outdueled the Big Train, Walter Johnson, in a specially arranged match game at Fenway Park, 1–0. Wood ended that season with thirty-four wins, ten of them shutouts.

Trivia mavens like to pose a tricky question: "When in 1961 Whitey Ford set a new mark for consecutive scoreless innings in World Series play, who was the pitcher whose record he broke?" The answer: Babe Ruth. That reply comes as a shock to people who think of the Sultan of Swat exclusively as a slugger. But the Red Sox southpaw began as a pitcher, and an excellent one. In 1915, when Boston boasted five starters in double digits, he won eighteen games. The following year Ruth, a twenty-three-game winner, had the league's lowest earned run average, threw nine shutouts, and came out on top in five encounters with Walter Johnson. When in 1918 the Red Sox won the World Series in six games, two of the victories went to the Babe, who had a 1.06 ERA. In that series Ruth's streak of scoreless innings reached 29⅔.

It is true, though, that Ruth gained immortality not on the mound but at the plate. By smashing eleven homers in 1918, Ruth tied for the major-league lead. In 1919, to give him more at-bats, the Sox moved him to left field on days when he did not pitch. The Babe responded by setting a new major-league record with an astonishing total that seemed unlikely ever to be matched: twenty-nine. Moreover, despite his humpty-dumpty figure, Ruth was a skillful fielder. In 1919 he made only one error in 223 chances, and his rifle arm accounted for fourteen assists and six double plays.

None of this mattered to Harry Frazee. A theater impresario, the Red Sox owner found himself short of cash to finance his Broadway shows. So in January 1920 he did the deed. Frazee sold Ruth to Jacob Ruppert, the beer-baron owner of the Yankees, for $125,000. In addition, Ruppert advanced $350,000 as a mortgage on Fenway Park. Hence, besides losing baseball's greatest star, Red Sox fans had to endure the humiliation of having their ballfield owned by the detested Yankees. Not until 1933 would the park belong to the Sox again. Outraged fans likened the transfer of the Babe to the sale of Faneuil Hall or the Boston Public Library. As Ed Linn has written, "If Frazee had been a bag of tea, he'd have been trundled onto a frigate and thrown into Boston Harbor." In his very first season in pinstripes, Ruth showed Boston what it was missing: 158 runs scored, 137 driven in, a batting average of .376, and an eye-catching 54 home runs, breaking the all-time major-league record, one he had set, by 25.

The sale of Ruth did not end Frazee's dismemberment of the Red Sox. In short order he sent Ruppert the Yankees' future third baseman, Jumpin' Joe Dugan; the stylish shortstop Deacon Scott, who held the record for consecutive games until it was broken by Lou Gehrig; and some of the finest pitchers in the majors. In 1922 Bullet Joe Bush left Boston for the Yankees. His twenty-six victories played a big part in their capturing the pennant, and his nineteen wins the following year helped them gain their first world championship. Even more important to the Yanks in 1923 was another Red Sox castoff, Sad Sam Jones, who won twenty-one games. That year the Red Sox also let the Yankees have southpaw Herb Pennock, who would win 162 games for New York and be undefeated in World Series play. Pennock chalked up so many victories for the Yankees that he was elected to the Cooperstown Hall of Fame. No less valuable was another Red Sox alumnus, Waite Hoyt, who chalked up 227 wins after leaving Boston. When on July 11, 1923, Frazee sold the team, the new owner, J. A. Robert Quinn, did not receive a single player from the world champions of 1918; all of them had been sold, traded, or had skipped away.

It did not take long for the Red Sox to pay the price. In its capsule account of 1922 baseball, *Reach's Guide* reported somberly: "Boston last season reaped the fruits of four years' despoliation by the New York club, and for the second time in American League history this once great Boston team, now utterly discredited, fell into last place—with every prospect of remaining in that undesirable position indefinitely." That forecast came painfully close to the mark. In the first dozen years after Ruth was let go, the Red Sox ended up in the cellar nine times. In 1923, for the second year in a row, they were dead last. Under manager Frank Chance (of "Tinker to Evers to . . ."), the Sox wound up thirty-seven games behind the Yankees with their infusion of former Boston stars. After moving up a notch to seventh in 1924, the Red Sox fell back into last place once more in 1925, 49½ out. They scored the fewest runs of any team in the league and, thanks to poor pitching and awful defense, let in the most runs.

Things, it seemed, could hardly get worse, but they did. In 1926 Boston lost 17 consecutive games, an unenviable performance that no other team in either league matched during the decade, though the Sox came close the following year when they dropped 15 straight. By losing 107 games that season, the 1926 Red Sox set a club record, one that a few years later they would manage to surpass. During an eight-year stretch from 1925 to 1932, the Red Sox landed at the bottom of the standings all but once, and that year the best they could do was sixth. In these years Boston never ended a season better than 43½ out of first place. For three years in a row, from 1925 through 1927, they lost more than 100 games each season, a sorry feat they repeated in 1930 and 1932. From 1927 through 1929, during the Great Bull Market, Boston's stock plummeted with winning percentages of .331, .373, and .377 and finishes as much as 59 games behind. When Ruth hit his record-breaking 60 homers in 1927, the entire Boston team totaled only 28. Eleven of the Babe's 60 clouts came courtesy of Red Sox pitchers. By the Fourth of July that year Boston counted 15 victories, 54 defeats, and in head-to-head clashes that season, the Yankees, already being described as a "dynasty," won 18, the Red Sox 4. Much of the success of the hated New Yorkers in the 1920s could be traced to acquisitions from their obliging northern rivals. "The Yankee dynasty," said a former Boston pitching ace who had been traded to New York, "was the Red Sox dynasty in Yankee uniforms."

It appeared that everything the Red Sox touched turned to ashes, in one instance literally so. On May 8, 1926, Fenway Park's third-base bleachers burned down, and no one much cared. The Boston management got a boost when in 1929 Massachusetts legalized baseball on Sunday, a move expected to keep the turnstiles revolving on a day when men and women were off from work, but on too many Sundays pouring rain washed out games. The Red Sox made a smart move when they hired the savvy Jim Price, a renowned baseball man, as club secretary, but in January 1929 Price took his life by slashing his wrists.

The Red Sox fared no better after the onset of the Great Depression. In April 1930, half a year after the Wall Street crash, President Herbert Hoover inaugurated a new season by throwing out the first ball, then sat through nine innings as Walter Johnson's Washington Senators went down to defeat at the hands of the Sox. Boston, though, would win only fifty more games all the rest of the season. Even in this bleak period a few individuals ran up impressive statistics, but the players were one-dimensional. In 1931 Earl Webb, a rough-hewn Tennessean who had gone down into coal mines at the age of twelve, set an all-time major-league record for doubles with sixty-seven, but he was no glove man. "I've seen some mighty bad outfielders," he once said, "but none of them had anything on me." Two sluggers, Dale Alexander, who won the league batting crown in 1932, and Smead Jolley, gave the Sox unfamiliar firing power, but Jolley may have let in as many runs as he scored. On one memorable occasion a ball rolled up Duffy's

Cliff between his legs and then, as it made its downhill return, rolled through his legs a second time.

Meanwhile the Red Sox continued to play giveaway with the Yankees. When in 1930 they once again dealt a player, they seemed to do so for good reason. In 1928 pitcher Red Ruffing had lost 25 games, the most by anyone in the league. In 1929 he was in the "L" column 22 more times, again the worst record. But the Yankees saw in the strapping, hard-throwing right-hander promise that eluded the Sox, and he quickly proved them right. In his first season with them, Ruffing won 16 games, the first of more than 200 victories for New York. In 1932 he led the league in strikeouts (190), and in 1938 won more games than any other pitcher in the American League.

The 1932 Red Sox roster had a third baseman with the appropriately Back Bay name of Urbane Pickering, but more of Boston's hopes rested on a flame-throwing pitcher, Big Ed Morris. Playing in 1928 for a last-place team, Morris contrived to win nineteen games. He tailed off thereafter, especially after he hurt his arm fighting two Detroit policemen, but the Sox still had a lot riding on him. By the end of the 1931 season, it was reported, "he had a lot of his old-time smoke on the ball." But at a farewell fish fry given in his honor on the eve of his departure from Alabama for the Red Sox spring training camp in Savannah, Big Ed got into a brawl with a gasoline station operator who believed that the pitcher was making a play for his wife. Morris, a 6-foot 2-inch bruiser, tripped and fell after knocking down his rival, and as he lay on the ground, the aggrieved husband knifed him twice in the chest. Two days later, Morris died.

Big Ed's death foretold the disaster that awaited the Red Sox in the 1932 season. In mid-June the manager quit after his club had run up a pitiful record of 11 wins and 47 defeats. In the course of the season, the Sox were whipped 111 times, and with an abysmal percentage of .279 finished 64 games out. No Red Sox team had ever had so many losses. The Red Sox averaged only 2,275 spectators a game. Fewer fans bought tickets that year than at any time in the history of the franchise. Amateur Twilight League contests often outdrew those at Fenway.

Not only the Red Sox but the Red Sox Nation experienced the Great Depression as a time of desperation, and the disintegration of the team in which Boston had once taken such pride mirrored what was happening to the city. Some 100,000 workers—blacks in the Roxbury ghetto, Italians in the North End, Irish in Charlestown three-deckers—had no jobs. Early in 1930 a man collapsed on the sidewalk of a downtown street, dead of starvation. When the state minimum wage commission accused Harvard of paying its charwomen two cents under the miserable hourly minimum, a thoughtful university official got the commission off its back by firing the women. To find a few days' work for the unemployed, the city abandoned the use of mechanical snowplows and handed the men shovels. In this context, the financial problems of the Sox seem trivial. Still, their owner, Bob Quinn, had to borrow on his insurance to come up with enough cash to pay for spring training in 1933. Fans worried that Quinn might not be able to keep the team afloat much longer. Nobody could imagine, especially in a period when even many men of wealth were hoarding their savings, that anyone would want to buy the inept Red Sox and their rundown stadium. It came as a shock, then, when on February 25, 1933, Quinn summoned the press to hear an astonishing announcement: he had just shaken hands on a deal with a young man who had purchased the club and Fenway Park for 1.2 million dollars. In return for that huge sum, he received, in the words of Boston sportswriter Bill Cunningham, "perhaps the most dilapidated piece of diamond merchandise to be found on the major-league shelves."

Thomas Austin Yawkey, the new owner, had a passion for baseball and the inherited wealth to indulge it. The sport was in his blood. Foster son and nephew of a former owner of the Detroit Tigers, he had chased balls for Ty Cobb as a boy, and at Yale, where he studied at the Sheffield Scientific School, he had tried, but failed, to make the Eli nine. He measured his life by baseball milestones. "I was born the year my father bought the Detroit club," he said. Yawkey purchased the Red Sox four days after coming into a large legacy at the age of thirty. "I want a ball club the crowd will love—every man jack on it," he told Cunningham. "I want to hear those bleachers thunder again the way they used to in the old days."

Finally Boston had an owner who loved the Red Sox and who carried a bulging wallet. Yawkey enjoyed taking batting practice and tossing the ball around with the players. He and his wife even picnicked in center field. With a suite at the Ritz and a vast hunting estate in South Carolina, he had money to burn. Recognizing that he lacked the knowhow to run the club despite his early tutelage with the Tigers, Yawkey hired as vice-president and general manager Eddie Collins, who had sparkled at second base in Connie Mack's million-dollar infield, and had been Yawkey's childhood hero. Yawkey had even made a point of going to the prep school in Tarrytown, New York, where Collins had been a legendary star, and he took pride in having won the Edward Trowbridge Collins Award as the school's best athlete.

With the 1933 season only a few weeks old, Yawkey began to spend. He bought Rick Ferrell, a first-rate catcher, from the St. Louis Browns, and Billy Werber, a speedy infielder, from the Yankees. The swift Werber, who would lead the league in steals the next season, soon delighted Red Sox fans by his daring on the base paths, in one game dumbfounding the Tigers by reaching second base on a walk. Later in 1933 Yawkey struck a deal with financially pinched Connie Mack, who for the second time in two decades was holding a fire sale. From Mack's Philadelphia Athletics Yawkey acquired three players. Two were past their prime: pitcher Rube Walberg, who in 1932 had won seventeen games for Mack; and Max Bishop, who held the all-time best fielding record in a season for second basemen. The third member of the trio, Robert Moses Grove, was the best southpaw in the majors.

Lefty Grove had been a twenty-game winner for seven seasons in a row and had led the league in strikeouts seven times. On a 1931 visit to Japan he entered a game in the eighth inning and struck out the side in both the eighth and the ninth—on only nineteen pitches. Some of his success he owed to intimidation. In an article titled "The Terrible-Tempered Mr. Grove," Red Smith wrote that Lefty "stood six-foot-three and wore an expression of sulky anger stuck on top of a long, thin neck." He even threw at his own teammates. At the A's spring training camp in 1930, rookie Doc Cramer homered off Grove in an intrasquad match. On Cramer's next trip to the plate, Grove drilled him in the back with a fastball. As Cramer iced his bruise after the game, Grove went over to him and snarled, "You didn't hit that one, did you, busher?" He hated losing—maybe, it was speculated, because he had so little familiarity with it. In 1931 he had gone 31 and 4. No longer young, Grove still figured to give the Red Sox the quality pitching that had been so sorely lacking.

"The first thing we've got to do," Yawkey declared, "is to get this club out of the cellar." No one supposed that was going to be easy. The team Yawkey had inherited, wrote a Boston columnist, was "a tatterdemalion aggregation of cripples, has-beens and would-bes, playing in a poor folksy park in a poor folksy way." Oddsmakers rated their chances of winning the 1933 pennant at 500–1. But in 1933, Yawkey's first year, Boston did climb up. Though a seventh place finish does not seem anything to get excited about, the Red Sox made the biggest advance in winning percentage of any team. To improve that performance in 1934, Yawkey installed a new manager: Bucky Harris, who had won renown as the "boy manager" of the Washington Senators. At spring training camp in Sarasota, Harris told his players, "We'll only have one rule this season: be in bed before twelve o'clock. Some of you will do some tomcatting and I may do some myself, but, if you do, get it done before twelve."

Over the winter of 1933–34 Yawkey lavished another million dollars on reconstructing Fenway Park. Employing hundreds of union workers, he financed the biggest private construction project in Boston during the Great Depression. (Only the building of the Mystic Bridge, a public project, was more costly.) Yawkey's huge investment in razing the unlovely old park and creating a new Fenway was making steady progress when on January 5, 1934, the fourteenth anniversary of the sale of Babe Ruth to the Yankees, a five-alarm fire destroyed the nearly completed wooden bleachers. Though insurance did not fully cover the loss, Yawkey, undaunted, resolved to rebuild the stands in concrete and, despite the setback, to fulfill his pledge to have the renovated park ready on Opening Day.

When fans filed into the new Fenway in April, they were awestruck. More than 10,000 seats had been added, and the roof was painted "Dartmouth green." In left field, Yawkey had scaled down Duffy's Cliff, slightly shortened the distance to home plate, and considerably raised the height of the barrier. (Not for another two decades, though, would it become the "Green Monster," since in these years advertisements plastered the fence.) A new scoreboard in left field featured an innovation: red lights for strikes, green for balls. (In 1936, to protect store windows on Lansdowne Street, a high screen was added on top of the left-field wall.)

Yawkey had a lot more spending still in mind. In late May 1934 he pried another stellar pitcher, Wes Ferrell, Rick's brother, from the Cleveland Indians. By winning twenty or more games in each of his first four seasons, Ferrell had established a major-league record. Many consider him as, save for Ruth in his early years, the greatest hitting pitcher of all time. He set marks for most home runs by a pitcher in a season (nine) and in a career (thirty-six). Movie-star handsome, Ferrell easily matched Grove in hot temper. On one occasion, after a poor showing, he took out his anger at himself by ripping apart his glove with his teeth, and another time he got so mad at blowing a big lead that when he returned to the dugout, he twice socked himself in the jaw and battered his head against a concrete wall. Ferrell's favorite reading matter was the astrology chart in the morning tabloid, and he became peeved if he was asked to take the mound on a day when the planets were squabbling.

Ferrell made an immediate contribution to the club, winning fourteen games despite his late start, and those victories helped the Red Sox finish in the first division (fourth place) for the first time since 1918. Critics might jeer that the money spent on buying Grove and Ferrell meant that the Boston club should be called the "Gold Sox," but Yawkey brought an excitement to Fenway that had been missing for too long. The 1934 attendance more than doubled that of the year before. Harris, though, lasted only that one season, for Yawkey had his eye on another boy manager.

After the 1934 season Yawkey bought from the Washington Senators their twenty-eight-year-old player-manager, Clark Griffith, and the league's premier shortstop, Joe Cronin. He gave $250,000 and an expendable Red Sox player. In 1930, only his second season in the majors, Cronin had received the Most Valuable Player award, and in 1933 he had made the American League's All-Star team, as he was to do every year thereafter through 1941. Cronin was as outstanding as a hitter as he was mediocre as a fielder. Few shortstops have ever been as productive in driving in runs. "Oh my, yes, Joe Cronin is the best there is in the clutch," Connie Mack said. "With a man on third and one out, I'd rather have him hitting for me than anybody I've ever seen—and that includes Cobb and the rest of them." Cronin recognized that he could not have a better place to display his talents than Fenway. "A fellow with an Irish name like mine ought to get along well there," he remarked. It was said that "if Cronin could not draw the Irish of Boston through the gates, then never a man from Antrim to Kerry, nor from Clare to Kildare, could." Cronin was to last as manager for thirteen years, a record for the Red Sox, and go on to become general manager of the club and then president of the American League. What made the 1934 deal especially striking, though, was not that Yawkey had snagged his third star—Cronin, on top of Grove and Wes Ferrell—but that Cronin was Clark Griffith's son-in-law. Cronin in fact learned of the deal at the end of his honeymoon with Griffith's daughter. One columnist wrote, "I wish I could sell my son-in-law for $250,000. Any bidders?"

Only one letdown had marred the inspiriting 1934 season: the performance of Lefty Grove. His arm unaccountably dead, he lost as many games as he won (eight), and his ERA ballooned to 6.50. Chagrined at what was happening, Connie Mack wrote Yawkey: "Bob Grove isn't delivering for you. We believed you were getting a sound pitcher. Under the circumstances, the Athletics club will be glad to take Grove back and refund you the money." Yawkey responded: "We also made the deal in good faith; we knew we were acquiring a veteran pitcher, and it is no fault of yours that Grove has developed a sore arm."

Happily, Grove's travail in 1934 proved to be a fluke. In 1935 he again became a twenty-game winner, and his victories, along with twenty-five from Wes Ferrell, made possible another first-division finish, again in fourth place. For years to come, Yawkey was able to rely on his rangy southpaw. From May 3, 1938, to May 12, 1941, Grove won twenty games in a row at Fenway. In 1939, at age thirty-nine, he had the lowest ERA in the league for the ninth time. No other pitcher had ever come close to that mark. In his years with the Athletics when he relied on his fearsome fastball, Grove "wasn't a pitcher," Mack reflected. "He was a thrower until after we sold him to Boston and he hurt his arm. Then he learned to pitch, and he got so he just knew, somehow, when the batter was going to swing."

An incident in 1935, however, revealed how reluctant Dame Fortune still was to smile on Boston. In the bottom of the ninth in a game at Fenway the Red Sox trailed the Indians by four runs when they began a rally that appeared to be destined to pull out a victory. With two runs in, nobody out, and the bases loaded, Cronin smashed a vicious liner toward left field that had extra bases written all over it. But the ball bounced off the skull of the third baseman, Bad News Hale, into the hands of the Cleveland shortstop, who swiftly relayed it to second, where it went on to first for a game-ending triple play.

Shortly after the start of the 1935 season the Red Sox signed a backup catcher: Moe Berg, Princeton '25. His baseball skills were unremarkable, but sportswriters swarmed around him because they had never known anyone like him before. Berg, one of the few Jews in baseball, had been graduated magna cum laude in foreign languages, including Sanskrit; had taken advanced work at Columbia and at the Sorbonne; and was respected enough in his field to be asked to review *The Affirmative Particles in French* for a scholarly journal. A sturdy receiver with a quick arm and a lot of baseball savvy, he was so slow that his Princeton manager told him he would "get to first base just as fast wearing snowshoes." Fortunately, he was such a poor batter that his lack of speed on the base paths went virtually unnoticed. Berg, one hard-boiled player muttered, "can speak seven languages, and can't hit a curve in any of them." He attracted the press, though, because of the quality of his mind. Berg knew a number of languages at least passably well, and he dabbled in several others, including Bulgarian, Old High German, and Mandarin Chinese. As they were about to sail across the Pacific on a baseball junket, Babe Ruth asked him if he could speak Japanese, and Berg replied that he had never troubled to learn it. Two weeks later, Ruth was startled to hear Berg greet a man on the pier in Japanese. "Wait a minute," Ruth said. "You told me you didn't speak Japanese." Berg retorted, "That was two weeks ago."

Berg's behavior off the field bore no resemblance to that of the carousing ballplayer. "With the Red Sox in Philadelphia to play the Athletics," his biographer, Nicholas Dawidoff, has written, "Berg might hurry up to Princeton for a look at an exhibition of Islamic miniatures and calligraphy, to listen to Thomas Mann lecture on Goethe's *Faust,* or to visit one of his former professors' Greek classes." In the midst of his baseball activities he found time to get a law degree and pass the New York bar exam. "Moe," Billy Werber later recalled, "was sober, almost sorrowful, always carrying the *Wall Street Journal* under his arm." Berg had eight identical suits, all somber, and a set of identical ties. Asked why he wore only black, gray, and white, he answered that he was in mourning for the world. Since he often received invitations to receptions for dignitaries, he kept black-tie formal wear in his locker at the stadium. In the bullpen, his main abode, Berg bemused pitchers with monologues on Molière and Spinoza.

His activities in World War II are shrouded in mystery. After resigning a coaching post with the Red Sox to accept an assignment in Latin America from Nelson Rockefeller, Berg joined the Office of Strategic Services, forerunner of the CIA. Berg's Medal of Freedom for service to his country is for enterprises so top secret that his citation only hints at their nature. We do know that on orders signed by the head of the OSS, Wild Bill Donovan, Berg scurried around Europe in a trench coat, packing a .45 and rolls of cash, to dig out information on German and Italian efforts to build atomic weapons. On one occasion, it appears, the OSS ordered him to attend a lecture by Werner Heisenberg to find out if German physicists were close to building an atomic bomb for Hitler, and, if so, to murder Heisenberg in the lecture hall.

Moe Berg, though choice newspaper copy, had little influence on the fortunes of the Red Sox, but another 1935 addition made an immediate impact. In December 1935 Yawkey paid Connie Mack $150,000 for first baseman Jimmie Foxx, the most powerful right-handed hitter in either league. Foxx had already been chosen MVP twice. In 1932 he had come close to Babe Ruth's record by knocking out 58 homers. In his first year with the Red Sox, Foxx tattooed the friendly left-field wall in Fenway for a .338 average and finished third in the league in both RBI (143) and home runs (41). Yet despite excellent seasons by Foxx, Grove, and Wes Ferrell in 1936, and the acquisition, again from Connie Mack, of a fine center fielder, Doc Cramer, the Sox wound up a disappointing sixth.

Foxx, however, gave promise of better things to come. Cartoonists depicted him as "XX" because he was poison to opposing pitchers. With the sleeves of his uniform cut off to reveal his enormous biceps, he was a scary sight. Opponents called him "The Beast." "Jimmie Foxx wasn't scouted," one pitcher grumbled; "he was trapped." The pitching ace of the Yankees, Lefty Gomez, was a close friend—but not on the field. "You know that unidentified white object we discovered on the moon?" Gomez asked years afterward. "It was that homer Foxx hit off me." Once, Gomez allowed only a single hit. The man who spoiled his no-hitter? Foxx. In another game, Gomez gave up three home runs to Foxx. Little wonder that when in a close ballgame Foxx came to the plate, catcher Bill Dickey flashed three different signs, only to have Gomez shake him off each time. Exasperated, Dickey walked to the mound to ask Gomez what he would like to throw. "I don't want to throw that guy anything," Gomez replied.

After the unexpectedly low finish in 1936, Cronin and Yawkey decided that a shakeup was in order, and they got rid of the Ferrell brothers and

Billy Werber. Rick Ferrell was a pleasant guy, but no manager got on for long with his cantankerous brother, whose stay with the Red Sox did nothing to mellow him. He once thumbed his nose at some obnoxious Fenway fans, and twice threw a temper tantrum on the mound because of the sloppy play of Sox fielders. Cronin said of Werber, who had graduated with honors from Duke and had been awarded a Rhodes Scholarship, "He's too damned intelligent to be a ballplayer." According to one tale, when a teammate pursuing a pop fly cried, "I got it!" Werber lectured him that proper usage was "I have it." Perhaps as a result of these changes, the Red Sox improved in 1937. Though they ended in fifth place, they had the highest winning percentage since Yawkey took over. Powered by Foxx, Boston was becoming recognized as a hitting team. The Sox blasted out 100 homers and were third best in the league in getting runners across the plate.

In 1938 the Red Sox, fielding their finest club in two decades, rose to second place. Six of their starters hit over .300, with Ben Chapman at .340 setting a record that no Red Sox right fielder has ever matched. Jimmie Foxx won the league batting title at .349 while smashing 50 homers, driving in 175 runs, and compiling the highest slugging average. Foxx, it has been said, "fashioned the greatest year a Red Sox hitter has ever had in Fenway Park, where he hit .405, cracked thirty-five home runs, and knocked in 104 for a Ruthian .887 slugging percentage." In being chosen MVP a third time in 1938, Foxx became the first to win that distinction. Boston also featured a talented twenty-year-old at second base, Bobby Doerr, who knocked in 80 runs and was outstanding in the field. Another of the new players, third baseman Mike "Pinky" Higgins, whom the Sox got thanks again to Connie Mack, set a record during two doubleheaders in June by hitting safely a dozen times in a row.

It may seem absurd to say that in 1939 Boston almost put it all together, since the Yankees humbled them by seventeen games, but the Sox did do a number of good things. Jimmie Foxx, batting .360, larruped a league-leading thirty-five homers, and Bobby Doerr, Joe Cronin, and Doc Cramer all hit .300. Most important, the Fenway Faithful welcomed the arrival of two new players. One of them, third baseman Jim Tabor, who had been a standout at the University of Alabama, sometimes surprised his teammates by arriving at the park sober. Tabor in his debut season batted a respectable .289 and drove in a more-than-respectable ninety-five runs. In the opener of a

Fourth of July doubleheader he hit three homers. No Red Sox player had ever done that before. Moreover, two of them were grand slams. Then he came back in the nightcap and knocked another ball into the stands, giving him eleven RBI for the holiday.

Even more impressive was rookie Ted Williams, one of the greatest athletes ever to wear a Red Sox uniform. John Updike wrote of him, "No other player visible to my generation concentrated within himself so much of the sport's poignance, so assiduously refined his natural skills, so constantly brought to the plate that intensity and competence that crowds the throat with joy." A year earlier he had come to Florida for his first spring training. Skinny, his baggy uniform drooping to his ankles, Williams did not cut an impressive figure, but, as Billy Werber later wrote, "his eyesight was sharp as a falcon's," and he "struck with the speed of a cobra." He also was an insufferable braggart. "Wait until you see Foxx hit," one of the seasoned players told the raw beginner. Williams shot back, "Wait until Foxx sees me hit!" On another occasion he announced, "I want to walk down the street after I'm through and have people say, 'There goes the greatest hitter who ever lived.'" The cocky loudmouth said he'd show them, and he did, batting .327, smashing 44 doubles and 31 homers, scoring 131 runs, and leading the majors with 145 RBI. Some of his home runs were prodigious, notably one in Detroit in early May that cleared the right-field roof at Briggs Stadium. With his phenomenal eye for the strike zone, he drew 107 walks. Not until near the end of the season did "the Kid," as he called himself, become twenty-one.

For a time the Red Sox kept in hot pursuit of the league leaders. At the All-Star break, they were only six and a half games behind, and when play resumed, they took seven out of eight from the Yankees. But their pitching did not stand up, and their defense was dreadful. The left side of the Sox infield was a sieve; the never-dependable Cronin committed thirty-two errors, Tabor an awful forty more. The egocentric, lackadaisical Williams made nineteen errors, an unusually high number for an outfielder. At one point Cronin pulled the rookie out of a game because he was sick of seeing him loaf in the outfield and on the base paths.

In 1940 Boston closed to within eight games of the pennant, and, though that was only good enough for fourth place, the Sox showed great potential. They set a record when all four of their infielders hit more than 20 home runs: Foxx, 36; Cronin, 24; Doerr, 22; and Tabor, 21. For the twelfth year in a row, Foxx bashed 30 or more homers and batted in more than 100 runs. Against the Tigers that season, he had grand slams on two consecutive days. Ted Williams, with a .344 average (third best in the league), swatted 23 homers and drove in 113 runs. Another outfielder also made his debut as a .300 hitter: the Little Professor, bespectacled Dominic DiMaggio. The pitching and the fielding, however, once again fell short. On Opening Day, Grove had a perfect game through seven innings, but Williams ended the skein by muffing a fly ball. Grove gave him a tongue-lashing, and the press chewed him out—another episode in the career-long war between Williams and the media.

In 1941 Boston climbed back to second place, though they trailed the Yankees, buoyed by Joe DiMaggio's streak of hitting safely in fifty-six consecutive games, by seventeen. Foxx, no longer as potent as he had been, managed to drive home 105 runs, hit nineteen balls into the stands, and bat .300, a remarkable accomplishment given his physical condition. Since the latter part of the 1930s, he had been suffering from blinding sinus headaches that sometimes impaired his vision. In one game he could not see at all and simply stood at the plate with the bat in his hands and made no attempt to swing. The opposing pitchers, unaware of his predicament and in awe of his strength, walked him six times in a row, a modern major-league record. It may have been the desire for surcease from the sinus stress that led Foxx to turn more and more to the alcohol that ruined his life. In 1941, despite his handicaps, he was chosen to the All-Star team for the ninth straight year. No other American League player had ever had that honor.

The spotlight in 1941, however, focused not on strongman Foxx, but on lanky Ted Williams. He had risen so far so quickly that in the All-Star contest in 1941, only his third season, he batted cleanup. He came to the plate in the bottom of the ninth with two men on base and the American League down to its last out, trailing by a run. On the fourth pitch he drove a mighty blast that struck the facade of the upper deck of Tiger Stadium, a home run that gave his team a 7–5 victory. As the Kid, who had irritated sportswriters by his smug arrogance, clapped his hands and leaped into the air rounding bases, he seemed a reborn Little Leaguer abandoning himself to the joy of the game.

In 1941 Ted Williams had the finest season of any hitter in the last two-thirds of the twentieth century. In one respect he had the best year ever, for he reached base safely more than half the time (.553), a record no other batter before or since has come close to equaling. On the final day, his batting average stood at an astronomic .3996. Manager Joe Cronin offered to let the Splendid Splinter sit out the last two games, since, when the average was rounded out, it would read .400, but Williams would not hear of it. Contrary to myth, Williams had no choice but to play, because a mark of .3996 would always have enshrouded in doubt the claim that he was a .400 hitter; but it is to his credit that, having achieved his goal in the first game of a doubleheader, he persisted in appearing in the second game too. Over the course of the afternoon, he went six for eight, including a homer and a double hit so hard that it broke a loudspeaker high on the wall in right center. In the locker room later, Williams bellowed, "Ain't I the best hitter you ever saw!" His performance catapulted him to .406. No one since has hit .400. It might be thought that he did so well because an exceptionally lively ball inflated averages that year, but Williams's mark in 1941 was forty-seven points higher than that of the league's second-best hitter. The nightcap of the twin bill was also memorable for another reason. Lefty Grove made the final appearance of his 300-win career.

The 1942 Red Sox won more games than any Sox team since 1915, a record that put them yet again in second place. For the fourth time in five years, they had the highest team batting average in the American League. Dom DiMaggio, while serving as a volunteer airplane spotter, compiled the most impressive statistics of any centerfielder in the league, better even than Brother Joe's. Batting leadoff, he hit fourteen home runs. That year, the decision reached several years earlier by Yawkey and Collins to rely less on buying players from other teams and more on building a farm system under a shrewd former umpire, Billy Evans, began to pay big dividends. Young Cecil "Tex" Hughson recorded the most victories (twenty-two) of any pitcher in the league. He gave the Red Sox its first twenty-game winner since Wes Ferrell in 1936. In the infield, Cronin made way for newcomer Johnny Pesky, whose 205 hits led the league, at the same time that he had the most assists of any shortstop. Over eight seasons, Pesky, born John Michael Paveskovich, was to bat a glittering .313. The yellow right-field foul pole at Fenway was dubbed "Pesky's Pole" because of the many home runs he was said to have hit that just barely stayed fair. In truth, the designation owes more to the warm regard writers had for the likeable Pesky, since he hit just seventeen homers in his entire career, with at most only eight of them hugging the line. Once more in 1942, though, the standout player was not Pesky, Hughson, or DiMaggio, but Ted Williams. It seemed inconceivable that he could match his extraordinary 1941 season, but in 1942 he won the American League triple crown: most homers, most runs batted in, highest batting average.

With this outstanding array of players, Boston had legitimate aspirations to its first pennant in a generation, but World War II snuffed them out. The Red Sox may have been hit harder than any other team by the war. Of their best players, only Doerr, Tabor, and Hughson were still around on Opening Day 1943, and by 1945 these three, too, were in uniform. In 1943 the depleted Red Sox dropped all the way to seventh, though on Bunker Hill Day Joe Cronin, who set a new league mark for pinch-hit home runs in a season, knocked three-run pinch-hit homers in each game of a doubleheader. The following year, Boston was in the thick of the pennant fight near the end of the season, only to lose to the armed services, in the first two weeks of September, Bobby Doerr, the league's second leading hitter; Tex Hughson, already an eighteen-game winner, with the best percentage in the league; and Hal Wagner, their hard-hitting catcher. With the heart of the lineup gone, the Sox slipped to fourth. In 1945, the year Uncle Sam took the last of their prewar stars, Jim Tabor, they welcomed to their pitching staff Dave "Boo" Ferriss, mustered out for health reasons, who won twenty-one games in his first season. But they did not have much else going for them. Moreover, Joe Cronin's career came to an abrupt end when, by catching his spikes while rounding a bag, he broke his leg. It happened on Patriots' Day at—where else?—Yankee Stadium.

Red Sox players in uniform did Boston proud, while the Boston management struggled to make do. Johnny Pesky joined the Naval Air Corps; Dom DiMaggio enlisted in the Navy. Ted Williams, under fire in the press for seeking to maintain a draft exemption, became a Marine Corps pilot, though he did not fly combat missions until the Korean War. Earl Johnson won both the Bronze and Silver Stars and was commissioned a second lieutenant on the field because of his bravery under fire in the Battle of the Bulge. At home, the Red Sox improvised. To comply with government requests restricting travel, the Sox moved spring training in 1943 and 1944 from Florida to the Tufts University campus in the Boston suburb of Med-ford, where, when players ventured outdoors, they wore long underwear. The Grapefruit League gave way to the "Frosbite League." In the first ex-hibition game of 1943 against the Brooklyn Dodgers at Ebbets Field, the season, noted one reporter, instead of an "atmosphere of orange groves, flamevine and hibiscus, opens in the smoke and grime of Flatbush." In 1944 Joe Cronin complained, "This is the first time I ever wore overshoes to spring training." In 1945 the Red Sox switched to a small New Jersey town just outside Atlantic City. One of the few franchises to lose money during the war, the Red Sox had more than the usual reasons to welcome V-J Day.

Boston fans turned out in record numbers in 1946 — 1,416,944, in contrast to the 1932 attendance of 182,150 — to welcome home their heroes. There would have been many more spectators, but Fenway was too small to ac-commodate them. At some sellouts, the Sox management stationed sentries blocks away to ward off people who did not have tickets. The Red Sox pub-licity director said, "There were as many people heading back for the sub-ways an hour before game time as there were coming to the ball park."

The Red Sox gave their followers a lot to cheer about. The first three bat-ters in the lineup — Dom DiMaggio, Johnny Pesky (again leading the Amer-ican League in hits), and Ted Williams — all finished over .300. Bobby Doerr chipped in with eighteen homers and knocked in 116 runs, while slugger Rudy York, their new first baseman, rattled the fences. The Red Sox also had an impressive starting rotation: Boo Ferriss (a twenty-five game winner), Tex Hughson (twenty wins, a team-leading 172 strikeouts, and a 2.75 ERA), southpaw Mickey Harris (seventeen victories), and Joe Dobson (thirteen wins), as well as a dependable relief corps. During the season Ferriss and Hughson each had twelve-game winning streaks.

So spectacular were the Red Sox in 1946 that at midseason they placed no fewer than eight of their players on the All-Star team — Bobby Doerr, Johnny Pesky, Dom DiMaggio, Hal Wagner, Rudy York, Boo Ferriss, Mickey Harris, and Ted Williams, who gave one of the greatest perfor-mances in the history of the event. By the time he got up for his final turn at the plate to face the Pirates' Rip Sewell, Williams had already hit a homer and two singles. Sewell was famed for a bizarre "eephus" pitch that went twenty-five feet high in the air, arcing in a parabola before uncannily dropping across the plate in the strike zone. It came down so slowly and at such a weird angle that, if the batter did manage to hit it, he could not drive it very far. When, on his first pitch, Sewell served an eephus, Williams almost broke his back trying to get to it. Sewell zipped a fastball by him, missed on another moonball, then decided to strike Williams out with a third eephus. But Williams, with exquisite timing, smashed the ball into the right-field bullpen, then laughed his way around the bases. It was not only his second homer of the game, but the only one ever hit off Sewell's eephus.

Five days later the Cleveland manager, Lou Boudreau, resolved to do something altogether unorthodox to contain Williams. In the first game of a doubleheader, Teddy Ballgame had almost singlehandedly carried the Sox to an 11–10 come-from-behind victory by walloping three home runs and knocking in eight. In the second game of the twin bill, Williams doubled in his first turn at the plate. The Indians' manager had seen enough. The next time Number Nine came up, Boudreau shifted all his players rightward, clustering them in the part of the field where the drives of the left-hand-hitting Williams were most likely to go and abandoning the considerable acreage where the third baseman and left fielder usually played. Since Williams persisted in hitting as he always had—because he was a proud man, because he did not want his power taken away from him, because he did not want to tamper with his graceful swing—"the Boudreau shift" (which had first been employed some years earlier by Jimmy Dykes) often worked.

But not always. On September 13, 1946, the Red Sox, within one game of clinching the pennant, found themselves in a tight pitching duel with no certainty of victory. Once again their opponent was Cleveland. In the first inning, with Williams up, Boudreau put on the shift. The Kid, seeing the Indians positioning themselves in this exaggerated manner, foxed them by driving a long ball to the vacated left side. By the time the Cleveland left fielder had tracked it down and thrown it in, Williams had crossed the plate with the only inside-the-park homer of his career. "My heart was in my legs that day," he later recalled of his race toward home. "I was thinking about all the years that Tom Yawkey had been trying to give Boston a pennant. There were plenty of us players who were getting tired of finishing second, too." With Tex Hughson pitching shutout ball, the game ended 1–0, and the Boston Red Sox had their first pennant since 1918. On orders from

Beantown's irrepressible mayor, James Michael Curley, firebells and sirens screeched from Beacon Hill to Dorchester.

The Red Sox and Ted Williams had outclassed the rest of the league in 1946. The Sox started the season 21–4 and coasted in by a decisive twelve-game margin, seventeen games better than the Yankees. Williams had a fabulous year. Batting .342 and leading the majors in walks, total bases, runs, and slugging percentage, he won his first MVP award. In addition to his All-Star game heroics and his pennant-winning homer, another turn at bat was unforgettable: the longest measured home run in Fenway history. Williams drove a changeup 502 feet into the bleachers where it struck a fan in the head. "How far away must one sit to be safe in this park?" the man asked plaintively. Today that spot is marked in bright red amidst a sea of green seats.

The year did not end on this high note, as Boston fans know all too well. The Red Sox took a 3–2 lead over the St. Louis Cardinals in the 1946 World Series and needed only one more victory for their first world championship since 1918. Instead they became the first Red Sox team to lose a World Series. Williams, who hit only .200 and would never again get to play in a World Series, broke down in tears. After that, Red Sox fans reprised Country Slaughter's madcap scamper around the bases as the opening scene in a melodrama of postseason engagements that did not yield a happy ending until fifty-eight years later.

One must remember, though, how far the Red Sox had come—from the depths of 1932 to pennant winners and almost world champions. Granted, it was dismaying to get so close in 1946, only to fall short, as would happen too many times afterward. But there truly is something worse, a lot worse, than losing a postseason series, and that is not getting there at all. If it is crushing to taste defeat at the eleventh hour, try rooting for a team that year after year finishes in the cellar, that year after year opens the season with no hope at all, that year after year is a laughingstock. That was the Boston experience too often in the interwar years.

The Red Sox Nation would profit from a bit of perspective. Boston fans are not the only ones to have known disappointment. The Giants are thought of as a club that has enjoyed considerable success, but they, too, have had mortifying moments: the Merkle boner, the Snodgrass muff, the time Heinie Zimmerman chased Eddie Collins across home plate. Wrigley Field jests bear a morbid resemblance to those heard at Fenway. In one Norman Rockwell cover for the *Saturday Evening Post*, the Chicago dugout is vividly imagined with every Cub player clinically depressed. Since 1945 Cubs fans have not seen a single pennant winner, while Red Sox rooters have had four. Dodger supporters still groan about Mickey Owen's letting a third strike get away and Bobby Thomson's "shot heard 'round the world." Followers of the Minnesota Twins, the Baltimore Orioles, the Cincinnati Reds, the Milwaukee Brewers, the Atlanta Braves, and the Cleveland Indians have all experienced cheering their favorites on from April to October, only to see them lose in the seventh game of a World Series. St. Louis Cardinals boosters have had that happen three times, twice when the Cards held 3–2 leads in World Series games. Even Yankee aficionados, those undeserving children of grace, live with more than a few excruciating memories. On five separate occasions since 1957 the boys in pinstripes have been humbled in the seventh game of a World Series. Recollection of Bill Mazeroski's homer off Ralph Terry in the bottom of the ninth in 1960 still rankles, and as recently as 2001 the Yankees led Arizona in the final inning of the Series, only to see the Diamondbacks walk off the field the victors. There was no "curse of the Bambino" marking the Red Sox alone for perdition.

The history of the Red Sox from 1918 to 2003, familiarly narrated as a chronicle of unparalleled, unmitigated bad fortune, might well be conceived of differently. Looking back on the twentieth century, Red Sox fans have had lot to be jubilant about: Cy and Smoky, Tris and the Babe, Jimmie and Lefty, Ted and Tex, Yaz and Pudge, Freddie and Jim, Dewey and the Spaceman, Pedro and Nomar. The lines of direction from the Ruthless 1920s mostly trended upward. True, the Red Sox did not win a world championship between 1918 and 2004. But it is also true that World War II Boston finished in the first division two-thirds of the time. Not every team can say that. From 1925 through 1932, the Red Sox were consigned to last place, baseball's version of Dante's hell, seven out of eight years. From 1933, the year Yawkey took over, to the present, a period of seven decades, they have not been at the bottom of the American League even once. It may well be fatal to my argument to end by quoting a former manager of the despised Yankees, but, as Casey Stengel was fond of saying, "You could look it up."

3

Ted Williams: Boston Hero, Boston Legend

John Demos

Ted Williams was the hero of my childhood. And of many other childhoods, too. If you were a boy living in or around Boston between 1940 and 1960, you simply couldn't avoid knowing about—talking about—caring about—worrying about—and being intermittently thrilled about—this one-of-a-kind, larger-than-life-itself, man-child of a baseball player. (I'm not sure about the girls. My sister was crazy about a chunky shortstop named Junior Stephens, who actually tied Ted one year for the runs-batted-in lead. For the most part, however, girls of that benighted era were not expected to feel concerned with sports and sports heroes.) In fact the same level of interest could be found in boys living far from Boston. A longtime friend and college classmate of mine, who grew up in Idaho, remembers deciding that "one of the best reasons for going to Harvard was the chance to see Ted Williams play ball."[1]

The bare facts of Ted's life and career are easily recounted.[2] Born in San Diego, 1918. Salvation Army mother. Alcoholic, generally absent father. Juvenile-delinquent brother. Became a professional ballplayer right out of high school. Moved swiftly through the minor leagues (San Diego Padres, Minneapolis Millers); reached the majors, and Boston, and the Red Sox, in

1939. Had two separate stints of wartime service: flight instructor, World War II, 1943–1945; combat pilot, Korean War, 1952–1953. Retired as a player, 1960. Elected to baseball's Hall of Fame, 1965. Returned as a manager (Washington Senators), 1969–1972. Retired for good, to Florida. Avid fisherman and outdoorsman. Married and divorced three times; three children. Died 2002. (Alas, we have to add that his remains have been "cryogenically" preserved, in apparent hopes of his eventual resurrection. But this bizarre postmortem—arranged by two of his children, against Ted's wishes—need not concern us here.)

Ted's hold on me and the rest of my boyhood cohort involved a rare combination of sheer athletic performance, dramatic flair, and personal charisma. Some of this is suggested by the extraordinary proliferation of nicknames and tag-lines attaching to him: The Splendid Splinter, The Thumper, The Beantown Basher, Teddy Ballgame, Terrible Ted, or simply The Kid (his own favorite). I remember trying out each one of them in "broadcasts" I composed of fantasy games designed to feature Ted's heroism. I remember, too, how *lovely* they sounded as they moved through the approving air between my lips and my ears!

In fact, however, Ted needed no one to speak for him; his own voice was clear, loud, insistent, and frequently raised on his own behalf. He said what he thought and felt, often pithily, sometimes recklessly. And we can re-approach the matter of his heroism now by way of his own words . . .

> All I ever want out of life is that when I walk down the street
> people will say, "there goes the greatest hitter that ever lived."[3]

This is perhaps the best-known sentence in the entire corpus of Williams-on-Williams utterances. And it does seem the candid expression of a deeply felt wish. As such it invites careful response from those who followed Ted's career close-up (or followed other similarly lustrous careers both before and after).

To begin with: in 1941, in only his third season of big-league play, Ted's batting average finished at an astounding .406. It had been eleven years since any player reached the .400 level; and no one has done it in the six-plus decades that have followed. From this grew yet another of the Williams tag-lines: "last of the .400 hitters." For players and fans alike, .400 is truly a benchmark number, a beautiful number, a magic number. There is none other quite like it in the number-crazed world of baseball, and nothing remotely comparable in any other sport. .400 means two hits in every five times at bat, for an entire season. Batting championships have been won with averages of several dozen points less. And .300 is invariably considered an excellent year.

Ted's .406 average belonged to one of baseball's most memorable seasons.[4] Joe DiMaggio's record hitting streak—fifty-six consecutive games—filled almost two months in midsummer. The incomparable pitcher, Lefty Grove, was ending his career with the Red Sox; in July he got his three hundredth win (another benchmark statistic). The National League's Brooklyn Dodgers and St. Louis Cardinals fought to the last weekend in what some called "the greatest pennant-race ever." The World Series, a Yankee-Dodger "subway" affair, was taut and tight until Mickey Owen's dropped third strike—the most famous "boner" in baseball history—tipped the balance toward the Yankees. And all this diamond drama played out against the backdrop of war in Europe, soon to envelop America as well.

The particular drama of Ted's average built and built through the summer. It started slowly; in mid-May he was around .330. However, an astonishing hot streak put him at .436, his season high, by early June. Thereafter he was mostly above, occasionally a bit below, the magic number—until a little slump right at the end dropped him to .39955, with only a doubleheader in Philadelphia left on the schedule. The rest has long since become a cherished nugget of baseball lore. Rounded off to the nearest digit, Ted's penultimate average would have counted as .400; and Sox manager Joe Cronin offered to hold him out of the lineup on that last day. But Ted declined; "the record's no good," he said, "unless it's made in all the games." So: his batting line for the season-ending doubleheader? Game one: single, home run, single, single, ground-ball error. Game two: single, double, fly out. All told: six for eight; batting average firmly, and permanently, lodged at .406. (Today's sacrifice fly rule would have made it ten points higher.)[5]

If this was Ted's biggest and best season-long achievement, there were others nearly as good. In 1942, and again in 1947, he won the batting "Triple Crown" (league leadership in average, home runs, and runs batted in). And, perhaps more striking still, in 1957, at the athletically improbable age of thirty-nine, Ted actually flirted with .400—again—ending at a remarkable .388. In that same season he also managed his second-highest slugging percentage, .731, and his best-ever ratio of home runs to at-bats, 1:11. It was, by any measure, the finest batting year by an *old* player ever. His single-game heroics were far too numerous to mention here, save perhaps for one: his two-out, ninth-inning home run to win the All-Star game in 1941—another quick salute to that fabled season—a hit Ted would later call "the most thrilling of my life."[6] (This was before my own baseball consciousness began. So here's another that I do vividly recall: in the All-Star game of 1946 Ted went four for four, including a unique home run off Rip Sewell's notorious 25-foot-arc "blooper pitch.")[7]

Another key part of his heroics: remarkable farewells, followed by remarkable returns.[8] *April 16, 1946:* In the first game of the new season, Ted comes back from three years of wartime service and promptly strokes a 466-foot home run. *September 15, 1950:* Ted returns to the lineup after three months of recuperation from an All-Star game injury (elbow broken in a collision with the outfield wall while making a difficult catch) and bangs out four hits, including a homer. *April 30, 1952:* In his last at-bat before going off to fly combat missions in Korea, Ted hits a game-winning home run off Detroit stalwart (and fishing buddy) Dizzy Trout. (Was this one a friendly setup? The question does get raised.) *August 1953:* Ted is back from Korea, and after a period of arduous reconditioning—his thirty-six-year-old body has softened, and widened, quite a bit—he returns to the Red Sox for the season's closing month; homers spring off his bat (thirteen in a mere ninety-one tries), and his batting average during that brief run is a bracing .407. His very next year begins with a severe injury: broken collarbone in spring training, surgically pinned back in place. Then, *May 16, 1954:* Ted reenters the lineup for a doubleheader in Detroit and cracks eight hits, including two homers. Asked afterward about his collarbone, he says "It hurts like hell;" asked about such remarkable results, Yankee manager Casey Stengel quips, "I'm going to have all my players put pins in their shoulders." *September 1957:* Ted is felled, not for the first time, by a severe, pneumonia-like virus, but comes back after three weeks to strike home runs in four consecutive at-bats (two as a pinch-hitter). These, in turn, become part of a record string of sixteen straight times reaching base. "I feel terrible," he comments to reporters, "but every time I swing at the ball, it goes out of the park."

The very last was best of all. *September 28, 1960:* the end of a mostly forgettable season (with the now forty-two-year-old Ted's average down to a
mere .317), his absolutely final game. The moment has been forever preserved by John Updike in a hauntingly beautiful *New Yorker* piece "Hub
Fans Bid Kid Adieu."[9] Another writer, forty years on, would be foolish to
venture back very far into such Homeric territory, but the headlines at least
must be recorded here. Sox against Baltimore. Cloudy, damp day; ball
doesn't carry well; not good at all for the batters. Jack Fisher pitching for the
Orioles. In the third, Ted flies deep to center; in the fifth, deeper—up
against the fence—to right; in the eighth, deeper still—*over* the fence this
time—for a wondrously fitting exit home run. The official park attendance
that day was 10,454; but at least a million would later swear they were there.

It would be hard to overstate the cumulative impact of such times. *He's
here, he's away, he's coming back:* thus the recurrent rhythm. Include the
ups and downs when he was present and playing—the amazing hot streaks,
the occasional deep slumps, not to mention his frequently changing moods
—and you got a kind of yo-yo effect. It kept us endlessly on edge, and sharp-
ened our sense of his heroism.

And through it all we wondered—we still wonder—about the "greatest
hitter" question. How does one measure and compare the great ones? Certainly, it goes beyond the matter of singular achievements, to encompass
finally the shape of an entire career. Lifetime batting average? Ted stands
near, but not at, the very top; his .344 is fourth on the all-time list. (Ty Cobb
leads with .367.) Home runs? His 521 was third when he retired, fourteenth
now. (Hank Aaron's 755 is best.) Slugging percentage? His .634 is second to
Babe Ruth's .690. On-base percentage? Here he stands first, at .483. And it
goes on. In sum, he stands around the top, within hailing distance of the
top, in category after category after category.[10]

There are, moreover, special considerations, most of which strengthen
the case in Ted's favor. His two-part military service obviously, and very significantly, reduced his career-long totals. Nearly five years away translates
into approximately 180 home runs; include these, and Ted climbs to third
all-time. Similar adjustments for other categories (runs scored, runs batted
in, and walks, for example) produce similar results. The "percentage" numbers are trickier. But we may reasonably assume that Ted's first wartime stint
(1943–1945, age twenty-five to twenty-seven) deprived him of his absolute

peak years; at least they are "peak" for most players. His batting average over the two seasons just preceding was .380, a likely indicator for the ones he lost. Finally, Ted's 1950 elbow injury must also be factored in. Though it healed much better than at first seemed likely, it left a lasting imprint on his swing. His arm "extension" would never again be complete; as a result, he was a bit more vulnerable to the outside pitch. In 1951, the immediate post-injury year, his average fell to .319, his poorest to that point.

So where does it all come out? "Greatest ever"? Or not? In truth, there is no settling such a question, but this much can be said. If "greatest" means most complete combination of power and average, there are two clear candidates, and only two. Williams and Ruth; the Kid and the Babe. And if we use on-base percentage to break the tie, it's Ted by a hair. (All right, go ahead, accuse me of bias. Hero-worshipers can scarcely be trusted with such weighty judgments, and I may indeed be overreaching here.) Anyway: one of the *two* greatest, for sure.

> Hitting a baseball is the single most difficult thing to do in
> sports.[11]

Thus spoke the maestro, many a time. And who can doubt it? Where else is so much compressed into such a tight frame? A major-league fastball takes a bit more than half a second to travel from pitcher's hand to home plate. A curve or slider adds the dimension of lateral movement. In this tiny interval the batter must, first, gauge oncoming speed, trajectory, and ultimate location; second, decide whether or not to swing; and third—if swinging—initiate a complex set of motions designed to produce the maximally effective meeting of bat and ball. No two players swing in exactly the same way. Each has his own style; each practices it, refines it with experience, considers (and reconsiders) it, loves it. Swinging a bat comes to feel instinctive, primordial, delicious.

And no one had a finer swing than Ted. Smoother, quicker, cleaner, just flat-out gorgeous. The "coiled spring" start: feet apart, knees partly bent, bat cocked diagonally over left shoulder, head turned sharply to face the pitcher. The quick, short backswing, the fanny wiggle; then everything *forward*, as hips turn, front leg strides, arms extend. *Whoosh!* Contact! And follow-through: bat completes its long arc, with chest and arms fully rotated, legs straightening, eyes closed, as if in a kind of ecstasy, for the final millisecond. In sum: what teammate Johnny Pesky called "that great buggywhip swing."[12] I can see it now.

Ted's mastery of the swing led some to call him "the greatest *natural* hitter ever." But he wouldn't buy it; indeed, he resented it. As if his brilliance had dropped from the sky, or sprouted from his genes. No, he reminded us again and again, it was all a matter of "practice, practice, practice." Of course, he did have the physical tools—for one thing, a long, muscular frame. But even that had to be honed and developed. As a young player he was very much "the stringbean" (his own phrase), and he worked at the process of filling out. In those pre-weight-training days, he walked, he ran, he did calisthenics, he squeezed rubber balls, he exercised tirelessly. He grew stronger as he aged, at least up to a point; his home runs to at-bats ratio actually increased in his later years (even with the limitation of his injured elbow).

Clearly, too, he was possessed of quick reflexes and excellent hand-to-eye coordination. His eyes provided an especially lively topic of discussion.[13] There grew over time a kind of mythology about Ted's sight—that it was, in and of itself, a unique gift, virtually superhuman. Stories abounded: he could read signs that other people couldn't even see; he could shoot down pigeons in the Fenway rafters from clear across the park; he could count the stitches on the ball as it met his bat. In fact this *was* a myth, nothing more. Ted's eyes were better than most; but 20–10 isn't completely unheard of. And, as he grew older, his eyes—like everyone's eyes—began to weaken.

Ted's work ethic, around hitting, was total. His practice sessions went on and on, in every conceivable venue; "I say Williams has hit more balls than any guy living," he liked to claim. He carried bats around with him, and swung them at opportune moments. Thus did broken furniture, especially mirrors, in various hotel rooms become another part of his legend. Even with no bat available—for instance, in the outfield, with a game in progress—he would carefully go through the motions of a swing.

But there was still more to it than physical skill and practice; Ted's brain, no less than his body, was centrally involved. He viewed hitting as a "science," and was forever analyzing its most arcane details. He would be its intellectual, no less than its practical, master, an Einstein in his chosen field. He had studied physics in the service, as part of preparing to become a flight instructor, and he sought to apply aerodynamic theory to questions like the movement of a curveball. This technical expertise was combined with a much more *ad hoc* experiential approach, exemplified by his eager, endless *talk* of hitting—both as a teacher of young players coming up, and as a colleague of other "masters" with whom he was regularly in touch (Ty Cobb, Rogers Hornsby, Bill Terry, all of them predecessors in the .400 club).

As part of the same overall program, he maintained a capacious memory bank, in which to store a trove of impressions of all the pitchers he had ever faced and his past encounters with them. He studied umpires no less closely, and mentally catalogued their strike-zone preferences. (He was not above a little gamesmanship either; understanding both pitchers and umpires as well as he did, he would flatter them to gain an edge.) He was an expert, too, on wind currents, and mound heights, and other minutiae of each and every major-league stadium. He would not be taken by surprise, not be fooled. He would plan to the last detail. He would *know*.

His absolute first principle was taken from Hornsby: *get a good ball to hit*. And from this flowed his extraordinary batting discipline. Each trip to the plate was an exercise in mental concentration, a call to calculated, rigorous choice. By the time he had carefully dug his spikes into the loose dirt of the batter's box, he was ready, really *ready*. He would swing, or not, depending on all the factors he had previously studied. His enormous total of bases-on-balls (second, lifetime, only to Ruth) testified both to the pitchers' respect for him and to his own unwavering focus.

So: a "natural" he wasn't. And a worker, a practitioner, a devotee he certainly was. He attained star status in high school, but no more so than many others who did (and didn't) reach the major leagues. His first two professional seasons, with the minor-league San Diego Padres, produced unspectacular averages of .271 and .291 and a modest home-run total of twenty-three. It was only later—after San Diego—that his career, and talent, began to soar.

All this was, in turn, a great encouragement to his legion of young followers like myself. We, too, could swing bats endlessly in our bedrooms and backyards. (And, yes, we also broke some furniture.) We, too, could practice the discipline of *getting a good ball to hit*. We, too, could share talk, and tips, and the various fine points of our batting experience. That had been Ted's route, we knew; why not ours?

> I'll be back. Tell that to all of them. Vosmik, Cramer, and
> Chapman [the starting Red Sox outfield in 1938] think I'm just
> a fresh young punk, don't they? Well, you can tell them I'll be
> back, and I'll make more money in a single year than the three
> of them put together.[14]

Those were the words of a young (nineteen-year-old), hurt, and frustrated
Ted Williams at the end of his first spring training with the Red Sox. He was
being sent down to the minors for one more year of seasoning. His reaction—a kind of baseball equivalent of General MacArthur's famous "I shall
return," on being driven from the Philippines—is also part of Ted's legend.
Indeed, it epitomized some of the inner fires that would later mark his career as indelibly as his playing-field accomplishments.

Ted was repeatedly hurt by things done to or said about him. And he became repeatedly—correspondingly—angry. Perhaps this reflected his early
years as a sometimes neglected, frequently "embarrassed" child. He never
forgot the excruciating shame he had felt when obliged to hold out a Salvation Army plate on the streets of San Diego alongside his mother.[15] (Also
striking in this connection is the way he framed his "greatest hitter" goal:
"when I walk down the street, people will say . . .") Whatever the cause,
wherever its roots, Ted was a transparently sensitive soul. As he commented
ruefully near the end of his life, "in a crowd of cheers I could always pick
out the solitary boo."[16]

The quality greatly complicated his relationship with sportswriters. His
feuds with various "knights of the keyboard," as he mockingly called them,
were notorious. It was hard to say how these originated—a harsh word in a
postgame commentary, a profane rejoinder flung across the locker room—
but, once begun, they went on and on. And the writers gave as good as they
got, maybe better; skewering the mighty Ted sold papers. *He was not a team
player.* (But if so, why did he often play hurt or sick?) *He couldn't hit in the
clutch.* (But what about his ninety-eight game-winning home runs?)[17] *He
was not a leader.* (But how, then, to understand his widely acknowledged
helpfulness to younger players?) *He was not a good husband or father;* for
example, he was off fishing in Florida when his first child was born in
Boston. (But, he said, she arrived prematurely.) *He was a poor, even un-
patriotic, citizen,* as when he queried his military callup in 1942. (But, he

claimed, he was the sole support of his mother.) The list was endless, and Ted never forgot or forgave. When honored on the field at Fenway before his final game, he looked up at the press box and began a little speech by saying: "Despite some of the terrible things written about me . . . and they *were* terrible things . . ."[18]

He never forgot, never forgave, and never changed, either. On the contrary, he insisted on remaining true to what he saw as his personal core. "I've always criticized myself," he wrote in his autobiography, "for the times I've let other guys dictate what happened to me."[19] (Such times were few, however.) There were little things like his unwillingness to don a necktie. (Actually, this was less little than it seems now. In the 1940s and 1950s neckties for men were *de rigueur* in most public settings; Ted's open-shirt style was, to say the least, conspicuous.) There were somewhat bigger things, like his refusal to tip his cap to the fans. Both then and now, cap-tipping is a ballplayer's chief way of acknowledging cheers. Ted did it in his first year; but soon thereafter—piqued by some slight (or so he perceived)—he stopped, and wouldn't resume. Even on his last day, even after that last at-bat and final glorious home run, he circled the bases and entered the dugout—while the crowd roared in delirious appreciation—with hands held resolutely to his sides. About this moment Updike famously wrote, "Gods do not answer letters." And Ted himself said, "Maybe I should have . . . but I couldn't. It just wouldn't have been me."[20]

This insistence on his own way—this stubbornness, not to say arrogance —spilled over at times into his on-field play. In the middle of the 1946 season, as the Red Sox marched toward a rare pennant, opposing teams began to use a "Williams shift." Initially devised by Lou Boudreau, player-manager of the Cleveland Indians, the shift moved fielders way around to the right (where Ted would most often pull the ball); the left side, meanwhile, remained practically vacant. Would Ted adjust, and direct his hits the other way? His answer was yes and no; or, rather, no and yes. At first, and for some time thereafter, he seemed to feel provoked—insulted—by this novel defensive strategy, and pulled the ball just as before. He did lose some hits as a result. But later he would deliberately aim to left, at least on occasion; once he even bunted for a double that way. (Oh, the shame of it!)

He detested ceremony, and largely avoided the rubber-chicken circuit; as soon as the playing season was over, he would head straight for his favorite

fishing camps. He expressed open disdain for "big shots" and "front runners"—or, for that matter, "the necktie crowd." His friends included many
from quite ordinary walks of life, some met in serendipitous ways: Johnny
Orlando, the Red Sox locker-room manager and Ted's closest confidant
over the years; Sergeant John Blake, a Massachusetts state cop who pulled
him over on the Providence Turnpike one day; Johnny Buckley, a movie-
house usher who insisted he take his feet off the chair; Chrysanthe Fry, a
college student and aspiring pianist, who introduced herself at a local benefit. He chatted easily with cabdrivers, hotel porters, letter carriers, and firemen, and sometimes brought them along to the clubhouse at Fenway. He
was extraordinarily generous to children—The Kid doing for kids. Especially during his first Boston years he would scoop up whole groups of
young fans for an outing to nearby Revere Beach. Sick children appealed to
him most of all. His work on behalf of the Jimmy Fund, a Boston charity for
children's cancer research, was unstinting—not only in raising money, but
also in numerous, mostly unpublicized, hospital visits. And this continued
long after his retirement. When Boston sportswriter Dan Shaughnessy's
eight-year-old daughter Kate contracted leukemia in the mid-1990s, Ted
called again and again, visited, sent gifts and constant encouragement—all
this though he was himself old (approaching eighty) and chronically ill.[21]

Such remarkable, and repeated, acts of outreach must somehow have
tapped into his own unhealed wounds from childhood. But there were
darker residues as well. The worst came in his intemperate public outbursts
against writers, against fans, against fate, indeed (so it seemed) against the
entire world. A strikeout, an error, or perhaps just a lethargic play in the
field would be followed by some booing from the stands; this, in turn,
might bring on a full-blown Williams tantrum. Cursing, spitting, obscene
gestures: he did them all. We, his acolytes and admirers, cringed, just
cringed on his account. *If only, Ted, if only you wouldn't . . .*

He was much too inclined to blame others: the press, most obviously, but
also the Red Sox front office (for not sufficiently protecting him from "embarrassing" situations) and "gutless politicians" (for, among other things,
supposedly engineering his second callup to military service). Yet he was
also honest, sometimes unsparing, with and about himself. He freely acknowledged his "emotional, explosive" nature, his tendency to "pop off,"
his readiness to feel "persecuted." He admitted having been "a fresh kid,"

who did "a lot of yakking"—in order, he later said, to "hide a rather large inferiority complex." He was also a quick study—witness his success in wartime pilot training—and his curiosity was bottomless. ("I want to know why.
I think why is a wonderful word.") But he was poorly educated ("I was a
lousy student") and wished it had been otherwise.[22] When Harvard considered offering him an honorary degree, he quickly demurred, because he felt
his baseball accomplishments ill matched to that sort of distinction.[23] He
knew who he was—and wasn't.

> When Mrs. Yawkey asked me to throw out the first ball in
> Boston during the 1986 World Series, I was proud to do it. I'd
> long since made my peace with . . . Boston.

Ted's specific connection to Boston is itself an interesting question: how
deep? of what sort? with what consequences? If his long life were divided
into quarters, only the second belonged to Boston: the first was Californian,
the last two were centered in Florida. Ted never made a real home in
Boston; during most of his Red Sox years he rented a little suite at the
Somerset Hotel for the in-season months, and spent the rest far away. One
could say, too, that his everyday style and Boston's were not a good match:
open-neck versus button-down, spontaneous and in-your-face versus fitting-
and-proper, and so on.

His coming to Boston in the first place was hardly foreordained. Other
teams had been interested in this "gangly teenager" with "the perfect
swing"; the New York Giants, in particular, nearly got to him first. But in
the late summer of 1936 Eddie Collins, then the Red Sox general manager,
went west to scout two other San Diego prospects, saw Ted play more or less
by accident, recognized his talent, and pushed team owner Tom Yawkey to
rush him a contract. Ted himself was taken completely by surprise, and
needed a map to find out where he was going. ("I thought, Jesus, it's a long
ways.") Moreover, in the years that followed, Ted was nearly traded away
on two occasions—to the hated Yankees, of all teams, for the great Joe
DiMaggio, of all players—but both deals fell through just short of consum-
mation. In short: he almost didn't come; he almost left in midcareer; he
wasn't around except when he had to be; he wasn't a great fit, to begin
with.[24]

No matter: as time passed, Boston took Ted to its heart—and he, in his fashion, reciprocated. He would visit from time to time in the off-season; I remember attending a "sportsmen's show" in January one year, in order to see him demonstrate fly casting (an activity in which I otherwise had absolutely no interest). After his retirement he came back for the occasional "old-timers' game"; I went just to watch him hold a bat again. In 1991 the team and city organized an official Ted Williams Day. He returned, stood on the grass at Fenway, made a gracious speech of appreciation (with just a brief jab at sportswriters), and—best of all—donned a Sox cap and tipped it lavishly to the fans. A street adjacent to the park was rechristened Ted Williams Way; a bit later Boston's new harbor tunnel would also take his name.

His final public appearance was as part of the festivities before the 1999 All-Star game, held for the first time in many years at Fenway. He was in a wheelchair by then, and obviously frail; but something of the old fire still flashed from his eyes and on his face. As he was pushed slowly toward the pitching mound for the introduction, an unforgettable tableau took shape. The various All-Star players, from both leagues, began to move toward him, and then completely surround him. Some had baseballs for him to sign; others wished simply to shake his hand; others seemed too abashed to do more than stare. He knew them all by sight, had watched them play (on television); he offered them greetings and even (it seemed) a batting tip or two. This milling scene continued much longer than expected, and league officials had to plead for an end to it so that the actual game might begin. Even then some players lingered nearby for as long as they possibly could.

I understood, in that moment, a complicated piece of my own experience as a young fan decades before. I had idolized Ted completely, but at the same time always assumed that baseball's true immortals belonged to a *previous* generation. I remember listening, with great interest and respect and at least a twinge of envy, as older fans told firsthand stories of Ruth, Cobb, Gehrig, et al. Much as I would have liked, I dared not put Ted, or any other then-active players, on the same level. There is something about baseball that honors the past, honors tradition, honors history, to a quite exaggerated degree. And when I saw this attitude vividly enacted by a fresh crop of big-leaguers—themselves All-Stars, including several sure bets for the Hall of Fame—it brought a certain closure. Ted belonged with the immortals, maybe even at the head of the immortals, after all. And I had been hugely lucky to see him play for so many years.

> I realized [later on] . . . that the fans were always with me. I
> had a love affair with them, and they had a love affair with
> me.[25]

Yes, exactly so. There was indeed intensity—emotion—romance in the way he and we connected. Each trip to Fenway during the Williams years carried special feelings of anticipation. (Would Ted hit one today?) Each time at bat was, as he put it himself, "an adventure for me." The energy of those moments was electric, and quite impossible to resist. Updike again: "This man, you realized—and here, perhaps, was the difference, greater than the difference in gifts—really intended to hit the ball."[26]

It is, after all, hitting that sets baseball apart. Running, throwing, catching: variants of these belong to many other sports. But hitting, "the single hardest thing," is unique. (Cricket, you say? Hardly counts at all. A weird little game played by Englishmen in starched shirts and bowler hats.) It was hitting that all of us would-be major leaguers most strongly aspired to. And it was Ted who did it better than anyone, who approached perfection, who set us the loftiest of standards.

The romance was complicated—was deepened, actually—by Ted's personal foibles. His emotional ups and downs mirrored something in us as well; we rose and fell with him, as if in mute synchrony. Was he occasionally disappointed, frustrated, "mad" (a word he often used for himself)? Well, so, too, were we. Was he pleased, or openly joyful, after yet another brilliant hit? We saw that, and shared in it. Did he sometimes feel unfairly treated by an uncomprehending or unsympathetic world? No less so than we. Had he occasionally crossed the line of public decorum in egregious gestures of affront? We cringed, yes; we made excuses for him, yes; we even apologized on his behalf, yes; but, for all that, we understood. And his very stubbornness—perversity even—spoke eloquently to our own private struggles. He was himself, he knew himself, he expressed himself with honesty and abandon. *With honesty and abandon.*

> Was this not a kind of recipe-for-Life?
> From The Kid?
> To a kid?

4

The Year of the Yaz

John M. Carroll

Many Bostonians, New Englanders, and members of a tribe now designated as Red Sox Nation remember 1967 with warmth and great relish. In memory, it was a time of youthful joy and rebirth. Some remember a specific game or event within a game that they attended, viewed on television, or heard on the radio. Others recall where they were or what they were doing when a key play or game-winning hit occurred. Red Sox fans outside New England often employed extraordinary measures to participate in the epic season of 1967. Sportswriter and television commentator Peter Gammons, a student in North Carolina as the season came to a dramatic conclusion, recalls wearing out a car battery while straining to hear a WTIC radio broadcast out of Hartford, Connecticut, as the Red Sox battled Detroit in a key September game. Some exiled fans bought shortwave radios and listened to those Boston games broadcast over Armed Forces Radio. The real diehard out-of-towners phoned family or friends in New England and listened to pivotal innings or sometimes whole games via costly long-distance telephone. The year was more than a point that marked a turn of fortune for the Boston Red Sox, however; it was a time of great change for the nation as a whole.[1]

In 1967 America was experiencing the beginnings of changes in politics, foreign policy, society, and culture that would resonate into the twenty-first century. As the year began, the focal point of interest was the rapid escalation of the war in Vietnam. During 1966 the number of U.S. combat troops supporting the Republic of Vietnam had more than doubled from the previous year, to more than 385,000. More than 5,000 Americans were killed in the war that year, and another 16,500 were wounded. Neither military experts nor President Lyndon B. Johnson could outline a short-term plan for victory in Vietnam. In early 1967 a majority of Americans continued to support the war, but dissent and organized protest were increasing.[2]

A week before baseball teams broke spring training camps and headed north, civil rights leader Martin Luther King Jr. denounced the war at New York's Riverside Church. He maintained that the conflict diverted funds away from civil rights programs and other Great Society reforms, and further charged that African Americans, still treated as second-class citizens at home, were fighting and dying in proportionally greater numbers than whites in Vietnam. An ardent supporter of President Johnson and his reform programs, King now declared that "the Great Society has been shot down on the battlefields of Vietnam." The civil rights movement appeared to be converging with forces opposing the war and becoming more radical in the process. In 1966 the U.S. government reported forty-three of what it described as racial disorders. The number of disturbances or riots would increase fivefold in 1967. That spring heavyweight boxing champion Muhammad Ali announced that he would refuse induction into the U.S. Army because as a Black Muslim he was a conscientious objector. Although a few prominent African-American athletes (none in baseball) publicly supported Ali's position, World War II–era athletes Joe Louis and Jackie Robinson strongly criticized the heavyweight champion. At the time, it was not apparent that racial unrest and antiwar protests would be a hallmark of 1967 and even have some impact on major-league baseball.[3]

When the Red Sox opened spring training camp in Winter Haven, Florida, in late February, even the most optimistic fans realistically expected little better than a break-even season. The 1966 team had lost ninety games and finished ninth (out of ten) in the American League. Boston's beloved Red Sox had fallen on very hard times in the 1960s. Six decades earlier the Red Sox had been one of the most successful teams in baseball, winning five World Championships over sixteen seasons. After the 1918 season, however, owner and Broadway producer Harry Frazee, the most infamous name in Red Sox history, began selling or trading away the team's best players, including Babe Ruth, who was dealt to the New York Yankees. The New York team would dominate baseball for most of the rest of the century, and Boston fans would never forget it. Ernie Shore, one of those traded to New York, later stated sadly: "When they talk about a Yankee dynasty, I say it was really a Red Sox dynasty, in a Yankee uniform." For the next dozen years the Red Sox were the perennial doormats of the American League. In 1933 Thomas A. Yawkey, a southern-born, thirty-year-old millionaire, purchased the team and attempted to restore the Red Sox to their former glory. Yawkey first attempted to a buy a pennant on the cheap in the Depression-driven market by acquiring star players who were just a bit past their prime such as Jimmy Foxx, Robert "Lefty" Grove, and Joe Cronin. It didn't quite work. Boston improved dramatically, but could not overtake the Yankee juggernaut.[4]

Beginning in the late 1930s, Yawkey's pal and general manager Eddie Collins signed a group of exceptional young players who would help make the Red Sox one of the best teams in baseball for the next dozen seasons. Ted Williams, of course, was the centerpiece of the potent lineup, but he was amply aided by Bobby Doerr, Dom DiMaggio (Joe's brother), and Johnny Pesky, among others. Except for the war years, 1943–1945, the Red Sox challenged for the pennant throughout the decade. In 1946 Williams and friends finally brought a pennant back to Beantown. Heavily favored against the St. Louis Cardinals in the World Series, Boston lost in seven games. The Red Sox not only lost, but lost under a cloud. A controversial play or misplay by shortstop Johnny Pesky allowing the winning run to score in game seven would become part of Red Sox folklore. The failure of an injured Ted Williams to produce in the series as well as sub-par performances by other key players would lead some in the media to criticize "Yawkey's Millionaires." Despite the defeat by the Cardinals, the future looked bright for the Red Sox as midcentury approached.

The angst of Red Sox fans increased, however, when in 1948, after tying Cleveland for the American League lead on the last day of the regular season, Boston, starting a journeyman pitcher, was massacred by the Indians in the playoff game at Fenway Park. Nineteen-forty-nine sank Boston and most of New England into severe depression. Leading the hated Yankees by a game with two games remaining in the season at Yankee Stadium, the Red Sox lost both games and the pennant. In the early 1950s Boston futilely chased the Yankees as most of the Red Sox stars of the previous decade retired. Yawkey and his general manager Joe Cronin spent millions signing expensive bonus-baby-era prospects, but failed miserably. Branch Rickey of the Brooklyn Dodgers estimated that Yawkey spent over $3 million. "Everyone took Yawkey," Rickey said. "And for a fortune." Red Sox broadcaster Curt Gowdy assured fans in his calming Wyoming twang that the likes of Billy Consolo, Ted Lepcio, Jimmy Piersall, and other nearly forgotten names would lead Boston to a new golden era. By 1954 the youth movement was curtailed, and the Red Sox remained a decent but not overly talented first-division team into the late 1950s. The fans kept coming to Fenway Park in substantial numbers in part out of loyalty and habit and in part to see the amazing Ted Williams, who in 1957 at the age of thirty-nine fell just short of hitting .400 for a second time while powering thirty-eight home runs.[5]

By the late 1950s the Red Sox began to unravel both on and off the field. The Red Sox began a descent from a first-division team in an eight-team league to finishing eighth or ninth in a ten-team league. After Williams retired in 1960, attendance dwindled rapidly. Going to Fenway Park for Boston-area fans and New Englanders generally was not just attending a ball game; it was a pilgrimage, as sportswriter Dan Shaughnessy beautifully describes in his book *At Fenway*. Boston is a unique baseball franchise in that it represents not only the city of Boston and surrounding areas, but nearly all of New England and parts of eastern Canada. There are few real Red Sox fans who don't remember their first visit to Fenway Park: the hustle and bustle outside the park in what is now Yawkey Way; the overwhelming green of the grass, fences, and grandstands contrasting against Boston's ultrawhite home uniforms; and finally, this huge wall (at least to a kid) hovering above in left field. But by the early 1960s fewer people made the pilgrimage as the team languished, dissension wracked the club, and it appeared that authority within the organization was based more on cronyism than on talent.[6]

The Red Sox team had long had the reputation of being overpaid athletes who cavorted about in a country club setting. Carl Yastrzemski, who joined the team in 1961, recalled that a popular radio talk show host once mocked the self-centered, bickering Red Sox on the air by calling a local restaurant to make reservations for the team. When the maitre d' answered and accepted the request, the caller explained that it would require "twenty-five tables for one." In July 1962 the country club routine degenerated into opera buffa or perhaps the "two stooges" when 6-foot 8-inch Boston pitcher Gene Conley, who was the team's best starter and had been shelled a few hours earlier at Yankee Stadium courtesy of four Red Sox errors, and his pal infielder Pumpsie Green walked off the team bus, which was stuck in rush-hour traffic on its way to Newark Airport. Green appeared two days later in Washington, where the Red Sox were playing the Senators, and explained that the two men had stayed overnight in New York and then proceeded to the airport, where Conley attempted to fly to Israel. He was turned away by El Al agents because he didn't have a passport. Conley returned the following day, and both men were heavily fined. The bizarre incident seemed strange, indeed, in the pre–Vietnam War era. No one could imagine then that within a dozen years two Yankee pitchers would swap wives and families. Red Sox fans, who had seen Williams spit and Piersall squirt home plate with a water pistol, knew it was not a good omen.[7]

In 1963 Johnny Pesky took over as Red Sox manager at the insistence of Yawkey. He experienced two agonizing seasons in which the team sustained 85 and 90 losses. According to future manager Dick Williams, who was a reserve player with Boston in those years, "poor Pesky was constantly dumped on, by general manager Mike Higgins and the players." At the end of the 1964 season Pesky was out, and Higgins's pal Billy Herman took command. The following year the Red Sox reached their nadir in the Yawkey era by registering 100 defeats. Attendance declined from over a million a year in the period 1946–1960 to barely 600,000 fans in 1965. Herman's chief complaint was that "Yawkey babied some of the players—like Yaz. He was Yawkey's boy; and if he was mad about something he'd just go through the motions. Best player in the league—when he was in the mood." Herman was fired near the end of the 1966 campaign, which the Red Sox finished in ninth place. One of the few good things about the season was that the Yankees finished tenth.[8]

At the close of the horrendous 1965 season, Yawkey had named Dick O'Connell general manager, replacing Pinky Higgins. O'Connell, who had been a very efficient business manager, focused his attention on retooling the on-field personnel. His most important move, however, came after the 1966 season, when he hired Dick Williams to manage the Red Sox. Williams seemed a strange choice; he was authoritarian, bold, brash, overbearing, and sometimes outright nasty. He didn't seem to fit the Red Sox mold. Williams had been part of the "country club" in 1963 and 1964 and didn't like what he saw. Perhaps the reason O'Connell hired Williams *was* to clean out the country club. Although he had only two years of minor-league experience as a manager, Williams received an excellent baseball education as a minor-leaguer in the Brooklyn Dodgers organization and in thirteen seasons as a major player. He was schooled in the fundamentals of the game under an innovative system devised by Brooklyn Dodgers boss Branch Rickey.[9]

Williams brought another important dimension to the Boston Red Sox. He was the team's first manager who had played extensively with African Americans at the major-league level and coached them in the minor leagues. When he broke in with the Dodgers in 1951, Williams was snubbed by most of the veterans, but was befriended by Jackie Robinson, whom he had met in California during the filming of Robinson's life story. Although he grew up in St. Louis, which was strictly divided by race, Williams was stunned by the racial harassment Robinson received, especially during spring training in Florida. Williams received more education on the race question simply by playing for Brooklyn, which was the most integrated team in baseball during the early 1950s. The Red Sox, on the other hand, were the last major-league team to integrate—a dozen years after Robinson's milestone achievement in 1947. Most people blamed Yawkey, who spent much of the off-seasons at his South Carolina estate, and his general managers from Eddie Collins to Pinky Higgins. The Texas-born Higgins once told a reporter, "There'll be no n——s on this ball club so long as I have anything to say about it." Under Collins's reign, the Red Sox, under extreme political pressure, gave Jackie Robinson and two other African-American players a "phony" tryout in Fenway Park in 1945. Boston sportswriter Cliff Keane recalled that after the so-called tryout "somebody up back of the building yelled, 'Get those n——s off the field.'" Four years later, Boston reputedly had a chance to sign Willie Mays, but failed to pursue the opportunity. Historian Jules Tygiel maintains that "whether by conscious design, or benign neglect, the Red Sox racial policies emanated from the top of the organization." One probable conclusion is that the deterioration of the Red Sox during the 1950s and the team's near implosion in the early 1960s can be traced, in part, to its long-standing racial policies.[10]

Even when the team did integrate, the Red Sox organization was far from enlightened on the race question. In the spring of 1966, for example, veteran pitcher Earl Wilson, Boston's second African-American player (Pumpsie Green was the first), was refused admittance to two Winter Haven nightclubs on account of his race. Wilson related the incidents to sportswriters who wrote about racial conditions at Boston's new spring training site. In June Wilson was traded to Detroit for journeyman outfielder Don Demeter. Wilson would win forty games for the Tigers over the next two seasons. The Red Sox would have five African Americans (excluding Hispanic players) on its roster during the 1967 season. Most of the black players would resent and even hate Dick Williams throughout the season for his hard-nosed methods and sometimes abrasive personality. A few years later one of those players, center fielder Reggie Smith, would call Boston a racist town and criticize the Red Sox organization. It is significant, however, that in 1967 and in the years that followed none of the five African-American players would accuse Williams of racism. No one can know Williams's precise racial views at the time, but the evidence suggests that he was an equal-opportunity tyrant.[11]

The new Red Sox manager brashly predicted that the team would register more wins than losses in 1967. For a team that had finished ninth the previous year with 90 defeats, it seemed a stretch to say the least. Few Boston fans following the Hot Stove League of hopes and promises complained as spring training approached. Oddsmakers were more realistic, making the Red Sox a 100–1 shot to win the American League race. When training camp opened in Winter Haven in late February, Williams installed a regimen of drills emphasizing fundamental baseball and asserted complete authority over the team. He recalled that he arrived "bearing many rules for the players, most of whom had either played with me or under me. Meaning, they knew I knew all their bullshit." When two pitchers showed up late for practice a few days after camp started, Williams loudly chewed them out and decreed that all players at the team motel would be awakened at 7:00 A.M., three hours before practice.[12]

To get his message across, Williams set his sights on Carl Yastrzemski, the team's best player, Yawkey's favorite, and the team captain in 1966. He had it announced through General Manager Dick O'Connell that there would be no more captains. Williams later admitted that he might have done it more gracefully by asking Yaz to resign. Then he vehemently added, "and maybe I should have asked everyone on the team how many games they wanted to play. And maybe I would have lasted in Boston six months. And had my goddamn living room repossessed. The hell with grace. I wanted wins . . . My ass was on the line on a one-year contract, and during that time this team was going to do everything Dick Williams's way, not Millie Putz's way, nor Yaz's way."[13]

Yastrzemski came up with the Red Sox in 1961, the year after Ted Williams retired. He was supposed to be the Second Coming, the slugging left fielder who would fill the shoes of the Splendid Splinter. The problem was that Yaz was a 5-foot 11-inch, 160-pound line-drive hitter who specialized in singles and doubles. He developed into a superb outfielder and played Fenway Park's difficult left field better than anyone ever had. Although he hit well and won the league batting title in 1963, Yastrzemski didn't deliver the home runs (his best effort was twenty in 1965) or RBI that were expected from him. Yaz obsessed over everything concerning baseball, from trying to fill the void left by Williams to which way the wind was blowing on a given day to mentally replaying a game for hours in the clubhouse. He was moody and usually stonewalled the media. "There were times after a bad game," Yastrzemski recalled, "that I'd sit in front of my locker with such dark thoughts that I'd think about jumping off Mystic River Bridge." He grew up on a potato farm in rural Long Island; Yastrzemski's father, an excellent baseball player himself, spent most of his free time grooming his son for a major-league career. When the Yankees and other teams balked at meeting the elder Yastrzemski's signing demands of a $100,000 bonus plus a free college education, Carl Sr. shipped his son off to Notre Dame on an athletic scholarship. At least young Carl would be the first Yastrzemski to graduate from college. Finally in 1958, Yaz signed with Boston for his father's $100,000 asking price and dropped out of Notre Dame after the fall semester. To fulfill his father's dream of a college education for his son, Yaz dutifully attended college in the off-season for the next half-dozen years, finally earning his degree from Merrimack College.[14]

Yastrzemski did not react, at least publicly, to being dethroned as captain. He later claimed that he had told Dick O'Connell the previous season that he no longer wanted the job. Even when Williams ordered Yaz into the single players' quarters after the left fielder's wife, Carol, left Winter Haven to tend to their children in Boston (a team rule concerning single players staying in the same hotel had not been previously enforced), Yastrzemski remained mute. Early in the regular season, when Williams benched Yastrzemski for lack of hitting and the press expected Yawkey's pet to explode, Yaz said nothing. One explanation might be that Williams was a feistier version of Yaz's domineering father. He was a father figure whom Yaz could relate to. Years later Yastrzemski explained his renewed dedication to the team and motivation this way: "What had I done really, my first six seasons? The club had a combined won-lost record of 434–535. Six straight seasons with attendance under a million. Four managers. And a bunch of second-division finishes." He was determined to turn himself and the team in a new direction.[15]

Yastrzemski may have weathered Williams's Prussian-style camp without apparent effect, but most players were enraged by his methods. The Red Sox skipper even managed to alienate Ted Williams, who had volunteered to help out with the outfielders. When Teddy Ballgame began instructing pitchers about rotation on the ball and other assorted issues while interrupting the volleyball games prescribed for their conditioning, the new manager chewed out the game's greatest hitter. Ted left camp a few days later, not to return. Someone heard him mutter as he exited, "Volleyball! What is this game coming to?" Dick Williams did manage to maintain an amicable relationship with Tony Conigliaro, the team's budding young superstar right fielder; but Conigliaro didn't like Williams. In 1964 the veteran Williams was ordered to room with rookie Conigliaro to provide a steadying influence. For two months, Williams recalled, "I never saw him. Not late at night, not first thing in the morning, never. I was providing veteran influence to a suitcase." Later that season, after Williams found a new roommate, Conigliaro was fined $1,000 for breaking curfew. He blamed Williams for being a snitch. They managed to coexist in Winter Haven, in part, because Conigliaro was batting .558 before being sent to Boston for an extensive examination of his injured shoulder. As spring training ended, Williams wondered when being a major-league manager would start to be fun.

"I had pissed off the entire team, alienated the greatest star ever [Ted Williams]," he remembered, "and everyone said the team had next to no chance of winning the pennant."[16]

The Red Sox home opener on April 11 was postponed because of near-arctic conditions in Boston. It might have been a good omen; on that date fifty-five years earlier, the H.M.S. *Titanic* had left Queenstown, Ireland, for New York. The next day only 8,234 fans showed up for the first game, deterred by the bitter cold. Boston edged Chicago, 5–4. Dick Williams put his mark on the game and indicated a new direction for the traditionally heavy-footed Red Sox by ordering three steals, all successful. One of the season's memorable games came two days later at Yankee Stadium. Rookie southpaw Billy Rohr no-hit the Yankees through eight innings. Tom Tresh led off the New York ninth by scorching a blue darter over Yastrzemski's head in left field. David Halberstam, a *New York Times* reporter who was home from assignment in South Vietnam, sat and watched as Yaz, playing shallow, "went back, and dove just at the right moment, his body tumbling into a complete somersault as he made the catch. It ranks," Halberstam wrote in 1986, "with the Gionfriddo catch as the greatest I have ever seen, made more remarkable by the fact that it saved a no-hitter." After the second out, Elton Howard broke up the no-hitter with a line single to right field. The crowd booed Howard, but Jackie Kennedy, who was attending the game with her son, John, hugged the boy with delight. Yastrzemski seemed shocked that the Kennedys were Yankee fans. Rohr became an instant celebrity, appearing on the *Ed Sullivan Show*, and the Red Sox made the national news for the first time in 1967. As for Billy Rohr, he would win only two more games in his major-league career.[17]

On April 15, as the Red Sox lost a 1–0 squeaker to the Yankees at the Stadium on Horace Clarke's two-out single in the fifth inning, more than 200,000 protesters were marching in Manhattan. The demonstration was organized by the Spring Mobilization Committee, which sponsored a similar event in San Francisco; there 50,000 people marched to Kezar Stadium, where Coretta Scott King delivered an address. In New York her husband, African-American radical Stokely Carmichael, and folk singer Pete Seeger were part of the largest demonstration against the war in Vietnam to date. As Terry Anderson has noted, by 1967 the antiwar movement was expanding rapidly, "including students and professionals, blacks and whites, ministers and rabbis, children and grandparents, even some from the new Vietnam Veterans Against the War." At Sheep Meadow in New York's Central Park, where the march concluded, 60 students organized by the Students for a Democratic Society burned their draft cards. More than 100 young protesters came forward spontaneously out of the crowd to perform the same act, a federal crime. Just two years before, about three-fourths of young people in their twenties favored the United States sending troops to Vietnam. Now, protesters, including many young ones, "marched daily around the White House chanting 'Hey, hey, LBJ, how many kids have you killed today?' and 'Ho, Ho, Ho Chi Minh, NLF is going to win.'"[18]

For Red Sox players and major leaguers in general, the Spring Mobilization demonstrations and the war in Vietnam may have seemed of little importance in their lives or their daily routines. But in fact many players were closely connected to the Vietnam issue. The relationship between the military and professional athletes in time of war had changed dramatically since World War I. In that war, some citizens and the many in government and military service considered professional athletes who did not either join the armed forces or take a job in a war-related industry slackers. By World War II, however, the military viewed athletics in a very positive way in terms of physical training and especially for their role in raising morale among both civilians and those in the military. The government sanctioned major-league baseball throughout the war, but most able-bodied players either joined one of the armed services or were drafted. The same was mainly true in the Korean War as players were drafted or called up with their reserve units, as in the widely publicized case of Ted Williams. All this changed with the Vietnam War because President Johnson refused to declare a national emergency and call up military reserves and National Guard units. Professional athletes took refuge in the National Guard or reserves in droves. Thus, although most pro athletes supported the American mission in Vietnam, many were resisting the draft much as students were doing by remaining longer in college, going to graduate school, or joining the Peace Corps. Historian David Zang cites one instance in which the Dallas Cowboys had ten players in the same National Guard division at one time. To be fair, it should be pointed out that professional teams were probably more responsible for this system than the individual players. In 1967 the Boston Red Sox had six reservists on their roster, including key players Tony

Conigliaro, Jim Lonborg, and Rico Petrocelli. The Department of Defense had recently ruled that all reservists would have to be in active units, which meant that they were subject to being called up for training during the summer.[19]

On April 16 Boston lost an eighteen-inning 7–6 game to the Yankees, squandering numerous opportunities to win. Williams exploded at first baseman George Scott, who was 1–8 in the game. In a postgame interview, he stated that talking to Scott was "like talking to cement." Scott, an African American who grew up in the segregated South, had joined the Red Sox in 1966 and had not played under Williams before. Williams later recalled Scott as "a likeable guy with a weight problem in both his belly and his head." They feuded throughout spring training, with Williams alternately benching Scott or banishing him to right field. It wasn't clear which Scott disliked most. What most players disliked about Williams was his tactic of criticizing them publicly rather than in the privacy of his office. "He had the habit of going to the press," Yastrzemski recalled. "So when he knocked Boomer [Scott] with his 'cement' comment, I got angry." Yastrzemski later pronounced that if he had read in the papers "that talking to Yaz was like talking to cement, I wouldn't have played for the guy." In midsummer, after another weight violation and benching, Scott recalled that "I was six inches from going after Williams . . . but my intelligence told me no." In retrospect, Scott said he loved Williams "because he had the ability to drive me, to get the maximum out of me." Williams meted out similar treatment to his African-American third baseman, Joe Foy, who was also periodically overweight. "He'd drop the weight and return to hit a couple more home runs," Williams recalled, "and then we'd cuss each other out." Williams had the wisdom, however, to make Coach Eddie Popowski his second in command. After Williams exploded, mild-mannered Popowski would calm the waters in a kind of good-cop, bad-cop routine. To what extent were the Red Sox plagued by racism? Sportswriter Leonard Schecter, who traveled with the team in the spring of 1968, observed that baseball people "have only a flimsy understanding of the outside world. Stereotypes are their only connection with life out there. There is less prejudice in baseball than there is outside of it, yet a baseball man will refer to Willie Mays as a 'nigger,' mean none of the implications of the word, yet cling to it emotionally as he does to all stereotypes."[20]

As the weather in Boston gradually began to improve in one of the cold-est springs anyone could remember, the Red Sox showed significant im-provement over 1966, but hardly appeared to be a pennant contender. On May 15 the team was in fourth place with a record of 13–14, six games be-hind the Chicago White Sox. Patrolling right field from Pesky's Pole to the bullpens and cheap bleacher seats beyond, once known as Williamsburg, Tony Conigliaro noticed that many young fans in the bleachers wore their hair long, dressed in ragged, colorful clothing, and razzed him more vocif-erously and skillfully than fans had in previous seasons. He was witnessing the vanguard of a counterculture movement that would soon engulf the na-tion. A city of colleges and universities, Boston was overrun with youthful students most of the year. By 1967 a good number of them openly opposed the Vietnam War, and some were "dropping out" of conventional society. At Harvard, a short distance from Fenway Park across the Charles River in Cambridge, radical students had shouted down Secretary of Defense Rob-ert McNamara with cries of "murderer" and "fascist" and had virtually driven South Vietnam's ambassador off campus when he arrived to deliver a speech. Similar incidents occurred at many of the city's other prestigious schools. With the Red Sox struggling to play .500 baseball, it was not appar-ent at the time that hawks, doves, and apolitical fans as well as businessmen, little old ladies, and long-haired students wearing beads would soon put aside their differences in terms of politics, age, and social status and unite behind the Olde Town team in one of the most exhilarating summers in the city's history.[21]

One of the key reasons for Boston's resurgence in 1967 was the quality of its pitching staff. The main man was Jim Lonborg. A usually mild-man-nered Californian, his teammates called him "Gentleman Jim." The son of a college professor and a straight-A student in high school, Lonborg at-tended Stanford University and was playing minor-league baseball during the summer when the Red Sox discovered him. A gangly 6-foot 3-inch sinker-ball specialist, he had minimal success with Boston in 1965 and 1966, posting a record of 19–27. Yastrzemski believed that Dick Williams played a big role in transforming "Gentleman Jim" into the dominant pitcher in the American League in 1967. In a game in early May against the Angels in An-aheim, Lonborg lost a no-hitter, a shutout, and finally the game on a wild pitch in the course of three innings. As he headed for the dugout, Red Sox shortstop Rico Petrocelli ran over and said, "Good game, Jim. Tough luck." Williams exploded and shouted, "Tough luck? My ass!" as he and Lonborg began jawing at each other. Although he didn't always approve of Williams's methods, Yaz conceded that Lonborg became a lot meaner after that episode. Williams agreed that Lonborg got tougher, brushing back hitters and even hitting them when the situation required it. "No longer were pussy .200 hitters beating him," Williams recalled. By the end of May, Lonborg was already 6–1 and on his way to a season record of 22–9 and the American League Cy Young Award.[22]

Behind Lonborg was a cast of starting pitchers who infuriated Williams when they faltered as the dog days of summer approached. Williams periodically banished Lee Stage and Darrell "Bucky" Brandon to the bullpen and sent rookie Billy Rohr to the minors. General Manager Dick O'Connell, however, acquired a couple of pitchers who would take up the slack. Puerto Rican–born Jose Santiago, who was signed in 1966, suffered through the early months of the season with a sore arm, but would emerge as the team's number-two starter and finished the season with a record of 12–4. On June 4 O'Donnell would make one of his shrewdest trades in acquiring pitcher Gary Bell from Cleveland. A ten-year veteran, Bell, who was nicknamed "Ding Dong" because of his bizarre personality, was 1–5 with the Indians, but would win twelve games for the Red Sox during the season. Closer John Wyatt was acquired by O'Donnell in a 1966 trade with Kansas City, which also brought the Red Sox a valuable utility player in Jose Tartabull. A veteran of both the Negro Leagues and the Mexican League, Wyatt had plenty of experience with poor playing conditions and nasty managers. He clearly didn't like Williams, but he held his tongue. It's widely rumored that he doctored the baseball and/or threw a spitter. Williams didn't care. "As long as he was getting batters out," Williams later wrote, "he could pitch it out of his ass." The manager fondly recalled the day Wyatt got caught in a rundown and some things fell out of his jacket pocket. "No big deal. Just some cigarettes and matches, his car keys . . . and a tube of Vaseline." Wyatt would win ten games for the Red Sox in 1967 and save a good number more. The following spring, after a row with Williams, he was sold to the Yankees and was angry. "I've played for about 11 managers," Wyatt said, "and I never saw one like that . . . If that man's your enemy forget it." The 1967 pitching staff was not the best in Red Sox history, but it was the best since 1949, when Boston had had two twenty-game winners and lost the pennant to the Yankees by one game.[23]

While the Red Sox were on the road in Cleveland in early June, O'Connell made another important trade, this time with the White Sox, which brought utility infielder Jerry Adair to the Red Sox. Adair would prove to be an invaluable addition to the team. Dick Williams was ecstatic about the acquisitions of Bell and Adair. "I think this gives us a shot at the pennant," he announced, but only a few people really believed it. There was even bigger news back in Boston. A race riot erupted in the Roxbury and South End sections of the city on June 2 after police stormed into a Grove Street welfare office, where African-American women were staging a sit-in protesting poor service and treatment by the welfare staff. After the event, rioting and looting quickly spread through Roxbury and into sections of the South End, where most of the city's African-American population of about 65,000 resided. One police officer was wounded by a sniper in one of the worst riots in the city's history. Almost 2,000 policemen dressed in full battle gear patrolled Roxbury and part of the South End. The rioting ended after three nights with seventy-five injured, sixty-five arrested, and substantial property damage. Boston mayor John F. Collins denounced the rioting as "the worst manifestation of disrespect for the rights of others that this city has ever seen." This was just the beginning of the summer of racial unrest. In the first nine months of 1967 there were 167 so-called racial disorders. Of those, thirty-three required governors to call out the state police, while eight required that the National Guard be summoned. The worst riots were in Newark and Detroit. In the Motor City forty-three people died and 1,300 buildings were destroyed. The Tigers were forced to cancel games in the midst of the cataclysm.[24]

Race relations in Boston were tense during most of the twentieth century. In the previous century the city's small African-American community had resided on the northwestern slope of Beacon Hill. The arrival of waves of new immigrants and political gerrymandering, however, forced them into the South End in the early 1900s and eventually into Roxbury by the 1930s. As a result of World War II, the city's black population almost doubled, to over 40,000, but was limited to these restricted areas by white segregationist attitudes. The beginning of urban renewal projects in the 1950s further squeezed African Americans as whole blocks of houses were razed in the

South End without additional housing provided elsewhere. With the beginning of the civil rights movement and rising expectations among African Americans, Boston's black community became like a boiling cauldron. Boston's African Americans were not Red Sox fans. During the 1920s and 1930s, Negro leagues were the main focus in the black community. Semi-pro teams, playing in the South End and Roxbury, attracted crowds upward of 10,000. Will Jackman, a submarine-style, right-handed pitcher, was a local hero. After Jackie Robinson made his debut with Brooklyn in 1947, the local teams became less important in terms of community pride. By 1950 those black Bostonians who did attend major-league games made their way to Braves Field to watch rookie speedster Sam Jethroe, who once had a try-out with the Red Sox. The city's African Americans duly took note that the Red Sox were the last team in major-league baseball to integrate. Dan Shaughnessy was right on the mark when he wrote that "a Fenway gathering resembles the crowd at a rugby match in Pretoria." As late as the early 1990s, a *Boston Globe* survey indicated that African Americans made up about .2 percent of a typical crowd at Fenway. In 1967 Boston's black community was one of the few that resisted the unifying effect of a drive for the pennant.[25]

By the beginning of June, Yastrzemski was on a hitting tear that would continue for the rest of the season. He would hit for average and with power, and, best of all, he was extraordinary in clutch situations. One explanation for the beginning of this magical season for Yaz could be traced back to mid-May. Mired in a slump, Yastrzemski sought advice and instruction from former Red Sox second baseman and then batting instructor Bobby Doerr. After watching Yaz hit in a morning workout, Doerr became convinced that Yaz was uppercutting the ball, causing an overspin that resulted in potential home-run balls' dying in the outfield. He suggested that Yaz raise his hands to the level of his left ear to correct the overspin problem, which the left fielder did and with devastating results. The year of the Yaz might have begun that day.[26]

Or it might have begun the previous winter, when Yaz went to the Colonial Country Club in Wakefield to start a light exercise program. He had never worked out much in the off-season because the fall and winter months were spent pursuing his college degree. George Berde, a former Hungarian Olympic boxing coach and head of the health club, gave Yaz more than he bargained for. In an era when it was not that common for baseball players to train rigorously in the off-season, Berde drove Yastrzemski for two hours or more a day six days a week, including weight training, which at the time was considered harmful by many baseball coaches. The result was that Yaz was stronger and in better condition than at any time in his career, and American League pitchers would pay for it.[27]

Another theory for Yaz's breakthrough season might center on Dick Williams. Over time the two men would come to dislike each other, but in 1967 the Red Sox manager was like the overbearing father who had motivated Yaz in his formative years—except Williams was meaner. In his autobiography Williams heaped high praise on his left fielder. "It [the Impossible Dream] started with Yaz, who was having what may be the best year of any player ever." After rattling off Yastrzemski's year-end statistics and noting that he was to win baseball's Triple Crown in 1967, Williams said, "I don't think anyone will ever have a year like this" because of the advent of multiyear contracts.[28]

With the urban riots spreading and escalating during July and protests against the war in Vietnam continuing as an average of 800 Americans died in Southeast Asia each month, *Newsweek* reported about the "Summer of Discontent." Others proclaimed the "Summer of Love." In July *Time* published a cover story on "The Hippies," introducing the subculture to many Americans for the first time. There were undoubtedly hippie enclaves in Boston in 1967, but the "Summer of Love" began in the city on July 14 with "the streak." On that date, the Red Sox were in fifth place, six games behind the Chicago White Sox. That evening Boston routed Baltimore 11–5 before 27,787 fans, with Tony Conigliaro hitting the longest home run anyone could remember at Fenway. The ball soared over the Green Monster, the screen above it, cleared Lansdowne Street, and landed on or beyond the Massachusetts Turnpike behind Lansdowne Street. Dick Williams recalled that "some people thought the homer meant we'd soon be playing out of this world. They were right. For 10 straight games we didn't lose once. It was a winning streak as strange and wonderful as an open parking spot in downtown Boston." After four straight victories at home, the Red Sox swept two games in Baltimore, with Yastrzemski connecting for his twenty-second home run. With Boston leading in the third game of the series 2–0 on July 20, only the heavy rains that washed out the game in the third inning temporarily cooled off the Red Sox.[29]

As the team headed to Cleveland for a four-game series with the Indians, Boston was abuzz with excitement. The Red Sox became front-page news, overshadowing a smoldering race riot in Newark, the Vietnam War, and the contentious mayoral primary contest among Mayor John Collins, Ed Logue, and Louise Day Hicks. *Boston Herald* sportswriter Tim Horgan was convinced that the Red Sox surge had reduced racial tensions in the city. According to Horgan, "the amazing thing is it's not just baseball fans. It's everywhere you go. Every porch you walk by someone has the ballgame on." One afternoon a motorist listening to an exciting moment in a game stopped his car at the entrance to the Sumner Tunnel, causing a massive traffic jam. He refused to enter until the inning ended because he knew his radio would black out in the underground chamber. Halfway around the world, in Saigon, David Halberstam, a New Yorker and converted Red Sox fan, was pessimistic about the futile violence of a war that appeared stalemated. Each morning he and Tom Durant, a Boston doctor, would encounter each other at the Associated Press office to wait for the results of Red Sox games. "I would meet him there," Halberstam remembered, "bonded by this need to escape, and this common passion, and we would follow the results of a wonderful pennant race and perhaps the greatest one-man pennant drive in modern baseball history by standing over the AP ticker." Halberstam would sit there and "could almost see Yaz as he was in Fenway, the exaggerated stance; it was oddly exhilarating . . . In what for me was a bad season," Halberstam recalled, "his [Yastrzemski's] was a marvelous season and reminded me of the America I loved, and which otherwise was so distant."[30]

In Cleveland the Red Sox swept four games from the Indians to extend their winning streak to ten games, the team's longest since 1957. En route to Boston, the team was in second place, one-half game behind Chicago. A year earlier, Boston had been buried near the bottom of the pack, twenty-nine and a half games behind the leader. As the Red Sox plane approached Logan Airport, the pilot announced that something strange was happening at the airport. The flight was diverted to an alternative landing runway as some 15,000 delirious fans jammed the main terminal and spilled over onto the tarmac. When the team arrived at the terminal by bus, joyous Red Sox rooters mobbed the vehicle and rocked it with glee. The Callahan Tunnel, leading to the airport in East Boston, was completely clogged, resulting in the worst traffic jam in Logan history. One airport official estimated that the throng was larger than the crowd that had greeted the Beatles a year earlier. Dick Williams wryly remarked that the crowd "was more people than the Red Sox had averaged in attendance in the last 10 years."[31]

The Red Sox started August, baseball's proverbial dog days of summer, in second place, two games behind the White Sox, with Detroit, Minnesota, and the California Angels all bunched within five games of first place. Yastrzemski remembered the month as one of highs and lows, with the team "sometimes delirious with victory, other times shocked by adversity." For Yaz, the night of August 18 "marked two turning points in the history of the Red Sox. It started us on a seven-game winning streak that positioned us for the greatest pennant race Boston ever saw, and it effectively began the end of Tony Conigliaro's career as a slugger who could dominate the game." In the fourth inning of a scoreless game with the Angels, California pitcher Jack Hamilton struck Conigliaro just below the left eye with a pitch that many suspected was a spitball. A pall came over Fenway Park at the sharp cracking sound of the ball striking Tony's cheekbone and the sight of him crumpling motionless at home plate. Conigliaro's season was over. He would eventually recover to play baseball again, but with his vision distorted he was never the same player.[32]

Two days later, on a warm Sunday afternoon, the Red Sox extended their winning streak to four games in a most improbable manner. Trailing the Angels 8–0 after three and a half innings in the second game of a doubleheader, Boston stormed back. When Yastrzemski belted a three-run home run (his thirty-first) in the fifth inning to cut the deficit to 8–4, Fenway and the whole city erupted. At Nantasket Beach on the South Shore, a roar echoed along the five-mile expanse of sandy shoreline as radio-toting Red Sox fans sensed a comeback in the making. Light-hitting infielder Jerry Adair, acquired earlier in the season from the White Sox, tied the game in the sixth with a single and then hit one of his rare home runs in the eighth, which turned out to be the winning run after Jose Santiago got out of a bases-loaded jam in the ninth. It seemed like a miracle. But more improbable events, or miracles if you prefer, continued to occur. On August 27 in Chicago, Boston led the White Sox by a run in the last of the ninth, but the Pale Hose had the tying run at third with one out. Pinch-hitter Duane Josephson hit a line drive toward utility outfielder Jose Tartabull in right field as the speedy Ken Berry tagged up at third. Tartabull, an excellent fielder with a weak throwing arm, caught the ball knee high and made an exceptionally strong throw to the plate, but it was too high. Veteran catcher Elston Howard, acquired from the Yankees earlier in the month, proceeded to make the play of the season. With his back to Berry, Howard leaped to spear the ball one-handed, came down with his left foot to deflect Berry's spike from touching home plate, and made a swiping tag to retire Berry all in the same motion. No one at Comiskey Park could remember a better play by a catcher. Since Howard could not see Berry coming, some observers suggested that the Red Sox catcher had radar or that it was plain luck. Many Red Sox fans had their own theory: a miracle.[33]

Going into September, the Red Sox led the American League by half a game, with Minnesota, Detroit, and Chicago all bunched within a game and a half of the top spot. It was the closest pennant race in history and would remain so through Boston's last twenty-seven games. During the stretch run, the Red Sox dropped in and out of first place with regularity as if on a seesaw. Yaz carried the team on his back for the final twenty-seven games, hitting .417, with nine home runs and twenty-six RBI. Statistics do not tell the whole tale, however, because he played superbly in the field and did his best hitting in clutch situations. Midway through the month, Boston fans braced themselves for the worst as the team seemed on the verge of sliding out of contention. After losing three straight games to Baltimore at Fenway, the Red Sox traveled to riot-torn Detroit for two games against the league-leading Tigers. Trailing 5–4 in the ninth inning of the first game, Yaz belted his fortieth home run of the season to tie the game. In the tenth inning, Dalton Jones, a utility infielder filling in for the slumping Joe Foy, delivered the biggest hit of his career as he launched what would be the game-winning home run into the right-field upper deck. The next evening the Red Sox rallied from a 2–1 deficit after eight innings to win 4–2 and move into a tie for first place. Boston completed the road trip by winning four out of six games in Cleveland and Baltimore. With four home games remaining to complete the season and only half a game behind the league-leading Twins, the Red Sox appeared to be in a good position to win their first pennant since 1946.

On September 26, an off day for Boston, the Red Sox moved into a tie for first place when the Twins lost. Then disaster struck. The lowly Cleveland Indians, who had lost seven straight games to the Red Sox, won two games in a row at Fenway Park. Boston scored only three runs in two days on a Yastrzemski home run. Yaz recalled going into the locker room after the second defeat and congratulating Lonborg and other players on a great season while thinking about next year and getting to the next level. A few moments later, however, the team received the news that the Twins had lost. The Red Sox still had a slim chance for the pennant. That night Dick Williams sat in his car outside his apartment, a six-pack of beer at his side, straining to hear distant reports on his radio of the White Sox–Athletics doubleheader. He remembered "hoping and wishing and trying to will the White Sox to lose both games before I went nuts or my car battery died." Incredibly, the last-place Athletics won both games. Suddenly it seemed that no contending team had enough energy left to seize the American League pennant. The four contenders managed to lose seven of nine games played in the first three days of the final week of the season. The Red Sox still had a chance for the league championship if they could defeat the Twins in the last two games of the season at Fenway Park.[34]

As Saturday's game with Minnesota approached, Red Sox fans were filled with both hope and anxiety. Many remembered the infamous two games at Yankee Stadium in 1949. Game one began badly for Boston. Jose Santiago was wild early and fortunate to trail only 1–0 after four innings. In the fifth inning, the complexion of the game changed as the Twins suddenly appeared snakebit. A bad-hop single that appeared to defy the laws of physics and the failure of pitcher Jim Perry to cover first base on a grounder to the right side of the infield, one of the most practiced plays in baseball, contributed to a two-run Red Sox rally. After the Twins tied the game at 2–2 in the top of the sixth, George Scott hit a long home run into the center-field bleachers to put Boston ahead 3–2. Yastrzemski put the game on ice in the seventh inning with a three-run home run into the Twins' bullpen. Fenway Park erupted. In the two games, Yaz would make an incredible seven hits in eight at-bats, accounting for six RBI. "Yastrzemski continued a streak," Dick Williams later said, "that cemented my feeling that his season was baseball's best ever."[35]

On October 1 nearly 36,000 fans somehow crammed into Fenway Park. Boston ace Jim Lonborg started for the home team. He was 0–6 lifetime against Minnesota. To change his luck, Lonborg had stayed the night before at the Boston Sheraton, engaged in a meditative exercise to relieve tension, and fallen asleep reading William Craig's *The Fall of Japan.* He pitched well enough through six innings, but trailed 2–0 mainly because of shoddy defensive play by the Red Sox, including a rare error by Yastrzemski. Meanwhile the Twins' twenty-game winner Dean Chance mowed down Red Sox batters and appeared to be on the way to his sixth shutout of the season. The most important hit that day and maybe the season came in the bottom of the sixth and traveled only twenty feet. Despite trailing by two runs, Williams sent Lonborg up to hit for himself. The 6-foot 5-inch, 200-pound Californian promptly laid down a perfect bunt toward third base. The sight of the gangly Lonborg racing to first base and halfway to Pesky's Pole in right field aroused the Fenway crowd while the Twins appeared bewildered. Jerry Adair and Dalton Jones followed with slap singles that loaded the bases. Then Yastrzemski delivered two runs with a sharp single to center field that tied the game at 2–2. The fans were now in an uproar, and the Twins began to unravel with a series of misplays and an error. Boston proceeded to score three more runs in the inning without hitting the ball out of the infield. Minnesota mounted a comeback in the eighth inning, but it fell short. When Twins pinch-hitter Rich Rollins lifted a soft pop-up toward shortstop with two out in the ninth inning and the Red Sox leading 5–3, fans in Fenway Park, Boston, and most of New England were primed for a long-awaited explosion of joy that would help expunge more than twenty years of frustration.[36]

When Petrocelli caught the ball, the ball park erupted in ecstasy. Most Boston players made a hasty dash for the clubhouse, but Lonborg tarried and was swept up by the swarming crowd, which elevated and transported him, as if he were levitating, toward the right-field foul pole. The frantic fans managed to defrock him and pilfer his shoe laces with his spikes still on his feet. He was finally rescued by Boston's Finest. One policeman re-marked that "this made Roxbury look like a picnic." Other rampaging fans dismantled the scoreboard, ripped up pieces of sod, and deposited handfuls of dirt in their pockets. Several sportswriters in the press box considered climbing down the screen behind home plate in their haste to reach the Red Sox locker room, but thought better of it when they saw a swarm of kids clawing their way toward them. Red Sox historian Ellery Clark described the scene as "a moment of Boston parochial emotionalism at its very best."[37]

In the Red Sox locker room, beer and shaving cream flowed freely. Dick

Williams quieted the ruckus temporarily when he told Lee Stage, who had already downed a couple of beers, "Careful, you're starting tomorrow." Suddenly it dawned on the celebrating mob that the Red Sox had only clinched a tie for the American League championship. It would take an Angels victory over Detroit to clinch the pennant. Otherwise Boston would play the Tigers the next day in a playoff game. The revelers quieted down to hear Ernie Harwell deliver the radio play-by-play of the pivotal game from Detroit. California trailed and then took the lead in the third inning, 4–3. Former Red Sox catcher Moe Berg, an intellectual, master of eight languages, and a spy during World War II, stood up and solemnly pronounced, "Despite the undiluted duality of baseball talent today, Yastrzemski must be considered and bracketed with all the men who were great at playing this sport." Finally it was over in Detroit, and the champagne was uncorked. Tom Yawkey, who hadn't had a drink in four years, raised his paper cup and sipped the juice of the gods.[38]

How had a ninth-place team the previous season won the American League championship? There is no certain answer. Three men made the biggest contributions. General Manager Dick O'Connell cultivated able players in the farm system and was determined to end the country club atmosphere in Boston by hiring Dick Williams as manager. With a one-year contract, Williams saw his main chance and proceeded to shock the team out of its lethargy. Yastrzemski simply had the season of his career and perhaps the century. Beyond that, the Red Sox were lucky. They were lucky that the league was evenly balanced among the contenders, that Al Kaline broke his hand, that Lonborg beat out the improbable bunt, and that their rivals collapsed toward the end of the last week of the season.

"The Impossible Dream," as Boston fans would call the Red Sox first pennant-winning season since 1946, did not extend to the World Series. The postseason playoff against the heavily favored St. Louis Cardinals was much like the rollercoaster regular season of ups and downs except that in the end it was the Red Sox who would walk off the field in the deciding seventh game at Fenway Park as losers. It was a series of two dominant pitchers, Lonborg and Bob Gibson. Lonborg pitched splendidly, but Gibson was magnificent, with three complete game victories and a 1.00 ERA. For Red Sox fans, the World Series provided many "what ifs" that would be discussed for years to come. Would the outcome have been different if

Lonborg had had proper rest and faced Gibson in games one, four, and seven? Could a healthy Tony Conigliaro have helped spark Boston to its first World Series championship since 1918? The one constant in the series for the Red Sox was Yastrzemski, who continued on a batting rampage with a .400 average, three home runs, and five RBI.

Despite the defeat in the World Series, the 1967 season changed everything about Boston Red Sox baseball. "Today," Dick Williams wrote in 1990, "Boston is considered perhaps America's top baseball town. The fans fill Fenway even when their team is lousy and losing. Baseball talk fills the radio and television airwaves even in the dead of winter." The once-carnivorous Boston media embraced the team even though it drove players and managers to distraction as the team failed to deliver a World Championship for thirty-seven more years. Fenway Park, which Tom Yawkey was hoping to abandon in 1967 for a new stadium, is now regarded by many as a Boston shrine in the same sense as Faneuil Hall or the Old North Church. Throughout the fall and winter of 1967, amid continued racial and war-related turmoil, Red Sox fans basked in the afterglow of a sublime season. Yastrzemski began collecting enough awards and trophies to fill several bookcases. In Vietnam, the Chinese lunar new year, "The Year of the Monkey," was beginning. Both at home and abroad it would be a year even more tumultuous than 1967. Many Red Sox fans would remember 1967 as "The Year of the Yaz." He and his teammates had accomplished something very special. "Very few people in sport can say they helped change the entire course of a franchise's history," sportswriter Bob Ryan wrote in 2002, "but that is precisely what the 1967 Red Sox did."[39]

5

The Boston Marathon:
America's Oldest Annual Road Race

Matthew Oshinsky and David M. Oshinsky

On April 18, 1994, in keeping with tradition, the *Boston Globe* printed its Boston Marathon Eve feature story for the ninety-sixth time in ninety-eight years. The story posed the question most commonly asked by those who would never dream of entering the race and are baffled by its lure: "Marathon Torture: Why Do Runners Run?"

The answers were predictably complex. Some runners spoke of setting goals and raising self-esteem. Others mentioned fitness, karma, and comradeship; still others loved competing against rivals, against the storied race course, and, most important, against themselves—the victory of mind and body over exhaustion and pain.

One point is clear: Marathoners are a diverse lot, bound together by the goal of running 26 miles for the sheer joy and accomplishment of running 26 miles. In Boston, the key to joining this unique and ever-expanding fraternity—the initiation rite—appears at the 21-mile mark, as the course begins to slope upward into a series of punishing hills. At this point, a longtime spectator recalls, "many runners are huffing and grimacing. Their strides have become slow, short, choppy. Some look up, searching for the summit; others look down, avoiding the view of the long road ahead. The applause from the spectators never lets up. Someone shouts, 'You can do it. You can beat the hill!'"[1]

It is at this moment that the runner truly asks "why," and either continues on to the finish line or surrenders to the self. One way or the other, the question has been answered.

Heartbreak Hill, about 5 miles from the finish line in downtown Boston, is the most fabled part of the most famous marathon in the world. When officials of the Boston Athletic Association first designed their course in 1896, they wanted something distinctive, a barrier, near the end, to remind competitors of their mortality. Heartbreak Hill—three hills, really—became that special symbol, a slow, steady incline that has punished elite athletes and ordinary plodders for more than a century, the exclamation point to this grueling 26-mile, 385-yard run.[2]

In truth, the BAA did not have much competition. The marathon had been run only twice before—at a onetime event in New York City in 1896 and, a few months earlier, at the first modern Olympic Games in Athens, Greece. To honor the achievement of the gallant warrior Pheidippides, who, legend said, had sprinted from Marathon to Athens in the year 490 B.C. with news of a military victory, the Olympic Committee designed a road race to cover the same distance. Part of the lure lay in the valor and patriotism of the runner, part in the fact that he dropped dead upon his arrival in Athens after delivering just three words: "Rejoice, we conquer."[3]

The BAA had sent a delegation to Athens to observe the 1896 Games. It had watched a Greek shepherd, Spiridon Louis, awe the 50,000 spectators in Panathinaikon Stadium by finishing the race in 2 hours, 58 minutes, and 50 seconds. BAA representatives were so taken by the challenge and danger of the marathon that they decided to create one in New England. A Boston Marathon would be the perfect way to combine extraordinary athleticism with civic boosterism. Louis, after all, had been transformed into a national hero the moment he broke the tape in Athens.

It seemed appropriate to hold the new BAA marathon on April 19, to commemorate Paul Revere's historic ride in 1775. Selecting a course, though, would take some effort. The BAA was determined to emulate the Greek model, but Boston's outer neighborhoods and thoroughfares were not as easily navigated as the more rural roads surrounding Athens. After a bit of study, Ashland was made the starting point, mainly because it was 25 miles from the only track-and-field stadium in Boston, the Irvington Street Oval.

The course led marathoners through Framingham, Natick, and Wellesley, up into Auburndale, over three successive Newton hills, down into Brighton, across Brookline, and finally into Boston. Those who entered the race did so at their own risk.[4]

Fifteen men accepted the challenge. On April 19, 1897, BAA hero Tom Burke, the winner of two sprinting medals at the recent Greek Olympics, called the runners to the starting line he had created with the heel of his boot. Lacking a pistol, Burke shouted "Go!" and the group took off for Boston, followed by members of a local ambulance corps. The race featured a rivalry of sorts between lithographer John J. McDermott, winner of the only previous American marathon, the 25-mile affair from Stamford, Connecticut, to Manhattan's Columbus Circle; and Harvard University's Dick Grant, the local favorite and the only runner in the field without a personal handler to give him water and lemon slices along the way. A few miles into the race, Grant found himself running stride for stride with a New Yorker named Hamilton Gray. To Grant's surprise, Gray passed him a canteen of water—a signal that all racers were competing together against a common enemy, the brutal course, as well as against each other. The gesture would become a Boston Marathon tradition.[5]

About halfway through the race, the runners began to struggle. Aside from simple exhaustion, they faced a choking cloud of dust kicked up by spectators, cyclists, and assorted vehicles following the competitors. Grant led the pack as it approached Wellesley College. Catching sight of his Harvard colors, the women let out a whooping cheer, starting another tradition that persists to this day. ("Whatever you do," implores the legend of the marathon, "do not falter at Wellesley.") Grant held on till the three hills at Newton before collapsing—literally—in a heap. Fighting leg cramps and blisters, McDermott entered Boston so far in front that he stopped for a short breather to watch a funeral go by. He reached Irvington Circle in 2 hours, 55 minutes, 7 minutes ahead of his nearest rival.

Ten of the fifteen runners eventually finished the race, the last taking more than 4 hours. Fearing permanent damage, McDermott vowed to retire. "This will probably be my last long race," he told the *Boston Globe*. "I

hate to be called a quitter and a coward, but look at my feet." Few would
have argued. McDermott, however, returned to defend his title in 1898, losing to a Boston College student named Ronald McDonald.[6]

As a sport, the marathon grew slowly in size and popularity. The BAA
moved the starting line to Hopkinton after the "official" distance for all future races was lengthened to 26 miles, 385 yards at the 1908 London Olympics in order to allow an ailing Queen Anne to watch the start from her balcony atop Windsor Castle. The event became a symbol of local diversity,
reflecting Boston's academic, commercial, and working-class roots. The
first fifteen winners included a student, a blacksmith, a carpenter, two
clerks, a plumber, a farmer, a mill hand, a printer, and six "unknowns."
Runners like Sammy Mellor of Yonkers, New York, and Timothy Ford of
Cambridge were able to bask in a day's worth of celebrity, making the
Boston Marathon a symbol of amateur integrity and competitive joy—a
place where average Americans could shine.[7]

Between his first victory in 1911 and 1930, the race was dominated by a remarkable runner, Clarence DeMar, who won it a record seven times. His
character seemed a natural—if regrettable—fit for the punishing 26-mile
course. The great sportswriter Joe Falls described DeMar as "a humorless
man, bitter at times . . . almost venomous." He ran the race in an angry
trance, kicking dogs and punching spectators who got in his way. "Once, at
Auburndale," DeMar recalled, "I was confronted by a youth with a pencil
and a book looking for my autograph. Spontaneously, I poked him in the
face and ran better for it. Running against time and signing autographs are
two feats that cannot be done at the same time. And I'll tell you, I landed a
good strong one on one bozo's nose and he knows why."[8]

DeMar, a Melrose native, worked as a printer for Boston newspapers. He
would often win the marathon, then shuffle off to his job that evening to set
the type of his own victory for the front page. DeMar's athleticism was well
disguised by a sunken frame, a balding head, legs that looked like rubber
bands, and a scowl that frightened children. He did not compete between
1912 and 1916, because doctors told him he had a weak heart. It was only
DeMar's perseverance and competitiveness that returned him to the winner's podium in 1922, 1923, 1924, 1927, 1928, and 1930.

One of the few things that could stop him in this period was the Great

War. The race was canceled in 1918—the only time that ever happened—following America's entry into World War I. Instead, on Patriots' Day 1918, the Boston Athletic Association staged an absurd relay race, with soldiers running in full uniform, including spit-polished boots. What was intended as a star-spangled tribute to the nation's fighting men turned into a ludicrous spectacle of exhaustion and discomfort. Public criticism was intense. Never again would Boston see a Patriots' Day without a proper marathon.[9]

DeMar's reign included the onset of the Great Depression. A bleak era lay ahead, and a bleak man wore the public face of the Boston Marathon. The event, like the nation, needed a breath of fresh air. It arrived, in the 1930s, in the form of two enormously gifted and popular local runners— Johnny A. Kelley and Ellison "Tarzan" Brown.

Kelley, from nearby Medford, had spent much of his childhood following his mail-carrier father on his daily route and caddying for tips at a local golf course. Each Patriots' Day would find him on Beacon Street, watching the marathoners run by. In 1928, a year after finishing high school, Kelley entered the Boston race but failed to finish. Even so, the experience was exhilarating. What began as a personal response to the Great Depression would mature into a lifetime calling. "There were no jobs anyway," Kelley remembered. "I worked here and I worked there [in the early 1930s]. There was nothing permanent, nothing steady. Running was fun. It helped kill time."[10]

The same held true for Ellison Brown, a young Narragansett Indian who had earned the nickname "Tarzan" for his diving exploits in the ponds and lakes around his hometown of Alton, Rhode Island. Brown was something of a local legend even before he entered the Boston Marathon, known for his intense character and bar-clearing brawls. Everyone had heard the stories about his winning two regional marathons in the span of 24 hours. He ran marathons as he lived his life—at full throttle. There was no strategy involved. He went as fast as he could for as long as he could, sprinting till he dropped. In the 1930s Brown proved the perfect media foil for Kelley—the untamed Indian against the determined Irishman. For the decade to follow, "Kelley vs. Brown" would lead the Patriots' Day headlines.[11]

Both men entered the 1935 Boston Marathon expecting to win. Kelley had finished thirty-seventh in 1933 and second in 1934. This was to be his year, the local newspapers claimed. Brown, making his Boston debut, showed up at the starting line in Hopkinton wearing a handmade shirt cut from the favorite dress of his mother, who had died two days before. Other favorites included Pat Dengis, a promising British runner, and Canadian Dave Komonen, the defending champion.[12]

The 1935 race is now part of marathon legend. Brown entertained the crowd beforehand by devouring one hot dog after another and washing them down with several bottles of orange soda. But his poorly made shoes failed him at the 20-mile mark; he ran the last 6 miles barefoot and still managed to finish thirteenth (out of a field of almost 200 runners). Kelley, meanwhile, had been given a packet of glucose pills by a team of Harvard doctors who were studying the metabolic effects of long-distance running. He took the early lead, gulping a pill every few miles. Dengis, timing his spurts expertly, pulled even with Kelley before the girls at Wellesley College and took the lead at the three Newton hills. Near the top, however, a stitch cut through his side, allowing Kelley to pass him as they approached the outskirts of Boston. Running strong into Kenmore Square, only a mile from the finish line, Kelley suddenly stopped, pitched forward, and began to throw up. As the crowd watched in amazement, he forced two fingers down his throat and spat the offending glucose pills onto Beacon Street. "Once I got rid of them," he told reporters, "I felt like I could run all the way to South Boston."[13]

His dramatic victory gave the city a new sports hero. Kelley was modest, courageous, ethnic, and thoroughly working-class. Like good men everywhere, wrote the adoring *Boston Globe*, he trudged anonymously to his job at a flower shop the next morning at 7:30, a wisp of a man in a gray sweat-shirt, a lunchpail under his arm, to commence another honest day's work. Few could have guessed that this was young Johnny Kelley, "the Arlington Irishman with the twinkling eyes and the chipmunk's saucy grin, who, 19 hours before, had led a crack field of distance runners over 26 miles in the annual Boston AA Marathon."[14]

For Johnny Kelley and the Boston Marathon, the days of obscurity were gone. More than 300,000 spectators lined the streets for the 1936 race, and local betting was brisk. Kelley was the crowd favorite, of course, but others stood a chance. The most intriguing rival was still Tarzan Brown, who had looked almost unbeatable in 1935 until his shoes fell apart. Since the winner would probably represent the United States at the upcoming Olympics in Berlin, the pressure was intense.

Brown took the early lead. Running flat out, as always, he was 500 yards ahead of the pack after only 6 miles. He flew through every checkpoint in record time—Framingham, Natick, Wellesley, Newton. This time, Tarzan's killing pace seemed to be working. He had even raced past the press cars. But as he neared the spires of Boston College, 21 miles into the race, Brown hit "the invisible wall." His legs tightened, he began to wobble, then to fade. Johnny Kelley, running a more measured pace, caught the leader near the peak of the third Newton hill. What happened next is part of Boston's star-crossed sports history, an event that ranks with Johnny Pesky's mental lapse in the 1946 World Series and Bill Buckner's creaky wickets exactly forty years later.

As Kelley passed Tarzan Brown, he gave him a pat on the shoulder, a gesture of sympathy—or, more likely, condescension—that enraged the struggling runner. In the words of a sportswriter who covered the race, "it was like Johnny Kelley had put a pin up the guy's ass." Tarzan charged down the hill, overtook Kelley, and never looked back. He even had time to stop for a few breathers before breaking the tape. Still furious after setting the course record, he told reporters, "I guess you white people can't say after this that the only good Indian is a dead Indian." From that day forward the steep inclines of Newton, where Johnny Kelley let his cockiness get the best of him, would be known as Heartbreak Hill.[15]

Kelley would win only one more Boston Marathon, in 1945. It was longevity that made him unique. Between 1934 and 1950 he finished third twice, fourth twice, fifth three times, and was runner-up seven times. For Kelley, like the beloved Red Sox, there was always "next year." He ran sixty-one Boston Marathons and finished fifty-eight, the last one at age eighty-four in 1992. Three generations of New Englanders saw him compete, and to those who lined the marathon course, the race was not official until they saw Johnny Kelley pass by. In 1999 Runner's World magazine described his exploits as "by far, in our opinion, the greatest running achievement of the century."[16]

Tarzan Brown met a harsher fate. He won only one more Boston Marathon, in 1939. His greatest moment had promised to be the 1936 Berlin Olympics, where he and Kelley were the American marathoners. Plagued by a hernia, Brown failed to finish the race. He did, however, stage a memorable brawl with a gang of Adolf Hitler's brownshirts in a beer garden near the stadium. By the 1940s, his running days behind him, Brown retreated into a life of alcoholism and sporadic work. He died in 1975, at age sixty-one, run over by a car during a fight in a Rhode Island parking lot. He was, perhaps, the most naturally gifted man ever to run in Boston.[17]

Until the late 1930s the Boston Marathon was a still a popular regional event, attracting top runners, but dominated by homegrown favorites like Kelley and Brown. The crowds were large and enthusiastic, but the flavor was strictly "Beantown." This image would change dramatically by the end of World War II, as the nation assumed new global responsibilities and sporting events took on an international flair. The charmingly provincial story of a local man taking the day off to "run for Boston" was coming to a close.

For the next three decades an American champion would be hard to find. The victors included the likes of Gerard Cote, the "fabulous French-man" from Quebec, who told reporters after his win in 1948: "Gentlemens! Gentlemens! One beer! One cigar! Then we talk about the race, eh!"; and Stylianos Kyiarides, undernourished and emaciated, whose dramatic, come-from-behind victory over Johnny Kelley in 1946 was celebrated as a triumph for the entire Greek nation, seven million strong, in its bitter post-war struggle to defeat Communism. (Kelley, the ultimate gentleman and perennial runner-up, embraced Kyiarides at the finish.) Through the 1950s and 1960s the winners of the Boston Marathon represented all parts of the "free world," including Finland, Sweden, Guatemala, Japan, South Korea, and "nonaligned" Yugoslavia. Anyone with the dream of being the world's best distance runner had to come to Boston to prove it.[18]

Amazingly, the only American to capture the race in these years was an-other local Irishman named John J. Kelley—no relation to Johnny. His victory in 1957 briefly raised hopes for an American resurgence in distance running. Unfortunately, what the two Kelleys had in common was the uncanny ability to come in second. John J. would be the runner-up in five Boston Marathons—almost matching his namesake's record of seven.[19]

Despite the marathon's growing international reach, the driving force behind it—the Boston Athletic Association—was little more than a "mom-and-pop" operation run by two cartoonlike old friends, Will Cloney and

John D. "Jock" Semple, Boston's favorite masseur. Semple's office, located in the bowels of the decrepit Boston Garden, home to the Bruins and the Celtics, was cluttered with rubbing tables, rolls of athletic tape, and tubes of Vaseline jelly. Each year, as marathon day approached, Cloney and Semple sifted through thousands of entries from around the world. It was a true labor of love for the Scots-born Semple—as evidenced by the photos that hung from the walls of his office, showing him greeting each year's marathon winner at the finish line, throwing a blanket around his shoulders, and escorting him to his traditional postrace bowl of beef stew.[20]

Semple and Cloney saw the storied race as a calling, and both were fiercely determined to keep it "pure." Jock had been a runner in his day, finishing as high as seventh in the Boston Marathon in 1930. Cloney, an ex-sportswriter, viewed athletic competition as the noblest form of combat, with a set of rules to match. That meant no women, no prize money, no expenses paid under the table, and no degrading publicity. In 1959, when a runner tried to compete wearing a clown's mask, Cloney ran the fellow down, tackled him from behind, and didn't stop punching until the police pulled him off. As the race grew larger, this problem naturally got worse. The 1960s were dawning, and as media and spectator attention steadily grew, so, too, did the impulse to make the marathon a stage for expression. Semple and Cloney began to patrol the event each year, looking for "imposters" like the ill-fated clown.[21]

It didn't always work. In 1967, buried deep in a pile of folders on Semple's desk, was an application from "K. Switzer" of Syracuse, New York. What Semple couldn't know—and K. Switzer didn't dare acknowledge—was that the applicant was female. The Boston Marathon was for "men only," and strictly enforced. You'll never see a woman playing for the Red Sox, the Celtics, or the Bruins, Semple liked to say, and you'll never see one running from Hopkinton to Boston, either. The marathon was a test of manhood. Allowing women to compete was both dangerous and disruptive; it would demean a great sporting event. As *Globe* sportswriter Jerry Nason put it: "Naturally, the Boston AA does not permit the babes to compete in their bunion derby—possibly because they'd get 369 boy entries from Harvard, MIT, and Boston U alone, if they did."[22]

These sentiments were not unusual. In 1928, Olympic spectators in Amsterdam had watched in shock as a number of women collapsed while competing in the 800-meter race, barely half a mile long. There were immediate calls in the press for a ban on all women's races over 200 meters. The International Olympic Committee obliged. These contests could hardly be considered healthy for such fragile human beings, especially in light of their reproductive responsibilities. Why jeopardize the future of the human race? The women's 800 meters would not be restored until 1960.[23]

A confrontation was inevitable. In 1966 a young woman named Roberta Gibb had been turned down for the race by Semple after sending for an application. Gibb, a self-described spiritualist, had discovered inner peace while jogging long distances, up to 40 miles a day. Her passion to compete was more personal than political: she simply loved to run. The Boston Marathon, she believed, was like a giant hippie commune in track shoes. She had to try it.

Gibb hid in the bushes near the starting line, then melted into the pack. Wearing a black nylon bathing suit and her brother's oversized Bermuda shorts, she somehow managed to avoid the visual radar of Cloney and Semple, finishing the race in a respectable—and unofficial—3 hours, 21 minutes, and 40 seconds. Those who spotted her along the way were wildly supportive, sensing that history was being made. A huge roar went up in Wellesley, and the press corps whistled and cheered. The next day's headlines read: "Hub Bride First Gal to Run Marathon" and "Blond Wife, 23, Runs Marathon." Some, of course, were stunned by the news. "It's hard to believe," said the Celtics' legendary general manager, Red Auerbach. "I can't get [my] guys to run around the floor, and a small broad goes out there and runs a marathon. I don't know what the world is coming to."[24]

Cloney and Semple were furious—and deeply embarrassed. They first denied that a woman had actually finished the marathon, and then vowed that it would never happen again. "The hell she ran," said Semple. "And I'll tell ye this—they don't belong in races where they don't belong, and I cannot get any more logical than that. And if they try to get in, they're gonna get thrown out." The gruff Scotsman would not disappoint.

Boston, with its many colleges and universities, was a center of social activism in the 1960s. There was strong sympathy for what Roberta Gibb had done, and growing public pressure to allow women officially into the race. None of which impressed the austere male gatekeepers, Semple and

Cloney, who stood guard on the press bus on a cold, drizzly Patriots' Day in 1967, scanning the crowd of runners for a female shape. Sure enough, only 2 miles into the race, Semple fixed on a sight he thought he'd never live to see. Not only was there a woman in the race, but this one was wearing an official number. How had that happened? How could Jock have possibly approved her application? Semple's face went crimson, but Cloney was one step ahead. Without warning, he jumped from the bus and took off in pursuit.

A marathoner he was not. Cloney gave up after several hundred yards and a torrent of epithets. But Semple, the former distance runner, flew past him, with the press bus in hot pursuit. His prey was competitor number 261, Katherine Switzer, a twenty-year-old Syracuse student who had come to run the marathon with her boyfriend, Tom Miller, and her coach, Arnie Briggs. Unlike Roberta Gibb, K. Switzer fully intended to make a political statement. And, clearly, Jock Semple did, too.

Their confrontation was brief but explosive. Semple approached her in full gallop, yelling, "Get the hell out of my race and give me that number!" He reached out and grabbed a handful of Switzer's sweatshirt. At that moment, Miller, a well-muscled Olympic hopeful in the hammer throw, came up behind Semple and flattened him with a body check that would have made the Boston Bruins proud. "Kathy! Run like hell," Briggs shouted. Switzer took off in full sprint, while the groggy Semple limped to the sidelines, vowing revenge. A few minutes later the press bus passed another woman on the course. It was the ubiquitous Roberta Gibb, running without a number. She would ultimately be stopped at the finish line by race officials, one yard short of completing the race.[25]

All of this was captured on film and flashed around the world. Switzer, Cloney, and Semple instantly became symbols: she of the surging women's rights movement, they of the cranky resistance to change. "I'm terribly disappointed that American girls force their way into something where they are neither eligible nor wanted," said a despondent Cloney. But that time had passed. Though some would poke fun at both sides in the controversy—"2 Girls in Marathon Don't Have Lovely Leg to Stand On," said the *New York Times*—a revolutionary change had occurred. For the next four years, women would run the race as "informal" participants. In 1972 Nina Kuscsik became the first official women's winner at Boston under the hesitant but hospitable eyes of Cloney and Semple.[26]

Over the next decade Switzer and Kuscsik would prove instrumental in organizing and executing the first ever all-female marathons in Atlanta (1978), West Germany (1979), London (1980), Ottawa (1981), and San Francisco (1982). Two years later the first women's Olympic marathon was run in Los Angeles, where, once again, a group of competitors collapsed beneath the broiling California sun. This time there would be no calls for a ban. Women had arrived in distance running at last. It had taken eighty-eight years.[27]

The 1960s were good years for the Boston Marathon, and for distance running as a whole. Vigorous exercise, once considered a hazardous waste of time—a hobby for eccentrics—was now seen as a patriotic virtue, eliminating complacency and flab. Its champions included a trim young president from Massachusetts and a group of sleek, fitness-obsessed astronauts who personified the nation's "right stuff." One exercised to sharpen the mind and body, and to fortify the soul. Furthermore, one often looked better for having done it.

Applications to the BAA continued to rise. In 1972 an American runner, Frank Shorter, won the Olympic marathon in Munich. His improbable victory helped legitimize serious distance running in the United States. Among the athletes inspired by Shorter was a recent Wesleyan University graduate from Hartford named Bill Rodgers.

A conscientious objector during the Vietnam War, Rodgers had come to Boston to do his alternative service at the Peter Bent Brigham Hospital. Having run track in college, with marginal success, he started jogging again to ease the tedium of his job and reverse the effects of a half-a-pack-per-day cigarette habit. "Billy Rodgers did not look like a young man with ambition," wrote one historian of the Boston Marathon. "He wandered between rebellion and destitution, like so many from the graduating class of 1970"— the class of Kent State and campus disruption.

Frank Shorter's victory set Rodgers's mind in motion; Jock Semple gave it proper focus. "Billy found his way to Jock's office," recalled author and runner Jason Kehoe. "The atmosphere . . . was supercharged with memorabilia . . . It represented all that was essential in the Boston Marathon, and Billy ate it up. Jock could see that not only was the young man a promising talent, but he also had an interest and enthusiasm for the history of the race." Semple believed he had found his great white hope.[28]

Rodgers ran Boston in 1973, but dropped out at Framingham. The next year he stayed with the leaders for about half the race, finishing a satisfactory fourteenth. In March 1975 he finished ahead of Shorter at the World Cross Country Championships. Everyone at the Greater Boston Track Club knew Rodgers was good, but beating Frank Shorter was something else. Rodgers became an early favorite to take the Boston Marathon that year. Patriots' Day 1975 was cool and overcast, with a west wind at the runners' back—perfect conditions. Rodgers got off at a moderate pace, but took control about halfway through. He kept widening his lead, despite slowing four times to drink water and stopping once to tie his shoe. As Rodgers bent over for his laces, Jock Semple charged off the press bus one more time. "Get going, lad," he screamed. "You've got a chance for the record!" Rodgers took off, finishing in a remarkable 2 hours, 9 minutes, 55 seconds, the best marathon time ever for an American runner.[29]

He would go on to capture three of the next four Boston Marathons, earning his place as the top-rated distance runner in the sport. "Boston Billy" was Jock Semple's dream come true: a homegrown world champion, a Johnny Kelley who could win. From 1975 through 1980 Rodgers was the undisputed king of the marathon at a time when the running boom hit its peak. In 1978 the number of people who finished a marathon topped 100,000. That same year, Jim Fixx's *Complete Book of Running* topped the *New York Times* bestseller list. Just as President Kennedy and the U.S. astronauts had transformed physical fitness into a patriotic pursuit, Fixx transformed running into a mystical one. Those of the 1960s generation who had grown older and a bit wider since Woodstock could get back into shape physically and spiritually. Running was at once peaceful and proactive. Together, Fixx and Rodgers symbolized a precious civic virtue: self-improvement. Rodgers was a late bloomer made good; Fixx was barely an athlete at all, more a popularizer with a perfect feel for what ordinary people yearned to accomplish.[30]

Together, too, they helped turn Jock Semple's quaint race into a modern spectacle. On Patriots' Day 1980 more than a million fans lined every inch of the course to cheer on the 5,000 official runners. Yet these surging numbers were deceptive. As distance running became a national hobby and more people crowded the starting line, the top marathoners began to stay away. Most of the entrants who lined up in Hopkinton that day were fitness buffs and weekend warriors, not elite runners. And the reason was simple: Boston, the holy grail of marathons, remained a strictly "amateur event," with no prize money for the top finishers. For some of the best road racers, a bowl of beef stew and a laurel wreath for the winner were no longer enough. Frank Shorter, the great Olympic champion, consistently skipped Boston because of the BAA's refusal to pay his travel expenses.

And then there was New York City. Ten years before, the New York Road Runners Club had inaugurated its own "marathon," a small event consisting of four laps around Central Park, with perhaps 100 spectators urging fifty-five runners to the finish line. But, in typical New York fashion, things grew quickly. Six years later more than 2,000 entrants raced through all five boroughs, crossed four bridges, and drew huge crowds along the way. By 1979 the New York Marathon was the largest in the world, attracting world-class runners with generous rewards. Its instant success spawned other marathons in Houston, Chicago, and Montreal, all paying big money to the top finishers, women as well as men. "Boston Billy" Rodgers won four consecutive New York Marathons in these years.

For the first time in decades, the Boston Marathon was in trouble. To compete with New York City, the BAA agreed to pay some "expense money" to top runners, but it wasn't nearly enough. Then, in 1980, the race itself suffered a major embarrassment. Though Bill Rodgers won easily that year, he was not the center of attention. The big story was the woman sitting next to him on the victory podium—a pudgy New Yorker with a mischievous look on her face. Rodgers was puzzled. He didn't recognize his counterpart. She didn't look particularly tired. He could not imagine how she had just run 26 miles. Nor, for that matter, could anyone else who had been following the race. As the two champions sat together for photographs, Rodgers leaned over and asked the mystery woman, "Did you win?" "Yes," she replied. Rodgers paused and rephrased. "Who are you?"

She was Rosie Ruiz, an unknown amateur from Cuba by way of Manhattan. To his credit, Will Cloney awarded Ruiz her medal that day without recrimination. He simply didn't know whether she had run the whole distance or not. But Jock Semple was livid, denouncing Ruiz as an imposter.[31]

Semple was right, of course. Ruiz, looking more for attention than for glory, had jumped into the race near Kenmore Square—very close to the finish line—and "won" quite by accident. Her plan, it appeared, was to finish third or fourth. Had she done that—had she waited a minute or two longer before joining the runners—she might well have pulled it off. But a winner comes under intense scrutiny, and Ms. Ruiz seemed to know nothing about running or training or even the marathon she had supposedly completed. For a week or so, she was the most famous female athlete in the world. Ugly arguments flared, often along ethnic and gender lines. "Now we'll have to have an official checker check the women," a weary Jock Semple told the *New York Times*. "Just another headache."[32]

The bad news kept mounting. In 1982 Newton mayor Teddy Mann threatened to close his roads to the marathon if the BAA didn't come up with the funds needed to cover the police overtime costs. Without consulting anyone, Will Cloney made a deal with local promoter Michael Medoff to raise the $400,000 it took to stage the race. Medoff found a number of sponsors, but kept a portion of the money raised for himself. When word of the deal reached the local newspapers, Cloney abruptly resigned. Aside from acquiring a handful of small sponsors, the plan had been a complete failure; the marathon was still in danger of collapse.[33]

In 1986 a major sponsor stepped in, putting Boston on the same footing as its competitors. With the backing of locally based John Hancock Financial Services, the marathon now awarded prize money for the first time. Instantly the world's top runners returned to Boston on Patriots' Day. Winner Rob de Castella of Australia took home $30,000 for finishing first, another $25,000 for setting a course record, $5,000 more in "performance bonuses," and a new Mercedes-Benz. On the women's side, Norway's Ingrid Kristiansen got $30,000 and the automobile. Once again, the marathon had saved itself by adapting to unwanted change.[34]

In 1990 more than 9,000 runners crossed the fabled starting line in Hopkinton. Ten years later the figure topped 15,000. The financial freedom provided by John Hancock allowed a new crop of runners—especially foreign runners—to take their stab at immortality. Ibrahim Hussein and Cosmas Ndeti of Kenya ushered in an age of African marathoners, winning six between them in the years 1988–1995. Ndeti matched Clarence DeMar and Bill Rodgers with three consecutive victories, becoming one of the preeminent runners in Boston Marathon history. The 1990s belonged to the Kenyans, who won nine times in ten races. And, much like Clarence DeMar sixty years before, no one is quite sure who will eventually come along to dethrone them.

Today the marathon is on solid footing, thanks in good part to the corporate largesse so common in bigtime sports. And it remains a very special event, the grandfather of long-distance races, its history a composite of the enormous social, economic, political, and demographic changes that have transformed the Boston area and linked it to the greater world. It's a race with a century's worth of legends and traditions and characters, all carefully remembered and lovingly passed along. There's a feeling of common purpose and community to this marathon that even the toughest of adversaries seem, intuitively, to understand.

In February 1988 Kathy Switzer flew from her home in Wellington, New Zealand, to visit an old man in a Boston hospital who was dying of cancer. "This was someone who was very, very key to my life," she recalled. "This man changed my life . . . Fate threw us together." She was nervous, not knowing whether Jock Semple would recognize her, or care to remember. "But when I walked in the door," she said, "he lighted up like a Christmas tree." Their bond was the Boston Marathon, and they spent the day reminiscing, telling jokes. "That," said Switzer said, "is how I will remember him."[35]

And that is how the rest of us, participants and admirers alike, can remember the Boston Marathon.

6

Rowing on Troubled Waters

David W. Zang

There may be no place in America that more quickly or surely separates jaunty hope from bedrock faith than the indoor rowing tanks at Harvard's Newell Boathouse. Here, mirrors and flowing water from a diesel-driven pump surround what appears to be an eight-man racing shell stuck in concrete. For more than a century thousands of Crimson oarsmen have poured their lifeblood and sweat into the tanks without moving the shell an inch, experiencing all of the suffering but none of the exhilaration that accompanies a well-rowed piece on the water. Dave Higgins, a former Harvard bow seat, describes rowing as a "struggle to force yourself into a cauldron of pain."[1] And when Higgins rowed, "cauldron" was an apt metaphor for more than the Newell tanks; everywhere he and the Harvard varsity eight went in 1968, it seemed they dipped their oars into churning waters.

They became that year the last collegiate team to win the United States Olympic trials. Their experience in Mexico City, where altitude drained them and politics and the media threatened to swamp them, exposed some deep divisions within athletics and the Olympic movement. Through it all, the remarkable man who held them together did so by subordinating his wishes to those of his athletes, an act of magic few coaches could replicate in the cultural firestorm of the Vietnam era.

That sort of paradox has been a hallmark of Harvard rowing since its inception. Boston has always been understandably proud of its "school in the clouds" even while maintaining a distant attitude toward it.[2] The Charles River separates the two, but for more than a century and a half it has also furnished a locus of commonality. As early as the 1840s, rowing clubs—begun by Irish longshoremen and Yankee bluebloods alike—gave the sport prominence in the city. At Harvard the rowing club made the school an integral part of Boston's sporting and social fabric by using its boats to ferry home drunken members after a night on the town while enacting a series of firsts that brought recognition to competition on the Charles.[3]

In 1846 Harvard's *Huron* raced a Boston boat, *Wave*, in the school's first match against outside competition. In 1852 Harvard won the first intercollegiate athletic event in history, outstroking two teams from Yale on Lake Winnipesaukee in New Hampshire. In 1858 the team rowed the first racing shell built in America; her captain, Benjamin Crowninshield, purchased six red silk handkerchiefs as headbands, thereby beginning the tradition of college colors and the identification of Harvard with crimson. On July 4, 1854, Harvard rowers participated in a series of races watched by 40,000 spectators. Later moved to the fall, the event became the famous Head of the Charles regatta. And in 1900 Harvard's English coach, Rudolph Lehman, incorporated indoor tanks into the design for the Newell Boathouse, another American first.[4]

By then Harvard and its Ivy League counterparts had established themselves as the national models for intercollegiate sport, protecting their zeal for athletics by aligning themselves with the British conceit of amateurism. Rowing was in fact the first sport that upper-crust Brits had singled out for testing amateurism's exclusionary principle, whereby gentlemen shunned any competitor who made his living with his hands. Eventually the claims of amateurism grew to include the grander assertion that participation in sport without recompense was a building block of good character.

Here, too, Harvard rowing claimed a first. After the Crimson won an 1858 race against the Young Men's Democratic Club's *Fort Hill Boy*, a boat manned by Irish longshoremen, the regatta chairman heralded it as proof that "scholars may cultivate manly and healthful exercises with advantage."[5]

And when Harvard's turn-of-the-century president, Charles Eliot, nearly abolished Crimson intercollegiate teams in 1906, he exempted rowing from his criticism, calling crew and tennis "the only honorable college sports."[6]

By the 1950s the idea of sport as a character-builder had been undercut at the collegiate level by wire service polls, national tournaments, cheating scandals, recruiting abuses, and the negotiation of national television contracts. In the Ivy League, where the philosophical inseparability of sports and curriculum made the very term *scholar-athlete* a redundancy, the strain of holding onto sport's century-old ideal of victory with honor showed most clearly at the University of Pennsylvania. Wishing to link itself with the academically prestigious Ivies in the early 1950s, Penn had gained entry to the league by surrendering its former football reputation as the "Notre Dame of the East," along with the accompanying crowds that had filled cavernous Franklin Field.

To new Quaker athletic director Jeremiah Ford II, the Ivy League looked like a place where "we can hate enough to beat each other but trust enough to schedule each other."[7] During Ford's decade-and-a-half tenure Penn got beaten so often (the first football coach Ford hired lost his first eighteen games) that the other Ivies couldn't wait to schedule visits to Philadelphia. But as the other schools took turns pounding Penn through the 1950s and into the mid-1960s, Ford never lost hope that his program might one day be a shining beacon to all of college sport. His hope rested in the example of his rowing coach, Joe Burk.

Burk embodied everything that Ford valued in sport. He was a soft-spoken, articulate gentleman who commanded respect, demanded commitment, never compromised principle, and won often. Alone among Penn sports, rowing under Burk had succeeded in the era when football was king and had continued to flourish even when the rest of the athletic program hit rock bottom (perhaps an autumn Saturday in 1965 when the soccer team outscored the football team for the fifth consecutive week).

Quaker oarsmen soaked up Burk's lessons, none more so than Harry Parker. A native of East Hartford, Connecticut, Parker arrived at Penn in 1953 weighing just 174 pounds. Before graduating in 1957 with a philosophy degree, he became the number-two man in Burk's heavyweight crew. After eighteen months as a Navy ensign, Parker won gold in the single sculls at the Pan-American Games of 1959. As the nation's top single sculler, he finished fifth in the 1960 Rome Olympics, then accepted a job as coach of Harvard's freshman crews. After his second season, he unexpectedly found himself in charge of the varsity when head coach Harvey Love died.

From the outset Parker proved himself at odds with the hoary traditions of college coaching—no peppery prerace speeches, no whipping-boys or favorite sons, no foot-stomping tirades, no inspirational banners slung above the Newell entries. Taking Joe Burk as his model, Parker summed up his low-key style by telling a reporter: "We don't have to say very much. Everything's all understood. Generally, all I have to do is push a button."[8]

Results were immediate. After just two years as head coach, Parker produced what Burk declared to be the "greatest American crew there has ever been, college or club."[9] In fact the varsity heavyweight eight of 1965 was so good that it put Parker where no rowing coach had ever been or will be again—on the cover of *Sports Illustrated*. A smiling Parker stood in the foreground, the anonymous rowers in the distance with their shell. The accompanying article praised Parker and his system, describing his regimen of interval workouts, his adaptation of mechanics used by the powerful German Ratzeburg crew, his team's Swiss-made shell, stiff English oars, and a new setup that dropped the old style of alternating rowers in port and starboard seats in favor of a new alignment that increased a boat's stability. The coverage was emblematic of what would become an increasingly common characteristic of American sport: the attribution of team achievement to the individual effort of a stellar coach or athlete. But in Parker's case it was ironic.

Harry Parker always knew that the athletes—not a system or a coach—were the final determinants of success. You can increase the stroke rate, smooth the catch of the oars, synchronize the movements of eight men, but you cannot significantly change the essence of rowing—forcing yourself into the cauldron of pain, or surviving what one writer has described as "an all-over, savage unpleasantness."[10] In the end a racing shell is moved by conviction.

Which is not to say that Parker was irrelevant. On the contrary, it was his deft mix of studied science and intuition that lent his assessments of muscle, heart, and mind their own conviction and turned Parker into an icon of American rowing. Like Burk, he was never shy about seeking out concrete solutions if science could supply them. Burk had devised a series of lights connected to Penn's indoor tanks to measure individual output. He used this "Wizard" to choose his varsity lineup. Parker used seat racing, a type of tryout in which a pair of rowers switched shells in a series of sprints to determine which one was moving a boat faster.

Still, Parker's distinguishing trait was his feel for the untouchable. He had something that Ted Washburn, Harvard's freshman coach in the 1960s, admitted he was "still trying to figure out" after several years of observation. Most of Parker's past oarsmen are still searching for ways to explain their coach's power. His words could be as spare and provocative as koans, but in their absence his mere presence was enough. As one of his former rowers told a reporter in 1968, "I am moved to rise when I hear his name mentioned."[11]

The intuitive, mystic quality was a good one to have in the 1960s, a decade when many of the nation's young sought to free themselves from technology's grip on twentieth-century life. Rowing is especially vulnerable to charges of robotism. Keeping a shell's path smooth and directed cultivates in oarsmen an unlikely grace, one that makes the sport appear to spectators as mere exercise that is neither exciting to watch nor easy to identify with. Indeed, in reporting on the Crimson in 1965 *Sports Illustrated* claimed: "It's hard when watching to believe the men are mortal and not metal."[12]

On the water, however, what looks robotic from a distance can exhilarate. Crews hit transcendent moments of synchronicity when the boat feels as if it has lifted out of the water. Rowers call the phenomenon "swing," and as early as 1843 the *Boston Post* took note of it, describing a race in which the boats were "skimming like flying fish along the surface of the water."[13] At Harvard, Parker knew how to keep the boats flying.

His first great team, the one that *Sports Illustrated* immortalized, was a highly motivated group. From that varsity eight came four doctors, three lawyers, and the beginning of a rowing dynasty. Parker said that in producing decades of good rowers he was "lucky rather than smart."[14] He might get by with that in describing his handling of his initial varsity crew, but his feel for the team that followed them was anything but lucky.

Although the 1965 team had talent, grace, and drive, they stood on the safe side of a cultural fault line, still part of the days when upper-crust white males ruled America and the world, when conventions of style and power were understood and deferred to, and when sport's positive contribution to society went unquestioned. Parker admits that they were "50s kind of guys, conventional, no rebels."[15] In contrast, Parker's second great crew, which arrived at Harvard in the mid-1960s, rowed in a changing world, one in which rifts opened suddenly between effort and fun, team and individual, science and spirit, elitism and the rights of long-neglected common folk.

Negotiating the strong cultural currents that pulled at athletes in the Vietnam era was no easy matter. And Parker, of course, had little control over what sort of undergrad showed up for his team tryouts. For many years recruiting rowers had followed a simple formula: show up at freshman registration and search for big men not already committed to other sports. Legend has it that Cornell sized a registration doorway to dimensions that helped the coach quickly spot new prospects. Parker's criteria for recruits were few: six feet tall, lean, with some athletic background. Pressed to be more specific about "some," he admits that it was really "anything." "We felt that we could teach them to row," he says.[16] The group that arrived at the Newell Boathouse in the mid-1960s, however, brought with them more athletic ability than Parker was accustomed to seeing.

Of those who would eventually row in the varsity heavyweight boat and make the Olympic team, nearly all had been good high school athletes with uncommon competitive drives. They had played football and hockey, basketball and squash; they had wrestled and run, and a few had even rowed. Collectively they had won nearly forty varsity high school letters in twelve sports. Still, the student body in those days was, according to Parker, "more all-around, less specialized," and the coach didn't know anyone in the university's admissions department.[17] In short, his new set of rowers was still Harvard material: bright, confident, and now, in the mid-1960s, politically aware. Elsewhere such traits were causing coaches to wring their hands. For those stuck in old ruts, the late 1960s became a quagmire.

The suspicions that many collegians had of technology paled next to their distrust of authority. Across the country, but particularly in the Ivy League, athletes questioned commonplace assumptions, challenged team rules that they judged to be irrelevant, and demanded a greater say in all team matters. Coaches who could not or would not adapt spent so much time fighting the brushfires of revolt that many left the profession or were forced out. In 1969 *Sports Illustrated* would devote four consecutive weeks to a series titled "The Desperate Coach." Harry Parker was not one of those in trouble. In fact, if his methods hadn't been so inscrutable and so impossible to replicate, he could have had fallen coaches studying at his feet. As well as any other coach in the nation, he understood and loved the athletes who arrived in the mid-1960s and matured during the decade's final days of turmoil.

To Parker, rules in a college setting smacked of timeless absurdity. Trying to dictate sleeping patterns to students was a "losing battle." Though he was aware of the political climate and knew that "allegiances to athletics alone wouldn't fly in the 60s," he made few conscious adjustments to the times. "I would just make the point," he says, that "you guys ought to be able to figure out what's good for you and what's bad." He didn't approve of alpine skiing in the middle of winter training, for example; when Dave Higgins injured a leg doing just that, he wrapped the injury in hopes of hiding it from Parker, but the coach figured it out. "I just remember realizing that Harry knew," says Higgins, "and kind of looking at me and not saying much of anything—the fear of disapproval was enough."[18]

Just as powerful as the disapproval was the hope, however slim, that approval might be culled from the silence. As Higgins notes, Parker "doesn't say a lot to inspire you, and . . . because the little words of praise are few and far between, you're looking for the crumbs." Teammate Andy Larkin believes that Parker was "actually a magician," having "studied wizardry under Joe Burk." Larkin swears that during a difficult workout, when Parker assented to a request from his oarsmen to switch directions to lessen the effect of a grinding wind, the gusts rearranged themselves so that the boat continued into the wind. Larkin contends that Parker "could say so little and people would do so much," an observation confirmed by coxswain Paul Hoffman: "In the end you rowed for Harry because he never asked you to." Fritz Hobbs understands the coach's appeal in even simpler terms: "You row with Harry, you're going to win."[19]

It is understandable that Hobbs would think that. As they headed into the 1968 season, Harvard had not lost a college race in four years and indeed had raised its sights well above the intercollegiate level. At the 1964 Tokyo Olympics a four-man crew from Harvard had won a bronze medal. From that point on, the Harvard rowers began thinking in terms of international glory. Ian Gardiner, now the chairman of the Friends of Harvard Rowing, stroked the varsity eight until mononucleosis wiped out his 1968 season. He remembers that as freshmen he and his classmates had begun carving the Olympic rings into the mantelpiece at Red Top, Harvard's training retreat.[20]

In 1967 the crew had won gold at the Pan-American Games in Winnipeg, then nipped the Russians for silver at the European Championships in France, in essence the world championships. A year later they were bigger and stronger. The spring season brought few stiff challenges. In the traditional race against rival Yale the Crimson finished so far ahead that the Elis did not even appear in the finish-line photo. Still, Harvard's dreams were clouded by the only other college team in the nation that also had Olympic aspirations, the only other college team that had also ratcheted up its performance: Joe Burk's Penn Quakers. "The whole deal was Penn," says Hobbs. "We knew it from the day the year began. They didn't like us, we didn't like them."[21]

The Harvard crew won their match race against Penn, and then beat them again in the eastern sprints. The final showdown would come in the Olympic trials at Long Beach, California, on a manmade inlet of Alamitos Bay, first used for the 1932 Olympic trials. Philadelphia's Vesper Boat Club, the defending Olympic gold medalist, was also entered, but the primary threat to Harvard was Penn. In putting together the crew that would challenge Harvard, Joe Burk had ditched his Wizard and another complex selection game he called Patience, which relied on the cumulative results of 125 workouts. He made two late changes, inserting into the boat two oarsmen whose names conjured images of Main Line dilettantes: Luther Jones III and Gardner Cadwalader. Neither was a dabbler. Jones was certainly not a Main Liner. Hailing from Blackfoot, Idaho, he had just completed his freshman year, and no one mentioned his name without a prefatory "immense" or "enormous." Cadwalader was a dogged competitor. He'd won a gold medal at the Pan-Am Games in the pairs with coxswain, and when approached by a writer before the trials race, he dismissed Harvard as a team too long at the top. "I say this race is going to be just guts," he said. "I think we're invulnerable."[22]

At the gun Vesper and Penn got off the line quickly—a bit too quickly in the opinion of Harvard's six seat, Larkin, who says a bit of a false start left the Crimson trailing from the outset. It was not a good sign. Harvard was not known for its starts, and in this race the oarsmen were going to need all their reserves at the finish. According to Larkin, Parker had already told his crew what was going to happen in the last 500 meters, and it "scared the shit out of me."[23]

After the first 500 meters Harvard trailed Vesper by half a second and

Penn by a second and a half. By the three-quarters mark, Vesper had dropped back, but Penn still led by a second and a half. Harvard began its final push, and as the bows of the two boats swapped places with each catch of the oars, it became clear that Harvard was picking up a few inches with each stroke—but not clear that they would amass enough inches to overtake Penn. Higgins, in the bow seat, remembers it as "the one time when in the last 500 meters the only thing on my mind was 'Let the finish line be farther away.'"[24]

The last 500 meters tested Parker's prerace prediction that "the prize will go to the crew which rows the toughest race." Both squads had rowed the distance all out. Scott Steketee, in Harvard's five seat, said that when the team took a "power 10" (ten strokes at full effort) in the final 500 meters, it was the only one he'd ever taken "that felt like every other stroke of the race." Adding to Harvard's task was an extra three feet on Penn's shell, half of it in the bow. "Seat-ways we were there," said Curt Canning, Harvard's senior captain, "but there was that matter of the length of the bow." When the two eights crossed the finish line, the naked eye could not separate one from the other. "All I knew," Parker said, "is that we were there with them. I thought there was a good chance we had won, but I was prepared to have it go the other way."[25]

It took seven minutes and an examination of sequential photos to determine that Harvard had crossed less than a foot ahead of the Quakers, an outcome determined by the fact that Penn was still on the catch, "oars in the water, unable to make that final thrust."[26] Both teams had the benefit of a brisk tailwind; even so, their times were extraordinary. In winning their first race two days earlier, Penn had established the course record at 5:56.1. Harvard's winning time in the finals was 5:40.55, with Penn at 5:40.60. Several of Harvard's oarsmen describe the win as the best race they ever rowed. A photo taken just after the race showed Higgins sitting on the dock, legs dangling like a boy watching clouds to pass a summer's day. The truth, he says, was that "I couldn't stand up. I was totally used."[27]

When Parker saw the photo of the finish, he uttered just one word: "Beautiful." It summed up his reaction to the Olympic trials, but it was also an apt description of the way his team had, for five years, steered its way through narrow passages that other teams and other athletes had been unable to negotiate.

For one, at a time when the surging fun crusade of the counterculture was busy ridiculing the Protestant work ethic, the Harvard crew managed to find pleasure in their experience. Many athletes in the late 1960s found the sports setting too regimented and too much like work; even youth league coaches echoed Bear Bryant and Vince Lombardi in their belief that character and a winning attitude were best forged through a daily dose of pain and discomfort—signals that reminded one of just how much sacrifice was involved. Parker believed that rowers "really need to enjoy the practicing because so much time is spent there." His practices were succinct and purposeful. He supplemented the demanding conditioning program with soccer games, running games, and practice races with random seating. "As much as we worked hard and had very high goals, we had fun," he says. "That was part of the tone of the program."[28] Most of his rowers agree.

They also found nothing objectionable about Parker's unique blend of science and spirit. While the American public had, throughout the twentieth century, become increasingly attuned to the idea of athletes as mere representations of their scientifically crafted conditioning programs and nutritional supplements, in the 1960s it also came to accept approaches to performance that were rooted in quasi-mystical conceptions. Muhammad Ali, passing himself off as part poet, defied the conventions of his "sweet science," winning boxing matches with artistry and clairvoyance that seemed otherworldly. Some coaches and athletes borrowed from religious and psychological tenets in trying to find the "sweet spot in time" that existed just beyond the grasp of the laboratory. Parker's system owed nothing to formalized schools of practice—scientific or mystical—but his rowers readily accepted his use of ergometers, seat racing, and new riggings while simultaneously assimilating his laconic and unerring mastery of relationships, strategy, and motivation.

At a time when extensive media exposure and attention to celebrity elevated some athletes, like Joe Namath and Walt Frazier, above their teammates, the Harvard crew also resisted the narcissism that social critic Christopher Lasch famously alleged was the hallmark of post–World War II American society—including its sports. This resistance owed something to the nature of rowing. There must be unison of effort and output to move a boat well; in addition, the distance between rowers and spectators (and the small number of the latter) makes star quality tough to spot in an oarsman in an eight-man shell. The eight-man boat is the fastest and the most face-less. Higgins explains the importance of the team in rowing: "You're push-ing your body into an area it doesn't want to go and it's a mental struggle and what motivates you to do it, I think, is the sense that you don't want to let your teammates down."[29]

After the Olympic trials victory Andy Larkin told the *New Yorker:*

> Each person in a shell rows alone, but the only glory comes as
> a unit. And it's *hard.* People keep asking me what's so hard
> about rowing, and I point out how tough it is to learn to hit a
> golf ball two hundred yards down the fairway. You know how
> many books there are about that. Well, rowing is getting eight
> guys to hit a drive two hundred yards at exactly the same in-
> stant, and doing it over and over again, faster and faster, even
> when you're all at the absolute end of your physical capacity.[30]

Still, for all of Harvard's success in avoiding problems that were bringing other athletes down and tearing other teams apart, the crew's decision to plunge into another area of controversy would lead to questions that could never be clearly answered and an Olympic performance that more than three decades later remains a painful memory. As Parker admits, "I don't go revisiting that time very often."[31]

That time began even before the Crimson beat Penn in the trials at Long Beach. It began more with a mindset than with an event. Parker had noted that the 1968 crew was "every bit as motivated" as the great 1965 team, but the later group was "much more politically conscious—they were right in the middle of it all. There was no way I was going to turn their heads."[32]

At the 1967 Pan-Am Games several members of the team had been struck by a briefing at which U.S. Olympic Committee officials had made two things clear: there was no room for politics in sport, and American athletes were to try particularly hard to beat the Communists from Cuba. In the mind of coxswain Paul Hoffman, this signaled the USOC's foolish attempt to sever Olympic ideals from reality. The reality that seemed most germane to him and several others was the effort of San Jose State sociology professor Harry Edwards to use the Olympics as a forum for discussion of the plight of the black athlete. In explaining why this issue was relevant to Harvard rowers, Hoffman says simply, "We couldn't just pretend that we were living in a cocoon. We were smart enough to know that we didn't know what was going on, and we were interested enough to find out."[33]

Hoffman's teammate, the number two seat, Cleve Livingston, was from California. The two decided that they would pay a visit to Edwards and find out more about his Olympic Project for Human Rights (OPHR). They came away from their meeting thinking that Olympic athletes should at least be allowed to have dialogue about issues in a "nondisruptive way."[34]

The OPHR argued the notion that sport did not offer black athletes an escape from racism, degradation, and privation in America, but was merely another institution in which those things were deeply embedded. Edwards had a boycott of the Games in mind, a measure aimed at exposing the Olympic movement "for what it is: a white nationalistic, racist, political tool of exploiting oppressive governments." The agenda of the OPHR was also enmeshed with wider issues: the perceived injustice in the government's handling of Muhammad Ali's rejection of the armed services draft, the allegedly racist policies of the New York Athletic Club, the segregated status of athletic teams from Southern Rhodesia and South Africa, and the racial composition of the U.S. Olympic Committee.[35]

After a summer's worth of discussion, some of the rowers were leaning toward making a commitment to Edwards's project. Just over a week after the Olympic trials, Edwards was scheduled to come to Boston to address the team. Following an "emotionally exhausting" week of conversation among the rowers, six of them decided, the night before Edwards arrived in Cambridge, to hold a press conference the following day to announce their interest in OPHR aims. They phoned Harry Parker, then drove to his Winchester home late at night to apprise him of their plan. It was the first he'd heard of it—and the event was going to be on the Harvard campus the next morning. The six made it clear that they were not going to boycott the Games. But, as Hoffman says, they were asking only for his support, not for his permission.[36]

Parker's response? "He was magnificent that night," remembers Hoffman. The coach asked only that the rowers be sure they'd thought through their position. "He didn't use his authority to try to dissuade us," says Higgins. The next morning Edwards, a large and imposing former track athlete, arrived at the press conference in dashiki, goatee, sunglasses, and black cap. It was a calculated style that triggered interest from the media and discomfort in whites. Next to him were Hoffman, Higgins, Livingston, Steketee, and the captain, Curt Canning. Larkin was supportive but too ill to attend.[37]

Canning opened the 3:00 P.M. gathering by reading a prepared statement that said in part:

> the struggle for racial justice is not simply a black struggle but one in which every man who counts himself free must be involved . . . We feel that working to correct racial injustices is the undeniable task of all athletes and all men, black and white . . . It is not our intention or desire to embarrass our country or to use athletics for ulterior purposes . . . [but] the position of the black athlete cannot be and is not in fact, separated from his position as a black man or woman in America . . . Surely the spirit of the Olympic Games cannot thrive on a hypocrisy that fails to acknowledge that even the highest individual achievement does not save a black athlete from the injustices visited upon him as a man.

The rowers proposed three things: to help all Olympians obtain information about the reasons for and goals of the black demonstration, to stimulate open-ended discussion, and to explore means of voicing support at the Olympic Games. Edwards made brief remarks in response, and a short question-and-answer session followed. A wire service photo went out the next day showing Canning, the clean-cut kid from Utah, seated with the black activist. From that moment on the Harvard crew became a lightning rod in one of the era's many cultural controversies, an unavoidable role that would heighten scrutiny of their performance in Mexico City.[38]

Parker's decision not to interfere in the matter and a public statement in which he praised the conviction, courage, and commitment of the rowers had set him apart from other coaches of the day, but he says that the involvement with Edwards was a "big thing" that "caught the other half of the crew and me by surprise." Actually, it wasn't quite half, but Steve Brooks, Art Evans, and Fritz Hobbs were noticeably missing from the conference. A crew that had spent four years becoming one unit was suddenly split in two.[39]

The team has had many years to think back on the implications, and the consensus is that the political split did not affect their performance on the water. Discussion remained open; friendships to this day remain intact. Hobbs says, "I listened carefully, it [OPHR goals] just wasn't that high on my agenda." Higgins maintains that the rowers "were just not going to let these things get in the way of either our friendship or our desire to compete and win a gold medal." Still, he refers to the divisions as "camps," and admits, "Fritz, Steve, and Art didn't want to put their names on this." Parker believes that the activism created some tension. "They might deny that—some of them might—but I think it was there." Though he doesn't believe that it affected their rowing, he says, "I think it was a mistake to try to be a crew serving another purpose."[40]

Regardless of the degree to which involvement with the OPHR may have shifted the focus of some of the oarsmen, the distraction was at best a slight impediment to performance when compared with the toll that Mexico City's altitude would exact. The decision to hold the Games 7,347 feet above sea level was one for which coxswain Hoffman says Olympic administrators "should never be forgiven." It meant that competition "had nothing to do with natural ability or training—it had simply to do with the quirks of adapting to that altitude."[41]

From the time that Mexico City entered its bid to host the Games in 1962, the city's altitude was a concern to the International Olympic Committee (IOC). The Mexican council that presented the bid to the IOC called altitude "a problem that has been artificially created, undoubtedly in good faith, but due to a lack of familiarity with the facts." The pneumology unit of Mexico City's general hospital testified that altitude "does not impair in any way the capacity to carry out sporting events and does not cause a pathology of any kind in human beings." The Mexicans pointed to past athletic festivals held at high altitude to bolster their claim that athletes would acclimatize within a few days.[42]

The Harvard crew's firsthand test of the effects of high altitude came in September at their training camp in Gunnison, Colorado. The IOC restricted altitude training to two and a half weeks. It was a period long enough to disprove the claims of the Mexicans. Art Evans, whom teammates regarded as a "great sprinting stroke" and the rower responsible for pulling the Crimson past Penn in the trials, could not row a full practice in Gunnison. Others also began to experience distress, a turn that made Dave

Higgins strangely optimistic. He'd always felt compromised by a lack of endurance. Now, as he adjusted to the new conditions better than most of the others, his sense of being on an equal footing convinced him "that we could win the gold medal." For those not adapting, however, the boat never felt as good as it once had.[43]

Parker had a dilemma. He was dedicated to the oarsmen who'd come this far, a fact that caused him to make what Fritz Hobbs deems "a rare mistake." It was clear that Evans could not adapt to the altitude. "He'd be in the boat, out of the boat, in the boat," Hobbs recalls. "Harry was in a tough spot emotionally."[44] To compound the problem, the rower who could have replaced Evans at stroke, Monk Terry, had won the Olympic trials in the four-man without coxswain. On top of it all, unlike in the 1967 season, during which the crew had rowed steadily in international competition, in 1968 they had no tuneups between the trials and the Games.

When the team reached Mexico City, it was battling two problems, according to Higgins: exhaustion from the long training period, capped by Gunnison's altitude, and the sensory overload of a first-time Olympic experience. In addition to the pageantry and color—in fact because of them—political chaos enveloped Mexico City. As Mexico prepared to become the first Latin American host in Olympic history, soldiers opened fire on 10,000 students who were protesting the nation's extravagant expenditures on sport in the face of widespread poverty. Many were killed and more than 1,000 injured.

A swollen press corps searched the athletic venues avidly for sensational stories. Six Ivy Leaguers who'd pledged support to a radical black movement were enticing fodder. The stroke from the 1967 team, Ian Gardiner, was in Mexico City to cover rowing and write about a possible Harvard success story. He says that the press was very interested in talking to the rowers, but the characterizations many of the writers settled on struck him as caricature. In a post-Games article *Newsweek* acknowledged that their hair was no longer than current college styles. Nonetheless, it noted, "they have been derided in Mexico as 'the grubby crew,' the 'shaggies,' and the 'hippies.'" "They weren't hippies, for sure," says Gardiner. "These were serious guys." They took the media criticism in stride. "We knew the risk of talking to sports writers," says Hoffman. "Their realities were pretty disconnected from anything observable." Hobbs was dismayed by "the arrogance of the press—to think that we—the smart little white guys from Harvard—were actually planning all this [OPHR actions]. What a crock! It really was."[45]

For the six involved with the OPHR, the media seemed a mere shill for the conservative hierarchy of the USOC, a group of men capable of far greater harm. As some of the first American athletes to qualify for the Games, the rowers had used the time between the trials and the main event to devise a system for notifying subsequently selected Olympians of the aims of the OPHR. The USOC took immediate note. A group, informally designated as an "athletes' liaison," was cobbled together, ostensibly to talk to all athletes about cultural matters. Its head was the famed black Olympian Jesse Owens, the man who had punctured Hitler's Aryan mythology in 1936. His acceptance of the role caused Harry Edwards to hang a photo of Owens in his office with the caption "Traitor (Negro) of the Week." The liaison, according to Hoffman, was a cover. The Harvard rowers were the first group the new panel wanted to talk to, he says, "just trying to find out what we were up to."[46]

Beyond attempting to open dialogue and offer support to the black athletes, they were up to little. Their actions—their entire stance—were, says Hoffman, not radical. "We were speaking the language of white civil rights workers," he says, characterizing themselves as "Yankees who knew what was right." Yet their self-perceived moderation did not satisfy Olympic officials.

USOC president Douglas Roby and media relations man Bob Paul were particularly strident in denouncing athletes whose political views differed from their own flag-waving exuberance. At a function welcoming U.S. Olympians, Paul approached Hoffman (who was wearing, he says, a "polyvinyl chloride outfit" that Sears provided for all the athletes) and tapped his OPHR button. "You've got to be in uniform," he told the coxswain. "No funny ties, no funny buttons." Hoffman, noting that sprint champion Wyomia Tyus was also wearing a button, told Paul that if he persuaded Tyus to remove hers, he'd remove his. Ian Gardiner thinks that such enmity was to be expected. "When you've got an activity going on that is important in and of itself, that then gets distracted by another important issue, there are going to be conflicts."[47] All the rowers thought that the interest of Olympic officials in hair length, buttons, and political leanings was obsessive, excessive, and autocratic.

The team did not march in the opening ceremonies held on October 12, husbanding their strength for the next day's opening race. Unfortunately, Art Evans's struggle with altitude had followed him from Gunnison. He collapsed partway through the race. Then a bolt broke on the rigging, robbing the boat of power from two oars. It was a hopeless situation, and the team sank from second to fifth. For four years they'd rowed without a single race lost to sickness or equipment failure. Now they got both in one race. The loss dropped them into the repechage, rowing's unique system of providing a second chance. In a few days they would row against all the other first-time losers—and the top two would claim places in the final. Two things worked against their chances: in all of Olympic history only one boat, a 1956 team from Yale, had survived the repechage and won a gold medal; the other problem was that altitude and sickness continued to plague them.

All endurance athletes struggled in the rarified air. Australia's premier distance runner, Ron Clarke, toppled unconscious at the finish of his 10-kilometer race. His team doctor said: "I remember thinking he was going to die." America's top miler, Jim Ryun, a student of altitude, kept a close eye on the rowing. What he saw on October 15 at Xochimilco, the manmade paddling and rowing venue, startled him. He noted eighty collapses in the first two days, events that filled the water with rescue launches, oxygen fixes, and dashed hopes.[48]

Repechage day was so filled with distress that Parker refers to it as "Black Tuesday." The coach remembers more than a dozen athletes—elite, highly conditioned, ultracompetitive athletes at the *ne plus ultra* event—quitting during races. Fritz Hobbs says that rowing at Xochimilco "took the oxygen deficit to a new level." Harvard, he says, was trained to go off the line all-out, which meant "you got to an oxygen debt area early," but which in Mexico meant that "you got there sooner, and when you got there, there was nothing left. It hit me hard; it was pain like I hadn't experienced."[49]

For the repechage, it was necessary for Parker to move Steve Brooks from the number-three seat to stroke, replacing the stricken Evans. Jake Fiechter, class of 1967 and a substitute at Mexico City, took the three seat, a move that forced him to return to a portside oar after spending his postgraduate time at starboard. Cleve Livingston, in the second seat, had gastrointestinal problems. Even so, the crew rowed an ironhearted race. Down by more than a length to an East German team that had beaten them badly in the heats, the team moved from last place to second, securing the last spot in the final. In his later report to the Friends of Harvard Rowing, Parker called the race "striking testimony to their courage and desire to do well." Alluding to the issue of involvement with the OPHR, he wrote: "Certainly they could never have performed as magnificently as they did in the repechage if there was any lack of desire on the part of even one member of the crew."[50]

Still, the issue followed them into the finals, when Paul Hoffman's OPHR button again became the focus of USOC officials. Hoffman had given it to Australia's Peter Norman to wear during the medals ceremony for the 200-meter track final. Standing on the second step of the victory podium, Norman was wearing the button to demonstrate solidarity with gold and bronze medalists Tommie Smith and John Carlos. When the two Americans raised their gloved fists skyward in the famous "black power salute," USOC leaders decided there might be basis in the rumor that Hoffman "had conspired to aid the demonstration." Smith and Carlos were sent home; Hoffman was summoned to a hearing the night before the rowing final.[51]

The slight coxswain was growing accustomed to trouble. American boxing coach Pappy Gault, a vehement opponent of Edwards and the OPHR, had accosted Hoffman during the week, throwing him against a wall and warning him away from the U.S. boxers. Hoffman's memory of the hearing is foggy. While the eight oarsmen waited at the Olympic Village to hear of their fate, the coxswain made a "strong effort to make sure we could row the next day." He recalls the setting as akin to a college admissions interview— "a bunch of old guys asking questions; me trying not to tell them what I really thought." Eventually he was sent to a hospitality room while his questioners debated his status until 10:00 P.M. Finally he was cleared for the next day's competition.[52]

In the final the team was again quick off the line against a field that included strong crews from Germany, Russia, Australia, and New Zealand. Harvard, drained by the effort of the repechage and compromised by the changes in its boat's alignment, raced on even terms for the first 1,250 meters before fading to last among a field of fading crews. "Even in the finals," Parker wrote, "when presumably only the most fit and capable crews remained, a number of oarsmen stopped rowing effectively before the race was over. One doesn't reach the finals of the Olympic Games only to stop rowing when it begins to hurt a little." Higgins says, "We busted our asses, but we were spent; halfway through there was just nothing there."[53]

The crew and its coach, though bitterly disappointed, knew that altitude, not attitude, had derailed their chances. Not everyone saw it that way. Despite 378 new Olympic records, some observers thought that the entire Mexico City Games had been victimized "by air too rich in rhetoric and poor in oxygen."[54] Joseph Sheehan of the *New York Times* deemed Harvard "soundly thrashed . . . outrowed, and outclassed." Perhaps, he speculated, the United Sates "should examine further the matter of organizing a national all-star eight, rather than turning over a job for grown men to a college crew."[55]

USOC president Douglas Roby was one of those most incensed. Embarrassed by the actions of the black athletes, who had opened an American wound for all the world to see, he was perhaps even more livid with the Harvard crew. Unable to recognize the irony of valuing least what he and other Olympic officials proclaimed to value most—a nation that was egalitarian, open, and tolerant—Roby settled on Parker as a target for his anger. Perhaps because the coach had not actively dissuaded his charges from voicing political concerns, Roby singled him out as the one most culpable. In a November 5 letter to the coach Roby revealed the depths of his anger and shame:

> At one time I, personally, was in favor of disqualifying you and
> your crew for acts grossly unbecoming to members of our
> Olympic Team. I am now glad that I did not encourage such a
> harsh action for I feel that the miserable performance of you
> and your crew at Mexico City will stand as a permanent rec-
> ord against you and the athletes which you led. As a boy I
> had great admiration and respect for Harvard and the men it
> produced. Certainly serious intellectual degeneration has
> taken place in this once great University if you and several
> members of your crew are examples of the type of men that
> are within its walls.[56]

Parker was too decent to reply or to make a public issue of Roby's unseemly and highly personal attacks. In his post-Games report he noted only an "over-reaction" on the part of Roby and the press. In thanking the Friends of Harvard Rowing back in Boston, he told them that the rowers "have accepted their disappointments as the price one pays for the opportunity to compete against the very best in the world."[57]

For the next Olympics both the USOC and some of Harvard's rowers had a chance to remedy the outcomes at Mexico City. The USOC changed its selection process, choosing a composite crew as Sheehan had suggested. But among the new crew of all-star oarsmen headed to Munich were Fritz Hobbs; his younger brother Billy, who had rowed in the pairs at Mexico City; Paul Hoffman; Cleve Livingston; his younger brother Mike, who had been a spare in 1968; and Monk Terry, all of Harvard. They beat the Germans by a stroke to win the silver medal.

In its insistence on challenging old dogma about sport and its place in American society, the 1968 crew was ahead of its time, a bridge to a future where athletes felt the freedom to speak out and make their own decisions. As the last college crew in the Olympics, however, the team seems to most Bostonians part of a long line of boats anchored to a distant past.

Perhaps the constancy of Harry Parker—he still coaches at Harvard and has amassed fifteen undefeated regular seasons, eight unofficial national crowns, six official national titles, and thirty-three wins against Yale in thirty-nine attempts—has given Harvard rowing its venerable patina. Surely the throngs that mass on the Charles see in rowing—despite its costly and high-tech shells, its measured approach to maximum performance—a throwback to a time when victory and honor coexisted without conflict, contradiction, or cash.

The accomplishments of the 1968 crew, then, compete against a longer, less threatening age. For many, the 1960s remain a dangerous and fearful time—even for brief visits. Nostalgia has not yet settled over the decade with the same fuzzy pleasurableness that attaches to the 1950s. It remains in public perception a chaotic span of excess and disjuncture. So it is that even when members of the crew reunited in 2002—Dave Higgins, Paul Hoffman, Cleve Livingston, Jake Fiechter, Andrew Larkin, and Kathy Keeler (Parker's wife)—they rowed to commemorate the sesquicentennial history of the Harvard-Yale rivalry. Here they were linked inextricably to a 150-year-old past that still matters a great deal in Boston, a city that still thrives on the memory of midnight rides, eighty-year-old curses on its baseball team, and a basketball dynasty now a half-century old. Meanwhile memories just thirty-five years gone streak past its consciousness, historical sunflares too hot to touch, too brief to celebrate.

7

Francis Ouimet at The Country Club

James Campbell

Historians—like sportswriters, detective novelists, western movie scriptwriters, and others of the scribbling classes—are habitual borrowers. Consciously and unconsciously, we recycle archetypes and tropes from other stories and narrative traditions to give structure and meaning to the tales we tell. The problem for the historian of Boston sports lies in choosing what to borrow. If Bill Russell's Celtics stand as the epitome of the Homeric ideal of "excellence," the plight of the post–Babe Ruth Red Sox has all the makings of classical tragedy, complete with paternal offense and a seemingly inescapable curse. The story of Roberta Gibb, the first woman to run in the Boston Marathon, reads like the script for a made-for-TV movie, a quintessentially American tale of obstacles overcome and virtue vindicated. The vicious race-baiting of black athletes—including, often enough, members of the home team—by the Boston faithful evokes less comforting American stories. Most recently, Bostonians have been treated to tales of Ted Williams's beheaded corpse hanging upside down in an Arizona cryonics laboratory, an image blending B-movie science fiction with a dose of gothic horror.

How then to tell the story of Francis Ouimet, the twenty-year-old amateur golfer who defeated the great British professionals Ted Ray and Harry

Vardon at the 1913 U.S. Open at The Country Club in Brookline? For nearly a century now, Ouimet's victory has served as the creation story of American golf, the signal event that transformed an elite pastime, still widely derided as effete and effeminate, into a game of the American masses. Unfolding on the very course on which Ouimet had caddied as a child, the story has all the elements of a real-life Horatio Alger novel: youth and innocence, luck and pluck, the golden promise of America. The story even comes with pictures, grainy black-and-white photos of the imperious Vardon, the grizzled Ray, and, most indelibly, of the downy-cheeked Ouimet strolling up the fairway beside his pint-sized ten-year-old caddy, Eddie Lowery.

It is a wonderful tale, broadly true in its particulars. Yet lurking within it are ironies and undercurrents worthy of O. Henry. Ouimet, as millions of American golfers know, grew up across the street from The Country Club, but he was certainly not a member; the whole reason for being of the club, and of the thousands of lowercase country clubs it inspired, was precisely to exclude such people as the Ouimets. (Even after his victory, the club refrained from offering Francis membership, instead granting him a year's free play on the course. He was finally made an honorary member in 1953.) Brookline was also a singularly unlikely venue for American golf's declaration of independence from Britain. Founded in the 1880s by "gentlemen" unsettled by the hubbub and social leveling of modern America, The Country Club was perhaps the single most Anglocentric institution in the United States. More poignantly, the 1913 Open, memorialized as the event that broke down the barriers of class exclusion surrounding golf, marked a watershed in the game's lamentable history of racial exclusion. Lost in Ouimet's triumph was the final U.S. Open appearance of John Shippen, an African American who had learned the game on Long Island's Shinnecock Indian reservation, where his father worked as a missionary. Shippen played in several U.S. Opens, including the 1896 championship at Shinnecock, where he braved threats of a boycott to finish fifth, but Brookline was his last appearance. Between U.S. Golf Association (U.S.G.A.) regulations restricting competitions to members of recognized clubs and the notorious "Caucasians only" policy subsequently adopted by the Professional Golfers Association, it would be another half-century before a black golfer again competed in the U.S. Open.[1]

Perhaps the greatest ironies cluster around Ouimet's amateurism, the appealing notion of the innocent American, motivated only by love of the game, triumphing over the mercenary British. Ouimet was indeed an amateur sportsman, and proudly so; much as he cherished his Open title, he valued his victories in the 1914 and 1931 U.S. Amateur championships far more highly. Yet the amateur ideal that Ouimet embodied was among the first casualties of the sweeping transformations of American golf that his victory helped to set in motion. Despite the U.S.G.A.'s strenuous (and occasionally ludicrous) efforts to defend the "character" of the game—Ouimet himself was briefly stripped of his amateur status because of his involvement with a sporting-goods venture—the future of American golf plainly lay not with Ouimet or even with Bobby Jones, his revered amateur successor, but with professionals like Walter Hagen, who finished fourth at Brookline and who, in his subsequent, colorful career, rarely played a stroke without a stake. Clearly, there is more to the story of Francis Ouimet's triumph at The Country Club than meets the eye.

The Country Club. The uppercase letters, the definite article, the absence of geographic specification: the term seems so pretentious as to be laughable. And yet Brookline merits the title. The country club, that most American and un-American of institutions, grounded at once in democratic principles of voluntary association and in undemocratic principles of hierarchy and social exclusion, was invented in Brookline.

The origins of The Country Club reach back to 1860, when seventy of Boston's most prominent gentlemen subscribed $100 each to establish a private club. Their motive was not golf—the introduction of golf into the United States lay a generation in the future—but horses. Horses were a ubiquitous presence in nineteenth-century America, but they had come to occupy a special place in the lives of old elites in cities like Boston, New York, and Newport, where the bloodlines in one's stable served as a marker of one's own breeding and status. The subscribers, all avid horsemen, sought a place within an easy carriage ride of the city, where men and horses could be refreshed without submitting to the kind of unwelcome mingling—human and equine—encountered at public inns and roadhouses. Plans included a clubhouse for the entertainment of wives and family and a racetrack, where members could exhibit and race thoroughbreds "freed from the presence and control of those persons who have made this sport objectionable to Gentlemen." In an era in which leisure activities still carried a taint of idleness and dissipation, the petitioners were at pains to stress that their club would include "nothing that could offend the taste of the most fastidious."[2]

The Civil War put paid to the gentlemen's plans, but the impulse persisted. If anything, the need for such a club became more urgent in the late nineteenth century as Boston, like other northern cities, was transformed by industrialization, mass immigration, and a commercial revolution that blurred established class lines. In 1882 representatives of Boston's beleaguered Brahmins met for dinner in the Commonwealth Avenue home of John Murray Forbes, a financier and pillar of local society. Born into a prominent merchant family, Forbes had made a fortune in the antebellum China trade before branching into railroad securities. Though ostensibly retired, he emerged in the decades after the Civil War as one of the country's most powerful railroad barons, with controlling interests in the Chicago, Burlington, and Quincy systems. Like many of his class and era, Forbes was a paradoxical fellow, waxing nostalgic for a simpler time while presiding over a process of unprecedented economic consolidation, extolling American values of opportunity and upward mobility while building institutions that evacuated those values of meaning. Forbes and his dinner companions found a solution to their predicament in the idea of a private, rural club. In essence, they proposed to create an association to preserve a way of life that they and their class had helped to annihilate.[3]

The gentlemen leased (and subsequently purchased) Clyde Park, a 100-acre horse farm in the still sparsely settled suburb of Brookline, which included a half-mile racetrack and a rambling farmhouse, once owned by Daniel Webster. They dubbed it The Country Club, apparently after a club that Forbes had visited in Shanghai during his youthful forays to China. The group issued a circular, inviting other prominent members of Boston society to join. The proposal clearly struck a chord: by the time the club opened in 1883 it had 600 subscribers, all recruited (in the words of the club's own historians) "from a single and sharply defined social stratum." The roster included twenty of the signatories of the 1860 petition, as well as the entire membership of the Myopia Hunt Club, which had been established in the outlying suburb of Winchester a few years before. In contrast to many later clubs, membership costs at The Country Club were deliberately set at modest levels—$25 as an initiation fee, with annual dues of $30, later raised to $50. The object, after all, was to attract not the merely wealthy, but rather the "right men," with the "proper spirit."[4]

Contrary to common belief, country clubs had no real precedent in Britain, where the gentry typically lived in the country and clubbed in the city. Yet from its earliest days The Country Club exuded an air of Englishness. As historian Richard Moss has noted, connection with an imagined Anglo-Saxon civilization offered embattled American elites a sense of historical depth in a nation seemingly bare of traditions, as well as a means to distinguish themselves from the roiling, polyglot society emerging around them. Brookline's initial membership list, with its Adamses and Bradfords, Cabots and Cottons, read not only like a roster of Englishmen but like a roll of *Mayflower* descendants, which to some extent it was. The old farmhouse, converted in the mid-nineteenth century into a hotel, was remade again in the image of an English country house, complete with leathery appointments and a retinue of faithful servants, some of whom would remain at the club for the next half-century. Like the great country homes of England, the clubhouse had both common spaces—a reception hall and formal dining room—and distinctly gendered spaces, including separate entrances for men and women, a ladies' boudoir (decorated with green furniture and Japanese floral prints), and smoking, billiard, and bar rooms for gentlemen. The whole place bespoke tradition and venerability, belying the club's recent vintage.[5]

Americans today associate country clubs with golf, but the game had not yet been introduced to the United States when The Country Club was established. The club did include facilities for several of the sports then fashionable among the society set—croquet, tennis, lawn bowling, later squash and curling—but the focus remained horses. Members laid out a steeplechase course and imported a pack of blue-blooded English beagles for foxhunting. The racetrack was enlarged and improved, and the area inside was drained and leveled for a polo field. New stables were built, as well as a large grandstand to accommodate spectators at the annual Country Club races. A meeting of "gentlemen-horsemen" (as distinct "from those of the commercial and semi-commercial" classes), the races remained a red-letter day on the Boston social calendar right through the 1930s, even as activities like polo and foxhunting disappeared. Competitors in the 1913 U.S. Open were forced to play approach shots over the racetrack on the opening and finishing holes.[6]

The marriage of golf and country clubs was consummated not in Brookline but at the St. Andrews Golf Club in Yonkers, New York. Whether St. Andrews—the club was obviously named after golf's Scottish birthplace—deserves its title as the cradle of American golf remains a source of some controversy. Canadians point to the priority of Royal Montreal, where golf was first played in 1873. Other claims go back further, to a short-lived South Carolina Golf Club established in Charleston in the 1780s, probably by Scottish soldiers, or even to the Dutch settlers of New Amsterdam, who played a game called kolven, a kind of cross between golf and ice hockey. But whatever the merits of such claims, and dozens of others besides, St. Andrews was the place where golf first took permanent root in the United States. Equally importantly, St. Andrews was the place where the linkage between golf and the country club was first forged.[7]

St. Andrews was the brainchild of John Reid, a transplanted Scotsman and avid sportsman, who laid out a three-hole course for himself and his friends in a Yonkers pasture in 1888. As the game caught on, the group moved to a new, six-hole course in a nearby apple orchard—hence the club's nickname the Apple Tree Gang. By the time the club had settled at its current location, its roster included many of New York's most prominent citizens, including Andrew Carnegie, himself a transplanted Scotsman, who saw the venerable, outdoor game as the perfect exercise for a society growing sedentary and dyspeptic. Like its Scottish namesake, St. Andrews established many of the American game's early traditions, from the vaguely regimental uniforms (red coat with brass buttons and blue collar in St. Andrews' case; green coat and primrose collar at The Country Club) to the deferential black servant serving drinks near the final green. St. Andrews was also the first U.S. club to import a Scottish professional, a custom that quickly became *de rigueur* among socially prominent clubs. Though little remembered today, these working-class Scotsmen were the true founders of golf in America, serving not only as teachers but as clubmakers, course designers, and greenskeepers.[8]

With its "royal and ancient" pedigree, golf was the perfect pastime for America's old elite, with its insatiable, if paradoxical, appetite for old traditions and new diversions. By the summer of 1889 a nine-hole golf club had

opened at Newport, summer home of many of the nation's wealthiest families; the club's members included railroad tycoon Cornelius Vanderbilt and
Theodore Havemeyer, whose family dominated the nation's sugar refining
industry. Not to be outdone, summer residents of the Hamptons, on Long
Island, built a course of their own, on land that was the ancestral home of
the Shinnecock Indians. Sparing no expense, the founders of Shinnecock
hired Stanford White, the nation's premier architect, to design an elegant
clubhouse, and Willie Dunn, an imported Scottish professional, to lay out
the course. In keeping with Scottish design practices of fitting a course to
the existing landscape, Dunn incorporated Indian burial mounds into his
design as hazards, an act of breathtaking insensitivity by today's standards,
but one that enabled him to capture at Shinnecock something of the character of traditional linksland golf.[9]

Once established, the game spread quickly. Chicago followed with a
brace of courses: the Chicago Golf Club, the nation's first eighteen-hole
course, established in Wheaton in 1893; and Onwentsia, on the city's tony
north shore, which opened the following year. The former course was designed by C. B. Macdonald, son of a wealthy Scottish-American family,
who discovered the game while a student at St. Andrews and went on to become American golf's most enthusiastic promoter. By 1900, when the great
Harry Vardon came to the Chicago Golf Club to claim his first and only
U.S. Open title, the city boasted more than two dozen golf courses. Overall,
the United States was home to more than 1,000 courses, the vast majority of
them private clubs of a decidedly elite stripe.[10]

Golf came to The Country Club in 1892. Its emissary was a woman, Flor-
ence Boit, who had discovered the game while summering at Pau, a French
resort and home to the first course on the European continent. Boit was so
taken with the sport that she persuaded her uncle, Arthur Hunnewell, a
resident of Brookline, to build her a pitch-and-putt course on his Wellesley
estate. The game caught on among Hunnewell's friends, including Lionel
Curtis, who successfully petitioned the executive committee of The Country Club to allow a trial of the game. Armed with an appropriation of $50,
Curtis laid out a six-hole course on the club's front lawn. The course
opened in April 1893 with an exhibition featuring Curtis, Hunnewell, and
G. E. Cabot, another enthusiast. If local legend is to be believed, Hunnewell, first to play on the 100-yard opening hole, inaugurated the course with

a hole-in-one. The gallery of club members surrounding the tee applauded politely; accustomed as they were to such sports as archery and shooting, they expected nothing less. The failure of Hunnewell's partners to match the feat produced some grumbling, but on balance the exhibition was taken as a success.[11]

The golf course at The Country Club evolved slowly in the two decades between Hunnewell's improbable ace and Ouimet's equally improbable victory. Virtually alone among the great American courses, Brookline was not designed by a single architect but rather grew as a kind of inspired hodgepodge. In late 1893 Curtis and his comrades, armed with an additional $50 appropriation, added three new holes and directed some of the existing holes away from the clubhouse, much to the relief of spectators on the piazza. In 1894 the club hired a Scottish professional, Willie Campbell, who strengthened the course, adding bunkers and yardage. A second nine was completed in 1899, but with the introduction of the rubber-wound "Haskell" ball a year later, the new course was almost immediately obsolete, forcing another major extension in 1903. The course was lengthened and rerouted again in 1908–09. This was the course on which Ouimet would win the Open.[12]

Not all members of The Country Club were pleased with golf's growing prominence. Older members, wary of higher dues and any dilution of the club's equestrian character, stoutly resisted additional appropriations for the game. In 1894 Campbell was ordered not to mow the fairways during the summer months as a cost-saving measure. (He solved the problem as any good Scotsman would, by introducing a herd of sheep.) Golf partisans, unable to persuade the executive committee to acquire adjoining property needed for the course, were forced on several occasions to purchase it themselves and hold it in trust until the club relented. In 1896 a group of golfers, frustrated with the club's tepid support, resigned en masse and reestablished the Myopia Hunt Club, which, despite its name, was chiefly devoted to golf. That same year, however, the club crossed a Rubicon of sorts when the polo field was annexed by the expanding golf course. This act of "piracy" enraged many older members, at least fifty of whom resigned from the club, but the future direction of the club was established.[13]

In American golf's early days, as in our own time, different clubs developed distinct customs and cultures. At summer resorts like Newport and

Shinnecock, the golfing and social calendars naturally centered on the summer months. The Country Club, on the other hand, featured spring and fall seasons and was virtually deserted in the summer, when Boston's wealthiest families retreated to homes outside the city. Clubs adopted different policies toward "the ladies"—Shinnecock initially included nine holes solely for women players—though in general they tended over time to reserve more and more of the prime playing hours for men. At Brookline women and men initially enjoyed equal access, but restrictions on women were introduced following the opening of the expanded eighteen-hole course in 1903.[14]

Beneath these surface differences, however, were profound similarities. The founders of America's first golf clubs were all deeply invested in preserving traditions, even if they had to invent them first. Clubs adopted distinctive uniforms and coats of arms; many coined their own Latinate mottos. Commerce was disdained, reflecting the aristocratic pretensions of club founders. (Some clubs prohibited all cash transactions, relying instead on chits and vouchers, a system that still prevails at many American country clubs.) Perhaps most important, the early clubs upheld a strict amateur ethic: golf was a "game," an avocation of gentlemen, certainly not something one did for money. While professionals were admired for their golfing prowess, they were also disdained as social inferiors. Early American clubs not only barred professionals from membership but actually prohibited them from setting foot in the clubhouse, a custom that persisted until 1920, when Inverness, in Toledo, opened its doors to professionals competing in the U.S. Open. Although photographs of Harry Vardon still adorn the walls of the clubhouse at Brookline, he himself never entered the building.[15]

In keeping with the quest for tradition, America's early golfers made much of the game's venerable Scottish roots. Golf was "ancient" and "honorable." While American games tended to be social and exuberant, golf, like the Scotsmen who invented it, was solitary, stern, laconic. For a writer in Scribner's, one of a host of popular magazines to assay the latest American craze, the game perfectly "illustrated the analytical and philosophical character of the Scottish mind," including a characteristically Presbyterian belief in ineluctable fate. (It was no coincidence, one wag noted, that the people who gave the world the theory of infant damnation also invented golf.) C. B. Macdonald, who learned the game amid the sheep hollows, burns, and hidden bunkers of the Old Course at St. Andrews, agreed. Other sports might strive to be "equitable" and "fair," but in golf, as in life, "the cardinal rules are arbitrary." There was no right of appeal and, in the absence of teammates, no one else to blame. The code was simple: "Take your medicine where you find it and don't cry."[16]

Yet even as they extolled golf's Scottish severity, the game's American proponents introduced changes that eroded the game's Old World character. In Scotland, courses were almost universally sited near the sea, on so-called links land, the expanse of treeless, grassy dunes separating sea from settled agriculture. Americans, on the other hand, insisted on building golf courses on any terrain, even carving courses through trees (an innovation, C. B. Macdonald warned, that ruined the game by foreshortening perspective and obstructing wind). To replace the hollows and hummocks that gave links golf its savor, American designers peppered courses with artificial bunkers and water hazards, features that not only diluted the "naturalness" of courses but also significantly increased the costs of construction and maintenance, thus contributing to the high cost of country club membership. To accommodate the diversity of climactic and soil conditions, Americans began to experiment with different types of grasses, as well as with fertilizers and watering systems, all to ensure the immaculate green carpet that American golfers would come to regard as their birthright. (Revealingly, the individual who pioneered golf course agronomy was William Taylor, the legendary "efficiency" expert, whose time-and-motion studies revolutionized American manufacturing.)[17] Such innovations wrought subtle but profound changes in the game. Hazards became visible from the tee. Soft, level fairways eliminated the capricious bounces that defined links golf. Imposed design became the norm, and "fairness" became enshrined as a design virtue. If links golf was the creation of Scottish Presbyterians, with its unseen hazards and inscrutable judgments, what emerged in the United States was a game of a decidedly Methodist temper, in which the adherent could, through the exercise of the methodical virtues, secure his own salvation.

There was an even deeper irony here. In their pursuit of Old World tradition and gentility, golf's American proponents invested the game with a social exclusivity that it had never possessed in the Old World. Though specific membership fees and requirements differed, all the emerging golf clubs jealously guarded their rolls. Shinnecock, for example, restricted membership to "those identified with the social life and interests of the immediate vicinity"—that is, to the elite families summering in the Hamptons. Chicago's Onwentsia required that new members be "personally known" to members of the board of governors, and even added rules for expelling members who besmirched the club's "character and good name." Onwentsia also seems to have been the first club to implement the practice of "blackballing," in which any two of the fifteen governors could, without explanation, reject a candidate for membership.[18]

All these qualities—the valorization of tradition, the emphasis on amateurism, the strict social exclusivity—were embodied in the United States Golf Association, the body that continues, in conjunction with the Royal and Ancient Golfing Society of St. Andrews, to oversee world golf. Originally established in 1894 as the Amateur Golf Association of America, the U.S.G.A. represented a coalition of five of the country's most socially elevated clubs: Newport, Shinnecock, St. Andrews, Chicago, and Brookline. In addition to establishing national championships and a set of common rules, the association took unto itself the responsibility of ensuring that the game's increasing popularity produced no dilution of its social "character." Membership in the U.S.G.A. was thus reserved for "representative" private clubs, which could be admitted with the approval of 80 percent of the existing clubs. A second, probationary status was created for clubs of lesser social standing. The purpose of the two-tier system, which persisted until 1937, was to afford humbler clubs a period of tutelage in the game's culture, after which they could graduate to full membership. In turn, participation in U.S.G.A. events, including the U.S. Amateur championship, the jewel in the association's crown, was restricted to members of recognized clubs, a measure that effectively excluded players from the small but growing number of public courses scattered across America. (Such players could, in theory, compete in the U.S. Open, the tournament established for lowly professionals.) But for the generosity of a member of Boston's Woodland club, who arranged a junior membership for the city's most promising high school golfer, the world might never have heard of Francis Ouimet.

Given golf's history of class, racial, and gender exclusion, it is a wonder that the sport ever became popular. Part of the answer lay in the genius of the game itself, which, when all social pretensions are stripped away, remains a supremely individual test. Country clubs may have their membership committees and blackballs, but golf is no respecter of persons. Equally important, American golf has been blessed with an extraordinary roster of popular champions, the vast majority of whom, ironically, have emerged from precisely the social classes that country clubs were designed to exclude. Walter Hagen was the son of a blacksmith. Gene Sarazen (born Eugenio Saraceni) was the son of an immigrant carpenter; he learned the game as a caddy at a Westchester country club. Ben Hogan and Byron Nelson also began as caddies, working together at the same Fort Worth club. Jack Nicklaus had a country club pedigree, but the champion he supplanted, Arnold Palmer, was the son of a greenskeeper. Nicklaus's great rival, Lee Trevino, offers perhaps the best example of all. A child of immigrants, Trevino grew up in a shack without water or electricity not far from a Dallas country club, where he learned the game as a caddy. After a stint in the Marine Corps, Trevino took a job as an assistant professional at a local driving range, where he earned $30 a week, plus whatever he could hustle from the local country club set.[19]

For the most part, golf's champions have adapted themselves to the codes and expectations of the American golfing establishment, which has warmly embraced them in turn. Working-class children like Sarazen, Nelson, and Palmer became the game's most revered elder statesmen, honorary gentlemen whose elevated social status was expressed in aristocratic honorifics: "the Squire" for Sarazen, "Lord Byron" for Nelson, and "the King" for Palmer. A few refused to adapt. Hogan treated golf society with the same cold fury he directed at his opponents on the course. Trevino, while infinitely more approachable, also remained acutely sensitive to the anomalies of his social position. Accepting the ceremonial handshake after one of his six major championship titles, Trevino ostentatiously spat in his hand, rubbed his palms together, and asked the startled official if he had ever shaken hands with a Mexican. During the peak of his career, he declined to play in the Master's championship at the then lily-white Augusta National, sacrificing an opportunity to join the handful of men to win golf's career grand slam. Even after relenting, he avoided the Augusta clubhouse, changing his shoes in the parking lot like any other day-fee player.

Francis Ouimet was American golf's first working-class champion, and its first honorary gentleman. Born in 1893, Ouimet grew up in a modest house on Clyde Street in Brookline, across the street from the seventeenth hole at The Country Club. He was the second of four children of Mary Burke Ouimet, an Irish Catholic of infinite patience, and Arthur Ouimet, a French-Canadian immigrant, whose brooding, bitter temperament over-shadowed the home. For Arthur, as for so many other immigrants, the United States was a land not of opportunity but of broken dreams. His first wife, also named Mary, died in childbirth; their infant son soon followed. With no education and a poor command of English, Arthur survived on odd jobs, often working as a gardener on the estates of local Brahmins, many of whom were members of The Country Club. The experience in-stilled in him an implacable hatred of golf, which came to symbolize all that he despised—idleness, exclusivity, pretension. Life in the Ouimet household would come to revolve around Mary's struggle to shelter the budding talent and strangely blithe spirit of her second son from the rages of his father.[20]

By his own account, Francis first entered the grounds of The Country Club as a "trespasser," cutting across the course on his way to and from school. While other children collected marbles, he collected lost golf balls, gutta-percha spheres with now-forgotten names like Silvertowns, Ocobos, and Henleys, as well as one prized "Vardon Flyer." Soon he and his older brother, Wilfred, a caddy at The Country Club, were batting the balls around a makeshift course in their back pasture, using a sawed-off brassie and tomato cans for holes. Francis taught himself to play by studying golfers on the course across the street. Whenever he saw a well-executed shot, he hastened to his backyard to attempt it himself.[21]

At the age of nine Ouimet joined Wilfred as a caddy at The Country Club, where he earned 25 cents per loop, along with a host of lessons in etiquette and comportment. Caddying today survives only in the poshest re-sorts and private clubs, but it was integral to the game's early days in Amer-ica. The relationship between golfer and caddy embodied an ideal of per-sonal service fast vanishing in the wider society, with the golfer cast as patron and the caddy, typically young and working class, cast in the role of faithful retainer. As in most such hierarchical relationships, the actual bal-ance of power was more complicated than it might appear; then as now, caddies spent much of their days laughing behind the backs of their hapless social superiors. In Ouimet's case, however, the experience seems to have worked exactly as advertised. He enjoyed caddying, and members liked him. One gave him his first full set of clubs. Another, having learned of Francis's own interest in the game, invited him to join him for a round, and then stayed behind to protect him from the irate caddymaster. (At the time, caddies were almost universally forbidden from playing at private clubs. The practice of allowing them onto the course at specified times began in 1913, as a direct result of Ouimet's victory.) Most important, caddying afforded the budding golfer an opportunity to watch and learn from some of the game's greatest players. In addition to Willie Campbell, the club's Scottish professional, Ouimet watched Arthur Lockwood, Chandler Egan, Jerry Travers, Walter J. Travis, Alex Smith, and four-time U.S. Open champion Willie Anderson, all of whom came to The Country Club for exhibitions.[22]

Ouimet soon outgrew his makeshift backyard course. With the nearest public course, Franklin Park, three trolley rides and a 2-mile walk distant, his trespassing at The Country Club became more purposeful. Rising at 4:30, he would sneak onto the course, hoping to complete a few holes before being run off by arriving groundsmen. Salvation came in the form of interscholastic golf. With the game now entrenched as a respectable pastime rather than a passing fad, several of Boston's elite secondary schools— Roxbury Latin, Newton High, the Fessenden School—began to field teams. Brookline High launched its team the year Ouimet arrived, apparently at his instigation. Afforded regular access to some of the city's finest courses, he soon established himself as the top schoolboy golfer in Massachusetts. By the time he left high school in 1910, he had won the state interscholastic championship, as well as The Country Club Cup, the premier amateur title in Boston.[23]

But Ouimet had already set his sights higher, determining to compete for the U.S. Amateur title. Reluctantly, he resigned his job at The Country Club, in deference to U.S.G.A. regulations that defined anyone who caddied after his sixteenth birthday as a "professional." To meet the U.S.G.A. requirement of membership in a recognized club, he persuaded the father of a teammate to sponsor him as a junior member at Boston's Woodland Club and then persuaded his furious mother to lend him the $25 initiation fee. Arthur Ouimet never learned of the loan, but when he discovered his son's intention to play in the 1910 U.S. Amateur championship, to be held at Brookline, he flew into a rage, declaring that anyone with time to squander at golf tournaments could work for his own living. Reluctantly, Francis agreed, leaving high school a year shy of his diploma. To make matters worse, he then failed by a single stroke to qualify for the matchplay portion of the championship, thanks to a double bogey on the final hole. In both the 1911 and 1912 Amateur championships, he again fell a single shot shy of advancing to matchplay, seemingly bearing out his mother's prediction that "the game of golf would ruin" him.[24]

While Ouimet's record suggested promise, there was nothing in it to portend his success in 1913. He began the summer by capturing the Massachusetts Amateur championship, playing with a mastery and a serenity that surprised even himself. In his semifinal match, he carded six straight birdies on the inward nine—2–3–3–3–3–3—on his way to a 28. At the U.S. Amateur, staged at Garden City, New Jersey, he breezed through qualifying and advanced to the second round of matchplay, where he staged an epic battle with defending champion Jerome Travers, finally succumbing on the thirty-fifth hole. By his own account, Ouimet was "scared to death" facing Travers, a legendary competitor who went on to claim a record fourth Amateur crown, but observers of the match were struck by his grace and grit. Among those most taken with the whippet-thin young golfer was Bernard Darwin, grandson of the famous naturalist and a fine amateur player in his own right. A Cambridge-trained polymath—he was, among other things, a noted Dickens scholar—Darwin chose to devote his formidable literary gifts to golf, serving for decades as the golf correspondent for *The Times* of London. "Mr. Ouimet was the find of the tournament," he wrote in his dispatches from Garden City. "He should have an excellent future ahead of him." Darwin would later serve as Ouimet's marker in the U.S. Open playoff and as chief burnisher of the Ouimet legend.[25]

Darwin had come to the United States to chronicle the exploits of touring British professionals Ted Ray and Harry Vardon. In an era in which British players were still regarded as far superior to their American counterparts, these two working-class Jerseymen were Britain's finest golfers. Ray, famous equally for his prodigious drives and for the pipe clutched constantly between his teeth, had won the 1912 British Open and finished as runner-up in 1913. Vardon (who, like Ouimet, was the son of a gardener) had won no fewer than five British Opens, reaching back to 1896. (He would claim a sixth in 1914.) Through the late summer of 1913, the pair barnstormed across America, playing exhibitions and dispatching all comers. Their final destination was Brookline, where they intended to wrest the U.S. Open crown from an upstart American, Johnny McDermott, who, in the absence of top British players, had won the title in 1911 and 1912. So elevated was their stature that the U.S.G.A. postponed the Open from June to September in order to ensure their participation.

Ray had never before crossed the Atlantic, but for Vardon the visit was a reprise of his celebrated 1900 tour, which had done so much to popularize golf in the United States. The 1900 tour had been underwritten by the Spalding Company, as a promotion for its new (though soon obsolete) gutta-percha ball, the "Vardon Flyer." For the better part of a year Vardon crisscrossed the continent, competing on unfamiliar courses against the best players America had to offer yet still managing to win eighty-seven of eighty-eight matches. (The sole defeat came on a Florida course with "greens" of rolled sand and oil, a concoction he had never encountered.) The tour climaxed at the Chicago Golf Club, with a commanding victory in the 1900 U.S. Open. Everywhere Vardon appeared, huge galleries turned out to see him. In New York the stock exchange closed for the day so that traders could see him tackle the new course at Van Cortland Park. In Boston, seven-year-old Francis Ouimet dragged his mother to a downtown department store to watch Vardon hit balls in a makeshift cage. In years to come, Ouimet would consciously model his own game—the overlapping grip, the upright stance, the flowing, rhythmic swing—on Vardon's.[26]

The years between 1900 and 1913 had not been kind to Harry Vardon. Tuberculosis had scarred his lungs. Nerve damage in his right hand had ravaged his once-reliable putting stroke. Yet he remained a peerless competitor, and few doubted that he would reclaim the U.S. Open trophy at Brookline. If he failed, Ray would certainly claim the title.

Though the Open was to be held literally across the street from his home, Ouimet did not plan to play. Despite his recent success, he did not consider himself a match for players of the caliber of Vardon and Ray. More important, he had just taken a vacation from his job at Wright and Ditson, a Boston sporting-goods firm, in order to compete in the Amateur championship. He entered the Open only after being prevailed upon by the U.S.G.A. president, Robert Watson, who was anxious to secure amateur participants in a tournament increasingly monopolized by professionals. Even then, Ouimet was afraid to mention his intention to his employers, who first learned of it when the pairings appeared in the local papers. When confronted, an embarrassed Ouimet promised to withdraw, but his employers, to their everlasting credit, insisted that he play.[27]

Even before Ouimet's stunning victory, the 1913 U.S. Open had attracted unprecedented interest, thanks to the presence of Vardon and Ray and the element of Anglo-American rivalry it injected into the affair. When defending champion Johnny McDermott insulted the visiting Britons at a press conference, newspapers all over the country picked up the story, forcing U.S.G.A. president Watson to issue a public apology. With a rain of journalists descending on The Country Club, Watson and his colleagues erected history's first "press tent," complete with a Western Union office. The U.S.G.A. also took the unprecedented step of deploying marshals on the course, in an effort to control the large, boisterous gallery. Surely the largest, if not the most boisterous, member of the gallery was former president William Howard Taft, who motored up to Brookline to watch the qualifying rounds.[28]

The story of Ouimet's victory has been lovingly told and retold for nearly a century now. With a record number of entrants, the tournament began with preliminary qualifying. Ouimet qualified easily, trailing only Vardon in his section. On the first day of the regular tournament—at the time, the Open's 72 holes were contested over only two days—he recovered from a dismal start to play solid golf, taking full advantage of the intimate familiarity with the course he had acquired as a caddy. He was ably assisted by his own caddy, Eddie Lowery, who had been drafted into service after Ouimet's regular caddy was hired away by a professional. Ten years old and four feet tall in his shoes, Lowery cut a comical figure, but he was fiercely competitive—he later became a distinguished amateur golfer in his own right—and fiercely loyal to Ouimet, braving a gauntlet of truant officers and the wrath of his widowed mother to reach The Country Club each morning. At the end of the day's play, Francis stood in a tie for seventh at 151, four shots behind Vardon, who was joint leader with Wilfred Reid at 147. Ted Ray recovered from a disastrous morning round with a course record 70 in the afternoon to finish at 149, tied for third.[29]

The final two rounds, played on Friday, would prove infinitely more challenging. Overnight, the first nor'easter of the fall blew in, bringing wind, plummeting temperatures, and pounding rain. With the rest of the field staggering through the mud and rain, Ouimet caught fire, notching four birdies in his first six holes. He finished with a 74, the low round of the morning, which left him tied with Vardon and Ray for the lead. Playing early in the afternoon, each of the Jerseymen shot 79 to finish at 304, an unprepossessing total, but one that seemed destined to prevail in the punishing conditions. Walter Hagen rallied, but was undone by a double bogey on the fourteenth hole. Other challengers fired and fell back. The onus fell finally on Ouimet, playing in one of the last pairings of the day.

Using the modern system of scoring against par, Ouimet owned a five-stroke lead on the field when he arrived at the fifth tee in the final round. Over the next hour he squandered it all, finishing the outward nine in an inglorious 43. On the tenth, his topped tee shot traveled scarcely fifteen feet, leading to another double bogey. His gallery, ecstatic only a few holes before, began to grumble and disperse. Ouimet steadied himself with pars at 11 and 12, but he still needed to complete the final six holes in two under par to qualify for the playoff. Nothing in the afternoon's play suggested even the remotest possibility that he would, but golf, as he himself put it, can be "a mercurial affair." His approach on the short thirteenth finished wide of the green, but he chipped in for a birdie, provoking a roar that brought thousands of spectators scurrying back. He parred the 3-shot fourteenth and made a scrambling 4 at the fifteenth. Desperate for one more birdie, he directed all his hopes to the sixteenth, the last short hole on the course, but made a hash of it, eventually holing a 9-foot putt merely to save par.[30]

The needed birdie came, fittingly enough, on the seventeenth hole, the hole that fronted his Clyde Street home, the hole he had played in secret a thousand times as a child. A fine drive and approach left him with a sliding, 15-foot downhill putt. With Vardon and Ray watching from the edge of the crowd, he inspected the line with only one thought in mind: "giving the ball a chance." "I struck that putt as firmly as any putt I ever hit," he later wrote, "saw it take the roll, bang smack against the back of the hole, and fall in for a three." All that remained was the eighteenth, a stern 400-yard par four, bisected by the racetrack, which the persistent rain had reduced to a quagmire. Ouimet drove in the fairway and laced a long iron straight at the flag. The ball hung in the long grass fronting the green, but he nursed a chip to four feet and rolled in the par putt, securing a place in Saturday's playoff. As sportswriters raced to the Western Union office to file their stories, Ouimet took a hot bath and walked home for dinner and a solid night's sleep.[31]

The rain continued the next morning as Ouimet arrived at The Country Club. Clumps of spectators already dotted the grounds, the vanguard of a throng variously estimated at from 5,000 to 20,000, but in all events the largest crowd ever to watch a golfing competition in the United States. Striking practice balls before the round, Ouimet felt utterly "numb." "I played golf for fun," he later recalled. "I considered professionals as something like magicians who had answers for everything. I felt I was in a playoff by mistake . . . It was a wonderful mood to get into." The only tension in the morning's preparations came on the way to the first tee, when a group of club members tried to dispossess Lowery of his caddying duties. Stressing the importance of the occasion, they cajoled and offered inducements, but the tearful ten-year-old refused to relinquish the bag. The episode was witnessed by Bernard Darwin, who would elevate into a parable of interclass fidelity. The lad "stood faithfully to his post and was not to be seduced," Darwin wrote; he was "a most heroic child, and as cool as his master." Whatever the merits of the characterization, Lowery's persistence did ensure golf its most indelible photographic image.[32]

The poise of both master and retainer would be sorely tested over the course of the eighteen-hole playoff. With Lowery chanting a mantra before each shot—"Keep your eye on the ball"—Ouimet played his best round of the tournament. The three players all completed the front nine in even par, but Ouimet nosed ahead with a par on the tenth and a birdie 4 on the par-5 twelfth. A birdie on the thirteenth brought Vardon back within a stroke, but Ray fizzled, surrendering any chance of victory with a double bogey on fifteen. The issue was decided, once again, on the seventeenth. Needing one more birdie, Vardon attempted to cut the dogleg with his drive but caught the lip of a bunker, ensuring a bogey. Ouimet, returning to the scene of the previous day's heroics, hit another fine approach shot and rolled in another curling putt to go 3 shots clear. He parred the eighteenth to finish at 72. For the first time, an amateur player had won the U.S. Open.

✳   ✳   ✳

According to legend, Ouimet's victory at Brookline ushered in golf's golden age, transforming a still-suspect "rich man's sport" into a game of the masses. "Overnight the non-wealthy American lost his antagonism toward golf," wrote Herbert Warren Wind, dean of American golf writers. Like most legends, the tale includes a fair measure of exaggeration, as any golfer who has let slip his fondness for the game to nongolfing friends can attest. Yet Ouimet's achievement clearly did spur the game's growth. Britain's finest professionals bested by a twenty-year-old American amateur, and a former caddy to boot: here was a story that even the dullest journalist could spin into gold. Newspapers across the country, even the sober *New York Times*, heralded the victory on the front page, elevating Ouimet to a paragon of all things American. Inevitably many accounts harkened back to the battles of Lexington and Concord, or at least to Longfellow's rendering of them, describing Ouimet's winning stroke as another "shot heard 'round the world."[33]

Ouimet himself was little fazed by the swirl of attention and adulation. He finished the season, packed his clubs away for the winter, and returned to his job at Wright and Ditson, albeit with a promotion and hefty raise. The following summer he accepted an offer of a free transatlantic passage from a group of wealthy Bostonians in order to compete in the British Amateur and Open championships. It was Ouimet's first trip overseas and, in retrospect, his most disappointing. Though he won the French Amateur championship, he struggled to cope with the hard ground and relentless wind of British links golf and made little impression in either the Amateur or Open (won by Vardon for a record sixth time). As always, however, he learned from watching others, adjusting his grip and shortening his backswing to produce a crisp, downward blow. The changes came too late to help him in Britain, but back in the United States they paid immediate dividends. In his U.S. Open defense at Midlothian, he finished a respectable fourth, a few shots adrift of Walter Hagen. Others might have resented surrendering the trophy, but Ouimet was buoyed by the result, which persuaded him, really for the first time, that his victory at Brookline had been something more than "a huge fluke." A few weeks later he claimed the U.S. Amateur championship, the title he had always coveted, defeating Jerry Travers in the final.[34]

Yet at the very moment that Ouimet was hoisting his prize, the world was plummeting into war. World War I put paid to tournament golf; even the game's most ardent defenders agreed that there was something unseemly about golfing in wartime. The British Amateur and Open championships were canceled for the duration; the U.S.G.A. followed suit in 1917, the year that the United States entered the conflict. In Brookline, The Country Club strove to do "its bit" for the war effort, subscribing an ambulance for the front and solemnly expelling all members who were citizens of nations with which the United States was now at war. (Presumably few Germans, Turks, and Hungarians belonged to the club in the first place.)[35]

American participation in World War I more or less coincided with the U.S.G.A.'s infamous decision to ban Ouimet from amateur competition. In early 1916 the association expanded its definition of professionalism to include "accepting or holding any position as agent or employee that includes as part of its duties the handling of golf supplies." The new rule was apparently prompted not by Ouimet's long association with Wright and Ditson, but by his decision to open a sporting-goods firm of his own, in partnership with a Boston businessman. Though he had yet to make a nickel from the venture, he had signed papers and was thus considered a professional. Even at the time, the decision prompted an outcry. William Travis, a former U.S. Open champion who had lost his amateur status a few years before because of his work as a writer for a golfing magazine, penned a blistering editorial, denouncing the U.S.G.A. as "high handed, intensely conservative, and archaic." Golf historians have generally shared that assessment. Perhaps the best that can be said about Ouimet's suspension is that it had little practical significance. With the wartime suspension of tournament play, Francis ultimately missed only one significant championship, the 1916 U.S. Amateur. (The Western Golf Association, not yet in thrall to the U.S.G.A., pointedly invited him to participate in the 1916 Western Amateur, which he won.) By the time play was resumed, Ouimet (who spent the war years as a lieutenant in the Army) had been quietly reinstated. The episode would scarcely be worth mentioning at all but for what it suggests about the U.S.G.A.'s continuing determination to defend its vision of golf's "character." The episode also suggests something about the character of Francis Ouimet, who, at the time and subsequently, kept his opinion on the suspension to himself.[36]

The U.S. Open and Amateur championships resumed in 1919; the British Open and Amateur resumed a year later. To celebrate the world's "return to normalcy," Harry Vardon and Ted Ray returned to the United States to compete in the 1920 U.S. Open at Inverness in Toledo. This time, result conformed to reputation: Ray claimed the title; Vardon finished second, a stroke back. (In one of those rituals of generational succession in which golf history abounds, Vardon was paired in the qualifying rounds with an eighteen-year-old amateur from Atlanta, Bobby Jones.) Ouimet did not compete at Inverness. Indeed, after 1915 he would play the U.S. Open only twice more, in 1923 and 1925, when he finished in a tie for third.[37]

Though he avoided the U.S. Open, Ouimet remained a fixture in amateur competitions. He remained a cornerstone of the Walker Cup, the biennial event pitting the best American amateurs against their British and Irish counterparts, representing the United States in the first eight competitions. (By a delightful coincidence, one of his opponents in the inaugural matches in 1922 was his old friend Bernard Darwin, who had been pressed into service after the regular British captain had taken ill.) He also continued to compete in his beloved U.S. Amateur, advancing five times to the semifinal round in the 1920s but never further. Friends whispered that he had lost his nerve, but Ouimet, with characteristic candor, insisted that his opponents, especially Bobby Jones, were simply better golfers than he. His assessment was vindicated in 1931, the year after Jones's retirement from tournament golf, when he claimed his second and final U.S. Amateur title.[38]

Much had changed during Ouimet's long quest for a second amateur title. As innumerable historians have shown, the decade of the 1920s marked the birth of our own times, as Americans shed the vestiges of Victorian self-denial and embraced the cornucopia of possibilities afforded by a consumer society. Radio and recorded music, movies and mass-circulation magazines, annual models and installment plans, underarm deodorant and the advertising industry: all these innovations and more blossomed in the decade after World War I. Not coincidentally, the 1920s represented a golden age in American sport, with figures such as Babe Ruth and Jack Dempsey emerging as national icons.

Golf stood at the forefront of this cultural revolution. The number of American golfers, a few hundred thousand in 1913, grew by an order of magnitude; by the end of the 1920s, close to three million Americans played regularly. The popularity of the game was underwritten by improvements in equipment, particularly mass-produced rubber-cored balls and steel-shafted clubs, which made the game not only more affordable but infinitely easier to play. Magazines such as *Vanity Fair* and the *Saturday Evening Post* featured regular articles on golf, exploring the game's foibles and endless fascinations. (Bernard Darwin's essay on carpet putting in the January 1925 issue of *Vanity Fair* brilliantly illuminates both.) *Architectural Forum* devoted a special issue to clubhouse design. Golf even gave rise to its own fashion industry, or at least to what passed for fashion among golfers. Gone were the scarlet coats and brass buttons of the game's early days, replaced by a new gentlemanly uniform of plaid and plus-fours. Golf had an even more dramatic impact on women's fashion, propelling the move toward less restrictive clothing—what would come to be called "sportswear."

As the number of golfers grew, so did the number of golf courses. The 1920s represented the pinnacle of American golf course architecture, with designers like Donald Ross, Alistair McKenzie, Seth Raynor, and Charles Tillinghast turning out dozens of classic tracks. A majority of these new courses were built for private country clubs, for whom a "signature" design had become a marker of social status. Many of the new layouts, however, were open to the public or even publicly owned. Not until the 1950s did the number of municipal and day-fee courses outstrip the number of private clubs, but the trend was already apparent in the 1920s.

To be sure, popular ambivalence toward golf had not completely disappeared; then as now, devotees were forced to defend the game against charges that it was effete, effeminate, exclusionary, even un-American. Babbitt, the title character of Sinclair Lewis's mordant attack on 1920s American culture, belongs to a country club, though to a less prestigious one than he might wish. F. Scott Fitzgerald offered a more subtle but no less damning portrait in *The Great Gatsby*, through the character of Jordan, a competitive golfer, whose signature attributes are lying and cheating. With the onset of the Great Depression, golf would become a convenient scapegoat for a host of American ills, a symbol of a decade of frivolity and excess. For one observer, writing in H. L. Mencken's *American Mercury*, the forced closure of hundreds of golf courses was the Depression's silver lining. Astute observers could already detect "a general elevation of the national mental health because of the decline in golf playing."[39]

Yet however the Menckens of the world might fulminate, golf's future in the United States was secure. Literally and figuratively, the game had become part of the national landscape. And it had all happened in scarcely a generation, the space in time separating a seven-year-old boy searching for lost gutties on his way to school and the same boy, now a man, claiming his second U.S. Amateur trophy thirty years later.

Francis Ouimet competed in the U.S. Amateur for the final time in 1940. In the years that followed, he settled into a comfortable life as a stockbroker and weekend golfer. By all accounts, he remained much the same man he had always been: humble, unassuming, devoted to golf. "Golf with me has always been just a game," he wrote in his memoirs, "but a game that can teach splendid lessons," including persistence, tolerance, self-control, humility, and equanimity in the face of good fortune or bad. Though in the course of his career he would work for two of Boston's professional sports teams, the Braves and the Bruins, he never played golf professionally, and he steadfastly declined invitations to capitalize on his name. (The sole exception was the Francis Ouimet Scholarship Fund, which raised money to provide scholarships for former caddies.) He remained a fixture at the Walker Cup, continuing as nonplaying captain until 1949. By that time, Ouimet, the man who had redeemed American honor by besting the vaunted British in 1913, had the ironic distinction of being as well known in Britain, where golf fans still attended to the amateur game, as in the United States—and certainly more revered. In 1951 he became the first American elected as captain of the Royal and Ancient Golf Club of St. Andrews, an honor later extended to that other great American amateur player, Bobby Jones.[40]

As the culture of American golf changed, The Country Club, always something of an anachronism, slipped slowly into senescence. While newer clubs built palatial clubhouses, members at Brookline took pride in their old farmhouse, with its worn wood fittings and faded mementos. As the official club historians revealingly wrote in 1932, "There is a personality about our house not unlike that of a true aristocrat of modest means." Proposed innovations—new tennis courts, the erection of an indoor curling rink, even a proposal to allow the serving of light lunches in the taproom rather than in the formal dining room—inevitably provoked resistance from curmudgeonly club members. ("You might as well serve meals in the lavatory," one elderly member grumbled at the latter prospect.) One of the most bitter disputes came in the 1920s as the club considered acquiring fifty adjoining acres for a new nine-hole course—what would become the Primrose course. The sale eventually went through, but only after fierce debate, threatened resignations, and even a court injunction. Assuming new debt, older members warned, would inevitably erode the character of the club, compelling an increase in dues or, still worse, the admission of additional members, until the club became "a huge, semi-public" institution.[41]

As such doomsaying revealed, invocations of tradition, hierarchy, and gentility remained common at The Country Club even as the larger society became more dynamic, democratic, and commercial. Determined to resist the excessive competitiveness that had "blighted the real fun of American sport," the club sponsored no weekly golf competitions. The annual club championship remained a matter of indifference to most members. While the club boasted of participating in the oldest international competition in golf (the annual joust with Royal Montreal Golf Club, begun in 1898), it pointedly selected a team composed not of its best golfers but of its finest gentlemen. This attitude, combined with the club's strict membership requirements and hostility to junior players, ensured that Brookline would produce no more great champions.[42]

Over the years the U.S.G.A. occasionally staged championships at Brookline, but the Open did not return until 1963, fifty years after Ouimet's triumph and four years before his death. The Open provided the occasion for a last reunion between Ouimet, honorary chairman of the tournament, and Eddie Lowery, now a successful businessman in California. Fittingly, the tournament issued in a playoff, though in this case the people's choice, Arnold Palmer, was beaten by Julius Boros. Rather than reviving The Country Club, however, the 1963 Open seemed only to confirm its obsolescence. Competitors complained not only about the poor course conditions, the wages of a harsh winter, but about the design itself, which most deemed unworthy of a modern major championship. With tiny greens, cross bunkers harking back to the days of the gutta-percha ball, and an assortment of blind shots, Brookline seemed not just old-fashioned but antiquated, a relic of another age.

But there was one last twist in the tale. Thanks in part to the appeal of the telegenic Palmer, golf's popularity surged anew. The golf boom, which continues today, can be measured in many ways: in the opening of thousands of new courses, a substantial majority of them public; in ever-escalating tournament purses and saturation television coverage; in the emergence of a space-age, multi-billion-dollar golf equipment industry. But the single most compelling index is simply the growth in the number of players. When Francis Ouimet won the U.S. Open, perhaps a quarter of a million Americans played golf regularly; by the end of the 1920s, the number had grown to nearly three million. Today the figure stands somewhere between twenty and thirty million.

As in American golf's early days, this burgeoning popularity has prompted mixed emotions among the leadership of the U.S.G.A. With its self-proclaimed mission of promoting golf in the United States, the association can scarcely help but applaud the game's growth, but officials also fret about diluting golf's "character" as millions of new players take up the sport, often with little or no instruction in its distinctive culture or code of etiquette. The U.S.G.A. response to the dilemma lies within the realm of what one might call commercialized tradition. Golf has always been alive to its past—among American sports, only baseball is comparably attentive to its history—but over the last few decades the U.S.G.A. has underwritten this interest with a more-or-less continuous marketing campaign, intended to preserve and protect the "character of the game." Network television, ever alert to the appeal of nostalgia in a rootless era, has embraced the campaign, larding telecasts of major championships with classical music, sonorous commentary, and sepia-toned images of past champions. Significantly, this new traditionalism has focused not only on great players of the past but on classic courses, the greatest of which have come to be discussed in the kind of reverential tones usually reserved for religious shrines or battlefields. Today as a century ago, golf plainly touches a deeply felt American yearning for a sense of place.

In this new climate, it was inevitable that The Country Club would be rediscovered and revalued. The very characteristics that made the course seem old-fashioned, even obsolete, in 1963 were precisely the qualities that most appealed to the U.S.G.A. when it returned the Open to Brookline in 1988, the seventy-fifth anniversary of Ouimet's victory. Indeed, in preparing the course for the tournament, the U.S.G.A. dispatched one of the country's premier course designers, Rees Jones, to Brookline with a collection of vin-tage photographs and a mandate to recapture the character of the course as it had been in 1913. Ouimet, dead for more than twenty years, was a palpa-ble presence at the tournament—in television coverage, in the U.S.G.A. souvenir program, even on a commemorative stamp issued for the occasion by the U.S. Postal Service. Inevitably, the championship issued in another Anglo-American playoff, in which American Curtis Strange defeated Eng-lishman Nick Faldo.

Buoyed by the success of the 1988 Open, the U.S.G.A. selected Brookline as a venue for the 1999 Ryder Cup, the biennial competition pitting Ameri-can professionals against their European counterparts. If Ouimet's playoff victory over Vardon and Ray represented (in Herbert Warren Wind's words) "the most momentous round of golf of all time," the "Battle of Brookline" must rank just below it. The galleries for the three-day event, among the largest (and certainly the most partisan) in the history of golf, thundered their approval as the American team rallied on the final day to reclaim the cup. Millions more around the world watched the event on television. As fate would have it, the issue was decided on the seventeenth hole, when an-other American putt, this one stroked by Justin Leonard, banged off the back of the cup and fell into the hole for the decisive birdie.[43]

If Ouimet was a palpable presence at the 1988 U.S. Open, he was posi-tively ubiquitous at the 1999 Ryder Cup. Television commentators intoned his name. A life-sized bronze statue of Ouimet and Eddie Lowery, based on the famous 1913 photograph, was installed outside the clubhouse. The fact that the decisive putt came on the seventeenth hole lent an almost mystical air to the proceedings. "This is Francis Ouimet's hole, and we felt his pres-ence," declared American captain Ben Crenshaw, who was shown on tele-vision kissing the seventeenth green after Leonard's putt fell.[44]

If Ouimet's ghost was indeed present for the proceedings, one cannot help but wonder what it was thinking. What would Ouimet, a sportsman in the truest sense of the word, have made of American spectators hurling epi-thets and beer at European players or, still worse, of the American team swarming across the seventeenth green in celebration after Leonard's putt, even as his opponent, Jose Maria Olazabal, faced a putt to halve the hole and retain the cup? What would this proud amateur make of American players' public threat to boycott the Ryder Cup unless each was paid a sizable appearance fee? How do we square the ubiquity of Francis Ouimet at Brookline with the ubiquity of Nike swooshes (more than a dozen of which adorn the wardrobe of Tiger Woods every time he plays in public)? How do we explain the reverence for The Country Club felt by millions of Americans, the vast majority of whom will never be allowed past the guard-house at the Clyde Street entrance?

Better not to ask such questions. Better, far better, to tell our stories— tales of innocence and underdogs, of hope and Horatio Alger, of a twenty-year-old slip of a boy and his tiny ten-year-old caddy, in whose aspect we might still glimpse, nearly a century later, the elusive promise of America.

8

The Lost Battle for Gentlemanly Sport, 1869–1909

Ronald A. Smith

> With athletics considered as an end in themselves, pursued
> either for pecuniary profit or for popular applause, a college or
> university has nothing to do.
>
> —"President Eliot's Report," March 1894

Early on he threw down the gauntlet, but he lived to regret it. In his inaugural address as president of Harvard in 1869, Boston Brahmin Charles W. Eliot called for a Harvard "aristocracy which excels in manly sports." In so doing Eliot inadvertently issued an athletic challenge for all institutions that aspired to be like the leading institution of higher education in America.[1] His call to surpass other colleges in sports put Eliot and Harvard in opposition to an upper-class attitude that college athletics should not be an end in themselves, but rather should be an adjunct to a general education. He need not have raised the competitive athletic bar that had already been elevated considerably in the post–Civil War era, especially between Harvard and America's second most revered institution, Yale. Indeed, Yale used Eliot's words against Harvard athletics as Yale attempted to surpass the elite Boston institution. A little more than a dozen years after Eliot issued the challenge, a Yale professor charged that Eliot had "expressed a desire to win in athletics; that Harvard had set the pace for Yale and drawn them into it."[2] By then Eliot may have wished that he had never mentioned attaining excellence in athletics. He would fight unsuccessfully against the tendency toward big-time athletics for most of his four decades as president of Harvard. Though it was unclear what direction intercollegiate athletics would take at the beginning of his tenure, by the end of the first decade of the twentieth century it was apparent which path had been taken. An emphasis at Harvard upon winning above all else had won out over gentlemanly sport.

Eliot was born into the Boston and Harvard elite. His grandfather was a highly successful merchant and one of the richest men in Boston. His father was the Harvard College treasurer and an ex-officio member of the Corporation.[3] It was expected that Eliot would attend Harvard, and he began there as a fifteen-year-old member of the class of 1853. Three years later, as he was about to begin his senior year at Harvard, the first American intercollegiate contest, a crew meet, took place. Eliot was not part of that contest, but he had been involved in rowing on the Charles River when the chief Harvard sport was to row into Boston on the wide lapstreak boats and stop at drinking establishments. The floors of the boats were used, he said, to bring home "members of the crew who did not propose to return sober from an evening in Boston."[4] During the summer of 1852 the railroad superintendent of the newly constructed Boston, Concord, and Montreal Railroad invited the crews from Harvard and Yale for an eight-day, all-expenses-paid trip to a vacation spot more than 100 miles from Cambridge if they would row a match at the quiet Center Harbor resort on Lake Winnipesaukee, New Hampshire.[5] Eliot was not one of the forty-one Harvard and Yale students who made the rail trip, but he soon learned of Harvard's victory.

Two years later Eliot began teaching at Harvard with a tutorship in math as one of thirteen faculty members and continued to spend some time rowing with the Harvard crews, even introducing crimson as the Harvard color as part of the rowing outfit in 1858.[6] Yet his goal was not to develop excellence in rowing, but to enjoy the sport. One time just before a contest with a Boston crew, he wrote his fiancée, Ellen Peabody: "I had rather win than not, but it is mighty little matter whether we beat or are beaten — rowing is not my profession, neither is it my love, — it is recreation, fun, and health. I am going to remember your injunction, and take the best possible care of myself, and row just as hard as I comfortably can, and not a bit harder."[7] This attitude was reflective of Eliot's upbringing and of the English aristocratic sporting code that permeated the upper class in America and to some extent Harvard athletics.

Although Eliot personally did not place a great value on winning, many late nineteenth-century Harvard athletes did. Harvard, along with Yale and Princeton, led the nation to the concept of big-time college athletics, something that came to mean commercialism, including large gate receipts, professional coaches, and an emphasis on winning, not just participating. The year that Eliot became president of Harvard, only about a decade after rowing for the college, Harvard sent a crew to challenge the best of the English, the Oxford University crew, in a four-mile contest in London on the Thames.[8] It was the same year that the first intercollegiate football game, really a soccer match, was played between Princeton and Rutgers. By then there was no question that winning, not sport for fun, dominated college athletics in America.

The desire to win, while always important in athletics since the ancient Greeks created the term, was softened by the English upper-class emphasis on achieving a gentlemanly sense of proportion, enjoyment, and fair play. Comparisons drawn between sport in English and American institutions of higher education were commonly made in the latter nineteenth century. "The English," wrote a knowledgeable American observer at the turn of the century, "seem to play more for the love of sport and less for a desire to beat somebody than their American cousins." An Englishman at the same time wrote: "The winning of a game being the only end that an American player has in view, he subordinated every other consideration," something that he claimed was not true of an Oxford athlete. An upper-class British traveler to America, John Muirhead, got to the point by questioning the emphasis upon winning in American college sport, asserting that "the desire to win must be very strictly subordinated to the sense of honour and fair play."[9]

The strict desire to win, as opposed to a sense of honor and fair play, was a concern to Endicott Peabody. Peabody was an American patrician by birth, educated in the English public school of Cheltenham and at Cambridge University. He returned to America and in 1884 founded and became headmaster of the elite Groton School for Boys in Massachusetts. With his gentlemanly background and a love of sports, he believed that the aim of sport in England "is recreation; in America it is victory." Peabody wrote: "In England there is not perfection by any means . . . but they do have one idea which appeals to the sportsman—athletics exist for the purposes of recreation; they are great fun." In America, by contrast, "we take the most promising men and make them practically perfect in our teams, for particular events." He believed that England was a better place to live than America, but America was a better place to work, for the "life of the ordinary man who is in earnest counts for a good deal more." American society, Peabody said, was "plastic," not unchangeable, as in England.[10]

The plasticity of American society that Peabody described meant that ordinary men who worked hard at their strengths could move ahead both financially and socially. The American belief in social mobility provides a key to understanding the emphasis upon the drive for perfection and winning in American intercollegiate athletics. Unlike England, America did not have a sharply defined, stratified society in the nineteenth century. To a great extent, performance rather than peerage determined a person's place in the social order. Alexis de Tocqueville, the keen observer of America, made the point a decade before the first Harvard-Yale rowing match: "The great advantage of the Americans is that they have arrived at a state of democracy without having to endure a democratic revolution, and that they were born equal instead of becoming so."[11] If Americans had no feudal system, no ancien régime, to revolt against and none to return to, and if Americans never had an established aristocratic class, as Louis Hartz has argued, American society would naturally differ from a society like England's, historically ruled by such an upper class.[12] A gentleman's code of social behavior easily translated into a code of sportsmanship, which befitted a rigid class structure. If a man did not have to prove himself continually in order to maintain his status in athletics or in anything else, there was less of a demand for excellence of performance. In America, such a gentleman's code of sportsmanship had much less chance of taking root.

In nineteenth-century America, when organized sport first appeared, there were, of course, elite gentlemen on college campuses, especially those at Harvard. But America's strong tradition of egalitarianism, not equality of talent but of equal rights, came into conflict with elite attitudes early on. Where opportunity for advancement exists, there is likely to be a greater struggle, and performance is more likely to be judged on the individual's pursuit of excellence. In athletics that pursuit often means winning. In an open society that acknowledges excellence of performance, status through winning seems only natural. One wins or one loses.

Nevertheless, Harvard was considered the most elite and aristocratic American college in the nineteenth century. Not only was it the first American college; it was the largest and wealthiest for much of the 1800s, and it had the most prestigious graduates. Nurturing Harvard was the most traditional upper class, the patricians of Boston, who saw themselves as an American aristocracy. Such a perception caused some to think that Harvard, more than other American colleges, ought to apply certain gentlemanly restraints to its athletics. Others, however, believed that Harvard had to either relax its gentlemanly ideals or lose out in its efforts to strive for superiority in athletics.

The presidency of Charles Eliot covered the years when Harvard confronted the paradox of attempting to play with a gentlemanly code of ethics while striving to defeat other colleges, especially its closest rival, Yale. It was a period when "the social character of Harvard College became increasingly 'Brahmin' in the sense of domination by Boston's social and economic elite."[13] Thus, while Eliot challenged Harvard to be the best in athletics as well as in intellectual efforts, he did not want this goal to be achieved at any cost; breeding and honor were not to be sacrificed to competitiveness. His enthusiasm for striving for excellence was tempered by his traditional upper-class attitude, carrying the implication there should be limits on athletic efforts. And yet "incidental pleasure," for which Eliot rowed in 1858, was not a logical means of achieving athletic superiority. Consequently, Harvard generally lost to Yale and Princeton in baseball, and especially in the important sports of crew and football. This lack of athletic success might well be attributed to the attitude that pervaded much of Harvard, an attitude akin to the aristocratic British viewpoint of participation imbued with a sense of enjoyment and fair play.

A number of individuals at Harvard attempted to conduct sport more like British gentlemen while competing with colleges that placed greater emphasis on winning. The Harvard gentleman's attitude of participating in

amateur sport, playing within the spirit of the rules, and being magnani-
mous toward opponents was more apparent, however, in its faculty, administration, and some alumni than in its student body. Harvard students, almost from the beginning, took winning seriously. By the 1860s, less than a
decade after the first contest, Harvard and Yale crews were contesting their
annual crew meet in a highly competitive manner, with little claim to
true gentlemanly sportsmanship. For instance, a donnybrook occurred at
Worcester, Massachusetts, in the 1860 regatta when police battled fans of
the Harvard crew, winners of a disputed race. For the next three years,
school authorities canceled the contests, presumably to prevent unruly behavior. Then, in 1864, in the midst of the Civil War, Yale hired the first professional college coach and defeated Harvard for the first time. A reporter
noted that "no friendly hands met at the close of the conflict."[14] After one
more loss to Yale, Harvard students asked former crewman William Blaikie
to help them. Blaikie traveled to England to study the Oxford rowing system, where, despite a gentlemanly tradition, the English had perfected
more efficient rowing methods. Harvard then introduced the Oxford rowing system. A series of Harvard victories resulted, one of which occurred the
year Charles Eliot became president. That year the Harvard crew accepted
an invitation to row against the Oxford crew in London. While the first Harvard crew was losing to Oxford in a four-mile race on the Thames, the second crew was taking on Yale in the annual challenge race. Harvard came
from behind to defeat the Elis by two lengths. One of the Yale oarsmen was
so angered by this bitter defeat that he drove his oar through the bottom of
his boat.[15]

The rivalry and desire to win continued in rowing into the 1870s and was
intensified by the addition of baseball, first contested in the 1860s, and football, a product of the 1870s. The Harvard baseball team had a record high
forty-four-game schedule in 1870, twenty-six of which were played out of
term time. In 1882 nineteen of its schedule of twenty-eight games were
played outside Cambridge, and eleven were played against professional
teams, including the Boston Red Stockings.[16] By the early 1880s the expansion and intensity of Harvard athletics had reached such a crucial point that
the faculty felt compelled to take action. They created a faculty Athletic
Committee assigned to control intercollegiate athletics in a more gentlemanly manner. The Harvard faculty desired to curb the attempt by students

to perfect "athletics practiced in a competitive spirit in emulation of professional athletes and players" and to return to an earlier form of "athletics
practiced for sport, social recreation, and health."[17]

The dichotomy between athletics for winning and athletics for recreation
in a gentlemanly tradition, institutionalized in the Athletic Committee,
continued throughout the nineteenth century and into the twentieth, and it
was exacerbated by Eliot, the governing boards, and the faculty. One year
after its founding, the Harvard Athletic Committee sent a letter to Yale re-
questing a conference of leading colleges to discuss policy regarding faculty
control of athletics. Though Yale at first declined, Harvard sent invitations
to thirteen institutions, eight of which, including Yale, eventually attended.
The conference adopted a series of resolutions aimed at preserving amateurism under faculty control. It also set regulations on eligibility and
agreed to play against only those schools that passed the resolutions. The re-
solves were then sent to twenty-one colleges with the proviso that they
would be enforced when five colleges adopted them. Only the Harvard and
Princeton faculties passed the resolutions, while students at every college
opposed them. The proposal died prematurely.[18]

The Harvard faculty, with the backing of President Eliot, continued its
drive to imbue college athletics with a sense of sportsmanship and con-
straint. In 1882 the Athletic Committee dismissed the students' chosen baseball coach, presumably for not meeting the gentlemanly standards of Harvard. In addition, it refused to explain why the crew could not hire a
specific crew coach. Soon thereafter the Athletic Committee asked the faculty to prohibit football because "the nature of the game puts a premium on
unfair play [which] . . . is profitable if it succeeds, is unlikely to be detected
by the referee, and if detected is very lightly punished." In the view of the
committee, football was "brutal, demoralizing to the players and to spectators, and extremely dangerous."[19] The faculty agreed, and football was
banned for a year.

Though football was soon reinstated, questions concerning amateurism
and the ethics of winning did not subside. In 1887 the Harvard Board of
Overseers, a group of elders with Boston Brahmin pedigrees who oversaw
but did not set policy, were asked to submit findings on whether undue
prominence was given to Harvard athletics. They concluded that "professional methods and professional standards gradually creep in until the

honorable emulation of gentlemen becomes a dishonorable struggle for a prize." They charged that "disputes over races, charges of trickery, complaints against umpires and referees have constantly occurred." The committee reached the opinion, with one dissenter, that Harvard faculty should prohibit all intercollegiate athletics for one year.[20] President Eliot, who favored one, two, or three intercollegiate contests a year, then appointed a committee of three knowledgeable faculty members to examine Harvard athletics. The committee did not propose abolition of athletics, but it did agree that "the passionate desire to win" led to "ungentlemanly behavior . . . professional spirit, [and] excessive desire to win."[21] Being intensely focused on winning was perceived as coarse and vulgar.

Harvard did not drop competitive athletics, but it continued to propose reforms that were generally rejected by its fellow institutions. In 1890 Harvard tried unsuccessfully to secure an agreement with Yale regarding the eligibility of players on freshman teams. In the same year it withdrew from the Inter-Collegiate Foot Ball Association because of objectionable practices of recruiting players and of fielding athletes who had previously received money for participation. Harvard further tried to eliminate all games played outside New England and to have a "dual league" with Yale. This effort was stifled by Yale and by interested Harvard alumni from New York City, who wanted to have the annual Harvard-Yale football game played in their city.[22] By the mid-1890s the faculty again voted to abolish football because of "unsportsmanlike and injury-producing elements of the game," but the Harvard Corporation upheld the Athletic Committee's opinion that Harvard could indeed compete "in the spirit of gentlemen."[23]

Toward the end of the 1890s a faculty conference was held at Brown University to discuss methods of eliminating objectionable features of intercollegiate athletics such as recruitment and offering athletic scholarships, professional coaching, and rampant commercialism. Harvard was one of six schools represented; Yale was conspicuously absent. The Brown Conference report proposed twenty rule changes, primarily those promoted by Harvard, and exposed almost as many malpractices in athletics. The group, dominated by faculty, spoke out again for the need for gentlemanly restrictions in American college sports: "We should not seek perfection in our games, but rather, good sport . . . What we all want is a good, manly struggle between fairly equal teams, who scorn to take unfair advantage."[24] What

Harvard officials and a few other faculty-controlled athletic institutions desired was the aristocratic view of competitive sports, a difficult achievement in a nation that lacked the traditional British view of sport.

As Harvard led the nation's colleges in the struggle to reform athletics through faculty control and by promoting a semblance of gentlemanly behavior, it was plain that at the same time the college was struggling to produce athletic excellence and to win, especially against its prime rival, Yale. The Yale rivalry tested Harvard's resolve to conduct athletics in the American tradition of the pursuit of victory while at the same time keeping within the bounds of the English upper-class notion of sportsmanship and gentlemanly reserve. William James Jr., a Harvard student in 1903, aptly summed up the problem when he said that Harvard was caught between beating Yale and preserving the ideals of athletics.[25] A captain of the Harvard crew in 1908 remarked to President Eliot: "It is a pity that Harvard could not find someone as her chief competitor with standards of sportsmanship more near her own."[26] President Eliot and the Harvard faculty, however, more than the students, were attempting to set the standards after the faculty Athletic Committee was formed in 1882. Until then Harvard had fared well against Yale in competition in the three major sports, rowing, baseball, and football. From the beginning in 1852 until 1882, Harvard led Yale by 16 wins to 6 losses in crew and 21 wins to 15 losses in baseball. Only in football did Harvard trail Yale, with 1 win and 4 losses. After 1882 until the end of the Eliot era, Yale dominated all three sports. From 1882 through 1909 Yale's record against Harvard was 19 wins and 7 losses in crew, 37 wins and 32 losses in baseball, and 18 wins and 4 losses in football.[27]

Several incidents in the early 1900s testify to the mistrust and suspicion surrounding the Harvard-Yale rivalry. In the fall of 1901 Harvard had won only two of the previous seventeen football games with Yale, and had not scored a point in three of the last four games with its prime rival. The spring before, Harvard had been tricked, it believed, when Yale changed its rules of eligibility to allow a law student, J. S. Spraker, to be admitted to the Yale Law School without an examination after he had failed to get into Princeton. Harvard students claimed that he had been brought into Yale only for athletic purposes. Spraker's winning of the high jump provided the points necessary for Yale to win the annual dual track meet. Early the next fall Harvard students, upset over Yale's chicanery, successfully challenged the eligibility of one of Yale's football players. Yale was, predictably, upset. It was then Yale's turn to question the eligibility of a member of Harvard's team, Oliver Cutts. Three days before the annual Harvard-Yale football game, the chair of the Harvard Athletic Committee received a telegram from Walter Camp, Yale's unofficial athletic boss and titular football coach. It read: "So much unsolicited evidence comes into our hands that Cutts taught football at the school from which he was receiving a salary that we find it difficult to prevent trouble and stop stories, both of which we desire. Can you give us necessary material to answer strong prima facie case."[28]

Oliver Cutts was a twenty-eight-year old, nearly 200-pound, second-year law student when he played right tackle for Harvard that season. Cutts had attended and played football for three seasons at Bates College before graduating in 1896. He was then hired to teach mathematics at Haverford Grammar School near Philadelphia and did so until 1900. Though he helped coach the Haverford football team and worked with students in the gymnasium, he was evidently not paid for that service. As a law student during his first year at Harvard, he did not play because Harvard had a rule prohibiting first-year law students from playing sports. The next year, though, the Harvard team welcomed him. On the morning of the Harvard-Yale game in 1901, Yale's Walter Camp produced one more bit of evidence from a Yale graduate stating that Cutts received a salary commensurate with joint service as teacher and athletic instructor. The Harvard Athletic Committee met for about four hours that morning, and in a close vote declared Cutts eligible to play, primarily on the basis of a statement from Cutts's principal at the Haverford school, who claimed that Cutts had not been paid for athletics and was thus an amateur. The game was played, Cutts starred, and Harvard won by the biggest score in its early history against Yale, 22–0.

Yale would not let the controversy die. Shortly before Christmas it presented new evidence to President Eliot: a copy of a check showing that Cutts had received payment for privately teaching boxing while at Haverford—thus making him a professional.[29] With this information the Harvard Athletic Committee declared Cutts ineligible. Chairman Ira Hollis was disgusted with the insinuations by Yale that his committee had been deceptive in its dealing with the Cutts case. He said that Yale, not Harvard, had been the "worst sinner" for not cooperating in the movement to produce needed rules and regulations in athletics. "Only Yale," Hollis emphasized, "has refused to take part in these discussions."[30]

The Cutts case finally motivated President Arthur Hadley of Yale to take some initiative for his student-run athletic program. He called for a joint Harvard-Yale undergraduate rules conference concerning eligibility. Out of the meetings came the 1903 Harvard-Yale eligibility agreement. This called for bona fide amateur undergraduate students to have only four years of eligibility, with transfer students required to reside at the college for one year before participation. No graduates were to play, and lists of eligible athletes were to be sent three weeks before the contests, with all protests to be made at least two weeks before the event. The formulation of written rules of eligibility was a move to bring about more ethical play, but, more important, it showed the lack of gentlemanly attitude in sport: if Yale and Harvard students had been true gentlemen, there would have been little need to codify behavior.

While Harvard and Yale continued to question each other's athletic motives, Yale kept winning—especially in football, where it shut out Harvard for the next six years. The Harvard-Yale controversy boiled over in a closely contested game in 1905, when a Harvard man, Francis Burr, was attempting to "fair catch" a Yale punt. Under the rules it was legal for Yale to attempt to play the ball. Burr was hit by James Quill, who "leaped into the air . . . missed the ball and, in his descent, fell on Burr with his elbow resting on Burr's nose," according to one of Harvard's players. "Blood spurted from his nostrils. But it was not a cowardly attack."[31] Harvard fans saw it differently. They believed that the Yale player had deliberately and flagrantly disabled the Harvard man. A storm of protest grew at Harvard at the very time that the death of a Union College player in a New York University game stirred the NYU chancellor to call a meeting of colleges either to abolish or to reform football. While that event led shortly to the creation of the National Collegiate Athletic Association, Harvard fans were more concerned about Yale. Harvard alumnus Richard Henry Dana, after condemning the Yale "brutality," asked President Eliot "if a flood of light" on football "would not force a reform."[32] LeBaron Briggs, dean of the Harvard Faculty of Arts and Science, believed that despite incidents such as the Burr-Quill affair, Harvard-Yale games should not be stopped. "I am not yet so pessimistic," he wrote Eliot, "as to believe that students of different universities cannot play against each other as gentlemen."[33] The Boston Brahmin–led Harvard Overseers, though, believed that the game of football was "essentially bad in every respect." The "trickiness and foul play" encouraged in many colleges should be condemned. The Overseers asked: "Is it not time for the larger and more important universities . . . to cry Halt?"[34] President Theodore Roosevelt, who only months before had helped resolve the Russo-Japanese War, for which he would soon win a Nobel Peace Prize, jumped into the athletic maelstrom of 1905 in an attempt to save the game that he thought best developed moral character. As a Harvard partisan who graduated in 1880, he corresponded numerous times with President Eliot trying to convince him that football should be reformed rather than abolished as Eliot desired. When Eliot, the Overseers, and the Harvard faculty called for the suspension of football at Harvard early in 1906, Teddy Roosevelt wrote in private that Harvard was "doing the baby act."[35]

The long-smoldering controversy between Yale and Harvard over the nature of college athletics was inflamed on the heels of the Burr-Quill controversy by an article published in the *Harvard Graduates' Magazine*. In an unsigned article, Yale and its administration were condemned for cringing "before the athletocracy." Yale, it stated, was only seeking general educational publicity by linking its name with Harvard in athletics. Further, and central to the theme of this piece, there was a charge that despite Harvard's sportsmanlike attitude toward athletics, "the temptation to imitate the practices which have brought victory to their opponents has sometimes proved too strong." The basic philosophy of athletics in the two institutions, the article emphasized, was different. "Harvard is pledged to the proposition that athletics in a university shall be subordinated to the real purpose of a university, that they shall be engaged in for recreation, that contests shall be waged in a spirit of sport, and that the standard shall be that of gentlemen." Yale, it stated, had "persistently opposed every attempt to curb, or regulate, or purify athletics." The anonymous author recommended breaking athletic relations with Yale, an institution that had consistently promoted an "anything to win" policy.[36]

This was not a new charge. A decade earlier, Harvard had broken relations with Yale over its attitude toward winning. The Harvard rowing coach in 1895 claimed that Yale had deprived Harvard of many victories "by their 'anything to win' methods. The alternative," the coach believed, "is to cease doing business with them for a time . . . or descend to the same methods. They do not seem able to act like gentlemen."[37] Similar charges had been made numerous times since Harvard had created its faculty Athletic Committee in 1882. More often than not it was the faculty and President Eliot rather than Harvard students who made the charges. William Thayer, editor of the *Harvard Graduates' Magazine,* noted this fact in 1905 after the scathing article on Yale had been published and reactions had surfaced. In a reply to President Eliot, Thayer remarked that "Harvard authorities have been struggling to set a higher standard, which our athletes cannot hope to reach unless they give up making concessions to competitors—Yale first of all—who avowedly prefer a lower standard. To judge from discussions of the past four weeks," Thayer believed, "our athletes resent the suggestion that they have ever had, or ever wish to have, a higher standard than Yale's."[38]

What was Harvard to do? Should it set higher standards of athletic conduct or should it play by the rules established by most American colleges, which stressed winning over anything else, especially gentlemanly play? President Eliot, the Harvard Corporation, the faculty, and a few alumni favored the English upper-class system of gentlemanly sport. Most of the student body and an increasing number of alumni favored beating Yale and showing Harvard's athletic superiority. The dean of the Harvard Faculty of Arts and Sciences, LeBaron Briggs, said in 1908: "The students love their athletics and their college and dislike seeing their chance of victory diminished by the shifting policy and restriction not subjected to by other colleges."[39] The Harvard faculty continued to condemn what it regarded as the evils of college athletics and even tried to pack the joint Athletic Committee, which since 1888 had had three members each from the faculty, students, and alumni. In 1907 the faculty voted to have the dean of the Faculty of Arts and Sciences, the dean of Harvard College, and the dean of the Lawrence Scientific Schools as its three representatives. Once on the committee, however, the deans felt that their membership on it was "a profound mistake" and recommended the creation of an athletic director and a return to the previous faculty representation.[40] The position of director of athletics was created as the Eliot era came to a close, with the title of graduate treasurer of the Harvard Athletic Association. One could hardly expect an athletic director not to promote a winning attitude.

Other changes rather quietly altered the status quo at Harvard from a system based on the upper-class emphasis on fair play to one that encouraged winning in the American tradition. The failure of the Harvard authorities to preserve the English amateur spirit was evident in at least three episodes in the early 1900s. First, Harvard alumni of the class of 1879 gave the then-huge sum of $100,000 to build a football stadium. President Eliot, who in 1896 had suggested holding contests with no permanent seating arrangement, decided in 1901 that a permanent football stadium would prevent the campus from being "defaced by unsightly banks of cheap wooden seats."[41] A stadium was erected in 1903 that could seat nearly 40,000 spectators. By building the first steel-reinforced concrete stadium in America, Harvard motivated other colleges to increase the size of their stadiums and to increasingly commercialize and professionalize sport. It would be difficult to remain amateur in spirit if the outward manifestations of sports were commercial and professional.

A second major shift away from gentlemanly sport became obvious when the Harvard Corporation began to award scholarships not only for scholarly achievement but also for athletic performance. This is a difficult concept to prove with historical accuracy, but there is evidence that Harvard began to grant athletic scholarships around the turn of the century. The Harvard Athletic Committee in 1903 raised the question: Should the George Emerson Lowell Scholarships be given to students showing excellence in athletics but only mediocre work in scholarship? According to the university catalogue, the Lowell Scholarships were to be awarded at the discretion of the president and fellows, with the provision that "excellence in classics or in athletics is recommended as desirable." The Athletic Committee chairman wrote President Eliot:

> I understand that one of them is usually awarded to a student
> who has exhibited special excellence in the classics, the other
> is awarded to a deserving student who has shown excellence in
> athletics. The latter was held last year by Mr. O. G. Frantz,
> who during the previous year had held a grade of C in his
> studies. To outsiders, it might seem that the University is insincere in permitting a man who holds this scholarship to play on
> an intercollegiate team, and I think that the precise reason for
> awarding the scholarship should be carefully defined, so that
> we may not be misunderstood. I call your attention to an ac-

count of a publication in one of the New York papers as to
how Harvard is in the habit of procuring trained athletes.[42]

The fact that "Home Run" Frantz, a stalwart on the Harvard baseball nine,
received the scholarship with little evidence of scholastic achievement was
an indication of Harvard's change of heart. President Eliot penciled a comment below the letter he received from the Athletic Committee: "Corporation have accepted the trust and propose to execute it." There is little proof,
however, that athletic scholarships were common at Harvard. Very few of
those who held scholarships at Harvard in the early 1900s were on athletic
teams, and those who possessed them played little.[43]

A third indication of a change from the English elite ideal of sport was
the hiring of professional coaches. Possibly the most important of Harvard's
policies attempting to maintain an upper-class notion of sport was the preservation of amateur coaching. No issue in competitive athletics at Harvard
was more fully discussed. The hiring of a professional coach was probably
the act most responsible for promoting winning and excellence at the expense of amateur athletics.

Harvard's Archibald Coolidge saw the impact of hiring professional
coaches more clearly than most. Coolidge, like President Eliot, was the
grandson of a wealthy Boston Brahmin merchant. A graduate of Harvard's
class of 1887, a member of the Harvard faculty and of the Athletic Committee, Archibald Coolidge favored amateur coaching and the belief that winning was not the "chief object of sport"; it was rather "sport for sport's sake."
In a 1906 article titled "Professional Coaches," Coolidge agreed that continual losses to Yale had pressured Harvard to consider a professional coach.
After the Harvard Athletic Committee voted for a five-year contract for a
crew coach in 1904, and a highly paid position for a football coach in 1905,
Coolidge expressed despair at having abandoned a standard that the committee had "always tried to maintain." He asked whether "technical perfection [was] more important than true sport."[44]

Harvard had finally succumbed to the lure of the professional coach. It
had taken almost a generation. Less than half a year after the Harvard Athletic Committee was created in 1882, it voted to fire the Harvard baseball
coach, who was a professional and not a Harvard alumnus. At the same
time the crew was forced to agree to use only Harvard graduates as coaches,

not allowing the team to hire outside professionals. In the 1880s and 1890s the committee sometimes wavered on the question of hiring professional coaches. In 1888 committee members agreed to allow John G. Clarkson, pitching star of the Chicago White Stockings, to coach baseball for several seasons, and in 1892 the committee allowed Timothy J. Keefe, his peer from the New York Giants, to coach pitchers. The committee allowed the football team to employ a professional wrestler as a football trainer, provided that the team employed "a reputable physician" to supervise the team's health. In the same year the committee asked President Eliot if he opposed hiring William A. Bancroft for three years as crew coach for a total salary of $10,000. Eliot pressured the committee to reject the idea, saying that he would make a public statement giving reasons for "disclaiming all responsibility for it" if the appointment were made.[45]

By 1900 almost all major colleges had begun to hire professional coaches for sports they considered important. Harvard students and many alumni felt they could no longer bear the cross of this aspect of amateurism. Stated one student enthusiast: "The undergraduates want a man who will stand in the same relation to athletics at Harvard as that which Mr. [Walter] Camp holds to athletics at Yale."[46] William Blaikie, Harvard crew member of the class of 1866 and New York City lawyer, sent President Eliot a twelve-page letter on the same subject. He suggested hiring a crew coach for $3,000 a year. "Suppose you do it, and Harvard wins," wrote Blaikie; "will you ever grudge the effort?"[47] After wavering, the Harvard Athletic Committee hired a new crew coach for $2,000 a year in 1904, and in 1905 the football team was given permission to hire William Reid as coach for $3,500. At the same time the alumni were given permission, because of "extraordinary expenses," to raise an additional sum of $3,500, enabling twenty-six-year-old Reid to receive a salary 20 percent higher than that of any Harvard professor, and nearly as high as that of Charles Eliot, who had been president since 1869. "It is perhaps superfluous to add," wrote a disgruntled Archibald Coolidge, "that this remainder was almost instantly guaranteed."[48]

The fight for the professional coach was not quite over. With football at a crisis stage in America in 1905 and 1906, the Harvard authorities set up a Joint Committee on the Regulations of Athletic Sports to represent the Harvard Corporation and the Overseers. This committee recommended that "professional coaching be done away with as soon as possible." The Harvard

Athletic Committee listened, but defeated a motion to abolish all paid coaches after the academic year 1909–10. They would agree to amateur coaches only if Harvard's "important rivals" would do the same.[49]

Harvard in fact hired Percy Haughton as its football coach in 1908. Though a Harvard graduate, Haughton had been criticized as early as 1902 by a booster of Harvard athletics, Dean LeBaron Briggs. Even Briggs could not countenance Haughton's attitudes toward athletics. "Things that Percy Haughton did in baseball," Briggs complained, "almost everybody would condemn."[50] Haughton, whose attitude epitomized the American goal of winning, held secret practices from the middle of October to the end of November in his first year of coaching as he readied his team for the Yale game. For the first time in seven years, Harvard defeated Yale, 4–0. The English attitude of sport for sport's sake took a back seat, and during the next decade Harvard lost only two football games, only three of the next twelve rowing meets, but a majority of baseball games to its closest rival, Yale. Much of the success appears to have been the result of professional coaching and the abandonment of English ideals of sport.

The Harvard and Boston elite's attempt to preserve gentlemanly sport in the English tradition had failed by the end of President Eliot's era in 1909. Eliot himself had become somewhat depressed about human nature in general and pessimistic about possible reform in college athletics. Shortly before retiring, he wrote: "After all, education and civilization put gloss or polish of manners on primitive man, but do not seem to have changed much his real fiber, or his emotions and passions."[51] The gentlemanly ideal in sport at Harvard had been unsuccessful, it appeared, because that system had not produced what was important in American society and at Harvard, winning and excellence of performance. The gentlemanly restraints that Harvard had attempted to place on its athletes—generally imposed by the Athletic Committee, faculty, president, and governing boards—had thwarted attempts to perfect varsity athletics to the level achieved by its chief rival, Yale. Harvard authorities were trying to impose a system of values on American colleges based upon an upper-class notion of breeding and honor that did not have deep roots in America. If Americans were "born equal" or "born free," as Alexis de Tocqueville had suggested in the 1830s, a more open society would produce excellence in performance and a winning attitude. America's lack of an effective and formal aristocratic class with a belief in gentlemanly sports stymied Harvard authorities, including President Eliot, in their attempt to foster gentlemanly sport. By the first decade of the twentieth century, the model favored by the Boston Brahmin Charles Eliot gave way to the demands of American society and to Harvard's students and alumni. And from then on, Harvard, against its major rivals, began to win.

9

Sports, Politics, and Revenge:
The Patriots' Strange Journey Home

David Welky

The New England Patriots met the Oakland Raiders on January 19, 2001, in an American Football Conference division playoff game staged in near-blizzard conditions. The weather produced a sloppy contest in which the Patriots trailed 13–10 with just minutes to go. All seemed lost after a Raiders defenseman recovered an apparent fumble by quarterback Tom Brady, an unheralded reserve who became the season's Cinderella story when he replaced injured star Drew Bledsoe and led the team to the playoffs. But for once the football gods smiled on the Patriots. After reviewing the play, referee Walt Coleman ruled it an incomplete pass and restored the ball to New England. Adam Vinatieri drove a 45-yard field goal through the snow to send the game into overtime, then connected on a 27-yarder to clinch the game. It was the last National Football League game played at Foxboro Stadium. The Patriots defeated the Pittsburgh Steelers 24–17 on the road the following week, then shocked the powerful St. Louis Rams 20–17 in Super Bowl XXXVI. For the first time in their forty-two-year history, the Patriots were champions.

Boston worshipped its professional basketball, baseball, and hockey teams, but professional football was "almost an irrelevancy." The Patriots were the perpetual doormats of the NFL, and Foxboro Stadium was an unsightly pit in "the middle of a rustic nowhere," equipped with frozen aluminum benches masquerading as seats and "dust bowl" parking lots that emptied at glacial speed. The nearly miraculous victory in its final game seems eerily out of place. It was as if the stadium was trying to make up for thirty years of disappointments. Perhaps it was an apology for the power outage that interrupted the AFC championship it hosted in 1996. Perhaps it was an apology to the many Patriots owners it had broken and left financially destitute. Perhaps it was even an apology to all of New England, an act of contrition for creating so much contention between neighborhoods, politicians, and sportsmen over the previous thirty years.[1]

Bostonians like to say that their three main pursuits are sports, politics, and revenge, and the story of Foxboro Stadium and Gillette Stadium, the edifice that replaced it in 2002, contains generous portions of each. Each stadium spawned years of bickering that sprawled across township boundaries and state lines. These often-personal, occasionally ideological, and usually bitter quarrels exposed class, racial, and governmental fault lines within Boston, Massachusetts, and New England and riveted attention on the relationship between the business of sports and public policy. Just as important, the fight over football stadiums highlights an evolution in the ways that people identified with Boston as a city. Once relegated to the fringes, professional football became a key element in the urban psyche. Definition as a "big-time" city increasingly rested not upon population, economic wealth, or cultural tradition, but rather upon big-time sports. The original patriots would have shuddered at the notion that possession of a football team housed in a luxurious stadium conferred legitimacy and major-league status, but in an entertainment-driven era a city could not be great without an appropriately magnificent sports cathedral.

American cities have used sports franchises to build civic pride since the nineteenth century. The stadium disputes in Boston, however, occurred against a backdrop of antagonism between cities and teams and a developing belief that losing a professional team damaged a town's stature. By the 1990s, free agency applied to teams as well as athletes, as owners showed an ever-greater willingness to relocate whenever a more lucrative offer came along. Experts have long doubted the economic impact of professional sports, but cities that lost teams felt the sting of abandonment nonetheless.

Brooklyn has never been the same since the Dodgers left in 1958. Leaders of cities with deep economic and social problems seized on luring a team as a quick way to create a more positive atmosphere without having to address the complex and divisive issues that plagued them. As cities battled for teams, it seemed easy to determine which were winners and which were losers, which were on the rise and which were on the decline. Baltimore without the Colts—loser. Indianapolis with the Colts—winner. Hartford without the Whalers—on the decline. North Carolina with the Hurricanes—on the rise. Savvy team owners usually exploited this leverage to the fullest.

The New England Patriots almost became famous for having nothing remarkable about them. Great players were few and far between. Great moments, at least before 2001, were practically nonexistent. Some teams symbolize the character of their home towns—the gritty Pittsburgh Steelers, the rowdy Oakland Raiders, the larger-than-life Dallas Cowboys—but the Patriots were a team without an identity. Still, they acted as a powerful symbol in a different way. To citizens and politicians in Massachusetts, Connecticut, and Rhode Island, they represented a chance to have big-time status conferred upon them. The economic fruits of that status were questionable, but politicians were willing to bet millions that they would materialize.

Professional football has always struggled to find a home in the sports-saturated Hub. Most of its professional sports teams—the Sox, the Bruins, the Celtics—seem to have been born with the city and are as integral to its fabric as Puritans and Brahmins. Harvard and Boston College football also have deep roots and symbolically serve as the athletic representatives of its Puritan and Catholic past. NFL franchises, however, have come and gone without leaving a mark—and without raising concerns about the city's overall health. The Bulldogs relocated from Pennsylvania in 1929 only to be wiped out by the Depression. George Marshall's Redskins replaced them in 1932 but jumped to Washington, D.C., in 1937. The Yanks made a brief visit in the 1940s before moving to New York. Rival professional leagues also failed in the Boston market. The American Football League's Boston Bulldogs (1926) lasted less than one year. The Shamrocks (1936–37) and the Bears (1940) suffered similar fates.[2]

There was no reason to expect that the Boston Patriots would have more success than their predecessors. Jilted in their 1959 quest for an NFL franchise, Texans Lamar Hunt and Bud Adams lined up seven ownership groups for a rival AFL but needed an eighth to fill out the league. Hunt called Billy Sullivan, president of the Metropolitan Petroleum Company, a leader in Boston's civic and church affairs, and a lifelong sports fan. Sullivan had recently headed an effort to persuade NFL commissioner Bert Bell to transfer the Chicago Cardinals to Boston. Bell's sudden death, however, left the league too disorganized to consider franchise shifts. Hunt's call gave him another chance to own a team. Sullivan had a good job title but was hardly a baron. Paying the $25,000 franchise fee left him $17,000 in debt. He had to bring in nine partners at $25,000 apiece and sell nonvoting shares of stock to purchase equipment and pay player salaries. The franchise hung by a financial thread when it took the field in 1960.[3]

The Boston Patriots opened their preseason on July 30, 1960, and crushed the Buffalo Bills 28–7. The ninety-degree heat in Buffalo may have limited the crowd to 16,000, but the low media turnout—only two of Boston's five papers bothered to send a reporter—was due to apathy rather than temperature. The Patriots were virtually unknown in the city and the region; one area hotel clerk assumed that the team's reservation was for "one of those crackpot right-wing organizations like the John Birch Society." They received far less attention than the Red Sox and barely even found a niche within the city's football market. Knowing that they could not compete with college football on Saturdays and televised New York Giants games on Sunday, the Patriots played most of their home games on Fridays.[4]

They outdrew most AFL clubs, eventually attracting more than 28,000 a game, yet struggled to break even. Tough economics forced Sullivan to minimize expenses, demoralizing his players and solidifying the AFL's image as a "Mickey Mouse League." The team could not compete with the NFL for players and had no coordinated scouting system. Players sat on milk crates to study game films projected on bedsheets. Sullivan never sent his team on the road until the last minute so he could save on meal money. On one trip to Buffalo, players were told to either sleep on top of their bedding in their hotel rooms or be fined, as Sullivan had negotiated a discounted rate if they did not dirty the linens.[5]

The Patriots were hardly the only AFL team with financial woes. What made them unique was their inability to find a permanent home. While Boston's other teams have played in some of the country's most famous arenas, efforts to construct a stadium for professional football floundered for decades. Mayor Maurice Tobin proposed a million-dollar facility in 1939 but found little support for the project, and not even legendary Mayor James Curley could get a 75,000-seat stadium built in South Boston's Columbus Park in the 1940s. City Councilor Sonny McDonough's 1948 proposal for an 86,000-seat stadium also died on the drawing board. Mayor John Collins, a friend of Sullivan's, pressured Boston University to allow the Patriots to play in the Boston Braves' old stadium, which the school had taken over when the team relocated to Milwaukee. Soon afterward he announced plans for a $25 million privately financed stadium and convention hall in South Boston. Sullivan spent $6,000 on a model of the stadium, which was supposed to open in 1962, but that was as far as the project got.[6]

Collins's proposed stadium was part of a general downtown revival. Mayor John Hynes had launched revitalization in the mid-1950s, uniting the Brahmins and the Irish—"the people who owned Boston" and "the people who ran Boston"—behind the common cause of restoring the city to greatness. In a controversial move that left old-line neighborhoods forever suspicious of new development, he tore down ethnically and culturally diverse neighborhoods in the West End and replaced them with high-rent apartments, shopping centers, and parking lots. Collins followed Hynes into office with promises of a "New Boston." Relying heavily on Great Society–era federal funding, the mayor spearheaded the Government Center and Prudential Center projects and directed a $100 million makeover of the waterfront area.[7]

A downtown football stadium was supposed to be one of the jewels of the New Boston, but no one could agree on a plan. Twenty-seven stadium proposals foundered amid protests from area residents or disputes over funding mechanisms. An oppositional city council further complicated matters. By the late 1960s, most members of the council were committed to protecting their districts from the bold designs that had ripped up the West End in the 1950s and zealously asserted their authority over a series of activist mayors. The state legislature only added to the difficulties, as members from outlying districts rarely voted for any project that solely benefited Boston.[8]

So the Patriots lived a fugitive existence, seeking refuge in one safe house after another. They had no regular practice field. They scrimmaged on an East Boston public school field until local politicians accused them of depriving children of a playground. Harvard allowed them to play a few games in its stadium but permitted the use of only the visitors' locker room. The Patriots dressed in a nearby Ramada Inn and met under the stands at halftime. Boston University evicted the team after Sullivan paid for a new press box and remodeled the locker rooms. The Yawkeys allowed the Patriots to play in Fenway Park and even let them put in a new scoreboard and playing surface. The stadium's cozy confines, however, limited attendance revenue, a fact that hardly endeared it to AFL owners. Moreover, because the Red Sox selected game dates first, the Patriots often spent long stretches on the road early in the season. The Sox also grumbled that their tenants tore up their field. Boston College took in the peripatetic club in 1969, but this partnership also fell apart; BC complained of illegally parked cars and rowdy fans on campus during games, the athletic department objected to sharing its facilities, and student ushers claimed that the team never paid them. The school shut the Patriots out after a single year to avoid being "stuck with them forever."[9]

The union of the AFL and NFL brought matters to a head. The merger agreement required that each team play in a stadium seating at least 46,200 (not coincidentally the capacity of George Halas's home, Wrigley Field) by the spring of 1970. Sullivan hoped to move into Harvard Stadium, which held about 40,000, and expand it to meet the requirement. Harvard was of a different mind. Citing the "fundamental incompatibility" between "professional and amateur athletic contests," university president Nathan Pusey rejected Sullivan's request to use the school's facilities. Pusey was also eager to avoid the kind of disruptions that the Patriots had caused on BC's campus.[10]

Many Bostonians reacted angrily to Harvard's snub, often for reasons that transcended sports. *Boston Globe* sportswriter Bud Collins mocked Pusey's "patronizingly hilarious" objections and demanded that the community mobilize against his Ivy League arrogance. Mayor Kevin White, another activist executive and revitalization advocate, blasted Harvard for its "hardened indifference to community problems" and hinted that the city might have to revisit its tax-exempt status. The state legislature organized hearings in January 1970 to consider a bill to take Harvard Stadium by eminent domain. Sullivan again raised the class issue in his testimony supporting the bill, declaring that "not everybody had the privilege of going to Harvard" and demanding that the school share a tiny piece of its tax-free domain. The Joint Legislative Committee on Federal Financial Assistance voted twenty to one to strip the stadium from Harvard, but the movement soon stalled. Sullivan backed away from his combative stance, and Governor Francis Sargent refused to support the action. The bill, moreover, clearly violated the state constitution, which granted Harvard permanent rights over its properties. With Harvard and the governor holding firm, House Speaker David Bartley gave up on the plan and shifted the blame to the government, demanding that the state "cut the comedy and get some leadership."[11]

The comedy seemed unlikely to end by the NFL's March 15 deadline for finalizing stadium plans. The owners of Fenway Park, the only viable alternative to a new stadium, resisted demands to let the Patriots back in. "We own Fenway Park," insisted Red Sox general manager Dick O'Connell, "and we pay taxes on it . . . I'm sick of hearing about the Patriots." Nor did Bostonians seem overly concerned about the Patriots' plight. One poll showed that only 51 percent of Bostonians considered keeping the Patriots to be "important" or "very important." Thirty percent declared that keeping the team was "not important at all." *Boston Evening Globe* writer Bruce Davidson considered the team's likely departure "regrettable, but hardly fatal."[12]

Sullivan bristled at the lack of support for his team. "We've paid more for the privilege of being affectionate to the city of Boston than any other sports team in the country today," he complained. Public apathy forced him to consider outside offers. He pondered bids from Tampa, Memphis, Seattle, Birmingham, Jacksonville, and Portland even as he championed a drive to convert Dorchester's 10,000-seat, school-owned White Stadium into a 50,000-seat complex. The proposal met with strong resistance. School committee chairman Joseph Lee alleged that spectator sports made America "a weak nation" and refused to cooperate. The largely black Dorchester population also organized. In a time of escalating racial tensions in the city and ongoing concerns about the power of the government over minority neighborhoods, area activists saw the plan as an effort to replace a "major recreational area of the Black Community" with "a maze of parking lots, concrete and astroturf" that would benefit only the Patriots. Unwilling to provoke controversy and racial antagonism, Mayor White also opposed the idea.[13]

The governor and other political leaders said they would support a stadium plan, but no one took charge. In early February, however, a new hope emerged from an unlikely quarter. Former St. Louis Browns chief Bill Veeck, the owner of Suffolk Downs racetrack in East Boston, approached Mayor White and Governor Sargent with an idea to fund a new stadium with profits generated from twelve days of racing added to his track's annual schedule. White, who had his eyes on the governor's office and wanted favorable publicity, treated the suggestion as a done deal and told a hastily assembled press conference that the track would fund a $16 million facility in Neponset, about two miles south of downtown. Unwilling to let White take sole credit for the project, Governor Sargent called his own press conference to announce the same deal.[14]

The news cheered Patriots fans and stunned Boston and Massachusetts politicians, who had not been consulted. Already angered by being kept in the dark, legislators in districts near the Neponset site howled about the "traffic bottlenecks" a new stadium would produce and again raised the specter of enormous construction projects obliterating working-class neighborhoods. Many objected to using gambling money to construct a public facility. Number-crunching legislators also recognized that some state money would be needed to complete the stadium. Representatives from outside Boston resisted spending state money to assist the city. Veeck, who was only trying to help, was astonished at how swiftly the mire of Massachusetts politics sucked him in. "I should have known better than to get involved when one mentions 'stadium' in Boston," he lamented, "especially in an election year."[15]

As NFL owners debated the Patriots' future, Mayor White and Boston Redevelopment Authority (BRA) chairman John Warner, a White appointee, launched a citywide public relations campaign to boost the Neponset stadium but could not persuade residents of its value or ease their resentment about not having been consulted before the plan was announced. "Nobody spoke to us at all," complained one antistadium leader, "and we don't like it. We don't consider ourselves second-class citizens." The proposal encountered more problems when it was brought before the Boston City Council. Besides taking issue with the plan's economics, the nine-member group had plenty of political motives for stalling. In the brutal game of Boston and Massachusetts politics, football issues became, well, a political football. Some of the council members had run against White for mayor and resented their loss enough that they refused to work with him. White's enemies on the council also knew of his gubernatorial ambitions and did not want him to get credit for a headline-grabbing project. Some harbored ambitions of winning the mayor's chair but knew that, should White become governor, he would back BRA chairman Warner for the position.[16]

With all this activity, it took a few days for anyone to pay much attention to what was happening in Foxboro, a sleepy town midway between Boston and Providence, Rhode Island. On March 17 E. M. Loew, a movie-theater mogul and the president of Bay State Raceway, told the Foxboro Board of Selectmen that he was willing to give the Patriots land to build a stadium next to his horse-racing track on Route 1 in exchange for a cut of the team's parking revenue. Foxboro voters informally approved Loew's offer by a four-to-one ratio in a door-to-door poll taken on March 22. The vote eased the pressure on the Boston City Council by providing hope that a stadium would be built even if the city refused to pay for one. Freed from fears of voter retribution, on the day after the Foxboro poll the council voted seven to two to kill the stadium. An embittered Sullivan blamed the city for forcing the team to leave and acidly hoped that it would forever enjoy the "rat-infested dump" that could have been turned into a stadium.[17]

The Patriots accepted Foxboro's offer on April 4, pending the town's formal approval of Loew's land grant. The outcome was never really in doubt, as Foxboro's advisory board, planning board, financial committee, and Board of Selectmen all backed the plan. For them, football was a way to put their town on the map. It promised new revenue for the town, a boost to local business, and abundant free advertising for the community. The citizenry assembled on April 13 in the Foxboro High School gym and approved the proposition 1,852–84. The decision nearly reduced Sullivan to tears. After a decade of wandering, his Patriots had a home. With the Foxboro deal finalized, Harvard relented and allowed the team to use its facilities for the 1970 season.[18]

The stadium package did little for the Patriots other than give them a home. The team agreed to pay Foxboro 25 cents for every admission, up to $100,000, and an annual rental fee of $300,000, plus an additional $40,000 a year for office space. A five-man Stadium Realty Trust (SRT) covered construction costs by issuing $5 million worth of stock and taking out an additional $2 million in loans. In exchange, the Patriots gave the SRT 11 percent of their first $400,000 in gross stadium revenues and 5 percent of the gross over $400,000. The deal limited the Patriots' chances of earning any substantial profits, but Sullivan had to sign on to keep the team in the Boston area.[19]

Crews broke ground in Foxboro on September 23, 1970, just 326 days before the first scheduled game. Good weather, good road access, and good digging conditions sped construction along, as did the stadium's very basic nature. Schaeffer Stadium—the brewery kicked in $1.4 million for the name—cost only $6.7 million, at a time when stadiums generally went for around $40 million. It was no frills all the way, a facility designed "for durability and maintenance rather than luxury." It had no fancy clubhouse, no private boxes, and no extra practice fields. Press facilities and team offices were rudimentary. Only 5,604 well-connected fans got to sit in chairs. The other 55,363 had to arrange themselves on 15.7 miles of aluminum benches —eighteen inches for each backside in the house. Still, the rising walls brought new life to the club. Season ticket sales jumped from 7,000 to over 50,000, and in the first year the team jumped from the bottom of the NFL in attendance to the top three. The move from Boston made the Patriots a regional attraction that drew from Massachusetts, Connecticut, and Rhode Island. Reflecting this fact, they changed their name to the Bay State Patriots, then to the New England Patriots after newspapers started calling them the "B. S. Patriots."[20]

The Patriots opened Schaeffer Stadium on August 15, 1971, with an exhibition game against the New York Giants. The United States Marine Band gave a pregame concert, followed by a 150-man barbershop choral group, a parade of area Minutemen, and a tribute to the recently deceased Vince Lombardi. The Patriots did their job by beating the Giants 20–14. Sullivan called it "the greatest night of my life." There were no seat numbers on the benches and no mirrors in the locker room, some of the women's bathrooms were not working, and most concession booths were out of food by halftime, but the stadium was a hit.[21]

The problem was the traffic. Officials had promised motorists that getting in and out of the stadium would be "a smooth operation," but the night turned into a "traffic holocaust." Six million people lived within fifty miles of the stadium, and it seemed as if all of them were on the highway.

With "grossly inadequate" access roads along Route 1, drivers became
snarled in a line that eventually stretched for five miles. According to sportswriter Ray Fitzgerald, it looked like "the last road out of a town after the announcement that Godzilla had just swallowed City Hall and was looking
for dessert." Hundreds of cars overheated on the road, and frustrated fans
abandoned hundreds more to walk the remaining miles to the stadium.
Thousands never made it to the game.[22]

The police eventually worked out the worst of the traffic problems, but
the drive to and from the stadium and the long waits in the parking lot always provided ample time for drinking and violence both inside and outside of Schaeffer. Disorderly Patriots backers tormented visiting teams. Fans
especially loved to cut hot dogs in half, let them freeze, then whip them at
the players as they entered and exited the field. Things sometimes got
much worse. One rowdy 1976 game against the Jets featured a stabbing and
more than sixty arrests for fighting. A drunken patron urinated on a medic
assisting a heart-attack victim, and frustrated drivers began building bonfires after being trapped in the parking lot for two hours.[23]

The next generation saw its share of chaos within the Patriots organization. In 1974 the Board of Directors, tired of Sullivan's micromanaging and
long-windedness and disgusted by the team's 27–54–3 record since moving
into Schaeffer, deposed him as team president. He received no severance
pay, no pension, and no recognition of his service. In a final insult, the
stockholders moved his seat from the front of Schaeffer's owner's box to the
back. Sullivan and his son, Chuck, regained control over the team the following year, but had to go millions of dollars into debt to buy out the other
directors and the holders of the nonvoting shares the team had issued in
1960.[24]

The Sullivans next moved to purchase the stadium from the SRT. Billy
Sullivan was the trust's largest shareholder, but was displeased with its operation, especially its failure to aggressively pursue the concerts and other
events it needed in order to turn a profit. The Foxboro government was
partly to blame for this, as it generally refused to allow potentially disruptive
acts into the quiet town. With the SRT running dry, the Patriots, who paid
the second-highest rent in the NFL, also had to shell out for Schaeffer's up-
keep. The team was already deep in debt as a result of low attendance
caused by poor play, and the Sullivans could not afford to keep subsidizing

the SRT. Financed by more loans, Chuck bought out the other shareholders in 1981. The Sullivan family now owned the Patriots and the stadium outright (and renamed it Sullivan Stadium), but Chuck's purchase of and subsequent upgrades to the facility cost $15 million that it did not have.[25]

Chuck Sullivan's decision to expand into music promotion seemed like a logical move. He owned a large venue and had promoted concerts in college. He brought such popular acts as David Bowie and the Police to Foxboro, but his decision to become the tour promoter for 1984's Jackson Family Victory Tour proved disastrous. Chuck vastly overpaid for the right to promote the tour, promising the Jacksons 83.44 percent of the "gross potential ticket proceeds"—in other words, what they would earn if every show completely sold out—and covering the tour's $1 million a week in overhead expenses. He had to put up Sullivan Stadium as collateral for the enormous loans he took out to cover his commitments. The concert tour became one of the biggest debacles in music history. Few shows sold out, and, in a final insult, Foxboro's selectmen prohibited the Jacksons from playing in Chuck's stadium for fear of attracting "undesirable crowds." Chuck lost millions on the tour, then tried to make it up by paying $18 million for the merchandising rights to Jacksons-related clothing. Michael Jackson promptly withdrew from the public eye for three years, and the Jackson fad collapsed, leaving Chuck even further in debt.[26]

Chuck's music business was losing money, the stadium was losing money, and the Patriots were losing money. The team went to the Super Bowl in January 1987 and still lost $9 million dollars that season. All told, the gregarious and likable Sullivans had managed to parley a $25,000 investment on a football team into $126 million worth of debt.[27]

The Sullivans desperately needed cash. They put the Patriots and Sullivan Stadium up for sale in December 1986 and soon struck a deal to borrow $21 million from a group led by Philadelphia restaurant owner Fran Murray in exchange for a three-year option to buy the Patriots for $63 million. Murray tried to exercise the option, but the Sullivans hesitated to give up their team even as their finances spiraled out of control. Chuck and Billy Sullivan postponed payment on several loans, Chuck's Stadium Management Corporation declared bankruptcy to protect the stadium from being auctioned off by its creditors, and the team had to borrow almost $4 million from the NFL in January 1988 to pay player salaries. The NFL finally intervened in March 1988, placing control of the team in the hands of a four-man committee entrusted with "wartime powers" over the future of the franchise. The Sullivans finally sold the Patriots in October 1988 to Victor Kiam and Fran Murray for $80 million.[28]

Kiam, the majority owner, had led a remarkable turnaround of the Remington shaving company and hoped to do the same with the Patriots. His tenure as owner, however, proved to be a financial disaster. His biggest mistake was failing to purchase Sullivan Stadium when he bought the team. His $19 million offer was topped by a group called K Corp, comprised of Robert Kraft and Steve Karp, which offered $25 million. Kraft, a longtime fan of Boston sports, had considered buying the team as well, but decided that the stadium was a better deal. As a stadium owner, he remarked, "you go to the game, and if the Patriots lose, you're disappointed for about 45 minutes. Then you ask, 'How much popcorn did we sell?'" K Corp sold a lot of popcorn. It extracted about $5 million a year from the stadium, largely because of the Patriots' punitive lease, which granted K Corp all of the team's concession, parking, and advertising revenue, demanded $1.2 million a year in rent (one of the highest in the NFL), and required the Patriots to hire security and clean up the stadium after games. This deal had been fine when the Sullivans owned both the team and the stadium, but it was ruinous for Kiam. The Patriots lost between $5 and $6 million dollars a year during his tenure.[29]

With Remington losing market share to Braun and Norelco and the Patriots hemorrhaging money, Kiam had to get out fast. In 1992 he sold the team to St. Louis multimillionaire James Orthwein, a member of the Busch beermaking family, for $106 million. The new owner also headed a group seeking an expansion franchise in St. Louis and claimed that he wanted to own the Patriots only until his hometown obtained a new team. The plot went awry when the NFL awarded new franchises to Charlotte and Jacksonville. Suddenly the odds of the Patriots remaining in Foxboro seemed long. Many assumed that Orthwein would relocate the team to St. Louis, but this option bore consequences that he could not accept. K Corp had an iron-clad lease and was willing to sue if the team broke it. In addition, August A. Busch III was pressuring his cousin not to move for fear of a boycott of Anheuser-Busch products throughout New England. Orthwein had little choice but to put the team on the market. The stadium had destroyed another owner.[30]

A new party got involved in September 1993, when Connecticut governor Lowell Weicker called the State Assembly into special session to consider building a stadium to lure the Patriots to Hartford, 60 miles southwest of Foxboro and 105 miles from Boston. It was still unclear who would buy the team—both former minority owner Fran Murray and novelist Tom Clancy were reportedly gathering investors—yet Weicker saw "potentially great benefit" for his state in the disorder up north. Many legislators feared that the Patriots were using Hartford to force Massachusetts to build a new stadium and help the team escape from its lease and questioned whether the state should subsidize a football team when the capital city was beset with gangs, crumbling schools, and layoffs in key industries. But most political leaders went along with the governor's $252 million plan. No money would actually be spent on construction until the Patriots committed to moving, and the prospect of making Hartford a big-time city assuaged concerns that the stadium would be a white elephant. Republican assemblyman Andrew McCall Norton rejected the notion that "even though the state is in bad times we must put on a hair shirt and never enthusiastically grab at something that might give a bit of pleasure to some people." The General Assembly passed the stadium bill on September 27.[31]

The doings in Connecticut inspired panic in Massachusetts. Long known for their apathy, Patriots fans rallied behind the team. "It was as if," wrote Sports Illustrated's Leigh Montville, "the plainest Jane in the secretarial pool suddenly removed her glasses after 33 years on the job and now was an unbelievable object of attention." Orthwein had hired gifted head coach Bill Parcells in January, and Drew Bledsoe, the team's first pick in the April draft, had the makings of a franchise quarterback. Now was not the time to lose the team. Weicker's proposed grab reawoke efforts to build a $700 million "Megaplex" in Boston that would include baseball and football stadiums and a much-needed convention center. Orthwein knew that he needed a new stadium to stay competitive and had lobbied for the Megaplex since the summer. Declaring that the Patriots would leave the state "over my dead body," Governor William Weld strongly backed the project as well.[32]

This apparent consensus brought Robert Kraft into the picture. Kraft had grown up in a tough Jewish area of Brookline and was devoted to Boston and Boston sports. He had owned Patriots season tickets since 1972, the year he took over his father-in-law's packaging company, Rand-Whitney, and launched International Forest Products. His privately owned holdings produced around $500 million in revenue a year. He wanted the Patriots to remain in the Boston area but realized that his antiquated stadium was inadequate for their needs. After Governor Weld assured him that the Megaplex would become a reality, he bought the team in January 1994 for $172 million. Mayor Thomas Menino promised those attending the ceremony marking the purchase that the team's return to Boston was imminent. Kraft's insistence that the team would not leave the area killed Hartford's plan to snatch away the Patriots.[33]

Kraft was a shrewd businessman, and he should have known better than to mistake politicians' promises for reality. Menino and Weld could coo in his ear forever, but they could not pass the Megaplex alone. Even though Kraft offered to make a substantial financial commitment—$215 million at one point—the proposal, like so many before it, broke up on the rocks of neighborhood politics. Kraft and Mayor Menino wanted the Megaplex in South Boston. Weld wanted it in Roxbury. Neither South Boston nor Roxbury wanted the Megaplex. Facing unyielding resistance, supporters shifted to alternative sites. Boston Navy Yard, Back Bay, North Station, and Neponset emerged as candidates, but the public, the mayor, and the owner could not agree on a location. Fearing a voter backlash that would cripple his reelection campaign, Menino bailed out in August 1995 and destroyed any chance of passing the Megaplex.[34]

With the Megaplex battle lost, Kraft redoubled his efforts to build a stand-alone stadium in South Boston, and he was willing to pay for it himself. Weld advised him to keep the project under wraps to avoid another firestorm and assured him that he, Weld, would win Menino's support. With secrecy appropriate to the development of a new weapon, Kraft began drawing up designs and lining up potential luxury-box tenants, but word of his project leaked in December 1996. South Boston erupted yet again as residents complained of being excluded from plans that could ruin their neighborhood. Menino was also furious about being kept in the dark—Weld had never fulfilled his promise to get the mayor's support—and, with one eye on South Boston voters, blasted the proposed stadium as "bad urban planning." Kraft was exasperated. He saw himself as the franchise's savior and could not understand why the city prevented him from keeping the team in the area. Trying to build a stadium in Boston, he moaned, was

more perilous than "going out to buy groceries in downtown Beirut." Powerful area bankers, who stood to gain from any expensive redevelopment
projects, also came out against stadium detractors. "Menino doesn't have vision," observed one anonymous plutocrat, "and the neighborhood [South
Boston] is parochial." Even the NFL got in on the action. The league
elected to make Providence, not Boston, the official host of the 1997 AFC
championship game between the Patriots and the Jacksonville Jaguars, a
move that Menino and others saw as a warning to play ball. "I guess Pawtucket was already booked," the mayor chortled. When Foxboro Stadium's
lights went out for eleven minutes during the game, some in the mayor's
party "hooted and jeered" at what they saw as a bush-league prank to high-
light the facility's inadequacies.[35]

The relationship between Kraft and Massachusetts politicians had
reached the breaking point. The owner was unused to the world of politics,
which he believed should operate like the world of business. He wanted
commitments instead of consideration, and his propensity for ill-timed
comments, such as threatening to move the team on Super Bowl Sunday
1995, did little to endear him to policymakers. He lost his only real ally
when Weld resigned in July 1997 to rally support for his nomination as ambassador to Mexico, and even he was losing patience with Kraft, who demanded direct and immediate access to the governor and treated his staff
with disdain. Menino's desire to assist the stadium efforts evaporated after Kraft declared that the mayor's "elevator doesn't go all the way to the
top floor." The owner also made an intractable enemy of House Speaker
Thomas Finneran, a conservative Democrat who ran the House as his personal fiefdom. The Speaker was suspicious of deals cut with elites and was
hypersensitive to anything that smelled of corporate welfare. Rumor had it
that Finneran particularly despised the Patriots owner because Mrs. Kraft
had once backed a political rival. The Speaker firmly believed that "citizens
should pay for their own entertainment, and franchise owners should not
ask the public for tribute." He responded to Kraft's pleas for state assistance
by deriding him as a "whining multimillionaire." As long as Finneran dominated the House, the Patriots had little chance of getting political support
for a new stadium.[36]

The Massachusetts stadium effort was revitalized only by a new threat to
relocate the team. In January 1997 Kraft invited Rhode Island governor Lin-

coln Almond to a playoff game, and the two discussed the possibility of the Patriots moving to Providence. A few days later Kraft considered stadium plans over dinner with the mayor of Providence, Vincent "Buddy" Cianci. Almond's staff began studying stadiums in other cities in preparation for their own proposal. The governor announced his support in July for a Providence stadium and, following another period of private negotiations with Kraft, laid a plan on the table in September. It envisioned a $250 million project that included about $130 million in public bonds, to be repaid through player income taxes, the team's corporate taxes, and a 7 percent surcharge on every ticket. Kraft would put up the rest of the money himself (although his share would be partly covered by the sale of $43 million worth of personal seat licenses that essentially required fans to "pay for the right to pay for the right to see a football game") and would be responsible for $95 million in lease payments over the life of the 68,000-seat facility. Kraft was also required to build a hotel, sports museum, shopping, and restaurant complex on the site—not much of a requirement, as he got the land for nothing and got to keep all of the profits it produced.[37]

Former governor Michael S. Dukakis denounced Providence's grab at the team as "an outrage," but few in Massachusetts seemed to care. After all, Providence was "just down the road." "It's not like the Patriots are moving to Connecticut," remarked one Bostonian. "They'll still be considered a Boston team." Others simply did not believe that Kraft would take the team out of the city he loved so much. He wanted to be the hero of Boston, columnist Mike Barnicle claimed, not of Providence, a town established "so travelers between New York and Boston might have a roadside rest area where pets could relieve themselves." The players seemed similarly unconcerned. Cornerback Jimmy Hitchcock insisted that it made "no difference" where he played so long as the stadium had a grass surface.[38]

Rhode Islanders did not exactly fall all over themselves to back the governor's plan. Many felt that Providence did not need a football team, certainly not one that cost millions to acquire. *Providence Journal-Bulletin* columnist Bob Kerr accused Almond of wasting money on an expensive project with a dubious economic impact. "Most of the time it [the stadium] just takes up room," he argued. "It doesn't make things happen. It doesn't set off a land rush of businessmen eager to put their factories and stores next door." He and others suspected that Almond wanted to produce a big trophy that he could wield in future political campaigns. Smith Hill, the ethnically diverse neighborhood picked for construction, also rose in opposition. "Who wants to live in the shadows of the stadium?" asked one resident. Residents protested the noise, litter, drugs, alcohol, traffic, and rowdy crowds that they believed Almond's project would spawn. Perhaps most damaging was the governor's opposition to submitting the proposal to a statewide referendum. As a candidate in 1994, Almond had objected to creating a parking garage in Providence without a vote, but now his fears of dragging the process out so long that Kraft would go elsewhere led him to shut citizens out of the stadium debate.[39]

The Rhode Island plan also sparked a battle for publicity and political turf between Almond and Mayor Cianci. Cianci was, to put it mildly, a colorful figure. He had served as mayor during the 1980s, resigning after he beat up his wife's lover and burned his face with cigarettes. After receiving a five-year suspended sentence, he became a popular radio talk-show host, then rode his blue-collar support to reelection in 1990. He was a man of questionable character and questionable friends who provoked nothing but scorn in Boston. Mike Barnicle labeled him "the only mayor in America with his own line of marinara and hair borrowed from Lassie. He is also one of the few who wear suits made of Valvoline and surround themselves with guys who appear to bathe in pesto sauce." Buddy Cianci had no deep love for Lincoln Almond and constantly tried to upstage him during the stadium negotiations. He supported the plan, but wanted everyone to know who was really in charge of the city. He demanded more input in the talks and threatened to "stop the whole thing" if the parties reached a deal without him.[40]

With Cianci nipping at his heels and Kraft nitpicking over details, Almond had a difficult time gaining traction for the stadium plan. Even so, Rhode Island's maneuvering inspired new action in Massachusetts. Paul Cellucci, serving as acting governor following Weld's departure, tried to stay out of the controversy but eventually got dragged into the fray. With Providence poised to steal the Patriots, Cellucci's probable opponents in the 1998 election began hammering him for the lack of "strong, focused leadership" on Beacon Hill. The Republican Cellucci did his best to deflect the criticism to the obstructionist Democratic Speaker, Tom Finneran, while preparing a counterproposal. He unveiled his plan to keep the team in Foxboro in a late-September news conference. Cellucci offered the team $50 million in public bonds to purchase land and pay for infrastructure improvements around Foxboro Stadium. Kraft would then pay $50 million to renovate the old facility. There were no representatives from the Patriots present, nor was Finneran anywhere to be found.[41]

It did not seem like much of an offer compared with Rhode Island's, but no one knew what Kraft would do next. Mike Barnicle thought the whole thing was hilarious. "It doesn't get any better than this," he told readers. "Three Italians [Cellucci, Cianci, and Menino], an Irishman [Finneran], and one swamp Yankee [Almond] all trying to bite each other's noses off over what one Jewish guy [Kraft] might—or might not—do." Almond mocked Cellucci's plan, telling Kraft that if he wanted "to buy a new car rather than a used car, he can buy the new car. The new car is in the showroom." And yet the used car was enough to derail negotiations with Rhode Island. Despite his public show of confidence, Almond worried that his state would end up paying more of the stadium's cost than he was comfortable with. Facing reelection in 1998, he was also fearful of stirring up voters. The lack of popular support in Rhode Island worried Kraft, too; he saw that he would lose his deal should Almond lose the upcoming election. In addition, he believed that the state was demanding too much money from him and was too reluctant to give him all the free land he wanted to build his complex. Both sides walked away from the deal in early October.[42]

Just in case the team had forgotten his position, Mayor Menino immediately reminded everyone that Boston was not an option for a new stadium. And so Kraft and his son, Patriots vice-president Jonathan Kraft, huddled with Massachusetts Senate president Thomas Birmingham and emerged with a deal to provide $52 million in state money for infrastructure improvements and $20 million to buy land around the stadium from Kraft. In exchange Kraft agreed to pay a $700,000-a-year lease and spend $220 million to build a new Foxboro facility. The package cruised through the Senate, 36–1, then ran into a brick wall in the House. Finneran objected to the land-buyback provision of the bill and showed no eagerness to work out an amended arrangement. Birmingham was "befuddled" by his fellow Democrat's intransigence and looked on helplessly as the Speaker kept the bill off the schedule.[43]

A new avenue opened up in May 1998, when Kraft learned of Connecticut governor John Rowland's plan to spend $1 billion to renovate the Adriaen's Landing area of Hartford. Kraft and Rowland had a friendly relationship and had informally mused about moving the team to Hartford. Now the Patriots' owner wanted to talk in earnest. The two worked out an agreement in private, then went public with a signing ceremony before a packed Old Judiciary Room in the State Capitol on November 18, 1998. Nobody expected the State Assembly to raise any problems. Jonathan Kraft considered it "a done deal, barring some circumstance of God." Hartford mayor Michael Peters declared that "we've got 10 yards to go with an open path to the end zone." For a city that had already lost the Patriots once, then lost the NHL's Whalers, then failed to land the Tampa Bay Buccaneers in 1995, Rowland's acquisition was no less than "a miracle." It was a chance for a city with a public image "somewhere between Gomorrah and Three Mile Island" to redefine itself and step into big-time status. It was an opportunity to give Boston, that "Big Apple wannabe," that "underarm of urbanity," a slap in the face. The *Hartford Courant*'s Jim Shea sarcastically wondered what the Patriots would do without their Boston fans. "Who is going to wander around stinking drunk?" he asked. "Pee in the stands? Start fights? Teach our children the latest off-color chants?"[44]

Some questioned Kraft's sincerity. The *Globe*'s Dan Shaughnessy insisted that a man with an ego as big as Kraft's would never trade in Boston for "the dead streets of America's Filing Cabinet" (a derisive reference to the many insurance companies headquartered in Hartford) and warned his neighbors to the south that they were "being used" to pressure Massachusetts. But most of Boston sensed that the Patriots were really leaving this time. Mayor Menino announced that he was sending Governor Rowland "a sympathy card" and dismissed the team's impending departure. "If it was the Red Sox," he laughed, "I'd be concerned." Finneran seconded the mayor's militant tone, declaring that he would never give tax breaks to "some fat-ass millionaire." Despite Finneran's bravado, he took the brunt of the blame for losing the Patriots.[45]

Rowland's plan offered $375 million for infrastructure improvements and a 68,000-seat stadium in downtown Hartford. In addition, the state offered $15 million to pay for a new practice facility and over $100 million to maintain the stadium over its thirty-year lease. It also guaranteed the sale of 125 luxury boxes and 6,000 expensive club seats—a provision that could cost taxpayers $17.5 million a year. Estimates suggested that Kraft would gross $100 million a year in stadium revenue. A few legislators privately voiced their concern that the deal was "overly generous" and wondered if the stadium would actually break even over its life. Rowland, however, stuck to his numbers while emphasizing the enormous psychological impact that winning the Patriots would have on the depressed city. He admitted that Hartford had deep economic troubles and crumbling schools, but envisioned Adriaen's Landing and the stadium that would be its showpiece as "the 800-pound gorilla" that would propel the city "into the next century."[46]

It soon became apparent that the plan would not pass without challenges. A study by the General Assembly's Office of Fiscal Analysis concluded that, far from breaking even, the project would cost taxpayers $257 million over thirty years. Close examination of the proposal revealed that it did not provide for adequate parking. Negotiations to remove a steam plant from the site also proved tricky. The plant heated and cooled most of Hartford's downtown, and its owners were not about to leave without what they saw as fair compensation. The site, moreover, was polluted with coal tar that would have to be removed before new construction could begin. Cleanup on a similar site in Atlantic City had taken four years and cost $14 million; such facts raised questions about how the state could meet its contractual obligation to open the stadium in 2001. Led by Connecticut resident Ralph Nader, oppositional citizens groups began coalescing. Deriding the governor as a "41-year-old twerp," Nader ripped the plan as "corporate socialism" and accused Kraft of stealing everything from the state except "the Capitol dome."[47]

Just as in Providence, the lack of debate on the measure made citizens worry that the stadium was being "shoved down our throats." There was only one public hearing on the bill, a four-hour "farce" dominated by prostadium lobbyists. The whitewash prompted the *Courant*'s Tom Condon to wonder whether this was all happening too fast. "This is a lot of money for an impulse buy," he fretted. Still, polls showed that a slight majority of Connecticut residents favored the plan, and it seemed likely to pass the legislature, which Rowland had called into special session to consider the bill.[48]

The Assembly met on December 13, just three days after NBC news featured the Hartford stadium on its "Fleecing of America" series. Though it forced some minor changes, most legislators lacked "a good grasp" of the plan. Representative Evelyn Mantilla voted for it despite her many reservations. "It's hard to be against it when you know the tide in favor is so strong," she explained. Just to be sure, Rowland spent the days leading up to the vote calling assemblymen into his office and twisting their arms to ensure a "yes" vote. The bill rolled through the Capitol on December 15. Connecticut had committed a lot for a football team, as the *Courant's* Jeff Jacobs recognized, but it was worth it. "This wasn't about football," he insisted. "It's about our future." Boston's Bob Ryan was more critical. "The ship of fools that is the Connecticut state legislature," he proclaimed, had "set sail" for the "Poor House."[49]

Although the game appeared to be over, there was actually much left to do. The $374 million bill that Rowland signed under the portrait of George Washington (the first Patriot, he joked) in the Old State House only established the outlines of the state's commitment to Kraft. It placed no binding commitments on Kraft. Negotiations between the state and the team continued in secret, and the two parties signed a 226-page development deal on February 12 at 1:10 A.M. Besides filling in the details of the financing, the agreement gave Kraft a number of chances to escape without penalty. Rowland believed that everything had been wrapped up. Kraft was more cautious—a Patriots spokesman called the signing merely "a significant milestone."[50]

The "shroud of secrecy" that cloaked the talks was troubling. State senator John Fonfara, the representative from the district where the stadium would be, had not seen the agreement before it was signed. Far more problematic, however, were the stalled negotiations over moving the CTC Re sources steam plant that sat in what was to be the south end zone of the new stadium. Rowland blustered about confiscating it through eminent domain, but no one had the stomach for the protracted legal struggle that would certainly ensue. The quasi-public Connecticut Resources Recovery Authority (CRRA), which converted trash into fuel around the state, was trying to work out a deal to take over CTG's heating and cooling contracts and pay for its move, but negotiations bogged down as both sides bickered about cleanup costs and relocation fees. Neither side seemed willing to budge despite intense pressure from the governor's office. The issue was not settled until early April.[51]

The site still had many problems. The soil-pollution issue remained unresolved, and developers had no idea what to do with the *Hartford*

Times building, a former newspaper office that now housed the city's fiber-optic network. Archaeologists were salivating at the prospect of digging in Adriaen's Landing, where they hoped to locate the remains of seventeenth-century settlers and perhaps even the home of Connecticut's founder, Thomas Hooker. A big find would bring the project to a standstill; one developer worried that "with our luck, there'll be a full Indian village under the steam plant." Most inexplicably, surveyors realized only in late April that the southwest corner of the stadium would hang over the Whitehead highway. This snafu would require either additional expense or moving the entire stadium. It was becoming obvious that Connecticut would not have a new stadium by 2001, as it had promised in the agreement, and even 2002 was an iffy proposition. Kraft was becoming impatient.[52]

Public backing for the Patriots' move began to erode as the project's enormous cost and limited economic returns settled into citizens' minds. Ralph Nader had helped to organize a group known as Stop the Stadium that spearheaded antistadium petitions and filed lawsuits against the plan. The press also grew more wary. In an increasingly typical piece, *Courant* political columnist Michele Jacklin condemned the secret negotiations, the exploding costs, and the one-sided nature of the deal. Kraft was set to become a "fabulously wealthy man," while Connecticut would receive only a vague psychic boost in return. Polls showed that support for the agreement and for Rowland was slipping.[53]

The NFL's entrance into the fray further disarrayed Rowland's plans. Commissioner Paul Tagliabue had endorsed the Hartford deal, then reversed his position in the spring of 1999, largely because of concerns about league revenue. The NFL feared that the movement of teams from large markets to smaller markets—the Los Angeles Rams to St. Louis, the Houston Oilers to Tennessee, the Cleveland Browns to Baltimore—would reduce the value of future television contracts. In March the league overwhelmingly passed Resolution G-2, which provided interest-free loans, to be repaid with the visiting team's share of club-seat revenue, to teams building stadiums in the six largest media markets. Boston was the sixth largest media market, and the NFL's vote made it financially possible for Kraft to construct a new stadium in Massachusetts. "This will be big for Boston," remarked one anonymous owner. "Most of us want that club to stay in Boston, and play in Boston." Kraft remained publicly committed to Hartford yet voted for G-2.[54]

The NFL was also moving behind the scenes to keep the team in the Boston area. Its private effort began in December 1998 after Steelers owner Dan Rooney listened to Kraft detail his stadium woes at an NFL owners' meeting. Rooney was horrified by the gridlock in the Hub and started working the phones to try to keep the team put. He got Tagliabue and Roger Goodell, the league's stadium expert, on board, then called Reverend J. Donald Monan, chancellor of Boston College and a powerful broker among the city's Irish executives. Monan put Rooney in touch with prominent area businessmen. Rooney's friend, Boston lawyer Paul Kirk, was also working the phones, and the two secretly put together a group called Operation Team Back. Most of the Team had connections to Boston College, where Cellucci and Finneran had attended law school, and all of them knew politics. The Team tried to convince state political leaders and the NFL that the business community would support a new stadium, then put the two parties in touch with each other. The veil of secrecy was lifted on April 16, when the Team revealed itself in a well-publicized *Boston Globe* editorial that informed readers that there was still "a window of opportunity" to keep the Patriots if Boston would only "rally to the cause."[55]

Kraft had an exclusive negotiating deal with Connecticut that prevented him from commenting on the new developments, but momentum was clearly shifting toward Boston as Tagliabue met with area business and political leaders in late April. Governor Cellucci and Speaker Finneran discussed stadium bills. Mayor Menino spoke vaguely but optimistically of a new Boston stadium, and Finneran told reporters that he was "very encouraged by the positive tone and direction" of the new talks—a meaningless statement, but friendlier than his earlier comments. After a series of closed-door conferences among Cellucci, Finneran, Senate president Birmingham, Kirk, and NFL executives, the state emerged with a plan that even Finneran could agree to. It called for the NFL and Kraft to finance a new stadium in Foxboro and the state to contribute $70 million in infrastructure improvements. The Patriots would pay $1.4 million a year to cover half of the state's financing costs.[56]

Few in Connecticut believed that this relatively stingy proposal would woo the Patriots back home. Kraft, however, remained ominously absent from the public eye. The agreement was in fact disintegrating. Kraft had to remain publicly silent, but Tagliabue would not have gotten involved without the powerful owner's approval. Partly because of his enormous ego and partly because of his loyalty to Boston, Kraft had always been reluctant to abandon the city. He worried about declining television revenues for the NFL—and, by extension, for himself—and questioned whether Hartford could sell out the scores of luxury boxes and thousands of club seats in the new stadium. His consultants, moreover, informed him that it would be impossible for Connecticut to complete the stadium by 2002. The team faced a May 2 deadline for exiting without penalty, and Kraft needed to make a decision. He explained his situation to Rowland and asked for an extension on his deadline. The governor was growing tired of Kraft's unwillingness to commit fully to the deal and refused. Still, he thought that both sides could work through their differences.[57]

Kraft announced the next day that the Patriots were not moving to Hartford. Even though he never mentioned Massachusetts, everyone assumed that this breakdown meant that the team would accept its offer. Connecticut was understandably livid. "No one walks away from a $374 million plan because a schedule might not hit the exact date he would like to see it happen," Rowland roared. He hinted at a lawsuit that would expose "the real reason" for Kraft's flip-flop. The Adriaen's Landing project was in chaos, and Hartford had suffered a "humbling blow." The *Courant*'s Jeff Jacobs branded the owner as "no better than a common tenement rat" and blasted the NFL for launching "the most withering and subversive attack by a major sports league on a single city in American history." The Boston press laughed at the losing city. "John Rowland is Charlie Brown," Dan Shaughnessy explained. "Bob Kraft is Lucy. And poor Charlie Brown is lying on his back because Lucy has pulled the football away at the last second. Again."[58]

The team announced a few days later that it would indeed remain in Massachusetts. Tagliabue returned to the Hub to ask business leaders to lease luxury boxes in the new stadium, and Finneran and Kraft at least pretended to shelve their personal animosities. The $70 million Massachusetts stadium/infrastructure bill, hailed by Finneran as "a model for the rest of the country," passed easily on May 18 after only one public hearing and very little debate. Hartford pushed forward with a scaled-down Adriaen's Landing project and elected to build a new stadium for the University of Connecticut just across the Connecticut River. Hoping to make amends (and avoid a lawsuit), the NFL sent Hartford a check for $2.4 million to cover the city's expenses from the Patriots project.[59]

The New England Patriots opened the 2002 season in brand-new $325 million Gillette Stadium, located just one-quarter mile from the ruins of Foxboro Stadium. It is a state-of-the-art facility bristling with giant video boards, television monitors, and sound speakers. The well-to-do can watch games from one of its eighty luxury boxes or 6,000 club seats. The owner who was willing to pay for his own stadium ended up paying very little. The NFL chipped in $150 million under its new stadium-financing system, and Kraft profited from his willingness to sell naming rights to everything except the players. The original sponsor, Andover-based direct marketing and investment company CMGI, offered $114 million over fifteen years for naming rights before bailing out as a result of the company's financial meltdown. The amount of Gillette's offer, which the company did not announce, is assumed to be similar to CMGI's. Kraft thought the deal made perfect sense. "The [Gillette] Mach 3 shaving system set new standards for consumers," he explained, "and the new Gillette Stadium is a major step forward in the design and construction of professional sports facilities." It was certainly a major step forward for commercialization. Visitors can park in the Taurus New England Ford Dealers Parking Lot, enter the stadium by way of the uBid.com Ramp, and relax in the Fidelity Investments Clubhouse. McDonald's ponied up $21 million to erect a restaurant near one end zone, and Pepsi signed up to be Gillette's official soft drink.[60]

The Patriots' new home will undoubtedly bring in huge revenues for Kraft, but Boston and Massachusetts can feel good that his profit will come at limited expense to them. Finneran's stubbornness, Boston's infighting, and Kraft's blustering produced a stadium deal that cost taxpayers much less than recent agreements struck in Baltimore, Cleveland, St. Louis, and Tennessee. Equally important, maintaining a professional sports franchise allowed Boston to preserve its status as a big-time city while denying Hartford the opportunity to improve its own status at the Hub's expense. Perhaps the classic Boston triumvirate of sports, politics, and revenge worked out for the best. Perhaps the bitter experience of building two homes for the Patriots taught the city, and other cities, important lessons in stadium building and urban politics. And perhaps we should wait for the completion of a new Fenway Park before suggesting that the Hub has finally figured it all out.

10

The Champion of All Champions:
John L. Sullivan

Elliott J. Gorn

The Irish who packed American cities by the hundreds of thousands in the 1850s were despised as an inferior race, as slavish followers of the pope, as destroyers of American democracy. So intense was this antipathy that a tidal wave of anti-immigrant sentiment broke over American politics in the mid-1850s and smashed the old party system, which had lasted since the time of Jefferson. Boston, arguably, was the most Irish city in America, and antagonisms there ran unusually high. Yet the Irish and their children were determined to make America their home, and by the final decades of the century they had attained modest success, mostly through steady work in trades like masonry, domestic service, and carting and hauling goods. Still, theirs was hardly a rags-to-riches story, and plenty of anti-Irish prejudice remained.[1]

From the perspective of the mid-nineteenth century, then, it was almost unimaginable that a son of Irish immigrants would become one of the most famous Americans of his era. Yet there he was, John L. Sullivan, prizefighting's heavyweight champion, who held that title from 1882 through 1892. In turn-of-the-century America it was considered an honor, as a popular song lyric put it, just to "shake the hand that shook the hand of Sullivan." His galvanic personality and his athletic achievements made him one of the nation's first true celebrities, and his status was affirmed by the fact that during his reign he became the first American athlete to earn more than one million dollars.[2]

Certainly no one would have predicted all of this for young Sullivan. A child of Irish working-class parents—his father was a hod-carrier—John's social horizons were very limited. Nor was Boston an obvious place to nurture colossal sporting achievements; New York City had much deeper athletic roots. Still, the solidarity of Boston's Irish, their unity in the face of strong social and cultural exclusion, gave Sullivan a base from which to launch his career.[3]

Sullivan's father, Mike, emigrated from County Kerry, and his mother, Catherine, from County Roscommon. John was born in Roxbury on October 15, 1858. He attended grammar school, then night school, before apprenticing in a series of trades, including masonry, plumbing, and tinsmithing. Such skilled crafts were about as high as most of Boston's Irish might attain, but Sullivan's pugnacious temperament—he quarreled repeatedly with bosses and fellow workers—kept jeopardizing these opportunities. If Sullivan's aggressiveness created difficulties on the job, it paid dividends in sports. His size and athleticism—at the end of his teens he stood 5 feet 11 inches tall and weighed nearly 200 pounds—made him a fine baseball player. He played for several semiprofessional clubs, and in 1879 was even offered a contract by the Cincinnati Red Stockings. As he reached adulthood, he also discovered the joys of Boston's bachelor subculture, in which men spent most of their leisure hours in the company of other men—in bars, at sporting events, in billiard halls—drinking, swearing, carousing, and fighting. Sullivan excelled at these activities, particularly the last. "At the age of nineteen," he recalled in his autobiography, "I drifted into the occupation of a boxer."[4]

"Drifted" was precisely the right word, though "occupation" was an unusual way to describe the life of a prizefighter in late nineteenth-century America. Even relatively respectable sports were just beginning to pay their players on a regular basis. The very Red Stockings whose offer Sullivan rejected was the nation's first professional baseball team, yet that club was only ten years old when he gave up the diamond for the ring. And while some might condemn as loafers men who played boys' games for a living, at least baseball was legal.[5]

Although prizefighting had its antecedents in ancient Greek and Roman games, the modern sport goes back only to late seventeenth-century England. The first great English champion, James Figg, emerged in the early 1700s, founded a school for teaching the manly art, and opened an amphitheater where he displayed his skills at sparring, swordsmanship, and cudgeling. The next English champion, Jack Broughton, received the patronage of the duke of Cumberland, with whose backing he fought prize battles, and founded the "London Academy" where he gave lessons. In 1743 Broughton promulgated the first rules of the ring, which with some modification governed boxing until nearly the end of Sullivan's career. They forbade strangling, hitting below the belt, or punching a fallen opponent— and little else. Under Broughton's rules, a round ended whenever a man was punched or wrestled to the turf, the next round began thirty seconds later with both men toeing a line called "the scratch," and the fight ended when either man could no longer continue. Under these rules, rounds lasted from a few seconds to several minutes (roughly a minute and a half on average), and there was no limit to their number. To ensure fair play, the fighters appointed seconds to assist them in the ring, umpires to settle disputes, and a referee whose decisions were final.[6]

At the height of its glory, from the late eighteenth through the early nineteenth centuries, boxing under the Rules of the London Prize Ring was considered the "national sport of England." Fights were illegal, and boxers played a cat-and-mouse game with the law, but aristocratic patronage generally assured that matches came off as scheduled. The great English essayist William Hazlitt captured the ring's glory in "The Fight," his account of the great 1821 battle between Tom "The Gas-Man" Hickman and William Neate. Hazlitt described the all-night tavern revels before the fight, noted the opinions of the trainers, boxers, and other "knowing ones" about the upcoming event, and painted the spectacle in colors still vivid today: "Reader, have you ever seen a fight? If not, you have a pleasure to come, at least if it is a fight like that between the Gas-man and Bill Neate. The crowd was very great when we arrived on the spot; open carriages were coming up, with streamers flying and music playing, and the country people were pouring in over hedge and ditch, in all directions, to see their hero beat or be beaten."[7]

One of the great bouts of this era involved an American. In December 1810 Thomas Molineaux challenged Tom Crib for the championship. They fought thirty miles outside London before a boisterous crowd. If reports in the English press are to be believed, those who witnessed the battle seemed less apprehensive that the title might pass to a black man than that its possessor might not be English. This brutal thirty-nine-round battle could have gone either way, but Crib finally won out through endurance—"bottom" as fighters called it—as much as anything else.[8]

Perhaps the most interesting thing about the Crib-Molineaux fight is that Americans paid it little notice. It went virtually unmentioned in newspapers on this side of the Atlantic, and little memory of Molineaux persisted after 1810. It is not surprising that whites failed to note the achievements of this former slave turned free black. Maybe his exploits were celebrated in African-American oral tradition—there is no solid evidence either way. But even had Molineaux been white, the new United States had virtually no modern sports, and boxing was as alien to most citizens in 1810 as cricket is to them now. Scattered fights arose in port cities, mostly among Irish and English immigrants, and a handful of men fought sparring matches and regular prize-ring bouts. But in the early 1800s Americans simply lacked a mental category in which to place this event, and not until midcentury would a great fight galvanize public attention.[9]

By then American cities possessed a large working class sharply divided along ethnic lines. New York City was the center of a new plebeian street life, one strain of which was the rough bachelor subculture. Ethnic and neighborhood factions coalesced, loosely organized gangs fought each other, and some men emerged from street battles to enter the formal prize-ring. Tom Hyer was a leader among native-born Americans; when the Whig Party or later the Know-Nothings needed muscle for ballot box stuffing or to lead an attack on a Democratic stronghold such as a bar or brothel, they often turned to this 6-foot 3-inch, 185-pound street tough. Irish-born James "Yankee" Sullivan fought in the London Prize Ring before being deported to an Australian penal colony. He escaped, sneaked back into his native Cork, and emigrated to America, where he soon led a Democratic Party faction in New York City. It was all but inevitable in this subterranean world that the paths of Hyer and Sullivan would cross.[10]

After repeated run-ins on the street, they signed articles of agreement to fight for $10,000, money raised largely by gamblers. Not only the sporting weeklies and the working-class penny press but even more respectable newspapers were filled with stories about the two men—stories that opened with disclaimers that covering the news did not imply approving of it. Because prizefighting was illegal, the fighters and a few hundred spectators met surreptitiously on the deserted Maryland shore on February 7, 1849. The battle lasted only fifteen minutes, and Hyer easily dominated the wily but much smaller (5-foot 10-inch, 155-pound) Sullivan. Not everyone was happy with the fight or its coverage. Former New York mayor Phillip Hone, now retired but still active as patron of the arts and lion of urban social life, noted with revulsion that the working-class *Herald* lavished attention on the event: "The appropriate organ of such disgraceful recitals, is filled this morning with the disgusting details." Officials might profess disgust, but Hyer's friends greeted his return to New York with fireworks, pageantry, and a brand-new title, "Champion of America." Long after the battle ended, lithographs of the two heroes decorated the walls of barrooms where men gathered to discuss the Great $10,000 Fight.[11]

For the next forty years prizefighting under the bare-knuckle rules was part of the urban American landscape. Followers of the ring were known as "the fancy," a group that consisted largely of young working-class males, gamblers, and sporting men, who together composed the bachelor subculture. New York City was pugilism's center, for here the greatest concentration of men and institutions—dance halls, brothels, gambling dens, saloons—nourished the culture of the ring. Of course prizefights deeply offended respectable people. The violence and raw passions at ringside, the drinking, gambling, and swearing, the rough ways of young working-class and immigrant men, all frightened the Victorian middle class, whose dominant values were sober self-control, hard work, devotion to home and family, decorous speech, and pious behavior. The prize-ring also represented a conflict over the very meaning of manhood. In the ring, masculinity meant aggression, raw physicality, bloodlust. But in parlors, churches, and countinghouses, manhood required steadiness and dependability.[12]

Boxing had its ups and downs for decades after the Great $10,000 Fight. The very culture of the ring, its anarchic qualities, always threatened to undermine the sport. By the time John L. Sullivan "drifted into the occupation of a boxer," at the beginning of the 1880s, prizefighting had reached a low. Violence at ringside, lethargic performances by fighters, and fixed matches contributed to a general decline. Newspapers wrote with disgust about pugilism—if they covered it at all—except to remark that in the old days the fancy could depend on the likes of Tom Hyer, Yankee Sullivan, John Morrissey, and John C. Heenan to give their best, and that the gamblers and sportsmen who arranged those early bouts had been more concerned with honor than with filthy lucre. Sullivan, in other words, entered a world of declining prospects.[13]

Yet change was in the wind. The prize-ring's problems grew out of its lowly status, its associations with urban riffraff. But other sports enjoyed a remarkable boom during the Gilded Age. After the Civil War baseball clubs proliferated across the land, college athletic programs—especially football—became central to student life, and basketball was no sooner invented than youths across America joined new teams and leagues. The athletic impulse had several origins. Many Americans worried that the shift from farms to cities made them indolent, flabby. More significant, the industrial economy was creating a margin of prosperity for many people even as it more rigidly divided work time from leisure time. Indeed, consumption of goods and services for pleasure became an increasingly significant part of a new economy of potential abundance. Sporting gear became emblematic of youth and vigor; tennis, golf, and yachting at brand-new country clubs offered opportunities for displays of wealth. At the other end of the social spectrum, playing or watching a game of baseball at a July Fourth picnic was an important gesture toward Americanization for immigrants. Even trends in science and religion were harnessed to the cause of sports. Social Darwinism—which applied the metaphor of evolution to the economy and politics—posited that survival of the fittest described how human societies functioned; sports extended the metaphor so that fitness for competition was exactly what athletics now promised. Moreover, "muscular Christianity," a movement that started in England, took root in late nineteenth-century America through organizations like the Young Men's Christian Association, which built gymnasiums across the country. Muscular Christianity, too, was a metaphor, expressing the desire of clergy and laypeople to participate in the active life of the age.[14]

Toward the end of the nineteenth century, sports no longer seemed antithetical to the old Victorian ideals of sober self-control, purposeful work, and virtuous self-improvement. On the contrary, a new sporting ideology propounded by men like Theodore Roosevelt and Yale football coach Walter Camp encouraged athletics as a route to clean living. Whereas in the early nineteenth century the word *sport* had most commonly meant a gambler and wastrel, by 1900 the term usually was connected to wholesome athletic games. Indeed, sports became a cornerstone of American masculinity. For a man like Roosevelt, sports' lessons in self-denial and mental toughness were invaluable. "There is a certain tendency to underestimate or overlook the need of the virile, masterful qualities of the heart and mind," Roosevelt declared. He feared that prosperity might make men soft, but added, "there is no better way of counteracting this tendency than by encouraging bodily exercise and especially the sports which develop such qualities as courage, resolution, and endurance." The new world of corporations created white-collar labor—attorneys, bankers, managers, clerks—and some Americans began to express fears that men might lose their vital masculine energy, that they might become "feminized." Muscles atrophied in office settings; bureaucracies neutered men spiritually. But sports inoculated Americans against overly safe and predictable lives. In popular culture, a new kind of hero, the athlete, took his place alongside pioneers and cowboys to reassert an image of manly individualism.[15]

Even that old outlaw, prizefighting, began to gain a measure of respectability. The ring came to represent "the raw side of human life" for many prominent men, such as Harvard psychologist G. Stanley Hall: "I have never missed an opportunity to attend a prize fight," he confessed in his autobiography, "if I could do so unknown and away from home, so that I have seen most of the noted pugilists of my generation in action and felt the unique thrill at these encounters." But for most respectable Victorians, prizefighting under the old rules was just too rowdy. Theodore Roosevelt, for example, called the sport "simply brutal and degrading" and condemned its fans as men who "hover on the borderlines of criminality." Yet Roosevelt loved boxing, fought with gloves at Harvard in the late 1870s, and years later invited former champion Mike Donovan to the White House for some good-natured sparring. Before the late 1800s, painters and novelists never dared to represent the ring, but by the turn of the century, artists began to see themselves less as upholders of high culture, more as adventurers on the frontiers of experience, so boxing scenes began to appear in the works of Frank Norris and Jack London, of Thomas Eakins and George Bellows. Even elite athletic clubs started hiring professionals, offering boxing lessons, and sponsoring tournaments. But always the distinction was drawn between illegal and degrading bare-knuckle prizefights, and wholesome sparring with gloves. Thus Duffield Osborn supported glove fights in his "Defense of Pugilism" in the 1888 *North American Review*, arguing that boxing, with its "high manly qualities," must be reformed and made available to respectable men before civilization grew overrefined and decayed into "mere womanishness," before "mawkish sentimentality" transformed men into "a race of eminently respectable female saints."[16]

So despite the declining fortunes of the old bare-knuckle game, Sullivan took the stage just as fighting with gloves began enjoying support from influential men. His fighting style and personality helped to transform boxing. "Sullivan is as fierce, relentless, tireless as a cataract," declared the writer and Irish nationalist John Boyle O'Reilly. "The fight is wholly to go in his way—not at all in the other man's." Dr. Dudley Sargent of Harvard, after carefully studying and measuring Sullivan's body, concluded that the champion was a model of "the brawn and sinew that conquers both opponents and environments and sustains the race." But these encomiums came toward the end of Sullivan's reign. When he first entered the ring, his chosen "occupation" remained a dubious one.[17]

Although prizefights under the old London rules remained strictly illegal throughout America, the police generally looked the other way during sparring matches fought under the Marquis of Queensberry rules—three-minute rounds, gloved hands, no wrestling holds—so long as the action did not become too violent. Young Sullivan fought plenty of street brawls in Boston, but he had no formal training. Still, when a fighter named Scannel challenged the crowd at Boston's Dudley Street Opera House one night, Sullivan strode down to the stage and laced on the gloves. A blow from Scannel to the back of Sullivan's head so angered the young man that he knocked the professional over a piano on the stage. Just out of his teens, Sullivan next fought a series of glove matches in Boston theaters and music halls against seasoned boxers; all of them fell to "the Highland Boy," as he was now known. He moved on to New York City with similar results. Next he accepted an offer to fight John Donaldson, the "Champion of the West," under bare-knuckle rules in Cincinnati. They fought in the back room of a beer hall for $53, raised by the handful of sports in attendance; Donaldson lasted only ten rounds and twenty-one minutes.[18]

With this victory, Sullivan challenged the world:

Cincinnati, Dec. 9, 1880

To the Editor of the Enquirer:

I am prepared to make a match to fight any man breathing for any sum from one thousand dollars to ten thousand dollars at catch weights. This challenge is especially directed to Paddy Ryan and will remain open for a month if he should not see fit to accept it.

Respectfully Yours,
John L. Sullivan.

Ryan, the reigning champion, told the brash young challenger to "go and get a reputation." Sullivan did. At Harry Hill's saloon in New York, a mecca for hungry young fighters, Sullivan took on all comers, offering $50 to any man who could stay in the ring with him four rounds under the Queensberry rules. No one succeeded. He took his challenge on the road to Philadelphia, Pittsburgh, Cincinnati, Buffalo, Louisville, and Chicago, earning as much as $150 per week, roughly ten times a laborer's wage. Then he fought a prizefight against John Flood, "The Bullshead Terror," on a moonlit barge towed up the Hudson River. Sullivan punched or threw Flood down for all eight rounds and collected the purse in just fifteen minutes.[19]

Finally Sullivan was able to raise substantial money and Ryan accepted a match. They agreed to fight for $2,500 a side somewhere within 100 miles of New Orleans. Richard Kyle Fox, the flamboyant editor of the recently revitalized *National Police Gazette*, backed Ryan, a move that ensured plenty of publicity for the fight. Sullivan and Ryan trained for weeks near the Crescent City, and fan interest far exceeded anything before. Thousands of men bought $10 tickets at the Louisville and Nashville Railroad office in New Orleans, tickets that specified no destination. They packed the train cars on the night of February 5, 1882. The great Cuban nationalist José Martí was on board one of those trains, covering the event for the *New York Sun*:

Now comes the drinking, the shouting, and the laying of bets . . . Now the reminiscing about the good old days in New York when electoral campaigns were bare-knuckle affairs in the al-

leys, the stories retold about how a certain McCoy killed Chris
Lilly in the ring, and how the bonfires burned along Park Row
after Hyer defeated Sullivan . . . Between swigs of burning liquor, some recall how Morrissey left Heenan for dead; others
remember the blow to the forehead with which McCool felled
Jones, that left him vomiting as if his brain had been shaken
from its moorings.[20]

At dawn the trains unloaded their cargo in the tiny depot of Mississippi
City. A ring was set up in front of the Barnes Hotel, and now gamblers in
the crowd shouted out odds, and bets as high as $500, even $1,000 were
consummated. Hawkers offered sandwiches and liquor to the crowd, and a
few enterprising souls sold replicas of the fighters' colors—for the champion, a white handkerchief with red, white, and blue border, images of an
Irish harp, an American shield, the seal of New York City, and the sunburst
emblem of the Finian brotherhood in the corners, and, in the center, an eagle straddling the globe with the words "Police Gazette, New York, 1882."
Sullivan similarly chose a white handkerchief with an eagle in the center,
but his border was green, and in each corner were crossed Irish and American flags.[21]

"When Sullivan struck me," Ryan said after the fight, "I thought that a
telegraph pole had been shoved against me endways." The battle lasted
only nine rounds averaging half a minute each. Declared the *New Orleans
Times Democrat* of Sullivan, "he forced the fighting from the start and
knocked his opponent about as though he were a football." At age twenty-
three, previously unable to keep a job, Sullivan had indeed discovered his
calling; he was Champion of America.[22]

The battle's aftermath proved a revelation. Demand for the *Police Gazette's* eight-page illustrated special kept the presses rolling for weeks. For
the first time, dailies across the country featured prominent stories about
this illegal match. As much as any other single event, the demand for news
of the Sullivan-Ryan fight fostered the development of modern sports coverage. Simply put, the fight made it clear to editors that sports sell newspapers. As the Champion worked his way back north, he was feted in Chicago, Detroit, Cleveland, Pittsburgh, Philadelphia, and New York; finally
returning to Boston, he received a thunderous welcome at the Dudley

Street Opera House, where he had first entered the ring just three years before. "The Boston Boy," as he was now known, was a hero in his hometown. The Irish, of course, who had suffered decades of ugly prejudice—for their poverty, their Catholicism, their "racial" inferiority—at the hands of native-born Protestants, made Sullivan into a god. But even the Anglo majority embraced him as their own. A poet caught the irony of staid old Boston lionizing the young roughneck:

> Just fancy what mingled emotions
>> Would fill the Puritan heart
> To learn what renown was won for his town
>> By means of the manly art!
> Imagine a Winthrop or Adams
>> In front of a bulletin board,
> Each flinging his hat at the statement that
>> The first blood was by Sullivan scored.

But this was only the beginning. Over the next decade Sullivan became one of the world's best-known public figures, Boston's greatest celebrity, and probably the most idolized athlete of the entire nineteenth century.[23]

Six weeks after becoming champion, Sullivan declared himself "disgusted" by all the boasts and rumors appearing in the newspapers. He challenged any man to meet him for $5,000 a side for the championship. More important, he renewed his challenge to face all comers for three four-minute rounds with the gloves, now offering $1,000 to anyone who could stay in the ring with him. Three-round Queensberry bouts were a goldmine for Sullivan, because for a gifted boxer like himself, they presented little danger. He held a series of these "picnics," as he called them, in New York, Brooklyn, Boston, and Rochester, easily dispatching all opponents. Sullivan next hooked up with a traveling variety show, assembled by sleight-of-hand-artist-turned-impresario Harry Sargent. After jugglers, wrestlers, and clowns, Sullivan came onstage, boasted that he "could lick any sonofabitch alive," and challenged the house. If there were no takers, he sparred with one of the members of the troupe. Occasionally local police might intervene if a match grew too violent, but for the most part the subterfuge of gloves and timed rounds did their work. Indeed, during the 1880s Sullivan went on three major tours that carried him across the country, and eventually overseas to England and Australia. Bare-knuckle fights netted him only a few thousand dollars over the course of his career, but these "knocking out tours" made Sullivan a millionaire.[24]

The Champion explained in his autobiography why he favored Queensberry matches, and his reasons centered on the fans:

> Where such an audience assembles [for a bare-knuckle fight] there will always be found a certain class of dishonest men practicing their nefarious work, whereas under the Marquis of Queensberry rules, the contest usually takes place in a hall of some description under police supervision, and the price of admission is put purposely high so as to exclude the rowdy element, and a gentleman can see the contest, feeling sure that he will not be robbed of any of his valuables or in any way be interfered with. Under the Marquis of Queensberry rules the manly art of self-defense, of which I am considered an authority, is conducted for the benefit of gentlemen, not rowdies. Fighting under the Marquis of Queensberry rules before gentlemen is a pleasure; to the other element it becomes a brawl.

Sullivan said nothing here about fighting style or technique; rather, he preferred glove matches because the crowds were orderly and respectable. Unprecedented numbers of American men could now see great ring heroes in action without compromising their safety or their reputations.[25]

The ring never became as pure as Sullivan claimed. The new rules helped take the sport away from the most disreputable gamblers and allowed it to be run more like a business. But the scent of barbarism remained, and this was an important part of the ring's renewed appeal. Middle-class men felt secure attending matches, finding there a little controlled atavism, a cathartic release in watching others bleed. The rise of boxing was part of a larger rediscovery of risk-taking and pleasure-seeking among American men. The old productive verities of hard work and sober self-control now found themselves competing with the freer new ways of a consumer culture. Without ever intending it, Sullivan became emblematic of the new order. Impulsive, a bon vivant with gargantuan appetites and an electric personality, John L.'s appeal extended beyond working-class and ethnic communities to embrace whole new groups of American men, many of them workers in bureaucracies and corporations who felt cut off from the flow of "real life." Sullivan epitomized action in an age that feared inertia.[26]

Old-time fans still considered the old bare-knuckle style the only real way for a boxer to prove his mettle, and Sullivan recognized that bare-knuckle matches offered valuable publicity for his glove tours. The Boston Boy held a few regular prize battles during the 1880s, but all paled in comparison to his 1889 match against Jake Kilrain. Sullivan had been champ for seven years by then, and his love of drink and nightlife had taken its toll. His fans grew impatient as his weight ballooned and as ugly rumors of spousal abuse, public drunkenness, and random acts of brutality made the papers. Sullivan's health broke down completely just before his thirtieth birthday. He claimed to suffer from typhoid fever, gastric fever, inflammation of the bowels, heart trouble, liver complaint, and incipient paralysis, but acute alcoholism was a more succinct diagnosis. Still, with fans clamoring for a real fight, Sullivan rose to the challenge.[27]

Kilrain (his real name was Joseph Killion) was a formidable athlete, a champion rower and a good boxer. With $20,000 a side and the championship at stake, Sullivan put himself in the hands of the wrestler William Muldoon, who forced the Strong Boy to endure months of hard training. Meanwhile *Police Gazette* editor Richard Kyle Fox bent every effort toward stirring interest in the fight. Finally, the boxers and thousands of fans gathered in New Orleans. The governors of six southern states declared that they wanted no part of the affair, but on the night of July 7, 1889, three trains left the Crescent City. The next morning they unloaded 5,000 men in the town of Richburg, Mississippi, where a local sawmill proprietor built a ring and some rough bleachers. As the clock passed 10:00 A.M. and the temperature soared toward 100 degrees, the fighters made their way into the ring. The athletic Kilrain weighed thirty pounds less than Sullivan, but the Champion looked equally fit. Declared one newspaper, "He was not the flabby Sullivan familiar to New Yorkers and Boston men of late. His feet bounded off the turf. His shoulders rolled with the old swaggering air of eight years ago. He looked the Boston Boy of early days."[28]

Kilrain won first fall by throwing Sullivan, and first blood with a blow to his ear. But the match belonged to the Champion. Sullivan stalked Kilrain the whole fight, and the journalist from the *Gazette*, William Harding, noted that "his eyes flashed, his lips were set and he seemed to become larger and more massive than he was." Kilrain backpedaled and fell at light blows, infuriating Sullivan, who berated him throughout the fight: "Stand up and fight like a man"; "I'm no sprinter, I'm a fighter"; "You're a champion, eh? A champion of what?" The only doubt came in the forty-fourth round, when Sullivan began vomiting. He drank throughout the battle a concoction of tea laced with whiskey, and a rumor went around the stands that Sullivan's stomach was retaining the whiskey but giving up the tea. They fought seventy-five rounds, lasting over two hours. Finally Kilrain's second, fearing for his man's life, threw in the sponge.[29]

For the first time, daily newspapers unabashedly flashed the results of the fight to their readers, often with banner headlines across page one. Serious poets memorialized the battle, but one bit of vaudeville doggerel caught on with unusual tenaciousness:

> His colors are the Stars and Stripes,
>   He also wears the green,
> And he's the grandest slugger that
>   The ring has ever seen.
> No fighter in the world can beat
>   Our true American,
> The champion of all champions
>   Is John L. Sullivan!

At the request of the governor of Mississippi, Massachusetts remanded Sullivan back to the scene of the fight, but local courts refused to convict him on charges of assault and battery and of staging a prizefight. Although his trip back south resembled a royal progress more than a criminal proceeding, legal fees cost Sullivan a small fortune, and he had no taste to ever enter the bare-knuckle ring again. In fact the world had witnessed the last title fight under the old rules.[30]

Sullivan returned to touring, now with a theatrical troupe in a play written especially for him, *Honest Hearts and Willing Hands*. He loved the limelight, and he was getting too old for the austere life of training. Sullivan drank his way across North America, then overseas to Australia, loving the adulation of the crowd, reveling in his celebrity status. Yet his fame finally depended on his ring prowess, and once again, after a few years' layoff from serious fighting, fans clamored for his return. Early in 1892 he published a new challenge to "any and all the bluffers who have been trying to make capital at my expense." He specified Frank Slavin of Australia, "as he and his backers have done the greatest amount of blowing"; Charlie Mitchell of England, "whom I would rather whip than any man in the world"; and James J. Corbett, "who has achieved his share of bombast." Above all, Sullivan specified that the fight must be governed by the Marquis of Queensberry rules, "as I want fight, not foot-racing." The next championship battle, in other words, would be won with the gloves.[31]

What he did not say, but had declared several times previously, was that he would not fight a black challenger. Certainly Peter Jackson of Australia wanted a match, and he would have been a very formidable opponent. But in this era of spreading Jim Crow segregation, lynching, and disenfranchisement, a curtain of racism now fell over the ring, just as it fell over other major sports such as baseball and bicycle racing. Sullivan was popular enough to resist such pressure, to insist on the rough-edged equality that the ring always presented to poor men like himself. He chose instead to follow the cultural trend that deepened segregation in American life.[32]

Corbett and his manager, William Brady, seized the opportunity the Champion presented them. The young Californian was not a street fighter like Sullivan; he had attended college, been a bank clerk, learned sparring in a gym, then taught the manly art in exclusive men's clubs. Corbett believed himself too quick for the aging Sullivan, and made his challenge with supreme self-confidence. Brady, a theater promoter with connections to elite institutions like the New York Athletic Club, had no problem raising the $25,000 stake for the fight. Understanding where the real money lay, he even wrote a play, *Gentleman Jack*, for his young protégé to star in after the match.[33]

The Sullivan-Corbett fight differed from all previous matches. When the two boxers signed articles, they met not at the old *Police Gazette* building, but at the offices of the *New York World*, which in ten years had gone from routine condemnations of the ring to calling itself "fistiana's authority." The *World*'s conversion exemplified the widening coverage of athletic events in new sports sections of daily newspapers across America. Moreover, the legal barriers to the prize ring were breaking down, and New Orleans led the way. In the late 1880s, silk-stocking athletic clubs in the Crescent City began sponsoring professional bouts, the contestants' fists encased in the thin padding of five-ounce gloves. As one paper put it, "steady businessmen, society bloods, and in fact, all classes of citizens are eager and anxious to spend their wealth to see a glove contest." In 1890 the New Orleans City Council voted to legalize Queensberry prizefights, provided that no liquor was served, that no bouts were held on Sunday, and that the parties involved donated $50 to charity. Scenting a chance to cash in on the newly sanitized sport, promoters built new arenas around town, hired their own referees, settled on six weight classifications, and began arranging bouts for talented young fighters.[34]

Because Sullivan was undisputed champion and had won under the old bare-knuckle rules, fighting Corbett with the gloves put his benediction on the new order. Ironically, although he had done more than anyone else to transform the ring, Sullivan would always be remembered as the last great bare-knuckler, and his opponent as the harbinger of the modern era.[35]

When the two fighters arrived, the city was in an uproar. The Olympic Club had organized a boxing extravaganza, with the Sullivan-Corbett match the culmination of three days of championship bouts. The *New York Herald* observed that the events were of national and international importance, and the *Chicago Tribune* marveled that now spectators arrived from distant cities in elegant trains, slept at the best hotels, and watched the fights in grand arenas. Finally, on September 7, 1892, 10,000 ringside spectators in New Orleans, as well as hundreds of thousands of fans in theaters and newspaper offices across the country—wired to the Crescent City by telegraph—held their breath as the fight began.[36]

It was no contest. Sullivan's out-of-shape body could not keep up with Corbett, who entered the ring eight years younger and 25 pounds lighter. After the Champion wearied himself slugging the air, Corbett began to land consistently, and in the twenty-first round rained down blow after blow until his defenseless opponent fell.[37]

The day after the fight, William Lyon Phelps, professor of English at Yale, read the newspaper to his elderly father, a Baptist minister. "I had never heard him mention a prize fight and did not suppose he knew anything about the subject, or cared anything about it. So when I came to the headline CORBETT DEFEATS SULLIVAN, I read that aloud and turned the page. My father leaned forward and said earnestly, 'Read it by rounds.'"[38]

A young journalist named Theodore Dreiser remembered meeting the great Bostonian a few years after the Corbett fight:

> And then John L. Sullivan, raw, red-faced, big-fisted, broad shouldered, drunken, with gaudy waistcoat and tie, and rings and pins set with enormous diamonds and rubies—what an impression he made! Surrounded by local sports and politicians of the most rubicund and degraded character . . . Cigar boxes, champagne buckets, decanters, beer bottles, overcoats, collars and shirts littered the floor, and lolling back in the midst of it all in ease and splendor his very great self, a sort of prize-fighting J. P. Morgan.

Here was Sullivan the hedonist, garish in every detail, flattered by hangers-on, luxuriating in the good life. With his own masculine prowess unquestioned, he gloried in leisure and excess. Dreiser went on:

> "Aw, haw! haw! haw!" I can hear him even now when I asked him my favorite question about life, his plans, and the value of exercise(!), etc. "He wants to know about exercise! You're all right, young fella, kinda slim, but you'll do. Sit down and have some champagne. Have a cigar. Give him some cigars, George. These young newspaper men are all right to me. I'm for 'em. Exercise? What I think? Haw! haw! Write any damned thing yuh please, young fella, and say that John L. Sullivan said so. That's good enough for me. If they don't believe it, bring it back here and I'll sign it for yuh. But I know it'll be all right, and I won't stop to read it neither. That suit yuh? Well all right. Now have some more champagne and don't say I didn't treat yuh right, 'cause I did. I'm ex-champion of the world, defeated by that little dude from California, but I'm still John L. Sullivan—ain't that right? Haw! haw! They can't take that away from me, can they? Haw! haw! Have some more champagne, boy."
> I adored him . . .[39]

Life after boxing was not always good to Sullivan. A decade after losing to Corbett, he had gained 100 pounds, pawned his championship belt, and

filed for bankruptcy. But he remained a celebrity, going on tour with theater companies, showing up at ringside, giving temperance lectures. It was
not the prematurely aged man standing before them whom audiences remembered, but the raw bare-knuckle slugger who had challenged the world
and beat all comers. Writing about his boyhood, the poet Vachel Lindsay
saw in the Champion the central symbol of the age:

> When I was nine years old, in 1889,
> I sent my love a lacy Valentine.
> Suffering boys were dressed like Fauntleroys,
> While Judge and Puck in giant humor vied.
> The Gibson Girl came shining like a bride
> To spoil the cult of Tennyson's Elaine.
> Louisa Alcott was my gentle guide . . .
> Then . . .
> I heard a battle trumpet sound.
> Nigh New Orleans
> Upon an emerald plain
> John L. Sullivan
> The strong boy
> Of Boston
> Fought seventy-five rounds with Jake Kilrain.

Sullivan helped usher in a new masculine tone in American culture. Heroic strife broke through Victorian cant. The Champion rejected the cluttered world of bourgeois sentimentality, but also the workaday ethic of shop
and office to live by his fists and his wits. For Lindsay, as for countless American men, this obscure Irish American from Boston became the very symbol of masculine renewal in turn-of-the-century America.[40]

11

Rocky Marciano and the Curse of Al Weill

Russell Sullivan

Rocky Marciano was one of us. He was born in the Boston area. He was raised in the Boston area. He lived most of his adult life in the Boston area. He spoke with distinct traces of a Boston accent. Like many of us, he made periodic excursions to the North End for Italian food. And, like many of us, he suffered with the Red Sox. On the basis of such background, character, and taste—coupled with the fact that he is, of course, the only undefeated heavyweight champion in history—Marciano can justly claim his place at the very top of the pantheon of Boston sports legends.

Yet Boston has never fully claimed Marciano as its own. Throughout Marciano's rise and then reign atop the boxing world in the early 1950s, there was always a slight yet perceptible distance separating the Hub from the Rock. Granted, many Bostonians of that era liked Marciano. Some even loved him. And nearly everyone in town rooted him on as he slugged his way to the top of the boxing world, ringing up an unblemished and unparalleled 49–0 record. Along the way, he became a celebrity and a source of civic pride in Boston.

But the passion was never there—at least the type of passion that other legends of Boston sport have elicited from the city. At first glance, Boston's lack of passion for Marciano is odd. He was, after all, the centerpiece of heavyweight championship fights infused with glamour and romance that captured the attention of the nation. He was "the heavyweight champion of the world" at a time when that title still meant something. And, as the king of a sport that was second only to baseball in terms of popular appeal, he was unquestionably one of the most celebrated athletes of his age.

He was also very much a man of that age, which, despite its surface simplicity, was not without its tensions or complexity. As a white man in a sport increasingly dominated by black men, Marciano reflected the curious, uneasy racial attitudes of his era—and became, to many, the Great White Hope. Moreover, as an Italian American in a society just beginning to embrace the concept of the melting pot, Marciano symbolized ethnicity at its midcentury crossroads.

In fact, in terms of symbolism, Rocky Marciano came to personify his entire age, standing for a set of qualities that were especially valued in early 1950s America: family devotion, loyalty, respect for authority, patriotism, piety, innocence, purity, hard work, decency, modesty, friendliness, and, perhaps most of all, simplicity. These were the qualities that were the springboard to the American Dream (an attractive wife, a few kids, a well-paying job, and a house in the suburbs with a white picket fence). More important, these were the qualities that made up the cherished American Way of Life—a set of values and a corresponding standard of behavior that served as the cultural antidote to the evil of Communism. Indeed, in this age of McCarthyism, with suspicion and fear permeating society, dissidence simply wasn't tolerated. Instead, conformity was demanded. And role models were sought (or invented) to fit the cultural consensus embodied by the American Way of Life. That Marciano in fact genuinely possessed many of the qualities at the heart of the ideal made it easy for the imagemakers to construct a larger-than-life image for the fighter, accentuating the positive and eliminating the negative (character flaws, peccadilloes). To his contemporaries, then, Rocky Marciano came to represent everything that was good and admirable in early 1950s America—an athletic personification of the American Way of Life.[1]

But all of this all took place on a national level. In Boston, Marciano may have represented a captivating "local boy makes good" story—but the plain fact was that the local boy didn't make good *here*. And that is the type of distinction that has always mattered in Boston, one of the most provincial places on earth when it comes to sports (or anything else, for that matter). The tale of Rocky Marciano and the Hub, then, is one of provincialism precluding passion.

Blame it on the Curse of Al Weill. For it was Weill, a New York manager of power and influence, who was lucky enough to stumble upon Marciano and squire him away from the Boston fight mob. It was Weill who directed Marciano's rise up the fistic ladder, a rise that saw Marciano fight extensively in Providence but only twice in Boston. And it was Weill who called the shots during Marciano's reign, placing his title fights in New York, Philadelphia, Chicago, and even San Francisco—but never in Boston.

It was the Curse of Al Weill that established the distance between the Hub and the Rock—and the Curse of Al Weill that prevented that provincial city from fully embracing the hometown fighter. Rocky Marciano was, indeed, one of us. But he was never really ours.

He would have been ours had Boston fight managers only paid a little attention to Rocco Marchegiano during the late spring of 1948. But they did not. And with good reason. Although the Brockton heavyweight, just one year removed from a failed tryout with a Chicago Cubs farm team, had made some noise in local amateur circles in early 1948, capturing three amateur titles—two in the mill town of Lowell, Massachusetts, and one in the big town in front of 4,749 fans at the old Boston Arena—he hardly flashed a world of potential in doing so. As Boston fight promoter Sam Silverman later remembered, "Of all the kids around, Rocky was the most unlikely to succeed. He was clumsy and awkward. He had no stance, no style, nothing."[2]

Actually, he did have something. In fact he possessed the most important assets that a fighter can have: a chin and a punch. As a result, his amateur strategy—awkwardly floundering around the ring and absorbing punishment from his opponent until he saw an opening to land a big one—was surprisingly effective. And the results gave Rocco considerable hope that he would be able to convince a Boston fight manager to take charge of his career. So in the spring of 1948, after he made the decision to turn professional, Rocco and his ubiquitous sidekick Allie Colombo traveled from

Brockton to Boston and began knocking on the doors of gyms and offices dotting Friend Street and Canal Street around the old Garden. The future heavyweight champion of the world was there for the taking.

No one took. In what turned out to be a gross fistic sin of neglect, the members of the Boston fight mob showed no interest in the Brockton fighter begging for a chance. One of the few to admit his mistake later was Peter Fuller, the son of former Massachusetts governor Alvan T. Fuller and an amateur boxer of some renown in the late 1940s. Marchegiano sent word through Jackie Martin (another prominent member of the Boston fight mob) that Fuller could become Marchegiano's manager if he were willing to pay Marchegiano the princely sum of $1,000. Fuller remembered seeing Marchegiano lose an amateur fight to Bob Girard of Lynn—a man whom Fuller himself later defeated in the ring. Using the power of comparative reasoning and the benefits of a Harvard education, Fuller asked Martin, "Why should I pay $1000 to a guy I can beat myself?"[3] To his everlasting chagrin, he rejected Marchegiano's offer.

Fuller was hardly alone. According to legend, several other movers and shakers in the Boston fight scene also passed on the chance to get a piece of the Rock. For instance, Rocco and Allie went in search of Johnny Buckley, the former manager of Jack Sharkey ("the Boston Gob" who briefly held the heavyweight crown during the early 1930s) and still a fistic force in the Hub. As the two Brockton boys were walking into Buckley's tavern, though, Buckley reportedly went walking out—to the racetrack. The few members of the Boston fight mob who actually paid attention to Rocco Marchegiano cited his awkward performances as an amateur, his advanced age (mid-twenties, late to be starting out in the fight game), and his obvious physical shortcomings (primarily his short arms) in marking him as a fighter with limited potential. In so doing, they let the future heavyweight champion of the world slip out of their grasp—and out of the Hub.

He slipped to New York and Al Weill. Acting on the advice of several confidants, Rocco and Allie decided to forget about Boston and instead seek a New York manager with big-time connections. Their particular target was Weill, a veteran New York manager who had come highly recommended. During a brief workout at the CYO gymnasium in New York City on a June day in 1948, Weill and Charley Goldman (the trainer who usually handled Weill's fighters) saw the same things that the Boston fight men had seen: an older boy with short arms who was all awkwardness. Still, because Marchegiano was a heavyweight with a punch, Weill decided to take him on.

It was the break that the fighter needed. Without Al Weill, Rocco Marchegiano (soon to shorten his name to Rocky Marciano because no one could spell or pronounce it) wouldn't have climbed as far or at least as fast. Weill had the association with Goldman that would provide Marciano with the masterful training that he needed to smooth the fighter's rough edges. Weill had the managerial experience that would provide Marciano with opponents who were ideal for his style and his emerging talent. Most important, in an era when a boxer's connections were often as important as his abilities, Weill had the power and influence that would provide Marciano with the big fights in the big arenas when he was ready.

If Rocky Marciano was lucky to have found Al Weill, Weill was even luckier to have found Marciano. For more than thirty years, Weill had used his canny knowledge of styles to guide three men to the championship of their weight classes: lightweight Lou Ambers in the late 1930s, featherweight Joey Archibald in the late 1930s, and welterweight Marty Servo in the mid-1940s. But he had never found a boy who could land him his sport's biggest prize—the heavyweight championship of the world—until that June day in 1948, when the future heavyweight champion of the world landed directly in his lap.

But Weill didn't realize it. And he, like his Boston counterparts, almost let Marciano get away. After trying unsuccessfully to convince Marchegiano to stay in New York, Weill decided to farm the fighter out to Providence, Rhode Island, where Weill had friends who could get the fighter some matches when he was ready. In the interim, said Weill, Marchegiano could come down to New York from time to time to work with Goldman. In other words, Weill stopped just short of giving Rocco Marchegiano a complete brushoff. There was no written contract, no agreed-upon financial split, no rigid training schedule, no master plan—just vague promises of some supervised gym work and a few fights in Providence.

As it turned out, Providence was an ideal training ground for Marciano. It was near his home in Brockton, which meant that his family and friends would always be there to root him on. It was a smaller city where he could develop without having to endure the white-hot spotlight of a big city like New York. And it was a great fight town, with a core of knowledgeable fans who consistently and passionately supported local boxing. It would also be the boxing home of Rocky Marciano for the first three years of his career. Between July 1948 and July 1951, all but eight of his thirty-four bouts would take place in Providence.

The top promoter in Providence at the time was Manny Almeida, who offered boxing shows nearly every Monday night at the Rhode Island Auditorium in downtown Providence. Silverman, the Boston promoter who had his hand in boxing ventures throughout New England, joined forces with Almeida behind the scenes to arrange the matches, hype the gate, and promote the Monday-night shows. Weill instructed Almeida and Silverman to line up some fights for his "discovery."

It didn't take long for the fans of Providence to discover Rocky Marciano. Between July 1948 and May 1949, Marciano rang up thirteen of his fifteen consecutive knockout victories in Providence, almost all of them in three rounds or less. Along the way he became a headliner for Almeida's Monday-night shows and a huge favorite with the Providence crowds. Marciano could hit. Marciano was exciting. Marciano was an Italian American, no small advantage in a city with a large Italian-American community. And Marciano won. By the end of 1949 he had a perfect 25–0 record and a reputation as one of the more promising young heavyweights in the nation. By that point he had become an adopted son of Providence.

Back in Boston, Marciano remained the reluctant prodigal son, out of sight, out of mind. Al Weill made sure of it. As soon as Marciano's knockout string started to approach double figures in late 1948, the manager's initial coolness toward the fighter disappeared. He was now hotly protective of his fighter. Shrewd, abrasive, manipulative, nurturing—as a boxing manager, Al Weill was all these things. Most of all, however, he was savvy about control. And he wasn't about to showcase Marciano in Boston, where members of the fight mob might have recognized their earlier mistake and tried to move in on his hot new heavyweight. So Weill kept Marciano laboring in the relative obscurity of Providence, where his crony Almeida could keep a close watch on his prized possession. The few in Boston fight circles who paid close attention to Marciano's lengthening winning streak during 1948 and 1949 saw it, with considerable big-city arrogance, as a minor-league, "Made in Providence" phenomenon.

Boston was forced to take notice in early 1950 when Weill matched Marciano against Roland LaStarza for his first big fight. Like Marciano, LaStarza was a young heavyweight with an unbeaten record who was seen as potential title timber. As a result, the LaStarza-Marciano bout generated a distinct buzz and heavy betting interest in New York. On a Friday night in March 1950, more than 13,000 fans in Madison Square Garden and fans in twenty-seven other cities (including Boston) on the fledgling NBC television network watched Marciano shake off a minor case of stage fright to capture a razor-thin decision. His reputation hardly improved in the process, though; the New York fight crowd criticized his performance and labeled him a not-ready-for-prime-time player. In Boston Marciano received kinder treatment, with some Boston reporters on the scene maintaining that Marciano had in fact dominated LaStarza. Even those who took a different view, such as Joe McKenney of the *Boston Post* (who concluded that Marciano was "a year or more removed from taking, or even contesting for the title") and "Colonel" Dave Egan of the *Boston Record* (who characterized the outcome as "a dubious decision"), spared Marciano their vitriol.[4]

Four months later Marciano crept further into the Boston sports consciousness when Weill at last let him fight in Boston. His opponent was Gino Buonvino, the former champion of Italy who had previously faced (and lost to) several big-name heavyweights of the era. Although the bout plainly fell short of a big fight, it was seen as a decent test for Marciano. It was also viewed as Marciano's coming-out party in Boston. The local hype reached its height several days before the fight when veteran Boston boxing promoter Eddie Mack exuded, "So he's crude! So what? . . . He's probably the best looking young heavyweight to come along since Maxie Baer," a comment that somehow incredibly overlooked the Joe Louis of the mid-1930s.[5]

It wasn't the faint praise but instead the weather that damaged the gate, with only 4,900 filing into Braves Field on fight night, July 10, 1950—a crowd far beneath the expectations of local promoters Silverman and Rip Valenti. It became a surreal experience for all involved. For one, the antique ring was several feet smaller than regulation, making Marciano and Buonvino look as if they were boxing in what Mike Gillooly of the *Boston Evening American* called "an enlarged birdcage." The ring was also in dilapidated condition: safety pins hung from the ringside, the ropes were hung far too loosely, the ring padding was like concrete, and the surrounding ring apron was small and substandard. The lights were also poor, causing the spectators in the grandstand at Braves Field to chant "Lights, lights!" throughout the fight. The fact that the bout was fought during a steady drizzle only added to its bizarre nature. "I'll never forget that night," a bemused Marciano would say two years later. "It was raining and they put the fight on early. And what a ring. It was really small and tilted. I felt like I was fighting uphill all night."[6]

At times Marciano looked as if he was fighting uphill. Although he knocked Buonvino down in the first round, he failed to finish his man. Then, in the second, Buonvino steadied and started to fight back. As the rounds wore on, Buonvino had to endure several crises, but also had several moments of his own, even managing to cut Marciano along the way. In the seventh, though, Buonvino began to tire visibly. Marciano knocked him down toward the end of the ninth, with only the bell delaying the end. Twenty-five seconds into the tenth and final round, with Marciano continuing to rain blows on Buonvino, referee Joe Zapustas stopped the fight.

In the aftermath, many Boston reporters fixated on the ring and all its inadequacies, with many sniffing some sort of conspiracy afoot to favor Marciano and his style. The few who focused on the fight itself were critical of Marciano. W. A. Hamilton of the *Boston Herald* found significant weaknesses in Marciano's defense and punching accuracy, concluding that "it will take more than he showed last night to convince veteran observers that he has the stuff to win the heavyweight title." Arthur Siegel of the *Boston Traveler* was even more blunt: the heavyweight field must be "a stinker" if Marciano was a leading contender, because the Brockton heavyweight was nothing more than "a good club fighter."[7]

For the next year Marciano retreated from Boston and from the national scene as Weill sent him back to Providence for further seasoning against a string of mediocre opponents. Marciano responded with a string of mediocre performances. He finally returned to the spotlight when he met Rex Layne in Madison Square Garden on July 12, 1951. A highly touted slugger from the West who owned a victory over Jersey Joe Walcott, among others, Layne was seen by many as the next heavyweight champion of the world. The bookies in New York made Layne the prohibitive favorite.

Meanwhile the hardened cynics in Boston hoped that Marciano would prove to be the real McCoy. This had in fact been the hope all along. In the aftermath of the LaStarza fight, for instance, Egan, while positing that Marciano's "equipment is too limited to carry him the full distance," also expressed his hope "that I'm wrong in my judgment of Marciano, for 'twould be nice to have a heavyweight champion hailing from Brockton." Now, on the eve of the Layne fight, Doc Almy, the veteran boxing writer for the *Post*, joined the chorus, recognizing that "simply by stretching our elastic neighborhood limits as far as Brockton we may consider Marciano as another Boston boy, one of our own." Almy, waxing nostalgic, enthused over the possibility that Marciano might join John L. Sullivan, Jim Maloney, Ernie Schaaf, and Jack Sharkey as the latest in the line of first-class Boston heavyweights. At the same time, though, Almy worried that "the Brockton boy's long series of so-called nursery bouts, fought in Providence and elsewhere along the pugilistic panhandle, will not stand him to good advantage now that he is moving back into the big time."[8] Others in Boston had similar reservations. Sure, Marciano was unbeaten. But whom had he fought?

Against Layne, Marciano answered his critics by scoring a spectacular sixth-round knockout. It would prove to be the key victory in his rise to the title. With a Marciano win, Siegel of the *Traveler* had correctly recognized on the eve of the fight, "Rocky will move into the upper brackets of his business. If he loses, he's just a workingman who may have to wait longer for a chance at the better money."[9] Marciano's convincing victory put him in the big time to stay. For many who saw matters through a racial lens, his defeat of Layne, also a white man, made Marciano the new Great White Hope. Race aside, he was unquestionably the hot new kid on the heavyweight block. His postfight appearance on that cultural barometer, Ed Sullivan's *Toast of the Town* television program, only seemed to confirm his newfound fame. Rocky Marciano had arrived.

In the wake of Layne, Boston scrambled to catch up to the unfolding Marciano drama. At the same time, the city prepared to host a Marciano fight one more time—and, as it turned out, a last time. On August 27, 1951, in his first fight after Layne, Marciano met Freddie Beshore in front of 9,523 fans in the Boston Garden. Those in attendance from the Brockton area got what they wanted: a Marciano victory courtesy of a convincing fourth-round knockout. The members of the Boston fight mob left the Garden disappointed, however. They had come to assess Marciano's progress since

Buonvino and his prospects for capturing the heavyweight crown. Such an assessment was impossible, however, given that the over-the-hill Beshore was plainly overmatched. Several years earlier, when Beshore was still a fine fighter and sniffing at the top of the heavyweight division, he might have constituted a decent test for Marciano. But not now. Against Marciano, the "hog-fat and out of shape" Beshore proved to be a sitting duck.[10]

To Boston, then, the Marciano story remained very much a mystery—one that neither the Beshore bout nor the Buonvino fight a year earlier had cleared up. On the basis of those spare live performances, Arthur Siegel of the *Traveler* observed, "It's hard for Bostonians to go overboard for Rocky." As Siegel explained, speaking for many Boston fight fans at the onset of Marciano's fame, "The boys who analyze affairs pugilistic can't reach unanimity on whether Rocky is a prodigy or a bum."[11]

As everyone was about to find out, Rocky Marciano was no bum. Two months after he flattened Beshore in Boston, Marciano was matched against the biggest name in the business (Joe Louis) on the biggest stage in the business (Madison Square Garden) with the rest of the nation watching on NBC. Marciano knocked out a washed-up Louis, ending the former champion's comeback and seizing the title of "uncrowned champion" in the process. As Gerry Hern of the *Boston Post* proclaimed, Louis had "lost to a guy he needn't be ashamed of. Rocky can carry on from here. He's a worthy successor."[12] Marciano had suddenly become the heir apparent. It now seemed only a matter of time before the new uncrowned champion would formally get his crown.

And that's exactly what happened. After four more bouts, Marciano got his shot at champion Jersey Joe Walcott in September 1952. Entering the thirteenth round behind on points, and with little or no chance to capture a decision in front of judges in Walcott's adopted hometown of Philadelphia, Marciano rose to the occasion, ending a classic fight with a classic knockout courtesy of a compact, deadly right. He would go on to defend his crown a half-dozen times (twice a year in 1953, 1954, and 1955) before suddenly retiring in the spring of 1956.

Along the way, Marciano emerged as a bona fide local celebrity who helped define early 1950s Boston. The turning point was Marciano's fight against Louis in October 1951. The fact that the local guy was preparing to fight the great Louis sparked enormous prefight interest in the Hub. And when the local guy knocked the great Louis down and then out, it became *the* story in town. Boston's hypercompetitive daily newspapers (which at that time included the *Globe*, the *Herald*, the *Post*, the *Traveler*, the *Record*, and the *American*) rushed to lavish attention on every aspect of the Marciano saga. They would continue to do so for the rest of his career, covering every conceivable angle, personal and professional. That Marciano frequently crossed paths with others in the ranks of power seemed to cement his status as one of the Hub's crème de la crème. Governor Paul A. Dever presented Marciano with a special license plate that read "K O" (presumably unaware that he was a notoriously dangerous driver). Archbishop Cushing let Marciano kiss his ring. Ted Williams gave Marciano his Red Sox cap. In early 1950s Boston, the Rock was on the scene and in the news.

But he wasn't immune from criticism. This was, after all, the generation of Boston sportswriters that Williams derisively labeled "the Knights of the Keyboard." While they knew their sports, they could be tough and even cruel. The prime recipient of their venom was, of course, Williams. Although they were far kinder to Marciano, they didn't always treat him with kid gloves, either. For instance, when Marciano, in his first fight after Louis, stumbled to victory against the hapless Lee Savold, sportswriters throughout the country heaped stinging, mocking criticism upon the man who would be king. Boston's scribes were no exception. Proclaiming that "Rocky never looked worse, not even as an amateur," Gerry Hern of the *Boston Post* mused, "The real story may be that the clock struck 12 for Rocky Marciano the other night and the Cinderella Guy turned and ran home leaving a glass slipper behind him." Declared the cantankerous Clif Keane of the *Boston Globe*, "Let nobody ever mention Rocky in the same breath with Jack Dempsey—or even Jersey Joe Walcott, for that matter."[13]

For the rest of his rise and throughout his reign, Marciano's ring performances—always effective but sometimes inartistic—would draw occasional criticism from the Boston press. In the wake of his greatest moment (the knockout of Walcott that made him champion), Harold Kaese of the *Globe* proclaimed, "We overrated our boy." Kaese then speculated that the new champion's reign would probably be brief, reasoning that "despite his courage, color and character, Marciano figures to be hit too much and cut too often to set any new records for distance." Four years later, in the wake of his greatest fight (the knockout of Archie Moore that brought him his forty-ninth and final victory), Kaese observed, "Marciano's fondest dream—to be regarded as a great heavyweight champion—did not prosper." Even a columnist like Hern, who usually wrote glowingly of the champion, would occasionally direct critical fire at Marciano, noting after he bludgeoned Don Cockell in their 1955 fight that his "timing was poor. He hit with little authority. He lacked confidence in his once great ability."[14]

Significantly, however, all of this criticism was about Marciano the fighter, not Marciano the man. When it came to Marciano's personality and character, never was heard a discouraging word in Boston. Part of this was due to the fading but still prevailing "Gee Whiz" sportswriting canons of the day, which dictated that sportswriters lionize the athletes they covered. Equally important was Marciano's excellent relationship with sportswriters. The fighter knew how to give scribes what they needed for their stories—and how to charm them and make them feel important. For example, when Bill Liston of the Boston Post arrived at Marciano's training camp in California before the Cockell fight, Marciano leapt to his feet, smiled, enthusiastically shook Liston's hand, and said, "Bill, how are you? It's good to see you. How's everything back home? Are any of the boys coming out to see the fight?" On another occasion, as he talked with reporters from around the country after his September 1953 title fight with LaStarza, Marciano put the spotlight on his hometown scribes by referring to the move of the Hub's National League entry and joking, "You Boston writers better not get fresh with me or I'll move to Milwaukee, too."[15]

There was little danger of that. Even before Marciano emerged on the national level as the athletic symbol of truth, justice, and the American Way, Boston's sportswriters were lavishing praise upon his qualities of character and spirit. After he knocked out Rex Layne in July 1951, for instance, Hern was impressed with how the victor greeted his fans in the Madison Square Garden ring after the match, "leaning over the top rope to shake the hands of excited Brockton and Providence people who had come here to see him." Gushed Hern, "This guy has all the touches a champion needs." Several days later Hern reiterated his point by quoting an ordinary citizen from Brockton: "He hasn't gone big time. Hasn't changed a bit, as far as I can see, and that's why all of us go to see him fight. We like him because he's a nice guy."[16]

One year later, as Marciano fought for the heavyweight championship of the world, Boston sportswriters broke into a spirited competition to prove to their readers that Rocky wasn't just a nice guy but in fact a great guy. The fighter became the prototype of the working-class hero. In a column titled "In a Game That's Noted for Its Punks, Phoneys, Rocky Stands for Class," Kaese declared, "He is somebody to root for. He is not clever, but is intelligent. He is not polished, but is solid. He is not sophisticated, but is natural. He is serious, modest, and patient." Echoed Hern, "The measure of Rocky Marciano is not only in his fists. The measure is in the warmth of his human relations." Liston of the *Post* went even further, quoting an unnamed priest who had recently met Marciano as saying, "That boy is no ordinary prizefighter. He is one of the most dignified, straightforward people I have ever met in my life. The people of the world should be informed of this boy's character and personality. Because if they knew him as I do now, he will become one of the most highly-regarded personalities in the history of sports."[17]

Sportswriters from all over the country (not just in Boston) were lauding Marciano in such a fashion during the early 1950s. What made Boston different was the paternalism of its sportswriters and fans. As a native son, he deserved and needed protection from the evil forces that lurked in boxing—and in Marciano's own corner in the person of Al Weill (whom Boston sportswriters, like sportswriters everywhere, didn't trust) and in the form of the International Boxing Club (IBC), the promotional power of the day that had close ties to Weill and thus Marciano. Like other prescient reporters around the nation, several Boston sportswriters saw the IBC as controlling, corrupt, and, in the words of Jerry Nason of the *Globe*, "somewhat sinister." Marciano originally suffered from the association. As Nason noted late in Marciano's rise to the title, even though "you could not find a finer young fellow than Rocky Marciano . . . despite your admiration for Rocky Marciano, the man, you cannot in your mind blot out the fact that he is a 'house fighter' for the IBC."[18]

Ultimately, though, the specter of guilt by association faded, and the Boston press cast Marciano as an innocent victim of the evil IBC. Exhibit A occurred before Marciano's second fight against Walcott in May 1953, when the IBC's publicists somehow convinced Walcott to climb into the ring with a goat in order to illustrate charges emanating from the Walcott camp that Marciano had illegally butted Walcott during their first fight. Alas, the goat didn't cooperate and refused to butt, even when Walcott got down on one knee and started to push the goat in the face. To the extent that reporters noted it at all, most were amused by the cheap publicity stunt. Not Nason. Why, he asked, had Walcott submitted to "that insulting gymnasium pose with the goat"? To Nason, "this one-sided name-calling contest has cheapened what is, with the World Series, sports' most staturesque [sic] event" — and had also tarnished the integrity and reputation of Marciano, "a man of humility and courage, and a great sense of responsibility at all times to the championship he holds." Concluded Nason, "Sorry for the soap-box session, kids. I just got heated up by this try out here to cheapen a pretty fine young guy."[19]

Indeed, throughout Marciano's reign Boston was quick to leap to the fighter's defense whenever anyone (particularly someone from the New York fight mob) criticized his record or abilities. For instance, after Marciano knocked out Walcott to become champion, Hy Hurwitz of the *Globe* speculated, "You will probably read and hear from some that Marciano can't be much of a champion if it took him almost 37 minutes of mauling to kayo the aged Walcott. What a lot of hogwash that kind of stuff is!" Three years later, toward the end of the champion's reign, Nason defended Marciano against charges that he was a "dirty fighter," pointing out: "Those who seek to smear the Rock with the 'dirty fighter' charge overlook the fact that no heavyweight champion, not even Joe Louis, has kept faith with the championship as Marciano has. He has enormous pride in it and his conduct has been willfully governed by it."[20]

No one, however, defended Marciano more often and more vigorously than Gerry Hern of the *Boston Post*. In the fall of 1953, for instance, Hern answered the question that he kept hearing from the New York cynics ("Who'd he ever lick?") with a one-word answer: "Everybody." Less than a year later, Hern blasted "those who persist in living in the past" for claiming that Marciano didn't measure up to champions of yesteryear. He was, proclaimed Hern, "the greatest fighter in the world at this moment. That doesn't include the historic past or the dreamboat future. It's just the present." In the fall of 1955, before Marciano's final fight against Archie Moore, Hern was still waging his one-man crusade against those "who confuse their hatred for the IBC with their appraisal of a decent, highly respectable man." Tongue planted firmly in cheek, he wrote: "There is the hope that the fight here tomorrow night will finally establish Rocky Marciano as heavyweight champion of the world." The title of Hern's column—"Rocky Doesn't Get Credit He Deserves as World Champion"—seemed to capture the sentiments of a generation of Bostonians who had shaken their initial skepticism about Marciano and were now vigilantly defending him at every turn.[21]

But paternalism doesn't always breed passion. Nor do acknowledged celebrity and genuine respect automatically kindle the flame. And that was the ingredient—unbridled, over-the-top passion—that was always missing for Marciano in Boston.

It most assuredly would have been there had Marciano's career not run so counter to the powerful forces of Hub provincialism—and had he fought at least one big fight in Boston during his rise or reign. A big fight in Boston would have helped bridge the gap that had opened when Marciano was made in Providence, not Boston. A big fight in Boston would have allowed the Hub to experience firsthand the excitement and glamour that surrounded Marciano's bouts in the early 1950s. A big fight in Boston would have sparked more passion and led to a fuller embrace for the local hero.

But a big fight in Boston never happened. Early on, there was hope. In the summer of 1950 Boston promoter Rip Valenti announced that he had offered heavyweight champion Ezzard Charles $50,000 to meet the up-and-coming Marciano in Braves Field. The fight never materialized. As Marciano went on to wage his most important pretitle bouts against Layne, Louis, and Harry Matthews in New York, Boston's fight crowd continued to try to bring the Rock back home to Boston. In the wake of the Louis fight, promoter Sam Silverman optimistically reported, "I'm getting a lot of encouragement from Rocky's direction. Don't be surprised if his first post-Louis fight is here in Boston."[22] Around the same time, Silverman supposedly offered the Marciano camp a $40,000 guarantee for a Marciano bout. Again, nothing materialized.

Silverman and Valenti kept trying. In the summer of 1952 Jersey Joe Walcott's manager, the shady Felix Bocchicchio, unable to obtain a manager's license in New York because of his criminal past, contacted Silverman about the possibility of staging the title fight between the champion

Walcott and the challenger Marciano at Braves Field. Eventually, though, Bocchicchio struck a deal with Weill and the IBC that placed the historic fight in Philadelphia. Several months later, with the now-champion Marciano having just successfully defended his title in the rematch against Walcott in Chicago, Boston was mentioned as one of the leading candidates for the next Marciano fight. Again, nothing materialized. Marciano went on to defend his title five more times, four times in New York and once in San Francisco. But never in Boston.

Why? The prime reason often cited, both at the time and through the years, involved "legal entanglements" that Marciano and his men allegedly faced in Massachusetts. Marciano had in fact been involved in a lawsuit with his amateur manager, Gene Caggiano, concerning several alleged contracts that the two entered into in early 1948 stating that Caggiano would manage Marciano if he decided to turn professional. When Marciano subsequently bolted for New York and Al Weill, Caggiano sued Marciano, seeking control of the fighter and a share of his earnings. The case quickly became bitter, with Caggiano claiming that he received several threatening letters and phone calls promising that he would end up in a block of cement if he didn't drop the case. But the persistent would-be manager pressed on—and actually won the first round in Suffolk Superior Court in late 1950. On appeal, however, the Supreme Judicial Court of Massachusetts reversed the decision, ruling in a published July 1951 opinion that the Marciano-Caggiano contracts were too indefinite and uncertain to be enforced.

That should have sealed the matter of *Caggiano v. Marchegiano*. But in the fall of 1951, just days after Marciano's landmark victory over Louis, Caggiano revealed with some fanfare that he was planning renewed legal action against Marciano and his men. One year later, after Marciano beat Walcott for the title, Caggiano was still threatening. The specifics behind the threat were always vague, and the underlying legal grounds were somewhat shaky. No matter—the mere existence of the threat was supposedly enough to keep Weill from setting foot in the Bay State for fear of being served with a subpoena. As Harold Kaese of the *Globe* noted in 1955, "Weill is fearful of getting involved in a law suit, brought by a former manager of Marciano, if the champion fights here." A year earlier Silverman had also supported the myth by stating, "I'm not kidding myself any longer. Weill refuses to come into Massachusetts. I don't believe he has ever been in Brockton, Marciano's home town."[23] In fact, and contrary to any fears that he might have harbored concerning Caggiano, Weill was in Brockton for Marciano's wedding in December 1950, Marciano's post-Louis parade in November 1951, and Marciano's retirement luncheon in April 1956. Caggiano's legal threat, then, was probably a red herring—and, at best, merely a secondary factor in Weill's decisionmaking calculus concerning a Marciano fight in Boston.

More at the heart of the matter was greed, always a powerful motivator. And that factor led Weill to place Marciano's big fights not in Boston but New York City. Weill himself was, by nature and personality, a New York guy to the core. He also correctly viewed New York as the unquestioned capital of the boxing world during the early 1950s. New York had the biggest outdoor ballparks (Yankee Stadium and the Polo Grounds) as well as Madison Square Garden, the crown jewel of indoor sports arenas. New York had the biggest sportswriters (Red Smith and Jimmy Cannon) in an era where newspapers still trumped television in terms of influence. And New York had the influential fight mob—the loose and somewhat shady assortment of promoters, managers, trainers, and mobsters that habitually congregated in the rundown, smoky, unwashed environs of Stillman's Gym in Midtown.

In Al Weill's mind, all of this made New York the ideal site for a big fight featuring his meal ticket, Rocky Marciano. No other city offered as much attention. No other city offered as much gate potential. Most important, no other city offered as much money. So Weill kept Marciano in New York. And, when it came to matters of Marciano's career, Weill called the shots, even during his stint as IBC matchmaker from May 1949 to August 1952—when, in a ruse that fooled absolutely no one, and in clear violation of boxing rules and ethics, Weill installed his stepson Marty, a salesman from Dayton, Ohio, as Marciano's on-the-record manager while continuing to manage Marciano on the side all the while.

Formally back in the managerial saddle during Marciano's reign, Weill occasionally held out the possibility that Marciano might fight in Boston—if it was worth his while, of course. "Will he fight in Boston?" Weill told Nason in the spring of 1953. "Why not? There's no reason why he shouldn't. He'll fight where the money is." In reality, though, Weill doubted whether Boston's fans would pay the premium $40 per ticket that he and the IBC

wanted to charge for Marciano's fights. Would Boston have in fact splurged
on the Rock? "Of course," Silverman contended. "New England fans
would pay that price to see Marciano in with a good opponent." Weill remained unconvinced. As one of Weill's cronies at the IBC told Nason,
"Silverman might talk, but we aren't convinced that Boston is a 'big' money
town." Silverman himself seemed to know it. "Weill, Al Weill, is the real
reason," said Silverman of Marciano's Hubless reign. "I know that Rocky
has asked Weill at least 20 times for a chance to fight in Boston. He'd like to
have a hometown match. But Al won't do it."[24]

Silverman himself was a pivotal figure relating to the other factor that
kept Boston from landing a big Marciano fight: a developing promotional
feud that pitted the local promoters against the national matchmakers at the
IBC. Alternately known as "Subway Sam," "Suitcase Sam," "Unsinkable
Sam," "Sad Sam," "Satchel Sam," "Suburban Sam," and "Substitute Sam,"
Silverman was one of those characters that only the ring seems to produce,
with a persona that included martinis, Chinese food, fast Cadillacs, and
omnipresent cigars. He was also the dominant figure on Boston's boxing
scene from the mid-1940s until his death in 1977. Along with erstwhile part-
ner Valenti, Silverman was at the peak of his promotional power in the early
1950s. Any IBC Marciano production in Boston, by necessity, would have
had to include Silverman on the local end. That Silverman had a personal
and professional relationship with Marciano (he had, after all, promoted
all his early fights in Providence in behind-the-scenes fashion) seemed to
make him a choice from central casting.

But there was a problem: Silverman didn't get along with Weill and his
cronies at the IBC. The relationship was frosty from the beginning, as the
flamboyant and independent Silverman bristled over the IBC's controlling
ways. And then, in April 1953, Silverman promoted a lightweight championship fight in Boston for the IBC that pitted Jimmy Carter against local
hero Tommy Collins. In front of a shocked national television audience,
Carter knocked down Collins ten times before Collins's cornermen finally
threw in the towel. Fans and sportswriters across the country were outraged
at the carnage—and directed much of their anger at the IBC. The IBC,
in turn, blamed Silverman. Then someone connected to the fight mob
bombed Silverman's house in Chelsea with several sticks of dynamite.
(When questioned about the bombing, Silverman, who wasn't home at the

time of the explosion, asked incredulously, "Bomb? What is this bomb stuff? There ain't no bomb. It was just a defective refrigerator.")[25] Metaphorically as well as literally, the relationship between Silverman and the IBC was starting to blow up. The formal split would eventually come in January 1956, with Silverman filing a $9 million lawsuit against the IBC that was eventually settled out of court.

For the time being, the festering feud that erupted after the Carter-Collins bout in the spring of 1953 was enough to give Al Weill—no longer an IBC employee but still an IBC man through and through—one final reason to keep Rocky Marciano out of Boston. In May 1953 IBC publicist Murray Goodman stated that Boston would not get a Marciano fight "for a long, long time" unless there was a change in local promoters (plainly referring to Silverman) as well as some assurances that such a fight would draw. Around the same time, an unnamed IBC source told Nason that Boston was unlikely to get a Marciano fight because "it's going to take a long time for Boston to recover from that awful Carter-Collins thing. I mean a long, long time." The source added that IBC czar Jim Norris "presumably has no use for that promoter up there," again referring to Silverman. From the Boston side of the promotional battle, Rip Valenti was sniping at Weill for various sins, transgressions, and personal slights. Plainly, Nason concluded, "There are no valentines or May baskets exchanged among Weill and the IBC on one hand and Silverman and Valenti on the other . . . But the real joker will be the fact that Marciano, caught in the cross currents of a tricky business, may never be seen as a heavyweight champion, in action, in the city on whose outskirts he was born and bred."[26]

By June 1954 Silverman and Valenti seemed to be resigned to the fact that Boston had been closed out of the heavyweight scene. "I've given up on it," Silverman admitted. When asked whether a Marciano fight in Boston was even a possibility, Valenti replied, "Never! In my opinion Marciano himself does not want to fight in Boston." Actually Marciano would have relished the opportunity to defend his title in the Hub. But it wasn't going to happen—a fact that Weill made abundantly clear in the spring of 1955 when he decided to match Marciano against Don Cockell in another city besides New York. He chose San Francisco, at least in part because he was close friends with the local promoter there, Jimmy Murray. "If Marciano has such a great following in this section, why doesn't he fight here?" pleaded Kaese. "Just once. Why—if he beats Cockell—won't he make his next defense in the Fall at Fenway Park?"[27] As long as Weill was calling the shots, however, that wasn't going to happen.

In other cities, the fact that a hometown hero never made a significant hometown appearance might not have mattered. In Boston, it mattered considerably, harnessing what should have been unbridled passion for the Rock.

Ironically, there was that type of passion for Marciano just twenty miles to the south of the Hub. That the good people of Brockton, Massachusetts, felt passion for Rocky Marciano was never in question. They psychologically linked themselves to his fortunes and emotionally drew on him for their identity. Many attended his fights in New York and elsewhere, betting heavily on their hero. Those who remained behind in Brockton on fight night breathlessly followed the proceedings as they unfolded on television or radio (as the rest of the city came to a complete stop). And when Marciano won, Brockton usually went into bedlam. The celebrations in the city were especially raucous the nights Marciano beat Louis and captured the crown from Walcott, with Brocktonians honking car horns, forming informal motorcades, snake dancing, waving banners, and mobbing Marciano's regular hangout, the Ward Two Memorial Club. A week or so after those two fights, as well as after the Layne fight and on the occasion of his retirement, the people of Brockton threw Marciano a parade, complete with all the trimmings. The largest was the one after he took the title from Walcott, drawing more people (between 60,000 and 100,000, depending on the estimate) than had turned out for President Roosevelt's and President Truman's earlier visits to the city.

All of this was proper and natural. After all, Marciano was from Brockton. And Brockton was of a size that it could afford to go gaga over the Rock. Boston, on the other hand, was bigger, more diverse, and more sophisticated—all factors that helped quell such frenzy for Marciano. Still, the contrast between Brockton and Boston in their reactions to local hero Marciano is striking. For while Marciano was a famous face in early 1950s Boston, he never was part of the Hub's psychological or emotional core. When he scored his greatest victories, Bostonians did not celebrate wildly. And Boston never threw a parade for Rocky Marciano. To get a taste of all that, Boston had to send press emissaries to Brockton to report on the goings-on there. In that sense, when it came to Marciano, Boston was always looking in from a distance.

The populace in early 1950s Boston did, of course, follow Marciano's career. And when he fought, people in the Hub paid close attention. On the Friday night that he fought Louis in October 1951, for instance, the streets of Boston became deserted as people crowded into bars and restaurants to catch a glimpse of the television and see if the local boy could make good. When he did make good, there were cheers all around. The cheers among Marciano's legions of fans in Boston continued for the rest of his reign. Many plainly felt a special connection to the champion. Boston's scribes felt the same way. "Boxing was a different, special kind of thing when Rocky was champion," Boston sportswriter Larry Claflin recalled years later. "Being a Boston fight writer was being sort of big time because the champ came from our town . . . the Boston crowd flocked to his training camps and his fights."[28]

But the mere fact that the Boston crowd had to flock to Marciano presented a stern challenge to the Hub's provincialism. And the problem was significant, given the larger role that sports was now playing in American culture. As Benjamin Rader has observed, by the middle of the twentieth century sports had emerged as "a central feature of American culture" and "one of the sinews which held modern society together." Among other things, sports could, according to Rader, "enhance a sense of individual identity and belonging." The same holds true today. And in this overall calculus, despite our electronic age of wide-ranging communication and connection, *place* continues to matter greatly. To become part of the fabric of a place, it is crucial that an athlete or a team perform regularly in that place. Even those athletes or teams with some civic connection cannot trigger those powerful feelings of identity and belonging if they are not on home turf but, instead, slightly removed from the scene.[29]

Nowhere is this presence more true than in Boston. Indeed, when it comes to our sporting consciousness, what happens here has always mattered the most. Events playing out on the national stage certainly receive our attention, but usually in a fleeting fashion. Instead, it is the drama surrounding our teams (the Red Sox, Bruins, Celtics, and Patriots) and our events (the Marathon, the Beanpot, the Head of the Charles) that trigger our passion. As a city infused with a proud provincialism, Boston likes that which makes it unique and distinctive. In sports, those factors have always translated into heightened interest in our teams and our events.

And, of course, our heroes. The vast majority of our sports heroes during the last half-century—Williams, Yaz, Orr, Espo, Bourque, Russell, Cousy, Havlicek, Bird, Flutie, Roger (before he defected), Pedro, and the newest hero of the Hub, Tom Brady—played for our teams or took part in our events. Rocky Marciano was the exception. He was our hero, certainly, but he didn't perform on our home turf or take part in our events. Instead, he performed in faraway New York for a New York manager in front of a New York crowd. Marciano may have been *from* Boston, but he was never *of* Boston.

For those of a sporting nature in early 1950s Boston, this contradiction presented a conundrum. Occasionally the resulting frustration would spill out in public, as when Rip Valenti complained about what he called the "Marciano wing" in the Boston press, explaining that "Rocky has never done anything for boxing in Boston and they give him all the headlines."[30] Aside from such rare rants by canny fight men trying to position their fighters, Marciano's lack of local connection to Boston was neither articulated nor delineated in the early 1950s. But the issue was there, lurking as an implicit part of the subconsciousness of Boston sports in the early 1950s. And it had its impact. For Boston was never really sure of what to make of Rocky Marciano.

Ultimately, then, it should come as no surprise that Boston largely forgot about Rocky Marciano.

Certainly the final milestone of his career, his April 1956 retirement, received a great deal of attention. In a final show of paternalism, Nason, Hern, and several other Boston sportswriters had previously urged Marciano to do precisely that—retire before his legacy, reputation, or physical health declined. When Marciano followed through and stepped away, the development triggered a flood of tributes and praise. The same was true— but even more so—when Marciano suddenly and tragically died in a plane crash thirteen years later. For several days Boston became engulfed in Marciano memories. The *Globe* ran a masthead editorial titled "A Boxer and a Gentleman"; the *Herald Traveler* ran one that elaborated at length on

Marciano's Horatio Alger–like heroism. For a few days, at least, Boston, in its grief, embraced Rocky Marciano.

Four months later, in January 1970, Marciano was one of the gladiators in Superfight, a surreal spectacle that featured Marciano and a then-exiled Muhammad Ali acting out rounds generated by a computer. The event (shot just before Marciano's death in the summer of 1969) resulted in a Marciano victory in the thirteenth round. More than 7,000 fans filled the Boston Garden to witness the proceedings. Some of those in attendance (such as Valenti) got teary-eyed when Marciano "won." Others filed out of the Garden yelling, "Long live Rocky!" In a bizarre sense, Marciano had, at long last, fought a big fight in Boston.

Since then, though, Marciano has largely faded from the Boston sports consciousness. Of course the Marciano name still occasionally bubbles to the forefront. But the Marciano legacy in Boston has proved to be far less enduring or passion-provoking than those of Williams, Russell, Cousy, and several other Hub heroes who also performed around midcentury. Boston tends to remember them. Too often, it doesn't remember Rocky Marciano. The Curse of Al Weill that curbed passion for Marciano during his career has also obscured the memories of him in the years since his death. That Marciano, with his unmatched record and his host of unmatched skills as a fighter, is on the short list of the greatest heavyweights of all time only adds to the irony of all this.

Like another curse that has afflicted the history of Boston sports—the infamous Curse of the Bambino—the Curse of Al Weill resulted in the loss of a legendary athlete to New York. In terms of impact, the Curse of Al Weill cannot, of course, possibly compare to that of its far more celebrated sister curse, given that the Red Sox have now gone more than eighty-five years without winning a World Series. In a certain sense, though, the Curse of Al Weill was crueler. At least Boston had the Babe for six years. Boston never really had Rocky Marciano.[31]

1. In 1915 Babe Ruth turned twenty and helped Boston win the world's championship. In six seasons with the Red Sox he won eighty-nine games as a pitcher, and in the 1919 season he hit twenty-nine home runs, a major league record. His departure from Boston in 1920 remains the most controversial trade in professional sports.

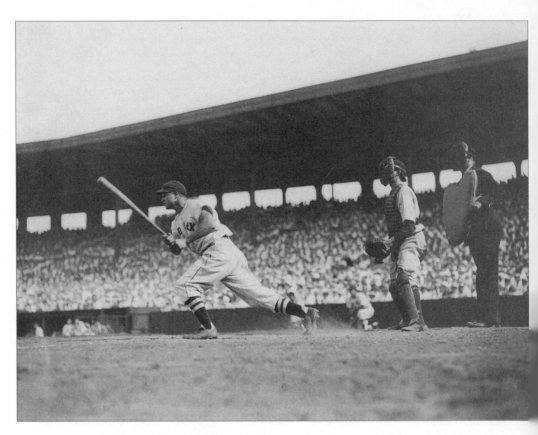

2. Jimmy Foxx could hit like Babe Ruth. In one seven-year period, which included three World Series, he averaged forty-one home runs per season. Unfortunately, he played those seasons for the Philadelphia Athletics. Foxx was traded to Boston in 1935. Though he did not lead Boston to a world championship, "Double X" was no disappointment.

3. If ever a baseball player looked as if he had been cast in Hollywood, it was Ted Williams. He was Gary Cooper with a perfect swing and an unforgiving edge. What he cared about he did better than anyone else, and what he didn't care about he didn't do.

4. According to the Boston calendar, 1967 was the Year of the Yaz. Carl Yastrzemski had a September that made the summer seem to last forever, leading the Red Sox past the Tigers and the Twins in one of the most thrilling pennant races in the history of major league baseball. Yaz won the Triple Crown; the Red Sox lost the World Series in seven games.

5. It seemed like a good idea to a group of Bostonians returning from the 1896 Athens Olympics. Why not run a race of about 25 miles (later standardized at 26 miles, 385 yards), winding through a swath of historical Massachusetts and ending in the center of Boston? The first race was run on Patriots' Day, April 19, 1897. Perhaps the most popular champion of the race was Johnny Kelley, who in the 1930s and 1940s gave lessons in the artless art of endurance.

6. In 1968 the Harvard heavyweight eight represented the United States at the Olympic Games in Mexico City. Eight muscular white men and a white coxswain, from mostly privileged families, improbably and controversially found themselves on the side of black rights advocate Harry Edwards. On the water and off, for them there were no half-measures.

7. Francis Ouimet had his moment as a very young man, and lived with that moment with grace for many years. Playing as an amateur, in 1913 he bested two seasoned English professionals, Ted Ray and the great Harry Vardon, in a playoff to win the U.S. Open championship at The Country Club in his hometown Brookline.

8. During the first generation of college football Yale and Harvard dominated the game. It was, largely, their game, and other colleges followed their lead. Violence, tramp athletes, every sort of violation of the amateur and gentlemanly code—Yale and Harvard blazed the trail for others to follow. Many educators, led by Harvard president Charles William Eliot, questioned the direction of the game.

9. Boston Patriots, New England Patriots, Hartford Patriots? The history of modern professional sports is in part the tale of franchise relocations. If a city holds out on building a new stadium or adding luxury boxes for too long, owners begin to look toward greener pastures or at least Providence. After prolonged negotiations, Boston didn't hold out. A look at the new stadium shows signs of commercialism everywhere.

10. John L. Sullivan, "the Boston Strong Boy," was America's first national athletic hero, and a fitting symbol for a time of tumult and change. He was the last bare-knuckle heavyweight champion. In his prime, a period before he was converted to temperance, Sullivan swore and drank and boasted that he could beat "any son-of-a-bitch in the house."

11. Rocky Marciano should have been another John L. Sullivan. Born in Brockton, a Red Sox fan, a tough, no-compromise fighter, he should have been the darling of Boston. But it never quite worked out that way. His manager Al Weill and trainer Charley Goldman (pictured) kept the Rock close to the island of Manhattan.

12. Tex Rickard is best known as the promoter of several "fights of the century" and as a sportsman who dreamed of an athletic empire. Madison Square Garden and the Boston Garden were cornerstones of that empire. The Boston Garden opened for business on November 17, 1928. Rickard died two months later.

13. Bobby Orr battles the Golden Jet, Bobby Hall. On the ice and off, Orr seldom made the wrong move. His game seemed magically effortless, and his life almost singularly charmed.

14. It was what they did best. Number 13 shot and number 6 defended. Wilt Chamberlain and Bill Russell were friends, but their association was defined by their rivalry. Chamberlain almost always won the statistical battles. Russell had to find solace in championships.

15. It happens every so often. An *annus mirabilis*. *Ulysses* and *The Waste Land* in 1922. *Stagecoach*, *The Wizard of Oz*, and *Gone with the Wind* in 1939. The Red Sox, Patriots, and Celtics in 1986. Almost, anyway. Close enough to believe that miracles can come true, even if they require waiting another eighteen years. Certainly Spike Owen, Roger Clemens, and Calvin Schiraldi have the look of a curse lifted.

12

Long before Orr: Placing Hockey in Boston, 1897–1929

Stephen Hardy

On Mother's Day 1970, Bobby Orr scored the Mother of All Goals to bring the Stanley Cup home for the first time since 1941. Orr's phenomenal play inspired a hockey boom in Boston. Towns and private investors built rinks to feed ice time to a growing legion of youth teams, filled with boys and girls who wanted to be Orr, and with parents who wanted to be Harry Sinden. It was not, however, Beantown's first hockey boom. Long before Bobby Orr graced the ice of Boston Garden and the screens of Channel 38, the Hub of the Universe was also a hub of homegrown "Boston" hockey. Long before Orr, Boston was a hockey town. Although New York, Chicago, Detroit, and other northern cities had supported professional and amateur teams for just as long, only Minnesota could rival Boston for positions on Olympic team rosters or for overall impact on "Canada's" game. Boston's hockey tradition is a case study in cultural diffusion, cultural identity, and chance. There is nothing "natural" about any aspect of it.[1]

To be sure, the Old Town enjoyed an abundance of local rivers, ponds, and lakes. The Charles and Mystic Rivers, Spy Pond, Ell Pond, Fresh Pond, Bullough's Pond, Hammond's Pond, Crystal Lake, and Lake Quonnapowitt, to name a few, all offered natural rinks for ancient pastimes like shinny, hurley, and hockey. These were all European folk games; native tribes played similar games. Players whacked a ball with a short stick—one-handed—toward, across, or through a goal, moving with the season, from field to ice. The term *hockey* or *hawkey* often referred to the stick, as Jacob Abbot explained in his 1839 book *Caleb in Town: A Story for Children:* "Now, a hawkey is a small, round stick, about as long as a man's cane, with a crook in the lower end, so that a boy can hit balls and little stones with it. A good hawkey is a great prize to a Boston boy." It still is.[2]

But these were not the foundation of Boston hockey. These were simple pastimes, with no recognized rules, no organization, no leagues, no records, no heroes to worship, and no fan following. While a frozen pond or lake might be dear to a skater's heart and memory, January thaws and February blizzards could snuff the game's life for a week, a month, or a year. Indeed, hockey was on thin ice when the "Montreal" game found the Hub in 1897. Within three decades, however, and long before Orr, the game was firmly embedded in Boston's sports tradition. The story contains elements common to the successful diffusion of other sports, such as baseball, basketball, and soccer. The list includes missionaries who introduced the game; athletes, coaches, and fans who embraced a novel activity; promoters and their media partners who saw a chance for mutual profit. But all of this required a careful cultivation of place—in this case both a facility (the Boston Arena) and a strategy to position hockey as a unique product.[3]

Boston's first organized hockeylike games were actually called "polo." Roller polo—some accounts trace its origin to Newport, Rhode Island—emerged in the 1880s as a popular spectator sport around New England and the Midwest. One set of 1884 rules provided the game's basics. Each team had seven players—goalkeeper, goal-cover and point-cover (the defenders), two backers (midfielders), and two rushers (forwards). Goals were six feet wide and from three to four feet high. The stick had a maximum length of four feet and diameter of one inch. It was essentially the old "hawkey." The ball was three inches in diameter. The game started with each team forming an inverted wedge. At the referee's signal, opponents rushed the ball placed at center ice. The game was on. There was no rule about offsides, but attackers could not stop within a 5-foot radius around the goal. Two or three team fouls, depending on location, equaled a goal for the opponent.

Matches were best-of-three or best-of-five "goals." There was no "intentional" striking, kicking, or tripping, but newspaper stories graphically described the slashing sticks, whirling fists, cracked bones, and bloodied heads. As one 1895 advertisement put it, "roller polo can arouse the sluggish blood, make the businessman forget his troubles, and afford much food for heated argument."[4]

In the early 1890s someone moved the game outdoors and dubbed it "ice polo." The first *Spalding Ice Hockey and Ice Polo Guide* (published in 1897) explained that although ice polo was linked to shinny, "it would seem nearer correct to credit its origin to the great and popular game of roller polo." By 1894 roller polo had reduced its teams to five a side: two rushers, a center, a halfback, and goalie. This is the same number reported in the *Boston Herald* in a December 1894 account of "Polo on the ice at Melrose."[5] Over the next few years Harvard and Boston College took up the game; schoolboys from Melrose, Medford, and other area schools formed the Suburban High School Ice Polo League; and amateur clubs took to the ice. Sporting-goods dealers like Wright and Ditson or Pitts, Kimball and Lewis provided ready-made equipment: India-rubber balls for a few cents, cheap Barney and Berry skates for as little as 15 cents, or Shamrock sticks for a steeper $2.00. At Boston College, President Brosnahan sanctioned the team's use of school colors as part of a wider publicity campaign.[6]

Even as ice polo was expanding in the Boston area, it was on its last legs. A new game was entering the United States, about to sweep all forms of hockey in its path, just as it had done in Canada. Known as the "Montreal" game, because of its birth in 1875–1877 at McGill University and the Victoria Rink, ice hockey had evolved from a fusion of field hockey and lacrosse into the clear forerunner of today's game. By the 1890s it featured a puck, a long, broad-bladed stick, face-offs, an offsides rule (no forward passing), a 4-by-6-foot cage, and seven players per side. Boston's first practitioners were probably a group of Harvard, Brown, and MIT grads who formed the Cambridge Ice Polo and Hockey team in 1897, playing home games on outdoor ice and away games at indoor rinks in New York, Montreal, Kingston, Ottawa, and Quebec.[7]

On January 19, 1898, Harvard converted to hockey in a game against Brown. It was, said the *Herald*'s headline, a "poor debut," as the Cantabs bunched up and generally "acted more like ice polo players" while losing

6–o. Brown spread out and used the open ice for "clean cut and accurate" passing. Brown's captain made the most "sensational" play, with a long lift from center ice. Puck control was in fact the great attraction of hockey. As the *Spalding Guide* noted in 1897, the broad hockey blade was designed to "shove or scoop" the puck in a two-handed sliding or lifting motion, as opposed to the polo player's one-handed strike. Although the puck could be lifted, it was mostly on the ice as a rusher tried to weave his way through the opposition, his teammates "following close behind or abreast of him" because they had to stay onside. Whereas the whack of a polo ball could send the rubber flying in any direction, hockey promised more scientific tactics. As newswriter and hockey publicist Fred Hoey recalled years later, "the hit-and-miss slam-bang feature of polo had no place in the new game."[8]

Within a few years area schools, colleges, and amateur clubs had converted to hockey. The game in Boston, however, still lacked the most important foundation of all—an indoor, artificial ice rink. An enclosed natural-ice rink had opened on Tremont Street as early as 1869, but it was out of business before ice polo or hockey came along. In 1896 the *Herald* speculated about plans for a rink to match the palaces in Chicago, Detroit, Pittsburgh, and Washington, D.C., but nothing developed.[9] As late as 1910, Boston hockey depended on the same old natural haunts, as well as some new flooded venues such as Franklin Field and Harvard Stadium. It was not easy to prepare a team on outdoor ice alone, as Harvard's longtime coach Alfred "Ralph" Winsor ('02) recalled in 1923. Pond, lake, or river "rinks" were simply open ice marked by goals of coats or stones. An errant pass or shot meant a long skate for retrieval, or a lost puck. Moreover, "a player was lucky if he found all his discarded garments intact at the end of practice." Local gamins were a menace. So were "frozen toes and ears" and soupy ice. All these factors created a serious disadvantage for Harvard in its rivalries with Yale and Princeton, both of which used New York's St. Nicholas Club rink for practice and games.[10]

The Boston Arena

Others realized the need for an indoor rink. One 1910 article, in *Baseball Magazine* of all places, recognized the "great demand" for a facility where skaters, hockey players, and curlers might "bid defiance to rain, snow and thaws." But, said the author, "conservative Boston is slow to move." William T. Richardson had tried to interest local investors, to no avail. He eventually found his money in Charles Abbey, a Chicopee resident. The Boston Arena Company, with Abbey as president and Richardson as secretary-treasurer, broke ground on October 11, 1909, in a St. Botolph's Street block between Massachusetts Avenue and Gainsborough Street. The Arena prospectus trumpeted the importance of location:

> From every viewpoint it is the most desirable in the city. It is in the midst of the new amusement centre of Boston—a district that is destined to be the very nub of the Hub. Near at hand are the new Museum of fine Arts, the Boston Opera House, Symphony Hall, Horticultural Hall, Chickering Hall, The New England Conservatory of Music, Mechanics hall, etc. Situated practically at the corner of Massachusetts and Huntington avenues, it is the most central point in the whole city of Boston.

Better yet, this area was served by trolley lines connecting the Arena to "every section of the city and its suburbs."[11]

The Arena was designed by the local firm of Funk and Wilcox. The principal architect was George C. Funk, a lifelong Brookline native and MIT graduate ('05). Years later, when the National Hockey League (NHL) was well established in the United States, *Popular Science Monthly* described George C. Funk as "Boston's ice engineer who built the first modern rinks in that and other large American cities" and who was "largely responsible" for hockey's American advance. Funk spared no amenities in designing the Arena, which had three components. The first was the "administrative" building, whose ornate façade opened to a 60-by-50-foot rotunda, offices, ticket booths, and writing and waiting rooms. Large windows opened from the rotunda to the ice surface so that fans could watch the action while they socialized. It was a giant proto-skybox. One level below were a skate shop, lounging and smoking rooms, lavatories, and locker rooms, all of which funneled by hallways to the ice surface in the main building, which was bigger than a football field. Its steel, concrete, and brick structure featured a truss-roof design that minimized the obstructed views among the 4,000 "polo chair" seats. The wooden roof was capped by a ridge of glass, which offered daytime skaters dazzling tints of light. Eighteen "intensified arc lights" burned for the evening activities. While the Arena was designed as a multipurpose facility, skating and hockey were its primary focus. The ice surface—90 by 244 feet—was the largest of its day and bigger than most rinks today. Maintaining cold ice in a warm rink was the work of the adjoining engineering building, where Funk used two 100-ton York refrigerating machines and a 400-horsepower Babcock and Wilcox boiler to push an ammonia/brine solution through some 55,000 feet of pipe under the ice surface. Funk's system, which he later revised and patented, was supposedly capable of maintaining a "skatable surface with a temperature as high as 110 degrees Fahrenheit." A "plenum vacuum" ventilation system drew outside air through a cleansing "water curtain" after which it was forced through a steam coil, heated to 55–60 degrees, and then distributed in the other buildings.[12]

The Arena opened in April 1910 to an array of skating and hockey programs. Fred Hoey, a *Herald* writer who served simultaneously as the Arena publicity director, recalled that "the hope and ambition of every Greater Boston hockey player was realized . . . outdoor hockey hardships were at an end. It was like a gift from heaven." Players and coaches could now count on a schedule of ice (at a cost). As the hockey season approached in early December 1910, the *Boston Post* bubbled with enthusiasm: "Great Year for Hockey" was a standard story line. The Greater Boston Interscholastic Hockey Association met to plan the year's schedule. Arena manager Jack Norfolk attended their meeting and announced that Monday and Friday afternoons would be set aside for the schoolboys. Norfolk also promised Harvard fans that their team was going to be tougher negotiating with Yale and Princeton. "Harvard has been generous in the past in showing willingness to go to New York," said Norfolk. The record shows they were more than generous. Every "Big Three" game from 1900 to 1910 was played in New York. The Arena shifted the balance of hockey power; Harvard now had "home ice." So, too, the amateur teams, with new contingents like the Boston Hockey Club, which the *Post* claimed "experts have picked as the logical opponents for teams from New York and the Provinces."[13]

But a 4,000-seat building would not last a winter on rental fees alone. The Arena was fan-friendly, but hockey still needed to build a broad base of fans. As Fred Hoey recalled, December 1910 was a bleak opening for hockey as spectacle: "sport fans were a bit skeptical about indoor hockey. Teams played to almost 4,000 empty seats. Something had to be done and done quick." Hockey had to distinguish itself in the broader marketplace of sport spectacle, then dominated by professional baseball, boxing, college football, and amateur track and field. Hockey had to position and brand itself.[14]

Urban Americans had already experienced a major shift in the way they purchased food, clothing, and personal products. The old dry-goods store, with its barrels of generic flour, crackers, and soap cakes and its shelves of cloth, had been replaced by grocery or department stores stocked with name-brand goods—Lux soap, Gillette razors, Uneeda biscuits. Manufacturers had learned the value of free samples, slick packaging, trading cards, and coupons in the fight for shelf space, name recognition, strong mental associations, and finally strong consumer loyalty. Fred Hoey and his fellow hockey promoters faced a similar task. They adopted a two-part strategy. The first stage was branding hockey as a special kind of sport; the second was branding different types of hockey. In both cases, hockey could count on a friendly press to craft and deliver the message.[15]

The first step was to import established teams from Canada—something like a limited trial offering. Not only did this move encourage new fans to watch hockey, but, as Hoey recalled, it attracted "former Canadians living in this area." As all sports promoters know, a packed house watching a skilled performance is the best way to turn a curious observer into a novice fan. The first exhibition was in December 1910—St. Michael's College of Toronto against the Boston Hockey Club. The press pumped the match. The BHC had old Harvard grads Ralph Winsor, Traff Hicks, and R. S. Townsend. St. Michael's had a "shining star" in Jack Spratt. On December 29, 4,000 fans watched St. Michael's earn a tough 5–3 decision, in a game that was sprinkled with Spratt's "wonderful rushing, dodging, and shooting." Mayor "Honey Fitz" Fitzgerald attended with his son Tom and his daughter Rose. So did a large contingent of the Canadian Club of Boston. Things went just as planned. It was, said the *Post*, "the largest gathering that ever watched a hockey game in this part of the country." On and off the ice, the world's coolest game was now Beantown's hottest. The *Post* ran one cartoon that showed a street urchin whacking a puck off the top hat of a stately gentleman. As the puck smashed a window, the would-be Jack Spratt yelled: "Hey—Lookout Mister!!!"[16]

In March the Arena gave local fans a bigger treat—an exhibition series between Montreal's Wanderers and Ottawa's Stanley Cup champions. The *Herald* emphasized that the "fine" Canadian amateur teams seen earlier that year "do not compare" with the professionals. Feelings would be intense; the officials would need close attention to "keep the men under control." The Senators featured Fred "Cyclone" Taylor, the "locomotive-like skater." The Wanderers matched him with "clever" Art Ross, who would make a long career of Boston hockey. Taylor and Ross led their teams in a split of two hard-fought games. Both men, said the *Post*, thrilled the "6,000 wildly enthusiastic followers" as they gathered the puck "time and again, and by clever dodging and hurdling" stick-handled "through their opponents the entire length of the rink." The exhibition was so successful that some worried about a letdown. Would the fans be satisfied with American amateur teams?[17]

American hockey needed some homegrown stars. A star with the skills of Taylor or Ross would galvanize the current fans and attract new ones. Individual skill in skating and stickwork was one of three key components hockey promoters used to brand the game. Fortunately, the rules of early hockey promoted stardom. The strict onsides rule eliminated forward passes, which encouraged individual rushes, stick-handling, and shiftiness to avoid crashing checks. By comparison, football had evolved into a "mass" game, which reduced the chance for brilliant flashes of individual skill. The forward pass, though legalized in 1906, was too restricted and the ball too round for accurate passing. Baseball had plenty of individual heroes displaying exquisite skill, but physical punishment was the exception not the rule. Hockey seemed to combine the best of football and baseball.[18]

Boston had its share of local talent, nurtured in the schoolboy leagues. Raymie Skilton, who first played at Rindge Tech, had a long career as a player-coach in the amateur circuits. Cambridge's George "Skeets" Canterbury had the skill (and the name) to stand out among goaltenders. The fact that many players came from Melrose and Arlington High Schools ensured their early dominance in the new Arena. Five of seven players on the *Herald*'s first "All School" team (1912) hailed from either Melrose or Arlington. For all this local talent, however, Boston's first superstar was Princeton's Hobey Baker, who had learned the game at St. Paul's School, in Concord, New Hampshire.[19]

Baker played dozens of games at the Arena, first for Princeton and then for the St. Nicholas Club. Whether he was the best player of his time was beside the point. He was promoted as the best player. After his sophomore year, the *Herald* concluded that he was "without doubt the best all-around player ever developed on this side of the border." As Fred Hoey argued after Baker had "hypnotized" a strong Boston Athletic Association seven in 1913, "the crowd went to the rink to see Baker. No player in the country has been so well advertised and no player has ever come through with more bells on." He was dashingly handsome, his blond hair flowing as he rushed the puck—an impossible image in today's age of helmet and face mask. Better yet, he was modest, as the press emphasized after every grudging inter-view. Of all the contemporary descriptions or later recollections, however, none captures his electric attraction better than a 1962 column by George Frazier, then the doyen of Boston's literati. "Always at college hockey games," said Frazier, "I am haunted by the redolent remembrance" of Hobey Baker

> as he was in the sinew and swiftness of his youth, in the
> nocturnes of half-a-century ago at the sanctified second when
> he would take the puck from behind his own net and, as the
> crowd rose to its feet screaming "Here he comes!" he would
> start up the ice like some winged messenger out of mythology,
> as fleet and as godlike as any of them, his bright birthright a
> blazing blur, and for a lovely little while God would be in
> His Heaven and the puck, more than likely, in the other
> team's net.

Whether they rooted for Harvard or MIT, Boston fans cheered for Baker.[20]

As early as his sophomore season (1911–12), Baker was clearly the man. If he was to be stopped, someone had to develop team play and tactics—the "science" of hockey, and the second component of hockey as a sport brand. Promoters of any sport in this era emphasized the "science" of their game. Boston produced the first coach to put an American spin on hockey's tac-tics. Alfred "Ralph" Winsor had played on the early Harvard teams, and had stayed to coach his alma mater (for no pay) while also playing and coaching in the local amateur scene for the BAA's "Unicorns." With both teams,

Winsor developed novel approaches to positioning. Years later he explained his revision of defense:

> In the first years, the two defense players stayed fairly close to the goal, one behind the other, and the first man used to skate out at the attacking combination with the intention of checking them with his body or stick. If the first man, the coverpoint, missed, the second player, or point, tried his luck. This method was found very faulty as the clever dodger had a chance to dodge each man consecutively and the defense had no chance whatever to stop a clever passing game.

Hobey Baker would lick his chops at that arrangement. So Winsor gradually moved the two defenders to a more parallel alignment, which denied the rusher such wide outside lanes. At the same time he developed a disciplined back-checking system, which would eliminate lateral passing options.[21]

The Winsor system worked wonders for Harvard hockey. From 1903 through 1917 his teams dominated the Yale series, 22–5. Against tougher and less-scheduled Princeton, Harvard went 10–6, including a 2–2 split during Baker's first two years. On January 24, 1914, more than 5,000 people packed the Arena for a showdown between the Crimson and early hockey's Golden Jet. The Tigers rolled into town with victories over top amateur teams, including the University of Toronto. The *Herald* admitted that most fans went to see Baker and expected him to prevail. But in "the most desperately fought college game ever played in this city, if not in this country," Harvard upset Princeton 2–1 when Leverett Saltonstall—a future U.S. senator—scored after 33 minutes, 40 seconds of overtime. Princeton outshot Harvard 36–23, and the Tigers dominated puck possession, in part because Winsor employed a passive forecheck, something like a neutral zone trap. As the *Herald* noted, the Crimson forwards did not "rush to meet Baker before he got underway." Most teams tried this and looked like turnstiles as Baker wove his way goalward. Instead, "the crimson players allowed him to gather speed and back up to their own goal until they reached a position where they could close in on him." Bend but don't break. Wait for the chance. And luck favored Harvard when an odd deflection landed at Saltonstall's feet for an easy poke-in. As much as anything, this game cemented Winsor's legend. Though Baker avenged the loss by taking two games and the inter-collegiate championship in New York a month later, it hardly mattered. Two years later, when a local amateur team smothered Baker's St. Nick's seven, John Hallahan reminded his readers that "Baker has been stopped before in this city." In Boston at least, the "Winsor system" had checked the irrepressible Hobey Baker.[22]

If the college game featured both individual skill and scientific team play, the amateur leagues accentuated hockey's third brand component—mayhem and bloodshed. Arena fans and writers were left to sort out the incidental from the intended. After one March 1911 exhibition between Canada's Queen's College and the local Victorias, the *Post* reported the game as "one of the roughest seen," in which "foul after foul" went unpunished," and "though the suspensions were many, they were not enough." While some postgame stories scolded the roughness, the pregame promotions were titillating. Before a 1912 game between a local club and Montreal's Westmounts, an unattributed *Herald* notice teasingly explained that the visitors were "considered the roughest players" in their league, banished after they had "caused a riot." Tripping was a common foul, and high sticks were a fact of life, with cuts to prove it. On the other hand, the nasty fouls were slashing, reckless body-checking, and roughing. Ralph Winsor recalled that the early game of hockey was little short of controlled brawling. With few or no team tactics, it was hit, hit, hit: "There were many hard knocks taken and given and the team which were standing on their skates at the end of the game generally won." Old-time hockey meant playing with pain and blood. The *Herald* wrote approvingly of MIT's captain Sloan, who left the ice only momentarily with a bloodied nose, got patched up, and returned to score in a 4–1 victory over Harvard.[23]

In the Arena's second full season, hockey promoters hatched an amateur rivalry laced with mayhem. The Boston Athletic Association wanted to start a hockey team. The BAA, best known for its establishment and custody of the Boston Marathon, was founded in 1887 as a means of pooling the resources of several smaller clubs and thereby better competing with the New York Athletic Club. It quickly became Boston's anchor in the expanding world of amateur athletics. If hockey was hot, the BAA wanted a team, so George V. Brown, the club's athletic director, spent time in the Arena, evaluating talent. After watching the Boston Hockey Club in action, Brown decided to convert this Harvard-stocked team into a BAA team, with Ralph Winsor as player-coach and himself as manager. It was a grand alliance. Brown and Winsor leveraged their strength with a favorable Arena contract guaranteeing the BAA prime-time ice. The BAA, with its Harvard flair, became the Arena's dominant amateur team, but it was also the target for bitter opposition. The Crescent club's Raymie Skilton decided to merge his club under the banner of the Intercolonials, expressly to defeat the BAA. As player-coach, Skilton was Winsor's doppelganger. George V. Brown had his own in a rising young buyer for a local grocery chain. Nicknamed "Pop," the Intercolonials' manager was, recalled Fred Hoey, "crazy about hockey," and his "unbounded enthusiasm was contagious." His name was Charles F. Adams. A decade later he bought a professional franchise and named them the Bruins.

The first match ended in a tie. The *Herald* emphasized the "bitter rivalry between the two teams" and the "forty minutes of slashing play which kept the big crowd thrilled." In a rematch for the "Championship of the State," the BAA eked out a 1–0 victory, marked by "rough attacks," players "spill[ing] about the surface," and sticks "flying in all directions." Fred Hoey admitted that "as press agent we could foresee a gold mine for the Arena if we could arrange a series." The March 1912 five-game series was for pride and a $100 cup—more than fair play could bear. Both teams packed their bench with ringers, drawing mutual howls of protest to no avail, as the cup agreement did not prescribe eligibility. It was, claimed Hoey, "the most thrilling and exciting series ever played on Boston ice." Sports fans "went nuts" and were "hanging on the rafters"; the games were "rough and tough," with "plenty of casualties," scraps, and flaring tempers. The Adams-Skilton franchise won the series, but dissolved within two years.[24]

With hockey available for boys and men, why not for girls and women? Surely they were playing, although the available record is slim. There is at least one story. In March 1917 the St. Nicholas Girls team played home matches with the Girls' Hockey Club of Boston. John Hallahan, the *Herald*'s hockey writer, covered the game in the Arena. He claimed that the match was a "first time" affair in America. This assertion is doubtful, but his overall account was positive, noting that "while hockey is altogether too strenuous a game at times for men, it did not prove too hard for women to tackle last night." In a concession to standard concerns for overexertion, the rink was reduced "to half its regular size," the three periods were reduced to 10 minutes each, and free substitution was allowed "throughout the struggle." In an aside that captured the essence of old-time hockey, Hallahan noted that "of course, there were several bumps, tosses, and falls, but no serious damage was reported, only that Miss Ruth Denesha had a couple of teeth loosened."[25]

Old-time hockey did not include helmets or face masks. But other items were clearly part of the brand. The puck and the stick had been crucial to the distinctions between polo and hockey. It took longer for entrepreneurs to recognize the need for specialized skates. The first guide book (1897) included ads for hockey, racing, and speed skates. All had a long, flat blade, while the racing and speed skates had a curved toe. By 1910 coaches and players had recognized the need to "rock" the blade with a slight curve to improve maneuverability. At Christmastime 1918 Wright & Ditson ran a large ad for "articles that promote health and happiness." This included seven styles of skates, including hockey skates from $2.00 to $5.00 a pair. Sticks ran from 50 cents to $1.00, pucks from 50 cents to $1.00, knitted caps for $1.00. The most exotic and expensive piece of equipment was the hockey glove, which ranged from $7.00 to $10.00 a pair, just slightly more costly than a Flexible Flyer sled ($3.00 to $8.50).[26]

By December 1918 the Arena had survived the lean years of the Great War, when college, school, and club teams trimmed or canceled their schedules. America was struggling to return to normal. President Wilson had arrived in Paris to a "Royal" welcome as he began his crusade for the League of Nations. The "Bolshevism menace" that threatened Europe was soon to threaten home—a political and cultural germ as virulent as the influenza that was ravaging the nation and the world. The Red Sox had won the World Series, but owner Harry Frazee began a player sell-off that culminated in Babe Ruth's departure a year later. Things were looking better for college sports as Harvard, Tufts, and Boston College all announced plans to return to prewar schedules and support. This was good news for the Arena.[27]

And then disaster. On the evening of December 17, 1918, several thousand boxing fans enjoyed a local card of action. As usual, the smokers filled the hall with a blue-yellow haze that drifted around the arc lights and tarred the roof's glass ridge. Fire marshals later decided that one cigarette butt must have smoldered undetected after the event, igniting in the early morning. At 5:41 A.M. a patrolman noticed the blaze and pulled the alarm at a nearby box. Despite a quick response, empty streets, strong water pressure, and little breeze, the "fireproof" main building was rubble within an hour. The wood seats, floor, and roofing had turned the brick-and-steel structure into a bake oven that burned and finally crumbled "like a box of metal-edged strawboard." Fred Hoey was somber as he considered even one winter without the Arena. While outdoor hockey was more invigorating for the players, the fans were now "educated" to the "comfortably warm Arena." They would hardly venture outside to freeze. Equally important, the top leagues could no longer depend on a schedule. Schoolboy managers might quickly shuffle their calendars, but not so the colleges and the amateurs. Nor could the exciting teams from Canada. When Arena president Charles Abbey traveled from Springfield a day later for his first look, local experts estimated the cost to rebuild at $400,000; they doubted if Abbey's group would bite. Fred Hoey wrote that hockey's very future depended on their decision.[28]

Rebuilding

For two seasons indoor hockey survived at the Pavilion, a small bandbox near MIT. George V. Brown described it as "a three lane bowling alley without the pins or pinboys." If the Arena was to rise from its ashes it needed some deep pockets. Enter Henry G. Lapham. A Brooklyn native and an 1897 Yale graduate, Lapham helped to develop his family's oil business—the Texas Corporation (now Texaco)—before expanding his own interests into directorships with banks, steamships, and power companies. A well-known philanthropist, he was a director of the Boys Clubs of Boston, and his social pedigree included membership in both The Country Club and the Algonquin Club. More important to our story, he was a longtime member of the BAA, was elected its president in 1920, and served on the American Olympic Association (forerunner of the USOC). In this capacity, Lapham worked closely with George V. Brown, the BAA's director of athletics and one of Boston's most prominent sports figures. Brown had managed the early BAA hockey teams in the Arena. Although he could not skate, he could see the rising importance of hockey in the Hub. He had a vision for a new Arena. Henry G. Lapham would be his money man.[29]

The Brown-Lapham connection epitomizes the opportunities that the still-young sport industry offered a man like George V. Brown. Born in 1880, the son of Irish immigrants, Brown was not from Lapham's world. After high school he attended Bryant and Stratton, a private career college in Boston, but his business was not oil or steamships or banks; it was sports. In 1900 he went to work for the BAA as an instructor, working his way up the ladder of amateur sports. Unlike baseball, rowing, or boxing, which developed in a commercial and professional environment before the Civil War, sports like track, football, golf, tennis, and hockey developed simultaneously with the amateur movement of the 1870s and 1880s. Amateurism was controlled by elites and rising bourgeois interests that wanted their own competitive space, free from the butchers, blacksmiths, and saloon owners who they claimed had ruined boxing, baseball, and rowing with gambling and match-fixing. But elite officers like Henry G. Lapham needed bright, responsible young men like George V. Brown to run their clubs. And so amateurism spawned a new form of patronage for a whole generation of men and women.[30]

By 1920 George V. Brown was a manager of the American Olympic team, secretary of the New England Football Officials Association, director of athletics at Boston University, and secretary to the Boston Interscholastic Rowing Association, to name just a few of his positions. Still, he was ready for more. Eighteen months after the last embers faded deep in the Arena rubble, the *Herald*'s Tom McCabe announced, "It's coming at last": a new and better Arena, with 5,000 seats, standing room for 2,000, a 220-by-90-foot rink, and design provisions for indoor track and boxing. The New Boston Arena Company was headed by Henry G. Lapham. The board included Joseph P. Kennedy. The general manager of the New Boston Arena was George V. Brown.[31]

Within seven months the New Boston Arena opened to a New Year's throng of 6,000 people, including governor-elect Channing H. Cox, local political dignitaries, and "high officials" from the still-active Army and Navy contingents of Boston Harbor. They enjoyed a gala ice carnival of fancy skating, novelty races, a historical pageant on ice, and a hockey burlesque played by clowns with brooms and a can. Real hockey followed a week later when MIT and Harvard hosted a weekend visit by a crack amateur team from New Brunswick. Harvard's Saturday-night match drew almost 7,000 fans, which Ed Cunningham characterized as the "greatest assemblage" ever to watch a hockey game in America. Only one week into the new Arena, Cunningham emphasized the "need for a balcony, which management plans to build."[32]

The Arena, like sport in general, was entering a golden age. As the 1920s unfolded, urban and industrial America experienced rapid expansion in both productivity and consumption. Greater Boston was not isolated from this phenomenon, even if local capitalists failed to invest in better infrastructure. The old mills and factories would do for now. Prosperity was uneven, to be sure, but many workers, especially in white-collar professions, enjoyed more time and income. American spending on recreation increased 300 percent during the 1920s. Movies, records, theater, and sports all boomed. At least for urban areas, the 1920s did roar. Bostonians had greeted 1925 "with jazz and din," announced the *Herald*, despite the "keen eyed efforts" of police and revenue agents, hustling from hotel to hotel in pursuit of Demon Rum.[33]

By the mid-1920s hockey was firmly placed as a special brand on the Boston sports scene. A *Herald* editorial titled "Ice Hockey" captured the core elements that had vaulted hockey from a minor sport dependent on freezing weather: "The scientist and the sports promoter have joined hands, the former with his ice-making devices, and the latter with his energy and his willingness to supply the proper inducements for teams and spectators." Hockey was now the bridge season between football and baseball. It had speed: "hockey players travel faster, probably, than any other athletes." It combined speed with "skill in the manipulation of the puck, the constant possibility that a lucky shot will turn the tide of battle, the mix-ups of little groups, the flashing of skate blades, the spills and the occasional conflicts which result in banishment of offending players." Better yet, the *Herald* sensed that American players were closing the gap with Canada.[34]

The Arena was at the center of this phenomenon, fusing the interests of promoters, players, and their fans. George V. Brown and the Arena Company had an obvious interest in "growing the game" among players and spectators at all levels of interest. The *Official Arena Program* for 1923–24 included a schedule for public skating sessions—three 3-hour blocks per day, costing from 25 to 65 cents, depending on age and time of session. Novices could rent skates for 20 to 50 cents or get a one-hour lesson for $1.50. Beginners were the first step on an escalator of involvement from shinny to the Olympics. With the Arena as guaranteed ice for part of their schedule, prep school and high school leagues expanded. Andover, Milton, St. Mark's, and Brown and Nichols cemented their hockey traditions. Public school leagues expanded in the city and its suburbs. Arlington and Melrose continued as powerhouses, but Newton vaulted to the top as well. When the United States Olympic hockey team prepared to compete for gold at Chamonix, two of the players were Newton grads.[35]

There is some evidence that African Americans organized teams and enjoyed Arena billings. In February 1929 John Hallahan promoted a game between the "Colored Panthers" and the St Joe's of East Boston. "The fans," he noted, "will have an opportunity to see the popular colored Panthers, who were a hit in last year's games." The "colored players" had lost only one game "in six starts." This statistic does not prove wide adoption among African Americans or wide acceptance from white audiences, but it does suggest that black players found ice time in an integrated environment. The same may be said for women's teams. In general, however, hockey was a white, male establishment.[36]

At the collegiate level, Harvard continued as a force, but its local rule was challenged by Boston College, which in the 1920s became a powerhouse and one of the Arena's biggest draws. Catholic families stocked the Eagle teams with a high level of talent. Boston College's star players of the period were the Morrissey brothers, Leo Hughes, and Sonny Foley. The *Boston Evening Transcript* (historically the paper for elites) described Foley as the fan favorite with Bakerlike praise: he "never loafs, never quits, never stalls . . . takes his bumps with a smile . . . is aggressive, talented, courageous, canny." And all this despite his "midget" size. The Boston University Pioneers enjoyed their first full season in 1923–24. Although the most notable hockey alumnus from the period was Mickey Cochrane, who had a Hall of Fame baseball career, the hockey star was goalie Sydney Silberberg, who was a four-year standout. MIT continued to present a competitive team.[37]

The top rung in the system was the U.S. Amateur Hockey Association, which had multiple entries from Boston in the 1920s. The USAHA was founded in 1920 by a small group of amateur sport administrators, including George V. Brown. Their objective was to create a national governing body that would be recognized by the Amateur Athletic Union and its stepchild, the American Olympic Association. The USAHA was Boston's top draw because it represented the pinnacle for most local players. Without professional rivals (the NHL was still restricted to Canada), the USAHA show-cased the most skilled talent. One of these was George Owen, who epitomized the Boston feeder system. A multisport standout at Newton High School, Owen next starred at Harvard, where he earned nine letters, never lost to Yale in football, and captained baseball. A smooth-skating defense-man, Owen also captained Harvard hockey for two years, and scored nine goals in only seven Yale games, including the game-winner in his last.[38]

When Owen played for Newton or Harvard, he carried the honor of alma mater. When he played for the Boston Hockey Club in the "eastern loop" of the USAHA, his club affiliation had two dimensions. To be sure, the BHC had heated rivalries with the local BAA Unicorns and the Maples. But the USAHA accentuated rivalries against other cities, and in this way emulated professional baseball, the top sport of the time. In the mid-1920s, the team that Boston loved to hate was the Pittsburgh entry, then nicknamed the Yellow Jackets. A mediocre team in the 1922–23 "western loop," Pittsburgh had watched the BAA waltz to eastern and national titles. The next season, Pittsburgh was the powerhouse, but not because of home-grown talent. The Yellow Jackets now included outstanding Canadian players Lionel Conacher, Roy Worters, Hugh Darragh, and Baldy Cotton. This roster captured the 1924 and 1925 USAHA titles and was so stocked with talent that it stepped right into the NHL in 1925–26. Boston hockey writer W. E. Mullins referred to them as "Pittsburgh's Canadians." The *Herald*'s gossipy "Bob Dunbar" column questioned why "Boston hockey" was "hooked up with Pittsburgh at all." After all, "the best hockey in Boston is played by our own boys," whereas hockey in Pittsburgh "is played mainly by a bunch of traveling mercenaries, who practically all are of Canadian birth and training." Parochial passions like these made the 1924 title series the top sports story, crowding out news on baseball's spring training or preparations for the marathon.[39]

Highly talented players and fierce urban rivalries were a recipe for both splendid play and mayhem—hockey's yin and yang. Descriptions of brilliant "dashes" down the ice were often matched by lurid accounts of cheap shots. After the 1924 final series with Pittsburgh, W. E. Mullins found BAA coach "Skeets" Canterbury "delighted" to get home without a "single serious casualty," given the Yellow Jackets' tactics of "slashing their opponents around the thighs and ankle . . . hooking around the face," and, worst of all, "the expert manner in which most of them could stick [spear] and use the butt ends of their mashies in massaging the ribs of their rivals." The bitterness peaked the next year when Pittsburgh's Joe Sills butt-ended the BAA's Leo Hughes in the face, requiring the removal of Hughes's right eye and possible loss of his left. Hughes, fresh from Boston College, was a darling of the Boston fans. Sills was a Canadian "mercenary." Boston threatened to quit the league unless President William Haddock, a Pittsburgher, stopped the "unnecessary and willful roughing" seeping into amateur hockey. Haddock sympathized but insisted that the game had not been out of control. In an accurate but undiplomatic conclusion he noted that "hockey, you know, is not a parlor game." This claim was true at all levels. That same month, the director of physical training for Boston's schools warned his hockey charges: tone down the roughness or find the sport banned. He meant business, having recently banned another rowdy sport—basketball.[40]

The fans were their own arbiters. Stanley Woodward, a rising star in sportswriting, covered the hockey beat for the *Herald* in the mid-1920s. His sensational prose included terms like "battle royal," "Roman Holiday," and the "slaughterhouse fans" of the Arena's northeast corner. After one slashing incident, Woodward said the offender "got out of sight quickly" to avoid a possible mob. Another runway skirmish among players, spectators, officials, and police came close to a "riot," snuffed only because too many people were jammed together. A close look at the Arena program of 1923–24 suggests that George V. Brown positioned the Arena as a place for fans of all stripes. The program contained a range of ads, from middlebrow Café Minerva or Professor Lerner's New Academy of Modern Dancing (which brooked no "freakishness") to the National Shawmut Bank, the State Street Trust Company, and E. M. Hamlin and Co., Bankers and Brokers.[41]

In all, George V. Brown and the Arena Company had cause to celebrate. In 1923, 300,000 fans came through the turnstiles for seventy-two evening games, an average of 4,166 per game. In January 1924 Brown explained that the Arena needed to expand. His experiments with lower ticket prices and doubleheaders had worked to a tee. Sellouts were becoming commonplace, with 2,500 standing-room patrons packing the nooks and crannies of the narrow concourse that surrounded the Arena's 4,000 seats. Fans were surging to the ticket windows between periods to buy tickets for the next week's events. The Harvard-Yale hockey game was becoming

as hot as its gridiron counterpart, with restrictions placed on advance pur-
chases. Brown promised to protect the fans from the clutches of ticket
speculators. And he promised even better hockey: "I am going to give
Boston the finest double-headers ever arranged in hockey history . . . I will
guarantee that every hockey team worthwhile seeing, which I can bring to
Boston, will play at the Arena." It was time to build the much-speculated
balcony. It was time to prepare for "the next upward move in Boston
hockey."[42]

The Bruins and the Garden

The next upward move had one meaning only—a professional franchise,
the penthouse of any hockey property. Despite speculation as early as 1911, a
local pro franchise did not emerge until 1924. Local promoters like George
V. Brown were content with revenues from the amateur and college
leagues, and the Canadian professional leagues (the National Hockey Association, 1910–1917, and its successor, the National Hockey League) had too
much internal squabbling to consider a southern expansion. By 1924, however, things had changed. The NHL was looking south to check the advance of a possible rival league. And Boston had one businessman eager for
a franchise.[43]

This was Charles Francis Adams, a native Vermonter who had cut his
business teeth in his uncle's wholesale grocery business in Springfield, Massachusetts. He had learned the art of sales, loans, and deals while pushing
tobacco and grocery lines in a beat that ranged from Chicago to Virginia.
By 1914 he had moved to Boston and hit pay dirt, buying the 150-store
Connor grocery chain, which he parlayed twelve years later into the First
National Stores. As treasurer, Adams could have enjoyed personal prosperity and prestige within the business community. He clearly sought to cut a
wider swath; sports would be the avenue. He had managed the Intercolonials in the old Arena, in the come-and-go amateur loops. By 1921 he
was on the board of directors of the New Boston Arena Company, where
he would have met regularly with both George V. Brown and Henry G.
Lapham. This was the great triumvirate of Boston hockey, a tense but working alliance that dominated the scene over the next two decades. The three
men also represented different archetypes in sport history. Lapham was the

elite amateur sports patron, content to stay behind the scenes; Brown, up-
wardly mobile from immigrant stock, was the professional sport manager in
service to his patrons. Adams was the self-made businessman, who found
his public persona in franchise ownership.[44]

In 1923 Adams formed an alliance with Thomas Duggan, a Montreal
promoter who had purchased NHL franchise options for New York and
Boston. Through backroom negotiations and public threats to build a new
facility, he pushed the reluctant Arena directors into a lease for ice time. By
September 1924 Adams was in control of a new Boston franchise, which he
called the Bruins. His most important move was to hire Art Ross as manager. Ross, a career professional, had the contacts to put a team on the
ice. But would they be more exciting than the BAA or Boston College or
Harvard?[45]

Professional hockey needed branding and positioning. The press was
happy to help. "There is a vast difference" between amateur and professional skating styles, ran one *Herald* story. "Professional hockey players execute plays with a minimum effort; amateur players as a rule waste a lot of
energy by useless skating." The pros were not just more efficient, wrote
Larry Paton after the Bruins' first exhibition game; they were faster and
more skilled, in part because they "are earning their living at the game."
Equally important, pro hockey allowed forward passing in the neutral zone,
a provision that quickened the pace. Ross, "an old fox at the game," added
science to speed, with "scoring plays, defensive tricks, and all that goes with
an effective and well balanced professional team."[46]

The Bruins took several years to be either. They opened on December 1,
1923, with a 2–1 win over the Montreal Maroons. The game, wrote Stanley
Woodward, was fast and rough, filled with "the most rugged body checking
that Boston fans ever have seen." The stands, however, were not filled. It
was a "scattered and rather chilly gathering"; the lack of crowd noise was
"deadening." It looked, said Woodward, "as if Boston will have to be educated to the professional game." Things went downhill from there. The
Bruins lost 11 straight games en route to a cellar finish of 6–24. Fred Hoey
later recalled that the franchise lost almost $40,000, or about three times its
purchase price.[47]

Could "Pop" Adams hang on? Some stories suggest that he wanted to
bail out and sell his team to the New Arena Company. In the end he held

firm. Over the next several years, Ross worked his magic to bring in talented players like Harry Oliver, Lionel Hitchman, Eddie Shore, Dit Clapper, and Ralph "Cooney" Weiland. Adams experimented with radio and target marketing. In 1926 Bruins games were broadcast on Boston's WBZA and Springfield's WBZ, with hockey writer Frank Ryan doing the play-by-play commentary. Ryan talked up the Bruins and their fans, especially the women. It was, recalled Fred Hoey, a strategy to build the fan base by convincing female listeners that Bruins games were the "in" thing. Adams himself joined the campaign with pitches to female fans in his press interviews. Demand rose high enough that the Bruins began a season ticket program. It was nice, remembered Hoey, that "sweet propaganda" could be so effective.[48]

By 1928 the Bruins were serious contenders for the Stanley Cup. The Arena had added a balcony in 1926 to accommodate the swelling crowds.[49] It would not be enough to satisfy Adams. In November 1927 Tex Rickard had arrived in Boston to announce plans for a new "fight auditorium" at North Station. Rickard was boxing's most famous promoter. But he also ran Madison Square Garden and its newest hockey tenant, which the local press got to calling "Tex's Rangers." In 1926 he had bid unsuccessfully for an NHL franchise in Chicago while trumpeting his plans for "Madison Square Gardens" in Chicago and Philadelphia. Hockey was central to his vision. In Chicago he pushed the ice game, claiming that "in New York, society comes to the games in evening wear . . . the sport takes hold of the women as well as the men." It was, he said, "better than baseball for interest in the scientific end."[50]

Rickard was shut out of Chicago and Philadelphia, but he had better luck in Boston. The Boston and Maine Railroad planned to replace its thirty-year-old station on Causeway Street, and Rickard convinced the B&M board to include a multipurpose coliseum as part of the project. He lined up prominent locals to serve on the board of the Boston Madison Square Garden Corporation, which would lease the coliseum from the B&M. The cast included Huntington "Tack" Hardwick, an old Harvard football star, who also served as Rickard's front man in Chicago. Also on the board were Homer Loring, the chair of the B&M; Judge Edward L. Logan; Bill Bingham, Harvard's athletic director; Charles F. Adams; and some of Rickard's New York staff. Rickard and Loring issued a formal statement that the Garden would be ready in a year and that the Bruins would be the anchor tenant, with boxing matches, horse shows, track meets, and assorted rallies to fill out the calendar. Rickard knew his marketing. With the North Station railhead serving 2.5 million people to the north and west of Boston, with adjacent subway and trolley lines, and with a new automobile "thoroughfare," the Garden could not fail.[51]

The terminal/arena complex was built on time, at a cost of around $4 million. It was an engineering marvel, and a novel exploitation of "air rights," as the arena stood directly above the terminal, connected by wide ramps or concourses that funneled the crowds in and out. George C. Funk designed the Garden itself, with seats for 14,500 hockey fans. Two balconies offered spectacular sight lines to the crowd attending the November 17, 1928, boxing match that officially opened the building. Three nights later, more than 17,000 hockey fans stormed the gates for the Bruins' home opener against the Montreal Canadiens. It was, wrote Stanley Woodward, "a riot, a mob-scene, a re-enaction of the assault on the Bastille." Almost 3,000 ticketless "shock troops" helped to swell the concourse with a flood that burst past police, ticket-takers, and ushers. Once inside the gates, "the crowd spread like rushing waters to every corner of the Garden, blocking the aisles, overflowing in every direction." Outside, the police quickly reorganized to block thousands more.[52]

In January 1929 the Bruins went undefeated in a drive that ended with the Stanley Cup. They were the hottest team that Boston had seen in years. Sellouts were standard fare, and tickets, wrote the *Globe*'s John Hallahan, were "as scarce as the Harvard-Yale football ducats."[53] Early in their streak, something happened that shook Boston's hockey world. George Owen turned pro. The *Post* and the *Globe* conveyed the collective shock. Owen was not the first collegian to do so; Dartmouth's Gerry Geran and Myles Lane were already in the NHL. But Harvard's George Owen was "the very symbol of amateurism." He had spurned earlier offers with the standard amateur line: "I play for the love of the game." He was well married and well ensconced in a local business. Clearly, the Garden and the Bruins had changed the rules of play. It was the challenge, said Owen: "I have seen professional hockey regularly since it came to Boston and I have always wondered whether I would be good enough to play it." He also admitted that "money had something to do with it" (his deal was for $25,000). He hoped that his decision would "not in any way affect his status in the community." He needn't have worried. Filling in for the injured Hitchman, Owen played his entire first game, matched with Eddie Shore, as the Bruins beat Toronto 5–2. "I enjoyed it more than any game I have ever played," said Owen. "Eddie Shore is a wonder." John Hallahan had followed the hockey beat for two decades. Owen's move fulfilled all his dreams. "The Bruins are glad and Bostonians are glad," he wrote, "that George made good." The NHL needed more Americans in their game. Owen's jump "is the biggest boost Greater Boston school hockey could receive."[54]

The Making of Tradition

In his book on Depression-era Boston, Charles Trout argued that the 1920s had "saddled Boston with inauspicious legacies." Conservative investors had joined conservative clergy and reformers in limiting the Hub's economic and cultural development. Ethnic politics, so skillfully wielded by James Michael Curley, had exacerbated the tension between rich and poor, Yankee and immigrant, capitalist and worker. The Great Crash continued a slide for America's Athens, in population and in commerce. By the end of 1929 the stockholders of the Boston Manufacturing Company, a founder of the nation's Industrial Revolution, had authorized liquidation. The Boston Grand Opera Company locked its doors. There were, wrote Trout, "dim signs that an era was ending."[55]

This statement also held true for Boston's sports scene. At the grassroots and high school levels, Boston offered a rich competitive environment that strengthened in the years to come. The future was less secure, however, for the Hub's major teams. Sunday sports—enabled for local option by a 1928 state statute—finally passed muster in Boston in late January 1929. It was big news for the Red Sox and the Braves; they could play games on the Christian sabbath. This move, however, could not ensure success on the field. Fans would wait through another world war before either team won a pennant. The fortunes of college football were uneven. Harvard teams packed the Stadium even as their schedules began to soften. Boston College and Boston University strengthened their schedules and produced a few outstanding teams. But any historical analysis would reveal that Boston's college teams had lost ground to their southern, midwestern, and western rivals. By the 1950s a strong college team from Boston was a rarity, and an unranked one at that. Basketball came on strong among the area's high schools and colleges, but no team could be called a national power. The Celtics were not born until 1946, and they would wait another decade for success.[56]

Ice hockey, however, was on an upward trajectory. The grassroots school programs fed talent to the college and amateur teams, which in turn stocked national and Olympic teams with "Boston" players. While George Owen would remain a rarity in American NHL markets—a local boy made good—this fact hardly mattered to fans. The Bruins were "our" team. They won Stanley Cups in 1939 and 1941 and were finalists in 1930, 1943, and 1946. Even when the Bruins slumped and the Celtics surged, hockey was still king. Boston was a hockey town, built on a foundation in place long before Orr. But there was nothing inevitable about Boston's hockey tradition. It grew more than anything from careful promotion and positioning— hockey's tradition was well placed.

When "Montreal" hockey arrived in the 1890s, Boston's landscape included a rich base of schools and colleges, which became incubators for players and fans alike, eager to use sport to promote their alma mater. These rivalries, however, could not have built hockey without the Arena. It was the crucial "place" in Boston hockey's calculus. Although no high school could pay rental costs for more than a core of league games and an occasional practice, that base alone could sustain the season through a long outdoor thaw. For the first time, there was a guarantee of ice. For the colleges, the amateurs, and the professionals, indoor facilities created the permanence, reliability, and credibility on which to build and sell a spectacle. The Arena (and later the Garden) also nurtured family dynasties that crossed from playing to officiating to coaching. Medford's Rileys were one. So were the Clearys. Bill and Bob played at Belmont Hill and Harvard before starring on the 1960 Olympic team, coached by Jack Riley. Their own father, Bill Cleary Sr., had been an outstanding high school and college referee back to the 1920s.[57]

The managerial dynasties included the Brown, Adams, and Lapham families. George V. Brown could not skate a lick; neither could his son Walter. Like his father, however, Walter had a knack for management, and he helped his father create a new team—the Tigers—in a new league—the Can-Am League—to keep some level of professional hockey alive at the Arena when the Bruins left in 1928. Although the Tigers were clearly minor-league, they were drawing 6,000 fans to the Arena in March 1929 as they surged to their own title. Walter's experience at his father's side led him into the world of international hockey tours and arena management, including the Boston Garden. Even as he later built the Celtics, he was a major figure in American and international hockey circles until his death in 1964. Like his father, he is enshrined in the Hockey Hall of Fame. Not to be outdone, both Charles Adams and Henry G. Lapham passed their reins of power to their own sons.[58]

God and glaciers had created the rivers, ponds, and lakes that are still etched in hockey's story. Today's middle-aged fans and coaches grow misty-eyed at the recollections of long days on Spy Pond or Crystal Lake, with stops only to shovel the snow, down an orange, or massage the toes. The Arena and the Garden, on the other hand, were man-made landmarks, situated with an eye on convenience and profit. Both buildings reflect what Michael Hollerin has called a new "culture of city building" that engaged "networks and ideologies of speculators, developers, surveyors, politicians, engineers, architects, lawyers, who influenced key decisions." The Arena and the Garden were intended to be places of permanence—focuses of community identity. As their surroundings changed, nothing was clearer than their permanence, and nothing was more central to their identity than hockey.[59]

Both the Arena and the Garden were multipurpose facilities. But hockey was literally cemented into their fabric from the beginning. Their investors saw hockey as an "anchor" tenant. These decisions, at least for Boston, made hockey *the* winter sport, with a decided edge over basketball. Both sports had emerged in the mid-1890s, and basketball swept the country as no sport had before or has since. By 1910 basketball dominated the winters in most American communities. It was cheap, it required little space, and it fitted into the gymnasiums or armories that already existed in small towns and big cities. These circumstances also held true in Boston, and a casual perusal of newspapers suggests that basketball was easily as popular at the grassroots and school levels. But in its early years basketball lacked a focal point in Boston. The Arena belonged to hockey, and in the Arena, hockey became both science and spectacle. Meanwhile basketball limped along as indoor training for football players. It couldn't find an identity. Nowhere was this lack of attraction clearer than at Harvard, the bellwether for Boston sports. Although basketball arrived with great excitement in the late 1890s, it never clicked with students or alums. The gyms and armories were dingy; the brawling play lacked any sense of science and skill. Worst of all, in 1909 Harvard's Athletic Committee approved a recommendation from the Student Council: abolish basketball. "The game has not flourished here," said their report, "and is regarded by many competent critics as among the least desirable of athletic sports in this part of the country." It took a decade for basketball to return. In Greater Boston, it has played catch-up ever since.[60]

By careful placement in the Arena and on the sports page, hockey was popularized as a sport *and* as a spectacle. As Tex Rickard, Charles Adams, George V. Brown, Fred Hoey, Stanley Woodward, and others all realized, the Arena and the Garden were shrines to crowds attracted by a combination of technology, craft, savagery, and mayhem. The buildings themselves were technological marvels. Sit in a warm seat and watch players compete on a frozen surface? Tell that to Thanksgiving Day football fans. But it was possible in the new arenas. Hockey was also fresh and authentic in a world grown heavy with routine and bureaucracy. A riveter facing a monotonous job on an assembly line, the insurance clerk shuffling papers all day, the telephone operator pulling and plunging jacks into and out of routers and switches—whoever saw the fruits of their labor? At night, however, they could hop onto a train or a trolley and watch Hobey Baker, George Owen, or Eddie Shore offer proof that individual skill still mattered, still stirred emotions. The fans might also see primitive displays of aggression and violence. Hockey was a complex product.[61]

Like cabarets and dance clubs, the Arena and Garden were new havens for the nightlife that Lewis Erenberg has so brilliantly interpreted. Here "men and women pursued a vital and experiential life, the flux and weave of movement and action that had been considered disreputable for the best people in the Victorian era." The Arena on hockey nights offered a respectable forum to watch violence, especially for women. And unlike football fans, the hockey crowd could see the individual battles. It was what Erenberg calls an "action environment." Hockey crowds were still interactive in ways that had faded slightly in baseball or college football. On March 21,

1929, as the Bruins began their postseason assault on the Stanley Cup, Gene Mack's cartoon montage of Bruins fans graced the *Globe*'s front page. Titled "Hockey fans in Class by Themselves When It Comes to Whooping It Up," one scene showed how the "crowds gather at the dressing room door to get a close up view of the Bruins." In the Garden's lower concourse, fans formed a gauntlet through which players filed to the ice. At a time when football crowds were swallowed in ever-larger stadiums that pulled them away from the field of play, hockey venues retained baseball's proximity, minus the dugouts and the foul territory. This close affinity with players carried over to the stands. The enclosed acoustics of the Garden or the Arena gave the fans (then called "bugs") greater effect. When the Rangers played cautiously in one game, a few "bugs" in the Garden's second balcony roared, "Play hockey, what are we paying our dough for!" That voice would never have resonated at Harvard Stadium.[62]

During the 1927 Stanley Cup finals against Ottawa, Stanley Woodward wrote that the Ottawa crowd was different from Boston's in some fundamental ways. "It does not," he said, "throw truck on the ice, except under greatest stress." Between periods, "it sings cheering songs," rather than "cursing and blackguarding the referees." Woodward was probably too kind to Ottawa's fans, but he hit a central point about hockey's attraction in Boston. Throwing curses, eggs, or lemons at a referee both reflected and built a sense of ownership. The game was still young, a frontier of opportunity, where players like Sonny Foley, administrators like George V. Brown, coaches like Ralph Winsor, referees like Bill Cleary Sr., and everyday fans could feel that their actions mattered. In the first three decades of the twentieth century, hockey was radically changing—dropping a skater, tinkering with offsides, creating separate zones, splintering the rules along professional, amateur, and collegiate lines. Boston figured into all of this. In Boston at least, hockey quickly shed its "Canadian" veneer. It was "our" game as much as anyone else's. Long before Orr, hockey had found its place.[63]

13

Number 4 Is the One:
The Emergence of Bobby Orr

Randy Roberts

Bobby Orr is the one. There always has to be the one. The one at the top of the list—the best, the greatest, the end of the discussion. Being Boston's greatest athlete is no mean feat. No city boasts tougher standards. Famed sportswriter Herbert Warren Wind said that his Boston counterparts tended toward "efflorescent exaggeration," by which he meant that the pros and especially the cons of any sporting situation stood in sharper contrast in Boston than anywhere else. Perhaps it is the Puritan legacy, perhaps the hard-nosed, blue-collar ethic. But it has always been easier to fall short in Boston than in any other city in the country. Being the best in Boston entails being the best day in and day out. It requires the athlete not only to play in Boston but to be of Boston.[1]

Babe Ruth could hit and pitch, but he just did not play in Boston long enough. His glory years, sadly, were played out in Yankee Stadium. Ted Williams was the greatest hitter who ever lived. Like Roy Hobbs in *The Natural*, when Williams retired people said of him, "He was the best that ever was." But his fielding always seemed an afterthought, and he kept sportswriters and fans at arm's length, almost as if he played the game just for himself. If it was lonely at the top, he seemed bent on keeping it that way.

Just as Ted Williams was baseball's greatest offensive force, Bill Russell was basketball's most intimidating defensive presence. And he was the greatest winner there ever was in a major sport. He hovered around the basket like an avenging angel at the gates of heaven, slapping away prayers cast up by the unworthy. But he was like Williams in two other ways. Russell was not athletically ambidextrous; his offense paled next to his defense. And like an avenging angel, he played with a certain palpable grimness. Now Larry Bird played flawlessly. Far too much has been made about his lack of "athletic" talent, as if basketball were nothing more than a track and field meet. Bird's combination of hands, timing, and vision was nonpareil. He played with heart on both ends of the court, and he exhibited a sense of pleasure in his work. He may not have been the most loquacious athlete—though his subtle humor is underrated—but he did his job off the court as well as on. In fact, his only problem is that he never bought into Boston. He knew himself. He was Larry Bird, French Lick, Indiana. Home-grown and proud. And everyone knew that when the season was over he was out of there. Boston was in his rearview mirror.

That's why Bobby Orr is the one. The total package.

Of course, like almost every other American who was not fortunate enough to be born in Boston, I was slow to realize it. In central Pennsylvania in the 1960s there were only two winter sports: basketball and wrestling. Hockey was a distant muffled echo, heard only on rare occasions. There were those cold spells, of course, when the creek froze and someone decided that it was time for a Sunday hockey game. We dug our sticks out of the back of a closet or a corner of the basement, trudged through the snow to the creek, and put on our skates—some figure, some hockey. Then we played a game that moved in straight lines, dominated by the few who were proficient at skating backward. Our primitive game lacked the geometry of basketball, and we had about as many stick-handling skills as we had kicking skills in soccer, a sport that we never played under any circumstances.

But hockey had its charms. There was something about the combination of sun and ice, sweaty undershirts and frosty faces, that had an undeniable attraction. And the activity connected us with something that was totally foreign. Hockey was like the French line in the Beatles' "Michelle": "Sont des mots qui vont tres bien ensemble." Familiar, but somehow distant from our landscape. At the time well over 90 percent of the players in the National Hockey League were Canadian, sons of farmers from Alberta and Saskatchewan, lumberjacks from Ontario, fishermen from the Maritime Provinces, and laborers from French Quebec.

It was the foreignness, the otherness, of the sport that drew us each year to watch a handful of Hershey Bears games. The Bears were a well-established minor-league team, a cut or two below the NHL, which only occasionally shipped a player up to the Boston Bruins. But it was professional hockey, which we assumed meant that the players would fight at the drop of a hat, or more specifically, a glove. We sat close to the action and employed all our finest adolescent power of persuasion to provoke fights. "Don't take that shit, Frenchy," one of us would shout, looking quite pleased with the quip. The understanding was that at least one player would assume that we were directly addressing him and feel that another player had committed some foul deed that demanded immediate chastisement. The ploy generally failed to achieve its intended purpose, but occasionally a grizzled player would glance over, flash a humorless pink grin, and make a silent rejoinder with one large, gloved finger. And sometimes, a player would even address us in his native French, in terms quite beyond our meager high-school-French exposure.

In the spring of 1966 *Life* magazine gave a face to our commonly held notions of professional hockey. It confirmed our worst fears and secret expectations. The story, "The Goalie Is the Goat," was forgettable enough, but the nearly full-page photograph of Toronto Maple Leafs goalie Terry Sawchuk was searingly memorable. The photo caption read: "Terry Sawchuk displays his hockey stitches and scars—applied for this portrait by a make-up man who did not have room for all of them." The photograph was of a real-life Frankenstein monster. Deep gashes cut across his forehead and disappeared into his hairline and eyebrows. Trenchlike scars crisscrossed his cheeks, bit into his lips, divided his chin. This wasn't a face, it was a battlefield! He had the sad eyes of a beaten dog, frightened, weary, potentially dangerous. The article noted that in his sixteen-year NHL career, Sawchuk had endured more than 400 stitches and various other injuries, including "a slashed eyeball requiring three stitches, a 70% loss of function in his right arm because 60 bone chips were removed from his elbow, and a permanent 'sway-back' caused by a continual bent-over posture." And Sawchuk was by no means unique. The sport, and particularly the position, created these man-monsters, these teeth-deprived, sewn-together, broken-bodied athletes. Well, we reasoned, Canada was a different country.[2]

Then in the fall of 1966 Bobby Orr exploded on the national scene like one of his famous starts, from standstill to full speed in nothing flat. There he was in the pages of *Sports Illustrated* with a face that looked as if it belonged on a 1951 Mickey Mantle rookie card. He looked nothing like Terry Sawchuk or the other rugged hockey scrummers that occasionally graced the national magazines. Orr was only eighteen, but he looked fifteen with his crewcut hair, smooth face, and almost innocent eyes. Perhaps his nose betrayed a hint of his profession. It looked as if it might have been broken once or twice. But that was the only facial indication. The Frank Deford story confirmed the visual evidence, noting that Bobby could "still smile through his own teeth" and had had his nose broken when he was thirteen. "Why, I don't even have 25 stitches and haven't lost a single tooth yet— touch wood," he told the writer. A few years later Herbert Warren Wind also observed that Bobby looked out of place in the NHL: "A handsome, long-jawed fellow, with light-brown hair and gray-blue eyes, he is usually taken in non-hockey conscious areas of Boston as just another college student." And that was after a few years of NHL ageing. At eighteen he looked as if he were auditioning for the Kingston Trio, as fresh-looking as a high school freshman. If ever a foreign athlete was adopted by an entire nation, it was Bobby Orr. In just a matter of four years, between 1966 and 1970, he created—his game, his will, his personality—millions of new hockey fans. And virtually all of them pulled for Boston.[3]

Orr appeared suddenly on the national scene, but his arrival in Boston was an eagerly anticipated event. To the Bruin cognoscenti, Bobby Orr was imbued with a messianic aura. He was the One for whom they were waiting. In a sport dominated by swift, powerful, brutal men, Bobby was already half legend at the age of eighteen, a figure out of fiction or, perhaps, mythology. He came, like Paul Bunyan, from the cold north, from a place where everything freezes in the winter and children spend all day playing games on ice skates. Or at least that was how the newspaper and magazine stories about Bobby made it seem. And they were not far wrong.

Robert Gordon Orr was born on March 20, 1948, in Parry Sound, Ontario, a town on the eastern shore of the Georgian Bay, about 150 miles north of Toronto. In the nineteenth century it had been primarily a lumbering town; it survived into the twentieth century with the help of an explosives-manufacturing plant and summer tourists visiting some of the Thirty Thousand Islands of Georgian Bay. Later sportswriters who journeyed to Parry Sound just to see the birthplace of Bobby Orr were struck by the town's grim circumstances—the unsightly black trestle of the Canadian Pacific Railroad looming over the town, the knifing boreas, the terrible winter temperatures. Winter seemed so long and so harsh that locals described summer as two months of poor skating on the Seguin River. It was, wrote Frank Deford unkindly, "a sad, friendly little place, the kind of town where the men stop to peer carefully into hardware store windows and where pretty girls turn fat before they grow old. It [was] a good place to play a lot of hockey."[4]

That was exactly what Bobby did, better than any other boy in Canada, where playing hockey is a passion and talking about hockey a way of life. Compared with other Parry Sound youths, Bobby got a late start. He was four when a friend of his father, Doug, gave him a pair of oversized skates; most of his friends began skating at three. But Bobby quickly overcame this handicap by playing endless games of keepaway with his friends and the Indians from Parry Island. By the time he was old enough to play on organized teams it was clear to everyone who knew the game that he had the gift. At the age of five he began to advance through the Canadian junior hockey ranks, from Minor Squirt to Squirt, then on to Peewee, Midgets, and Bantam. He often played with boys a few years older than himself, and he always dominated the games.[5]

All he cared about was playing the game. Raised in a house pressed tight against the tracks of the Canadian Pacific and in a family that seldom owned an automobile, Bobby's horizons were limited; not that he cared a whit. During the long winters he played hockey, returning home only for occasional warmth, food, and rest. In the short summers he practiced shooting against a rectangular piece of wood the size of a goal, ran at night, and lifted weights. He seldom talked about what he wanted or what he planned, but Doug Orr reckoned that by nine—maybe ten—Bobby had decided that he would be a professional hockey player.[6]

In Canada hockey talent does not go long unnoticed. Scouts discovered Bobby before he was a teenager. When he was twelve, playing with older boys on a Bantam all-star team, his squad advanced to the Ontario championship against a team from Ganonoque. Scouts from several NHL teams were on hand, including a bevy of Boston Bruin officials. They were all there to watch two highly regarded Ganonoque fourteen-year-olds. But their eyes seldom left Bobby Orr, the 5-foot 2-inch, 110-pound defenseman with the baggy pants and droopy jersey. Bruins general manager Lynn Patrick recalled, "There were players in the NHL who couldn't feather a pass the way Orr did that night—and Orr was only twelve-years-old . . . He was amazing. He could have played for the Bruins that year without embarrassing himself at all." Extravagant praise, undoubtedly, but it should be remembered that that year Boston was the worst team in the NHL.[7]

The courting of Bobby Orr had begun. Technically the Bruins could not sign Orr to a contract until his fourteenth birthday, but they could try to win his favor. The standard procedure was to contribute to the target's local amateur hockey program. The Bruins immediately dispatched scout Wren Blair to Parry Sound with a check for $1,000, a little something to buy sticks and uniforms courtesy of the Boston organization. This move bought goodwill, no small matter where small-town Canadian boys and their families were concerned. In addition, Blair arranged his schedule so that he could hover around Parry Sound as much as possible, watching Bobby play, talking with Doug, seeing if there was anything the local program needed. Of course, Bobby had not escaped the notice of the other NHL teams. Representatives from the Montreal Canadiens, Toronto Maple Leafs, Detroit Red Wings, and Chicago Blackhawks swarmed to Parry Sound as well, just in case they could do anything for the young prodigy and his family.[8]

In 1962 Bobby turned fourteen, legal age for a hockey player because he was old enough to sign a standard Junior A card. Playing Junior A was an important step in a player's career. It normally entailed moving away from his home and family, boarding with another family in a different town, playing eighty to ninety games a year, and, at least in theory, attending some school. Most of the Junior A players were much older than Bobby, bigger, stronger, more mature. Boston gave Bobby a choice between its two leading farm teams, the Niagara Falls, Ontario, Flyers and the Oshawa, Ontario, Generals. They also said that he could commute the first year and just play in the games. Bobby's parents gave him the final call. If he was old enough to sign, he was old enough to choose. On Labor Day 1962, on the kitchen table of his parents' home, he did just that. For $2,800—$1,000 in cash,

$900 for a fresh stucco job on his parents' house, and $900 for a used car—Bobby Orr signed his career over to the Boston Bruins. The Bruins' management also promised him a new wardrobe, but they never delivered on that verbal part of the arrangement.

He was still small and still light, but in 1962 he entered a man's world, a sports world very different from the one south of the border. In the late nineteenth and the twentieth centuries, sports in the United States had developed around the ideal of the student athlete. It was, to a large degree, a very American and very middle-class notion, suggesting that in the economically and socially fluid United States even athletic excellence was an avenue toward advancement, security, and respectability. A good athlete, regardless of his background, could attend college on a scholarship, graduate, and become a productive middle-class gentleman. And even if he made a temporary stop in professional sports, he would always retain the patina of respectability acquired by virtue of the college degree. This gentlemanly, middle-class ideal carried over into professional football and basketball, where players were commonly identified not with their hometowns but with their colleges or universities. The social implications were clear.

Professional hockey was the product of a different culture, one not so wedded to the universal faith in economic and social mobility. It was a working-class sport that tapped into the deep pools of farmers, lumberjacks, fishermen, mill laborers, and other men throughout Canada whose income was the product of their sweat. Add to this a generous portion of independent-minded, distrustful French Canadians, and you have a cross-section of hockey players. Even in the late 1960s only 17 percent of professional hockey players had graduated from high school; nor did they expect to see their sons rise far above them. Men of limited incomes and limited horizons, they saw in hockey their lives in microcosm. The sport demanded toughness. It was played along the boards and in the crease. And for every moment of flying beauty, when a skater would break free and descend, Mercury-like, on the goalie, there were probably a dozen fistfights and body-crushing checks. It was, in short, like life, where moments of glory were few and pain and injury always at hand in the form of threshers, combines, butcher's knives, saws, fishing nets, looms, and any number of other dangerous machines and instruments. For the men who played and watched hockey, the brutality was not gratuitous. It was essential.[9]

Derek Sanderson, one of Orr's teammates, understood the culture of hockey. He called hockey fans "the lunch-bucket crowd, guys who slug their guts out all week long and whose only enjoyment is a few beers and a hockey game." And what did they expect? Journalist Tom Dowling noted that the ethic of hockey is "solidarity and revenge." It is about men sticking together, forming a bond, being a band of brothers. Altogether, not unlike war. Again, Sanderson spoke to the point: "We got eighteen players and each'll fight for the other seventeen, and if someone gets taken out and can't get the bastard that did him in, then someone else will pick up the banner. Sooner or later we'll get him." It might not be in the next minute, that game, or that month, but sooner or later there would be a reckoning. There was no "let's win one for the Gipper" or "give it the old college try" in professional hockey. There was only "we'll get the bastard." That was the hockey world that Bobby Orr entered when he was fourteen.[10]

During his first year with the Generals Bobby commuted between Parry Sound and Oshawa—three hours each way in good weather—for the games. His father borrowed friends' cars and drove his son through snow-storms and along icy roads, often not returning home until two or three o'clock the next morning. The following year Bobby moved to Oshawa and boarded with a family from September to June. During his four years with the Generals he grew to almost six feet and put on weight. He became stronger, faster, and smarter. But even as a small boy he played like a vet-eran; he had something, some instinctual gift, which transcended size and age. In his first season with Oshawa he was selected for the league's second all-star team; in the next three seasons he was the league's premier player. In his final year he also led his team to the Ontario Hockey Association championship. And Ontario was the epicenter of hockey in Canada. By the time he was eighteen and old enough to play in the NHL Bobby was a phe-nomenon. He was, said a writer in Canada's national magazine *Maclean's* when Bobby was still only sixteen, "a swift powerful skater with instant ac-celeration, instinctive anticipation, a quick accurate shot, remarkable com-posure, an unrelenting ambition, a solemn dedication, humility, modesty, and fondness for his parents, and his brothers and sisters that often turns his eyes moist." He was, in brief, a Canadian cover boy, ready to change the face of his sport. And the oddest aspect of the extravagant praise was that it was all true.[11]

Boston waited. "Look, we considered him a savior," said Richard Johnson, an authority on Boston sports. In 1966, when Orr's Oshawa team
played the Niagara Falls Flyers, Boston's other major farm team, in an exhibition game in the Boston Garden, more than 10,000 fans turned out to get
their first look at Bobby. They had all heard the stories and longed to see
the player who management promised would change the fortunes of the
Bruins. And no team in the NHL needed a savior more. The Bruins had a
fabled history. The first NHL team in the United States, the Bruins won the
Stanley Cup in 1929, 1939, and 1941. In the first two, Eddie Shore, the brilliant, moody, brutally competitive defenseman, led the Bruins. In the third
championship, the Bruins' famous Kraut Line of Milt Schmidt, Bobby
Bauer, and Woody Dumart led the way. But the glory days ended with
World War II, and Boston fell on hard times. The team was decent in the
1940s, bad in the 1950s, and dreadful for most of the 1960s. For the first eight
years of the decade the Bruins finished out of the playoffs and generally in
last place in the NHL. For the Boston Bruins, the only unresolved question
going into those seasons was whether they could win more games than the
New York Rangers and stay out of the cellar. Mostly they did not.

The promise of Orr lent hope to these seasons of discontent and misery.
In 1966, at age eighteen, he was eligible to play in the NHL, and Bruins
president Weston Adams and general manager Leighton "Hap" Emms offered Orr a more or less standard rookie contract of something in the neighborhood of $10,000 a year. But Orr was not a more or less standard rookie.
He was the One, the designated savior of the Bruins, the promise of a glorious future. And what was more, Adams and Emms had been saying as
much for several years. It was like a scene from the hit film *Oliver!* When
Emms made his offer, Orr politely said something to the effect of "Please,
sir, may I have more?" Orr then referred Emms to Alan Eagleson, the
player's agent, a man as different from the straight-shooting Orr as can be
imagined.[12]

For a polite, soft-spoken, seemingly conservative cover boy who only
wanted to play hockey, it was the action of a radical, anarchist bomb-
thrower. The owners of the six NHL franchises, a socially prominent plu-
tocracy, were unaccustomed to negotiating honestly with any of their players, and the Bruins' management in particular tended to throw around
nickels like manhole covers. The idea of dealing with Orr through Eagle-

son, a Toronto-based lawyer destined to become the gray eminence in Bobby's career, was repugnant to Emms. NHL general managers thrived on bending players to their will, signing them for their figure, not actually negotiating, and certainly not with a lawyer. Emms refused, muttering disgust at the very idea. But the Bruins needed Orr, had said they needed him, and had promised him to their faithful fans. Orr, Emms and Adams had trumpeted, was Boston's ticket to winning seasons and the Stanley Cup. They had to sign him. They knew it. Orr knew it. And Eagleson knew it.

By the mid-1960s the costs of doing business in professional sports had begun to rise dramatically. In 1965 Joe Namath, a strong-armed, weak-kneed quarterback out of the University of Alabama, had signed with the New York Jets for a reported $427,000, a sum that made all professional athletes regard their activities in a different light. The next year Sandy Koufax and Don Drysdale, the Los Angeles Dodgers' franchise pitchers, hired an agent and staged a joint holdout, demanding Namathesque salaries. They asked for a million dollars over three years. After a bitter dispute with management, Koufax signed for $130,000 and Drysdale for $115,000 for the 1966 season. With expansion and new leagues, and with the specter of free agency haunting the imaginations of team owners, the old order of imperial, autocratic management-labor relations was gasping its last breaths.

In this new economic world, professional hockey bordered on antediluvian. Its six-team league, odd alliance among the owners, and conservative, ethnically divided player pool immunized it against rapid, radical change. But the young Orr and the opportunistic Eagleson challenged the old order—and won a modest victory. After threatening to play for the Canadian National Hockey Team instead of the Bruins and waiting for Emms to come to him, Orr signed a record-breaking rookie contract: $80,000, which included a $25,000 signing bonus, $25,000 for his first season, and $30,000 for his second. The contract did not exactly break the NHL bank, but it did announce the dawning of a new economic age.

Eagleson was behind Orr's economic boldness. No one, however, directed Bobby's revolutionary approach to the game. And no one can really explain it. It is easy enough to describe what Orr did on the ice. He was a defensive player who thought, skated, stick-handled, and shot like an offensive player. With Orr on the ice, the Bruins had a perpetual power play. Instead of stopping the puck in his zone and pushing it out to a wing, Orr took off up the ice, trusting his speed, ability, and instincts to overcome his positional disadvantage. This put tremendous pressure on the opponent's defense, creating additional match-ups and uncomfortable spacing. With Orr as an extra offensive player, the Bruins got more shots, more goals, more time in the offensive zone and, at least in theory, more wins.

Of course, in theory, it also meant Orr was often out of position and opened the Bruins' defense to devastating counterattacks. But with Orr, that theory was not validated on the ice. He seemed to know intuitively when to attack, how far to attack, and the exact moment to fall back. It was that process, that calculus of athletics, that sportswriters attempted but failed to explain. Frank Deford, one of the first American sportswriters on the national scene to lavish praise on Orr, observed Bobby's "magic facility for heading toward an empty spot and attracting a loose puck toward him." The image of Orr as a magnet that attracted vulcanized rubber disks suggests something about the player's anticipation, but hardly explains it. Other writers rhapsodized about Orr's speed, his reflexes, his creativity. A few years into Orr's Bruins career, a *Boston Globe* sportswriter noted, "The most surprising thing about Orr is that he has anything left to surprise you with." Again, true, but hardly elucidating.

George Plimpton came a bit closer. During the summer of 1977 he trained with the Bruins in preparation for a brief stint between the pipes. As with his other athletic efforts, Plimpton demonstrated that his skill as a participatory journalist definitely inclined toward the noun and away from the adjective. In one conversation, Bruins defenseman Mike Milbury told Plimpton that greatness in hockey entailed the ability to seize opportunities. "One of the things about hockey," Milbury mused, "is that for a goal to be scored someone must make at least a small error. You can't discount the brilliance of a particular play, but usually the greatness of the great player is that he can take advantage of a small error." Milbury was not talking about Orr, but he was describing him. Orr had the ability to force his opponents to commit an error—to give him an opening—and the reflexes to adjust accordingly.[13]

As a source on his own greatness, Orr has provided few clues. "At times it's impossible for me to explain what I do on the ice, and why I do it," he said. On one occasion, he was moving with the puck toward the opponents' goal while being closely checked by two players. Then, suddenly, he was alone in front of the net. "I honestly did not know what I had done to get there; in fact, I was so surprised to find myself in that unguarded position that I missed the net completely with my shot." After the game he viewed the tape of the contest, watching himself break free by making a fast counterclockwise spin. The next day a photographer asked him to repeat the maneuver. "I spent twenty minutes trying to re-create that move, but I just couldn't do it. So how did I do it in the game? . . . It just happened, that's all I can say."[14]

"It just happened." Perhaps that is the best explanation for genius. How could a critic or a historian explain the creativity of Wolfgang Amadeus Mozart or Albert Einstein? It just happened that they had the capacity to see patterns invisible to others, to leap ahead while others plodded along flatfooted. Orr did not try to explain his movements. "I just trust my instinct. When it tells me to take a chance and make a certain play, I never worry too much about the possible repercussions if the play does not work for some reason." Teammate Gerry Cheevers voiced an important insight. "If Bobby has a problem, it's just that he has no fear. No fear whatsoever. If nothing else will do, I swear he'll use his head to block a shot. He's already been hurt bad, and he'll keep getting hurt. But that's his style. He won't change. He won't play it safe." This fearlessness characterized Orr's style from his first season with the Bruins. He did not fear injury, embarrassment, or success.[15]

Success came swiftly, but not immediately. In 1966 he took the ice for a team that had set new standards for ineptitude in the NHL. In the previous seven seasons the Bruins had finished last five times and next-to-last the other two. Never once during those seasons of seventy games did the Bruins manage to win thirty games, but many years they struggled to clear twenty wins. From 1961 to 1966 not a single Bruin was named to one of the NHL all-star teams. But the Boston faithful continued to take the T to North Station, spill onto Causeway Street, and make their way into the grimy, dimly lit, rodent-infested Boston Garden. During these years the National Basketball Association *was* the Boston Celtics. They won championship after championship, playing the game at a level that has never been matched. But they often played before a half-empty Garden. Not the Bruins. During the 1960s the attendance rose steadily and was always outstanding. Though the Gallery Gods complained bitterly at times, they also cheered for and genuinely cared for Leo Boivin, Bronco Horvath, Pat Stapleton, Jerry Toppazzini, Doug Mohns, Ted Green, and perhaps even Minnesota-born Tommy Williams, who for a time was the only American-born player competing in the NHL.

In Orr's first season (1966–67) the Bruins once again finished in last place, slipping below the twenty-win mark. Orr, though, did not disappoint. He seemed electric on the ice, playing as if he expected to win every game. He ended the Bruins' all-star drought, won the Calder Trophy as top rookie, and clearly laid claim as the league's premier defenseman. When the Rangers' Harry Howell was awarded the Norris Trophy as the top defenseman, he graciously accepted, commenting, "I am glad I won the Norris Trophy this year, because in 10 years it will be the Bobby Orr Trophy." It was clear that first season that all Orr needed was the right talent on the ice with him.[16]

The next season (1967–68) the pieces began to fall into place. The NHL had a history of odd, almost criminal trades—trades that gave off an odor of fishiness—and one of those transactions took place before the 1967 season. In a lopsided trade the Bruins sent Gilles Marotte, Pit Martin, and Jack Norris to Chicago for Phil Esposito, Ken Hodge, and Fred Stanfield. They also picked up several fine players in the expansion draft and in other trades, including Dallas Smith and Eddie Shack. These new players combined with such veterans as Gerry Cheevers, Johnny Bucyk, Ted Green, Ed Westfall, John McKenzie, Don Awrey, Tommy Williams, and Garry Doak. In addition, Derek Sanderson became a fulltime Bruin that year. The only unstable component was Orr himself. On the ice he was as brilliant and fearless as ever, and that was part of the problem. He paid the price. He took risks, and he took beatings. During the season he missed twenty-eight games as a result of operations on both knees, a twice-broken nose, a fractured collarbone, and a separated shoulder. Although Boston had the third-best record in the NHL, the team was swept by Montreal in the Stanley Cup quarterfinals.[17]

The Boston-Montreal series was a wonderful match-up. Between 1956 and 1969 the Canadiens won nine Stanley Cups. But the character of the dynasty was changing, its luster wearing ever so slightly. Maurice Richard, the Rocket, had retired at the beginning of the decade. Jean Beliveau, the long, elegant Le Gros Bill, was in the twilight of his glorious career. Gump

Worsley was certainly one of the finest goalies in the NHL, but on the whole the Canadiens seemed a team on a slow, incremental decline to something just below dominance. In contrast, the Bruins played with the confidence of a team with time on their side. Though they lost the series, they did not lose hope. "We knew things would be different the next year," recalled Phil Esposito.[18]

Part of Esposito's confidence resulted from his own play. In Boston, under the second-year coach Harry Sinden, Esposito found a home for his game. A large, powerful center who took up space in the slot in front of the net and had exceptional anticipation and hands, he was often the beneficiary of Orr's long breakouts and Boston's wings' ability to muck along the board and center the puck. In the 1967–68 season he finished second to Stan Mikita in scoring. The other part of his confidence came from the fact that he played with Orr. "Our team also improved as Bobby Orr improved. By the 1968–1969 season, Bobby had become the most dominant defenseman ever to play the game." Because of the way Orr played the game, he made his teammates better. When Bobby was on the ice, Esposito didn't have to go as far back to receive the puck, Eddie Johnston and Gerry Cheevers faced fewer shots, and the wings got more chances to score. It was all part of the "Orr Factor."[19]

While Orr matured and Boston improved, the other teams in the NHL declined in strength. In 1967 the NHL expanded, doubling from six to twelve teams and dividing into East and West Divisions. Suddenly men who could not have made an NHL team the year before became regular players. The impact of expansion was most visible in offense. In the years after expansion, players scored more goals and rewrote most of the scoring records. In the 1968–69 season, Esposito became the first NHL player to break the 100-point barrier, but even more remarkable, Bobby Hull and Gordie Howe also exceeded the mark. The next season Bobby Orr smashed 100 points from his defensive position, and the following year four Boston players—Esposito, Orr, Bucyk, and Hodge—did it. It was the NHL's version of a run-and-gun style of play. It was revolutionary. And Boston was the home of the revolution. To keep up with Boston, teams had to score more.[20]

Hockey authorities expected that in 1969 the Bruins would defeat the Canadiens en route to the Stanley Cup. Toe Blake, after coaching the Montreal team to eight Stanley Cups, had retired, and Beliveau was close to the end of his career. For most of the season the Bruins seemed prepared to meet the challenge. With Esposito smashing scoring records, Wayne Cashman and Jim Harrison filling in for injured players, and Bobby Orr electrifying spectators with his rink-length rushes, the Bruins skated around and through the opposition. And when they were not outscoring and out-skating the opposition, they were outfighting them. The 1968–69 Bruins did not invent winning by intimidation, but they put their stamp on the prod-uct. Mark Mulvoy of *Sports Illustrated,* playing off the popular rock group, called the team "Bobby Orr and the Animals," and they played the game with smash-mouth intensity—without helmets, without fear, and without respect for even their most venerable opponents. It was not just Ted Green, the longtime Bruins cop, who actually seemed to be mellowing. Even the youngsters were getting into the spirit of "Bruins hockey." Jim Harrison was brought up to fill in for an injured player, and after playing only a few games was challenging Gordie Howe, who had been a star in the league for more than twenty years. After slamming Howe into the boards and causing him to drop his stick, Harrison paused for a moment and then kicked the stick thirty feet down the ice. "He's what you'd call a disturber," general manager Milt Schmidt said later.[21]

In December 1968 the Bruins lost only two games, and the next month they did not lose one. Then Orr missed a series of games because of another knee injury, and the Bruins suffered without him. They faded in February and March, and finished second to Montreal in their division. In the play-offs they swept Toronto, then lost once again to Montreal, this time four games to two. In midseason a number of writers agreed with Mulvoy that they were witnessing "the start of what seems certain to be the next dynasty in the NHL." But at the end of the season it was a dynasty deferred, and again the Canadiens hoisted the Stanley Cup.[22]

The next year was the year. The year that Bobby Orr fulfilled his promise in spectacular fashion. But it began ominously. In a preseason exhibition game—an exhibition game!—against the St. Louis Blues Ted Green and Wayne Maki began to fight in front of the St. Louis net. Pushing and shov-ing quickly escalated into high-sticking, which Maki ended with a vicious stick blow to Green's head. Green collapsed, bleeding from the mouth and head, and was rushed to the hospital, where he underwent an immediate operation. There were fears that he might not live and a general consensus that if he lived he would never play again. (He lived and played the next season, though he had to learn to play right-handed.) The loss of Green, Boston's outspoken, emotional leader, forced Bobby Orr into a new role. He had always been a leader on the ice, but now he had to lead off the ice as well. "So—reluctantly, but oh, so beautifully—Bobby Orr took charge of the Bruins and the several rinks of the NHL," wrote Gary Ronberg.[23]

The season belonged to Bobby and the Bruins. Although they won two fewer games than the year before, they played with an intensity and abandon that awed spectators and intimidated opponents. They were viewed as modern-day Vikings, a collection of athletes with the ethics of a motorcycle gang. "Let's face it," said goalie Ed Johnston, "we're just a bunch of kooks and degenerates who get along." "People read that the Bruins are coming to town, and they think they're going to rob all the banks and rape all their daughters," commented a person close to the team. Yet their leader had the mop-top looks and the off-ice behavior of a choirboy. Bobby Orr, his hair now as long as a 1964 Beatle's, exceeded expectations. He became the first defensive player to score more than 100 points, breaking records for the most goals by a defenseman (33) and the most assists by anyone (87). He won the Norris Trophy as top defenseman, the Art Ross Trophy as top scorer, the Hart Trophy as the league's most valuable player, and the Conn Smythe Trophy as playoff most valuable player. No player has ever so dominated the game—before or since.[24]

That dominance was never more evident than in the Stanley Cup playoffs. It was an uncharacteristic year. Both Montreal and Toronto failed to qualify for the playoffs, assuring an American champion. The four best teams—Chicago, Boston, Detroit, and New York—were in the East Division; the West Division was comprised entirely of expansion teams. That meant, as it had the previous two years, that the team that won the East would almost assuredly capture the Stanley Cup. Both Chicago, the champions of the East, and Boston won their quarterfinals round, setting up a classic confrontation with all sorts of minidramas. It would be the Battle of the Bobbies: Orr and Hull; or the Battle of the Esposito Brothers: Phil and Tony. It would be a war.

It wasn't. Boston totally dominated Chicago, sweeping the series 4–0. Throughout the series Orr controlled the action, speeding up or slowing down the game as the situation dictated. He led offensive charges to capture a lead and then smothered the action to protect the advantage. Even the Blackhawks had to admire Orr's brilliance. "Hell, [most of the Chicago players were] just standing around watching Bobby fly, like they were in awe or something," said a Bruin.[25]

Everyone expected that the final series would be an afterthought, more of a coronation than a contested championship. The St. Louis Blues, the best of the West, had played in the two previous Stanley Cup finals, but they had lost 4–0 in both series. "I don't want to take anything away from St. Louis, because they are a good hockey team," outspoken Phil Esposito said, "but this final is anticlimactic, the same as last year after Montreal beat us. We've just got too good a hockey club." Proving the point, Boston won the first three games convincingly. In an attempt to neutralize Orr, Blues coach Scotty Bowman assigned a player to shadow Bobby all over the ice, with the effect of weakening the rest of his defense. The result: Orr scored slightly less but Boston, and especially Esposito, significantly more. "It doesn't bother me," Orr told a reporter. "If we can keep scoring six goals a game, they can send a guy to lunch with me." In game four, played in Boston, the Blues stiffened, sending the contest into overtime. Sudden-death hockey is always a problematic affair, subject to the whim of the puck, which is apt to slide or bounce in unexpected directions at unexpected moments. It was not that the series was in jeopardy; it wasn't. But winning the Stanley Cup in Boston was.[26]

Early in the overtime period, with the game on the line, Orr made three critical mistakes in a matter of a few seconds. As Syl Apps, a standout center in the 1930s and 1940s, explained, "First, he did the wrong thing at the blue line when he charged the puck. If it had got by him, the other team would have had a clean breakaway, and possibly the winning goal. After he had knocked the puck over to Sanderson, he made another mistake. He should have gone back to the blue line, but he headed for the net. Then he made his third mistake. Instead of lifting the puck over the goalie when he got Sanderson's pass, he slid it through the goalie's legs."[27]

Three mistakes that ended in arguably the most famous goal in the history of hockey, a goal that not only ended a rather dull series but culminated in the magical moment when Orr took flight, a moment captured by photographer Ray Lussier. Of course, what appeared as mistakes to a hockey traditionalist were in reality examples of Orr's genius. He had trusted his instincts, without the slightest fear of consequences. He knew the safe play, he understood the dangers, but, as he later observed, "I instinctively skated toward the St. Louis goal." And that, in part, was what separated Bobby Orr from the pack.[28]

Bobby Orr was only twenty-two when he slid that shot between Glenn Hall's skates. He was only twenty-two, but he had become the most celebrated athlete in North America, revered above and below the border, venerated in Boston. In December 1970 he was named Sportsman of the Year by *Sports Illustrated.* No one questioned his ability on the ice. League president Clarence Campbell, normally a laconic Scotsman, said, "I've seen all the greats since the 1920s, and I've never seen a player with the skills of Orr." New York Rangers coach Emile Francis agreed: "I thought he would be a superstar when he was 27. But he's only 22, and he's already the greatest ever."[29]

But Bobby Orr, as a man and as a symbol, transcended what he did on the ice. At twenty-two he was—and would remain—a fixture at Boston charities, especially those organizations centered on children. He visited hospitals, churches, and schools, not for publicity and not for token stays. He did it because he cared, because, he seemed to sense, someone as blessed as he simply owed more than other people. Witnessing suffering, he confessed to a reporter, "cuts deep into me, and I'd rather not talk about it. It's very personal with me. Ask me about the broads or the booze, anything else."[30]

In an age of celebrity athletes, when the fame and money were increasing geometrically, Orr was the symbolic throwback, a relic of another time. By 1970 he had become the anti-Namath. Joe Namath was the new breed of superstar, a brash mixture of ego and glitz, part athlete, part pitchman, and part hustler. Orr was different. He did not crave the lights of New York City or tailor his pronouncements for the evening headlines. He was quiet and shy, not as an act or an image, but because he *was.* Of course, the NHL tried to exploit even this aspect of Orr. "Bobby Orr is a whole 'nother ball game, a whole new breed of superstar," said an NHL official. "He's modest, he's restrained, he's understated. He's the exact opposite of Joe Namath. Namath reached millionaire status as a kind of mixed-up antihero, but Orr will reach it as a hero in the classic sense." Comparing Orr with Namath was common at the time, but Orr never made the comparison. Molding an image was not one of his concerns.[31]

In 1970 Bobby Orr was young, and so were most of his Bruin teammates. They had the finest team in hockey, a handful of top draft choices, and a future full of possibilities. They were poised to become the Boston Celtics of hockey, or perhaps another Montreal Canadiens. But it did not happen. In 1972 they won another Stanley Cup, and they were a very good team throughout the decade. But Montreal of the old teams and the Philadelphia Flyers of the expansion teams dominated the Stanley Cup.

And the promise of Bobby Orr faded. He became a victim of his own best traits. Even at twenty-two his body betrayed an indication of his future. His face had become scarred. The skin was thicker above his eyes, his lip drooped slightly, his nose was flatter. Jack Olsen noted, "After five years in the bullpits of the National Hockey League, Orr does not yet resemble Marlon Brando in *On the Waterfront* . . . but he is en route. His nose has been fractured three or four times and he has taken 50 or so stitches, mostly in the face." But the worst scars were the least evident. His knees, after Joe Namath's the most famous in America, could not withstand his game. He had already had several operations, and the future would hold many more. By the mid-1970s they would effectively end his career. His body, an athlete's greatest gift, in the end betrayed him.[32]

That betrayal is common enough. Perhaps what was even more painful, a subject Orr does not discuss, was that he was also betrayed by his own trust. He trusted, without reservation, his family, teammates, and friends. His loyalty was blind. He put the business aspects of his career into the hands of Alan Eagleson and trusted his counsel. When other players began to question Eagleson's ethics and honesty, Bobby defended his agent. It was a trust badly, and sadly, misplaced. After Orr's injury-riddled season of 1975–76 and fourth knee operation, Eagleson arranged for Orr to leave Boston and sign with Chicago. Eagleson told Orr that Boston refused to make an acceptable offer, that the team questioned Bobby's physical condition. In fact Boston had made a significant effort to re-sign Orr. Eagleson arranged the move for his own purposes, which had nothing to do with what was best for his client. The result was that Bobby Orr finished his career two years later in a Blackhawks uniform. It should never have happened that way. He deserved to play out his career with the Bruins—and Boston deserved it too.[33]

In the years of expansion and growth, of national television contracts and million-dollar contracts, Bobby Orr was the face of hockey. He was the one that fans in expansion cities turned out to see; he was the one that children in the mushrooming youth hockey programs dreamed of playing like. It is difficult to imagine hockey today without the career of Bobby Orr. He was the one who made it all happen.

Shortly after Orr departed for Chicago, George Plimpton spent time in training camp with the Bruins. After practices the players gathered at a local bar to drink beer and talk hockey. They told stories, ridiculed players past and present, and laughed. They sat for hours, drinking and talking and laughing. But Plimpton noticed that when the talk turned to Bobby Orr— and it always did—the players' tone changed. "They told stories about him with a kind of reverence, with no interruptions, or horseplay around the table, and if a waitress came around to take orders for another round of beers, she waited until the story was done, and very likely, being a Massachusetts girl, she would lean in to hear the rest of it because there is no one, ever, who matched Orr for the adulation he received in New England for his brand of play."[34]

Plimpton vividly recalled one story. Bobby was killing a penalty against Oakland, playing the old game of keepaway with the puck, when he lost a glove at mid-ice. "He was not deterred at all. Wheeling around behind his own net, one bare hand on the stick, he came back up the ice with the puck, going at top speed, when suddenly, almost as an afterthought, he reached down and scooped his bare hand into the empty glove as he passed it, never breaking his stride, and settling it into place, he went on through the two defensemen and challenged Gary Smith, the Oakland goalie. And Smith beat him, turning away Orr's shot . . . and the best part of the story was that *both* benches groaned, the Oakland bench as well, because the sequence had been so brilliant that it seemed to require a goal to round it out aesthetically."[35]

Plimpton was mistaken on only one point. Bobby Orr did not need the goal to round it out aesthetically.

14

The Battle of the Beards:
Russell and Chamberlain

Randy Roberts

I think it was something in their beards, some configuration of facial hair, that dictated their behavior. In 1965 Wilt Chamberlain sported a goatee, a tiny beboppish tuft of hair on his chin accented by a lower-lip spot and a thin mustache. The combination was a throwback to the heyday of the New York jazz scene, a time when Charlie "Yardbird" Parker and "Dizzy" Gillespie reigned at the Three Deuces and the Onyx Club. Wilt's goatee was Miles Davis cool. It linked him to James Baldwin and the black and white Beat writers who had asserted their naked individuality and regarded conformity as heresy. It said, in effect, "Here I am. Deal with me." With a hard emphasis on the *me*.

Bill Russell would have none of that. His beard was fuller and more defiant. He wore a glorious Fu Manchu, a bit long at the bottom but neatly trimmed on the sides. It attached Russell less to the Village cats than to what would become the Oakland panthers—Black Panthers, black leather jackets, fists raised in the Black Power salute. Nineteen sixty-five was still a few years before Huey Newton, Tommy Smith, and John Carlos, but in Russell's mind and beard the future was already taking shape. Miles Davis had not shown the way, but Malcolm X had. Power to the people, baby.

Russell's beard seemed to proclaim, "Here we are. Deal with us. Or don't. It doesn't matter. We're not leaving."

They were the two best big men of their time. They were rivals—and friends. But except for their height, they could hardly have been more different.

"Look at the board," a Celtic fan hectored Chamberlain from a safe distance in an upper section of the Boston Garden. If the Philadelphia 76ers center heard the barb, it didn't register on his face. His face was a monument to impassivity; nothing seemed to touch him. His team was being badly beaten by the Boston Celtics in the first game of the National Basketball League Eastern Division Finals. Celtic fans were raining abuse on Wilt, showering him with insults, holding him somehow personally responsible for . . . what exactly? For Philly's success in the 1964–65 season or for Philly's failure in this particular game? For being too tall or scoring too many points? For seeming not to care or just not to care about them?

That's it. Wilt's seeming indifference, his refusal to look at the scoreboard or show some facial indication of concern, was a direct insult to the Celtics faithful's own passion. Wilt's attitude—his casual nonchalance and regal, expressionless face—silently questioned the importance of his activity. It suggested that the first game of a best-of-seven series, played in the opponent's house, didn't really matter that much. In fact, no single game in a season of 100-odd games truly mattered. The Boston fans demanded some sign from Wilt that their own passion was not misplaced, that the loss hurt. But all they saw on Chamberlain's face was a distant look and sweat streaming down his goatee.

The 76ers had started fast in the game. Hal Greer, Philly's lean, muscular guard, scored 5 points in the first few minutes to bump his team to a 7–3 lead. But then Celtic coach Red Auerbach called for a full court press, and the Philly players began to resemble a team maneuvering on ice. They walked, kicked the ball out of bounds, threw errant passes, and missed shots with alarming frequency. Against this comedy of errors, the Celtics performed with passion, precision, and guts. Tommy Heinsohn, who led Boston with 23 points, had a sponge taped to his left foot to cushion an ailing arch. John Havlicek, who added 20 points, had had his knee drained before the game. Bill Russell, the team's center and central player, was on the court for every second of the contest. Although he only scored 11 points, he grabbed 32 rebounds and contributed 6 assists, doing "the job he was supposed to do," said Auerbach. It was such a total team performance that with four minutes remaining in the game and the Celtics leading 101–81 Auerbach lit his traditional victory cigar and relaxed on the bench.

Chamberlain finished with 33 points and 31 rebounds. Like Russell, he played the entire game. Even Auerbach, a flinty, stingy man when it came to praising opponents, said, "That's as good as I've seen him play." After the game reporters gathered around Wilt for comments, but he said almost nothing. He didn't seem upset, just not particularly interested. "They're tough," he said, adding little else. The game was over; the series was just beginning. Chamberlain's reticence suggested that this was no great matter, that here was no reason to get excited.[1]

Wilt Chamberlain had a reputation. He had always had a reputation. And only partially was it because of his height, although that was what everyone noticed first. His parents were just a shade above average height, and a few of his siblings were fairly tall, but it was difficult to advance a strong genetic argument for Wilt's growth. He was 29 inches at birth and just seemed to keep growing. At the age of twelve he had reached 6 feet, 3 inches, and then he sprouted about 4 inches in seven weeks. By the time he finished growing he was an inch over 7 feet.

By then he was also a basketball legend. At Overbrook High School in Philadelphia, he scored 74 points in twenty-four minutes in one game and 90 points in another. Virtually unstoppable, he had an outside and inside game, an all-around attack that featured dunks, one-handed jump shots, and two-handed set shots. And in the summers he learned more about the on-and-off-the-court game of basketball playing in the Catskills "Borscht Belt," an informal league attached primarily to Jewish-owned resorts that provided entertainment and chances to place friendly wagers for paying guests. There he played against and dominated some of the finest college and professional talents in the country. By his senior year at Overbrook he had become the first black high school player to develop a national reputation.[2]

College coaches coveted Wilt. It was 1955, college basketball had weathered the scandals of 1951 and emerged more popular than ever, and nobody was watching the recruiting game too closely. It was a year after the *Brown* decision, the year that Bill Russell led the University of San Francisco to a National Collegiate Athletic Association title, and college coaches were sensitive to the subtle changes in the country's racial status quo, especially if it afforded them a chance to improve their win-loss record. Chamberlain, nearly everyone agreed, was a ticket to multiple NCAA championships. "I had offers from damn near every state in the union—plus Hawaii, which wasn't even a state yet," he said. "Alphabetically, the schools ranged from Arizona State to Xavier of Ohio." The competition for Wilt was fierce, and eventually he chose the University of Kansas. Rumors of what it cost Kansas to win the Chamberlain sweepstakes filled sportswriters' columns. "I feel sorry for The Stilt," commented New York writer Lenny Lewin. "When he enters the NBA four years from now, he'll have to take a pay cut." Lewin was wrong. Chamberlain estimated that KU supporters probably paid him "less than $20,000," and he didn't take a pay cut when he signed with the National Basketball Association.[3]

In Philadelphia the weather was breaking. As so often happened in the city, residents had hoped for more from April than they were getting. The month had started with low, gray skies and cold, damp days. Rain and snow mixed in just the right amount to ensure that the city looked its worst. On the fifth, the day after the 76ers' loss in Boston, the sky turned blue, and the temperatures climbed from the thirties to the low sixties, offering a glimpse of spring. On April 6, as Boston and Philadelphia prepared for their second game, it rained again, but this time warmer, springlike showers.

Both towns seemed more concerned with the series than with the weather. The sportswriters in Philadelphia and Boston fueled the rivalry between the two teams, which as often as not they personalized as a clash between Bill Russell and Wilt Chamberlain, the two dominant big men in the NBA. Across America, African Americans were making their presence felt. In the year since Sidney Poitier won the best actor Oscar for his work in *Lilies of the Field*, black Americans had sung, fought, marched, walked, run, and died their way to the center of the American psyche. It was a year that witnessed the Supremes break into the Top Forty, the murder of three civil rights workers in Philadelphia, Mississippi, passage of the Civil Rights Act of 1964, the assassination of Malcolm X, and the beginning of the march on Selma, Alabama. During the year Bob Hayes became the world's fastest man at the Tokyo Olympics, Cassius Clay changed his name to Muhammad Ali, Martin Luther King Jr. accepted the Nobel Peace Prize, and Lorraine Hansberry and Nat King Cole died. Everywhere, it seemed, the nature of the racial equilibrium was changing, and the pace of that change was quickening.

Nowhere was this more evident than in the National Basketball Association. Until 1950 the NBA—and its Basketball Association of America predecessor—had been an all-white affair. Then, in the second round of the 1950 draft, Walter Brown, owner of the Boston Celtics, selected Duquesne University's Chuck Cooper. "Walter, don't you know he's a colored boy?" another owner asked. Brown thought for a moment then replied, "I don't give a damn if he's striped, plaid, or polka-dotted! Boston takes Chuck Cooper of Duquesne!" Later in the draft the Washington Capitols selected another African-American player, Earl Lloyd of West Virginia State. A few months later the New York Knicks bought the contract of Nat "Sweetwater" Clifton from the Harlem Globetrotters. As a result of these off-season maneuvers, in 1950 Cooper, Lloyd, and Clifton, collectively, became the Jackie Robinson of the NBA.[4]

Except unlike Robinson all three were strictly utility men, minor-role players visible only because of the color of their skins. Coaches insisted that they play tough defense, work hard under the boards, set bone-crushing picks, and let their white teammates take most of the shots. Dolph Schayes, one of the NBA's leading scorers who played with Lloyd in Syracuse, noted that his black teammate made his job easier. Lloyd "got the poor end of the stick as far as playing was concerned. He was always doing the dirty work, fouling out of the game. Actually, he helped me a great deal because with him in there I was free to rebound and get a lot of glory, since his game was to guard the other team's offensive ace." Clifton played a similar role. Although he was a fast, high-jumping player, he was expected to play a supporting part. "They [the Knicks] didn't want me to do anything fancy . . . What I was supposed to do is rebound and play defense . . . I'll put it this way: at the time they weren't making any Black stars."[5]

The numbers underscored their stories. Until the arrival of Elgin Baylor and Wilt Chamberlain at the end of the 1950s, no African-American player broke onto the league's list of top scorers. There such players as George

Mikan, Paul Arizin, Neil Johnston, Bob Pettit, George Yardley, and Dolph Schayes ruled. Most were tall and slow; a few were tall and quick. All were white. Even the few guards, such stars as Bob Cousy and Bill Sharman, who cracked the list were white. It was a paler time in the history of the sport.

Times changed faster than anyone, black or white, could have reasonably anticipated. During the 1964–65 season, six of the top seven scorers in the NBA, all five assist leaders, and four of the top five rebounding leaders were black. Of the ten players who started the second game of the Celtics-76ers playoff series, eight were black. Only Tommy Heinsohn on the Celtics and Al Bianchi on the 76ers were white, and both were near the end of their playing careers. The strength of Boston was its defense, anchored by three superb black players: guard K. C. Jones, forward Satch Sanders, and center Bill Russell. The power of Philadelphia resided in its offense, led by three talented black performers: guard Hal Greer, forward Chet Walker, and center Wilt Chamberlain. The two teams promised a classic matchup, but, more than that, they put to rest stereotypes—which were still alive in the early 1960s—that white players were the heart of championship teams.

Almost 10,000 people, a near-capacity crowd, jammed Philadelphia's Convention Center for the second game. Boston's players hated the Philadelphia fans. They considered them loud, obnoxious, and rowdy, always cruel to opponents, often vicious toward their own team, and mean-spirited, foul-mouthed, and a general blight on civilization. Bob Cousy, Boston's all-pro guard, recalled one particularly vile Philadelphia Warriors fan who had a regular courtside seat under the visitor's basket. During pregame warm-ups, Cousy wrote in an editorially more restrained era, the fan "shouted things so obscene that they are unprintable and utterly unbelievable." Cousy and other Celtics used to hope for a riot for a chance to even the score with the guy. Once Cousy did exact a modicum of justice. Struck by a golden inspiration, a sort of basketball epiphany, he instructed teammate Jack Nichols to stand directly in front of the odious fan while the Celtics lofted a few meaningless pregame shots. Then Cousy went to the foul line and fired his hardest pass at Nichols, who at the last possible split second stepped out of the way of the oncoming missile. The ball exploded into the unsuspecting man's face. Cousy and Nichols hurried over to admire their handiwork, and all the dazed heckler could mutter was, "What happened? . . . what happened?"[6]

By 1965 Cousy had retired from the Celtics, and the Warriors had departed Philadelphia for San Francisco, but the level of Philadelphia fans—now 76ers fans—had not improved much. Like other fans throughout the NBA, they hated Boston, the perennial world's champion Boston, and longed for the team's demise. Philadelphia's coach Dolph Schayes shared their feelings. As both a player and a coach he had a long history of losing to the Celtics, and after the series opening loss he openly criticized his team for playing soft. The Celtics, Schayes said, had been brutal in Boston. They "chopped us up pretty good Sunday. We're all scratches and bruises. They pawed, pushed, held and got away with a lot." He promised to retaliate in Philadelphia. With Wilt and Luke Jackson, two of the strongest men in the NBA, Schayes asserted that if Boston wanted to play "that way" his team would "oblige them."[7]

And oblige them they did. Everything the 76ers tried seemed to work; none of the Celtics counters did. Philadelphia's offensive strength was its inside game. Its game plan was simple: Get the ball inside to Chamberlain as fast as possible. With enough time Wilt could maneuver Russell close to the basket for a dunk or a peep shot. If the Celtics doubled Wilt he could push the ball back outside to Greer for a jump shot, to Walker for a drive or pull-up jumper, or to Jackson for an inside bucket. The Celtics' best counter was to keep the ball out of Chamberlain's hands or at least to limit his options once he had the ball. Their press was designed less to force turnovers than to make Philadelphia expend valuable seconds bringing the ball up-court. If Celtics could keep the ball away from Wilt for 15 seconds he would not have the time to maneuver for his best shot or the luxury of drawing a double team and passing off. Ironically, although Philadelphia had a higher-powered offense, the 24-second clock worked to Boston's advantage.

In game two Chamberlain was hot and Boston's press was not. After a close first period, Boston went cold, hitting only fifteen of fifty-one shots during the middle periods. And Wilt, hauling down a remarkable thirty-nine rebounds, consistently limited the Celtics to one shot. On the offensive end Chamberlain was equally effective, scoring 30 points and distributing eight assists. Perhaps even more important, the 76ers' guards and forwards effectively handled Boston's press by either using back-screens, employing long, crisp passes, or simply breaking down-court before the Celtics could set their press. Sam Jones finished the game with 40 points and led a late, futile charge, but in truth the Celtics found no answer for

Chamberlain's offensive and defensive prowess. After the game, Russell praised Chamberlain: "The big fella' was great, real great out there tonight. I ha[ve] to say he was fantastic . . . the finest performance he has ever had against me."[8]

Red Auerbach was less charitable than Russell. Perhaps his sour disposition after the game was the result of the punch he took. A Philly fan cold-cocked him as Auerbach was making his way to the Celtics' dressing room. "There wasn't a cop around," he complained. "Isn't that great?" Perhaps it was the result of the officiating, which he believed gave the 76ers a distinct advantage. "These giants—Chamberlain and Jackson—were in [the lane] all night. What can we do? We can't put a stop watch on them." Either way, Auerbach was in no mood to applaud Wilt's performance. To his way of thinking, he had been cheated out of one victory cigar.[9]

As so often was the case, Russell was more insightful—or simply more honest—than Auerbach. Insight and honesty were characteristics that mattered to the Celtic center. More than most athletes, he had the mind of a gifted scholar or a chess champion. He watched and he thought. On the basketball court this basic approach allowed him to anticipate what an opponent was likely to do at any given moment. Russell knew the strengths and weaknesses of his opponents, when they would try to drive and when they would pull up and shoot. His approach—know your opponent, understand the situation, anticipate the next move—carried off the court as well, where his opponents tended to be white and powerful. In a world informed by race, he was sensitive to its every nuance, and he was always prepared to speak his mind. His attitude did not make him the most popular player in the National Basketball Association, and that was fine with him. "I can honestly say that I have never worked to be liked," he wrote in 1965. "I have worked only to be respected. If I am liked, then that is an extra, valued bonus of the world we inhabit. If I am disliked, it is the privilege of those who wish to dislike me—as long as it is not based on prejudice."[10]

Bill Russell was no Wilt Chamberlain. He never had been. Wilt was a wunderkind, a rare basketball talent who was clearly destined for greatness from the first moment he picked up a basketball. He was tall and strong, fast and quick. Not only could he dunk over anyone and wow spectators with his trademark Dipper finger-roll; he was a surprisingly nimble ball-handler, an accurate passer, and, as he was apt to remind people, a fine outside shooter. The fact that he was a bricklayer from the foul line was merely a reminder that he was at least partially mortal, that he, like Achilles, had a flaw. Russell, on the other hand, was always a bit of a work in progress, the kind of player who, even after years as a professional, was apt to cut a new facet.

He undoubtedly owed his success to World War II. Russell was born in the dusty, rural poverty of Louisiana to proud parents who chafed under the constant restrictions of Jim Crow. When the war came, Russell wrote, his father "struck out for freedom," finding a job in a shipyard in Oakland, California, then sending back South for his family. Though the Russells were still poor and lived in a rundown part of the town known as "Landlord's Paradise," Oakland compared to Louisiana was "Paradise gained." But Russell recognized that in the North as in the South, racism and a double standard based on race were always as near as his shadow. They were present in the suspicious gaze of every policeman, the cold greeting of almost every teacher, and, saddest of all, in one's attitude toward oneself. Life at the bottom was not much of a life. African Americans, Russell later wrote, "become more and more frustrated. They lose respect for themselves and they lose respect for society. Pretty soon you develop a hatred for yourself. And then you lose all association. That is what happened to the Negro in this time, in this place."[11]

Russell knew the route to racial hell because he traveled partway down the path. He possessed perhaps the worst trait he could be plagued with in his time, in his place. Deeply sensitive, he keenly felt, almost like a lash, every slight, every negative word, every sign that he did not measure up. Looking for acceptance and a sense of worth, he tried athletics—badly. He was cut from the football team. He was cut from the basketball team. He was cut from the cheerleading squad. At his lowest point, when he was dejected and ready to take the final step toward self-hatred, a high school janitor gave him a gift of good advice. He had not seen Russell around the gym for some time and asked why. "These guys are just better than me. I couldn't make it," Russell answered. The janitor thought and then said: "If you think so, Russell, then they always will be."[12]

Perhaps that advice turned Russell's life around. Or perhaps it was the act of a kind junior varsity coach who gave the gangly youth the sixteenth slot on a fifteen-man team. Or perhaps, and even more likely, it was something inside Russell himself, some part of his father, some drive that refused to allow him to accept life inside a racial cage. In the next few years Russell grew taller and developed as a basketball player. Generally the height stayed well ahead of his talent, but by the end of his senior year the two inched closer. In an important game he scored 14 points—a high school career best—and gained the notice of an informal scout for the University of San Francisco. Word that Russell had some talent moved up the USF food chain, and eventually the school's coach offered him a scholarship. A few years later Chamberlain, who would have hung his head in shame at scoring only 14 points in a half, would have scores of scholarship offers and abundant choices. In 1952 Russell had one offer, and an easy choice. For a black youth, transplanted from the Jim Crow South to an unfriendly Oakland, one choice probably seemed like a hundred, maybe a thousand. How many of his neighborhood friends had any choices? He accepted the scholarship to the small school that it took him three trips over the San Francisco Bay to find.[13]

LBJ was in the news again. Since his inauguration, when he had wondered "how incredible it is that in this fragile existence we should hate and destroy one another," he had done his best to drum up support for America's war in Vietnam. In February 1965 he had dramatically responded to a low-level Communist attack on the U.S. installation at Pleiku by ordering air strikes against North Vietnam, an operation designated as Rolling Thunder. In March he had committed ground troops to Vietnam by sending two battalions of Marines to the air base at Danang. These troops differed from the earlier advisers; they were sent with orders to conduct military patrols. Then in April, the night before the third Boston-Philadelphia game, President Johnson suggested that Red China was underwriting North Vietnam's war of aggression. Retreat, he told his countrymen, was not an option. If America did not stop the Communists in Vietnam, the conflict would spread in a domino effect across Asia. He reaffirmed his sincere desire for peace but made it clear that he would not abandon an ally.

In Boston, Philadelphia forward Chet "the Jet" Walker blocked out the news of the day and prepared for a battle of his own. His career was a reminder that sports could—and often did—extract a terrible price. Like Russell, Walker had been born in the South and had moved with his mother to the North, to a place without "Whites Only" signs but with plenty of "white only" stares. In Mississippi, Walker had been painfully certain of his place; in Benton Harbor, Michigan, he was less sure. A nervous child who stuttered, afraid to talk and afraid of making mistakes, he was comfortable only in the project where he lived and, as he grew older, on any basketball court, where he excelled. The sport became his salvation. It provided him with an identity and perks. Teachers cut him slack, adults wanted to talk to him, women showed interest in him. Basketball moved him through high school and to college, and it even gave him a very limited sense of confidence, although he still harbored bone-deep insecurities and feelings of inadequacy.[14]

When he arrived on campus at Bradley University, an overwhelmingly white school in Peoria, Illinois, he "experienced the sensation of being noticed *and* ignored, but finally rejected, in a nice, middle-class way." His coach never displayed any interest in Walker as a person, and his clothes, language, culture, and background—let alone race—isolated him from everyone else, save the few other black athletes, on campus. Even worse, playing for Bradley meant that Walker had to make road trips for games in St. Louis, Houston, and Denton, Texas, to schools where students waved Confederate flags, threw lit cigarette butts on the floor, and screamed "Nigger!" And about all his coach could muster was a "that's just how things are" shrug.[15]

If playing in the South was soul crushing, playing in the North took a greater toll on Walker's body. During his sophomore season Walker led his team to a 24–2 record and a bid to the National Invitational Tournament at Madison Square Garden. Throughout the 1950s the Garden was "*the* arena," the focus of the basketball and boxing world. The Garden epitomized the very best and worst of sports. It smelled of beer and cigars, and seemed alive with the ghosts of Joe Louis and Joe Lapchick and the other sports legends who had fought and played their best there. But the Garden was also haunted by the ghosts of Jake La Motta and Jack Molinas, by fixed fights and point-shaving scandals. Unknown at the time to Walker, he experienced the worst. Jack Molinas, a very talented basketball player and an even better basketball fixer, arranged for Walker to drink a glass of orange juice laced with a drug that induced fever, cramps, nausea, and diarrhea.[16]

Walker should never have been allowed to play in the game that night, but he was and he did. He played in a haze, in spurts, running between the court and the locker room. He was dizzy and sick, and the world tilted like a funhouse. Bradley won the game, but Walker suffered lasting kidney damage. Years later he summarized his predicament: "I was a kid on the biggest night of my life. I was in pain and frightened and had to put myself in other people's hands. We're talking about 1960 here. I had no agent, no lawyer, no leverage. A kid from the projects, I was constantly trying to prove myself worthy of all this attention and opportunity."[17]

By 1965 Chet Walker had few illusions left to lose about sport. Always the two sides, the glitter and the garbage. The Boston Garden, with its championship banners, parquet court, storied history, symbolized success and tradition in the NBA, but Walker knew what was behind the veneer. Going into Boston was like descending into "Dante's inferno." At the airport cabbies yelled insults, people gawked, and the entire city seemed edgy. He felt it everywhere. "In the ride from the hotel to Boston Garden, it seemed the streets were always covered with slush as if the city was waiting for us to leave town before cleaning up." Inside the Garden was no garden. The opponents' locker room was "cold, damp, and dirty. Noise came up from the plumbing to drown out the coach's pregame talk. Rats and roaches lurked in that ancient building as if they'd signed a long-term lease." It was a locker room that was truly shared.[18]

And then on to the court, where Celtic fans abused Walker and his teammates—especially Chamberlain—and dead spots on the floor confounded them. There seemed to be a new dead spot for every important game, or perhaps the old ones just chose to relocate from time to time. In game three of the series the 76ers needed more than a map of the dead spots to win. Bill Russell was leaving nothing to chance. After getting the best of Russell in Philadelphia, Chamberlain had told reporters, "As far as I'm concerned, I've outplayed Russell individually. But the difference is that Boston has beaten the teams I've been on." Russell answered Chamberlain on the court, giving early notice that he would not permit his team to lose. He began the game with three straight baskets, made his first six field-goal attempts, and finished the quarter with 12 points. More important, he forced Chamberlain into either passing or taking low-percentage shots. Wilt made only one shot in the first half and added only one more in the third quarter.

By then the game was effectively over. After a 15–2 Boston spurt early in the second quarter, the 76ers never crawled closer than 9 points, and the Celtics cruised to a 112–94 victory.

Chamberlain's performance mystified Coach Dolph Schayes. In Philadelphia Wilt had challenged Russell, forcing him low on the block and taking the ball to the basket. In Boston Chamberlain positioned farther up the block and shot lazy, balletic fallaways. He was an enigma, not only to Schayes, but to everyone in the NBA. Sometimes it seemed as if he enjoyed being perversely unpredictable. What else could explain the timing for his attack on the entire league? In the middle of the most important series of his career, when he finally had a team that could rival Boston, he chose to assert individualism over any notion of team.[19]

The day of the third game the April 12 issue of *Sports Illustrated* reached the newsstands. It included the first installment of a two-part series by Chamberlain (with Bob Ottum) provocatively titled "My Life in a Bush League." "Oh, man, this is going to be better than psychiatry," Chamberlain began. And he continued as if he were stretched out on a psychiatrist's couch, moving randomly from one subject to another. It was a glimpse, as he promised, of "life inside a giant, baby."[20]

Being Wilt, Chamberlain said, was tough. Sure, he owned a $27,000 baby lavender Bentley Continental convertible, a forty-unit apartment house in Los Angeles, another twenty-seven-unit complex off Riverside Drive in New York, a couple of houses in Philadelphia, a piece of three trotting horses, Big Wilt's Small's Paradise in Harlem, and significant mutual funds. But all that did not add up to happiness. Every game he had to endure insults from fans, physical abuse from other players, bad calls from officials, and lately he had suffered from a chronic stomachache. But even that was not the worst part of being Wilt. The worst was simply playing basketball in a "bush league," a league populated by unprofessional owners, ill-trained coaches, and backbiting players. "I ask you," Wilt wrote, "Where else but professional basketball do you get (1) owners, (2) players and (3) coaches all knocking each other? . . . It creates a strictly bush atmosphere." And to support his contention, Chamberlain proceeded to "knock" NBA owners, coaches, and players.

The NBA system of elevating former—and occasionally current—players into the coaching ranks was one of his primary complaints. Case in point:

Dolph Schayes, his own coach. Schayes, Chamberlain emphasized, was too nice a man to coach. He was "so tender-hearted that someone sitting on the bench can look over at him with those big wet eyes, and he'll put them into the game—even if the man replaced is having a big night." Not only was Schayes too kind, Chamberlain hinted, but he was too dumb. Schayes's notion of sage advice was telling his players to fake more fouls. When a player argued that not everyone had the knack for faking fouls, Schayes said, "All right, I guess we'd better play it straight. But fake them when you can, huh?" Proof positive for Chamberlain that "the coaching system is right out of bushville."

Wilt's unstated goal in "My Life in a Bush League" was to distance himself from almost everyone else in the league. Not only was he the best in the game; he was the only one to see through the game. It was not a stand that endeared him to players, coaches, or NBA executives. "It looks as though everyone is out of step in basketball but him," said Red Kerr, Chamberlain's veteran teammate. Most of the other 76ers wisely kept their opinions to themselves. "I don't want to comment because we're fighting for the Eastern Division title," said Al Bianchi. "Money is what interests me right now." Dolph Schayes and NBA president Walter Kennedy refused to be drawn into the controversy. Both told reporters that they were too busy to read the article.[21]

Chamberlain showed no remorse for his words. He refused to suggest that he had been misquoted or that he did not mean everything that he said. In fact, he further distanced himself from his teammates by missing a team practice in Boston and flying back to Philadelphia in a different plane. "It appeared that Wilt had stuffed one in the wrong basket," remarked a Boston sportswriter.[22]

Perhaps. But a more likely explanation was that Wilt was just being Wilt, drawing the maximum amount of attention to himself. Throughout his career he evinced a certain discomfort with the idea that basketball was a team game. He grudgingly accepted the need for teammates, but he expected that the spotlight would always be pointed directly at him. Even later in his career, when he became a "team player," he expected the focus of every story to center on him as a "team player," as if he had invented the notion. Even as he demanded to be noticed as the brightest star in the basketball galaxy, he refused to acknowledge that he was in any way responsible for the failure of his teams to win championships. Poor management, inexperienced coaching, inept supporting cast—they lost championships, not Wilt.

Finally, the article revealed another troublesome aspect of Chamberlain's character. In moments of crisis, when the pressure to win was the greatest and the possibility of failure was the highest, he began searching, psychologically, for a soft place to land. He prepared excuses, talked about quitting, and, if so moved, did quit. In "My Life in a Bush League" he offered several reasons for speaking out, and "Reason No. 1" was "I'm at the top of this game and I'm thinking of retiring . . . I have now racked up all the all-time scoring and playing records—all the ones that count—and what else is there?" Only as an afterthought did he mention that in addition to scoring titles and rebounding crowns, a championship would be nice, but he added quickly, "I can't do that all by myself, right?"[23]

Chamberlain's tendency to deflect responsibility and slide toward the door became apparent during in his college days. When he enrolled at the University of Kansas, already one of the finest programs in the nation, sportswriters assumed that he would lead the Jayhawks to two, perhaps three, national titles. In his sophomore season—his first varsity year—he broke Kansas' single-game scoring record in his first outing and led his team to the 1957 NCAA finals. In the championship game against North Carolina, Wilt started slow and the Tarheels began fast. "My teammates . . . couldn't put a pea in the ocean," Chamberlain later wrote about the first half of the game. In the second half Kansas fought back, taking a 3-point lead into the final two minutes of the game. But North Carolina capitalized on a missed free throw and a turnover by Kansas and sent the game into overtime, finally winning it in triple overtime.[24]

The North Carolina game was the closest Chamberlain got to a national championship. The next year Kansas State won the Big Eight title and earned the NCAA bid, and sophomore Oscar Robertson at Cincinnati led the nation in scoring. Chamberlain complained that coaches devised new defenses just to stop him and that officials allowed his opponents to play unusually rough against him. By the end of his junior year he had tired of the college game, a game that featured double teams and clogged lanes. So he quit, later saying that if he had played another year at Kansas he might have burned out on basketball and never played in the NBA. Instead, he played a year with the Harlem Globetrotters, the one professional team in the world that could guarantee that he would be the center of attraction *and* win every game.

Game four helped Philadelphia fans to forget Chamberlain's assault on the NBA. It was more intense than the first three games, and for most of the contest it followed a pattern. Philadelphia led by 11 at the end of the first quarter, but Boston, behind the jump shooting of Sam Jones, Tommy Heinsohn, and John Havlicek, finished the half ahead, 56–51. The third quarter resembled the first. Hal Greer's jump shots, Chet Walker's drives, and Chamberlain's dunks erased Boston's 5-point lead and gave Philadelphia a 6-point advantage. In the last period the Celtics struggled back once more. Sam Jones was spectacular. Time and again he scored on his trademark long bank shot. With five minutes remaining in the game he hit 3 straight shots to tie the contest 106–106. With less than a minute left Boston led by 4.[25]

Chamberlain's play contributed almost as much to Boston's spurt as Jones's performance. In the last 90 seconds Wilt missed four straight free throws, and frustration was beginning to show through his mask. Then Luke Jackson made a jumper, Jones finally missed one, and Wilt grabbed a rebound, immediately calling time out. One second remained on the clock.

One second, in an age before game clocks were subdivided into tenths. Actually it might have been almost a full two seconds, or just a mere fraction of one second. It seemed a question for mathematicians, not players. After signaling time, Chamberlain slammed the ball to the floor. He knew that his foul shooting had cost the 76ers the game. After the time out, substitute guard Larry Jones inbounded the ball. The four other 76ers lined up across the court. Then Chamberlain dashed for the basket and Walker and Luke Jackson for either corner. Greer remained stationary and caught Jones's pass between the top of the key and the half-court line, 35 feet directly in front of the basket. He jumped and shot as the horn sounded. The ball lined straight, hit the backboard, and dove into the basket.

Red Auerbach argued fruitlessly with the referees. "It's impossible, just from logical thinking," he said after the game. "How can a man catch a pass-in, take a dribble, go in the air after flexing his knees and release the ball all in one second?" Greer correctly denied that he took a dribble. He said he just caught the ball and fired it toward the backboard, hoping for a fortunate bank. "I didn't have time to take dead aim at the rim."

The shot deflated Boston. In the overtime period the 76ers took an early lead and kept the pressure on the Celtics. Larry Jones, Greer, Jackson, Walker, and Chamberlain all scored in the final session. Wilt even hit his free throws. With the Philadelphia faithful cheering wildly, the 76ers won 134–131 and evened the series two games each. The game, and Chamberlain's lukewarm attempt to distance himself from his own words, put the focus of sportswriters back onto basketball. What had once been a best-out-of-seven series was now down to a best-out-of-three one.

It was sunny and mild in Boston for game five. But for the Philadelphia players, returning to the Boston Garden was like violating parole and being sent back to prison. Over a two-year period the 76ers had lost nine consecutive games in the inhospitable Garden, many of them painful, humiliating thrashings. Sunday's game certainly did not promise a gentler environment. "The shot," as it was being called, seemed the only topic worthy of discussion in Boston. Proposed Vietnam peace talks, the civil rights protest march in Bogalusa, Louisiana, Arnie's charge at the Masters—all seemingly unimportant compared with "the shot." "In darkened discotheque halls, in corner drug stores, and in rattling subway cars, they haven't stopped talking yet about Hal Greer's 'one-der' shot," commented a Boston writer. It "is the most talked about item here since Rudy Gernreich's topless swim suit." Bob Cousy, the ABC color commentator and Celtic legend, said emphatically that the shot had been good, but with all due respect to the great Cousy most Bostonians disagreed. And when Greer and his teammates took the floor a chorus of catcalls, insults, and brief opinions echoed from every section in the Garden.[26]

Greer played another fine game. So did Chamberlain. The other 76ers were awful. After two minutes the Celtics led 9–0, and they outscored the 76ers in each of the first three quarters. In the fourth quarter, after Russell drew his fifth foul and left the game, Philadelphia cut into Boston's lead. The final score was 114–108, but the game was never really close.[27]

Leading the series three games to two and still holding a home-court advantage, the Celtics should have felt confident. But Auerbach was concerned. His team's age was showing. Heinsohn reinjured his foot in Sunday's game, and Russell was exhausted physically and mentally from defending against Chamberlain. Auerbach told both players to skip practice, but the concession did nothing for Russell's sleeping problems. Always high-strung and temperamental, Russell fully accepted the team nature of basketball but knew that his role was essential to victory. The Celtics did not depend on one particular scorer. Sam Jones, Heinsohn, and Havlicek were all capable of scoring 30 or more points. But without Russell's rebounding and defense the Celtics would struggle. The thought caused the center to vomit before every game and created sleeping problems throughout the series. "For years I'd get 30 minutes or one hour's sleep a night during the playoffs—if that," Russell admitted. "I used to wear out a set of tires just driving up and down all night." But now he needed the rest and took sleeping pills. "I may be groggy the first hour after getting up but I can face jobs like Wilt."[28]

Winning was everything to Russell. Athletically, it was the way he measured himself. It was less important to Chamberlain. He was a Hercules, capable of heroic deeds. He scored 100 points in a single game and more than 70 four other times. He scored more than 50 points a daunting 118 times; in fact he averaged 50.4 for the 1961–62 season. He grabbed 55 rebounds in single game and twice averaged more than 27 for a season. By any simple tabulation of numbers he was the best who ever played the game, and that was pretty much how he judged himself. Winning was nice; he liked to win; but if his team lost, well, it had to be someone else's fault. How could any player who so consistently scored 30 or 40 points and hauled down 20 or 30 rebounds be even partially responsible for any loss? He was like the jazz virtuosos he loved so much, judging himself by his perfect riffs.

Russell's riffs were less noticeable. He had crafted his game to be part of an ensemble, and when performing alone he never appeared great. His moves with the ball were seldom either textbook efficient like Oscar Robertson's or classically graceful like Elgin Baylor's. Watching Russell maneuver for a shot was like seeing a flamingo take flight. The fascination was less in the effortless beauty than in the tortured process. But both somehow got the job done. But as part of a symphony that transformed defense into offense Russell was magnificent. Jumping fast, grabbing a defensive rebound high over the rim, and seemingly before he even touched the court firing a pass to an outlet man, Russell started countless fast breaks. From the time he touched the ball on one end of the court till it went through the basket on the other often took less than four seconds. It was so perfect and efficient a play that Russell could relax for a moment after his role was complete. There was simply no need to sprint to the other end.

If the Boston fast break was the pinnacle of Russell's athletic evolution, where was the base? Who could have predicted such an end for that gangly Oakland teenager who received only one college scholarship? He had what it took—height, strength, speed, jumping ability, and exquisite timing. But he willed greatness out of the accumulated slights, frustrations, hatreds, and desires of his past. Early in his sophomore season, he said, he made the decision. The University of San Francisco was playing Brigham Young University in Provo. On the first play of the game the smaller BYU center out-maneuvered him for a basket. "Why don't you try playing some defense?" a teammate carped. Russell burned inside. Then at halftime his coach criticized his play. "Right there at half time in Provo I decided that I was going to be a great basketball player," he later wrote. "Everything inside me poured itself into that decision; all the anger and wonder joined together with one purpose, and energy was coming out of my ears."[29]

In the next few years he became a student as well as a player of the game. He studied how players moved individually and how teams moved together. Most importantly for his game, he learned how "to predict where a pattern of action will lead, and then act to change that pattern to the advantage of his team." In the process he stole Chamberlain's future. It was Russell, not Chamberlain, who became the center of championship teams. USF won back-to-back NCAA titles during Russell's junior and senior years, amassing 55 straight victories during one stretch. In his thirteen years as a Celtic, Boston won eleven NBA championships.[30]

While he was winning championships, winning championships became an important part of who Bill Russell was. He cared about winning championships, not scoring 50 points or winning rebounding crowns. But by 1965 he sensed—his body told him—that he had only a few more years remaining as a world-class athlete. Yet he was not just an athlete who won championships. In the 1960s he became one of the most vocal athletes on the subject of civil rights. On the road, in NBA cities, and in Boston, he refused to accept second-class citizenship. Yet here, too, time was running short. Either white America was going to accept full integration, or not. Pondering the subject, he said to a reporter: "it becomes a question, you know, of will we go the way of the American Indian. What's better, to live as a subservient minority or 'die like a man'? To live or to die, that's what the signpost could read at the crossroads. Because two things could happen. You could have a race war, which we will undoubtedly lose. Or you could have a mass exodus."[31]

Winning—as a team and as a race. The stakes were always high, but no loftier than his expectations. Life on and off the court was a series of tests, and Russell did not have the psychological comfort of saying that if he lost he still had his lavender Bentley Continental convertible, baby. Game six in Philadelphia was another test. This one he failed. Chamberlain was magnificent. He led both teams in scoring, rebounding, and blocked shots. But the plays that were most uncharacteristic of the Chamberlain-Russell duel came in the last minute of the game. With Boston mounting a late rally and the score 107–104, Chamberlain tapped a jumped ball to Greer, who hit a 25-foot shot. Then at the other end of the court he blocked a Russell shot, tied up his rival, and won another tip. They were the plays, the crucial plays at the critical moments, that had defined Russell's career. Getting the job done when it just had to get done.[32]

The series seemed fated for this: one game in the champion's house. If the 76ers were to end the Celtics' stranglehold on the NBA, they had to do it in Boston Garden, in the seventh game, before an arena crammed with frenzied green-clad spectators. That is the way Hollywood would have scripted it. It had to be done in a game for the ages.

The day before the game Auerbach was pulling all the strings. How could his team win in Philadelphia, he asked reporters? The referees handcuffed his boys with fouls and allowed Jackson and Chamberlain to shove, bump, and goal-tend with impunity. And the Philly fans—forget about it. "Those people are something else. They've got a guy down there who sits near the bench and I'd pay 10 bucks to punch him in the mouth." Then in a closed meeting he told his team, "I just want to let you guys know something. No matter what happens, you're still all my boys." Knute Rockne could not have matched his performance.[33]

NBA games are rarely decided in the first quarter, especially seventh games. The Boston-Philadelphia contest on April 15, 1965, was no exception. Boston surged to an early lead. Nor are most NBA championship games decided in second and third quarters. Philadelphia charged back in the second period behind inspired shooting by substitute Dave Gambee, then Sam Jones and John Havlicek moved Boston into a comfortable 8-point lead at the end of the third period. But by then the dynamics of the game had changed. Tommy Heinsohn and Satch Sanders, the Celtics' top scoring and defensive cornermen, were in foul trouble, and 76er forward Chet Walker was playing his finest game of the series. In the last quarter, which saw occasionally ragged but always intense play, Philadelphia started to inch back.[34]

Late in the game Philadelphia's play turned from ragged to bad. For three minutes they failed to score and made several crucial turnovers that ended with Boston baskets. At 110–103 with just over a minute to play, the game threatened to end not with a bang but a whimper. All that remained was for Boston not to give a 76er a cheap 3-point play and to protect the ball. For a minute the game went as Boston planned. Wilt tipped in a ball, then made two free throws with thirty-six seconds remaining in the game. After Boston held the ball for twenty-four seconds, Chamberlain scored again, this time on an uncontested dunk. The score was 110–109. Boston's ball. Five seconds remained in the game. All the Celtics needed to do was inbound the ball and hold it for a few seconds.

Then, as happens in only great games, the action changed speeds. Everything slowed. Time became elastic and stretched like warm taffy, stretched like illustrations of the effect of Einstein's theory of relativity on space travel. Something so dramatic and so unexpected happened that it made spectators question their sight and knowledge of the game. And in the following decades the event would be so often discussed and so often replayed in super-slow motion that it is remembered as something that took place in a different time dimension. It was this fragment of the contest—a mere five-second snippet—that made what until that moment had been an ordinary game memorable.

As soon as Chamberlain scored, Russell took the ball. "I did not trust *any-one* else to throw that pass in but me because I always felt that I was the best passer," he explained years later. "It might not have been true. But I always felt that." The truth was that he was an outstanding passer, and his height allowed him to throw the ball over the head of most defenders. In this particular case, however, the defender, Chet Walker, surprised Russell. While

Russell stood three or four feet behind the baseline looking for an open man, Walker leaped out-of-bounds at him. Walker's unexpected jump, clearly an infraction, disrupted Russell's throw, and the ball brushed the guy wire, a long support wire attached to the lower balcony. By the rules, hitting the guy wire was no different from rifling the ball into the twentieth row. It was now Philadelphia's ball under their basket, and there were still five seconds in the game.[35]

Russell went wild, frantically arguing his case to the referee. Not realizing that Walker had crossed the baseline, Russell insisted that the Philadelphia player had touched the ball before it hit the guy wire. It had to be, just had to be, still Boston's ball. Russell raised his hands to the heavens, covered his face in anguish, dropped to his knees in supplication. He stopped short only of rending his garments. The cold Old Testament referee was unconvinced and unmoved. Philadelphia's ball.[36]

Dolph Schayes called time out, and the 76ers floated lightly and joyfully to their bench. One look at Schayes told Walker that the coach was lost. "It was obvious he didn't know what play to call. In desperation he just said, 'Get the ball to Wilt,'" which, given the fact that Chamberlain was the most prolific scorer in the game, was a fairly unimaginative call. But Wilt, who always wanted the ball, vetoed the call. He had missed thirteen out of nineteen free throws and dreaded going to the line with the game riding on the outcome. Schayes tried again, diagramming a more elaborate play that involved a pass to Walker, a backscreen, and another pass to Greer. "I don't think anyone thought the play would work; I certainly didn't," Walker later wrote. He decided that if he touched the ball, he was shooting. Period. "All the elements that players and fans spend their lives waiting and hoping for were right here. And I was ready."[37]

Gloom clouded the Boston huddle. Russell was still shaken. He implored his teammates. They had to do something. They had to redeem his mistake. For a player who had spent his career cleaning up teammates' mistakes, it was a more-than-reasonable request. He knew, positively knew, that the ball was going to Chamberlain. He glanced at Chamberlain as they lined up for the inbound pass: "From his eyes I knew it was going to be his play. I got ready to put my weight against his. For all the marbles. For all the money and the years, good and bad, the MVP trophies and the All Star Games and all the rest of it. For the whole career."[38]

As so often happens in sports, the final play was totally unpredictable. Chamberlain never touched the ball. Neither did Russell. Nor Walker. John Havlicek deflected the inbounds pass to Sam Jones, who then dribbled a few seconds and passed the ball back to Havlicek. As the game ended and Boston fans swarmed the court, Havlicek launched the ball toward the hoop. It was a shot not of a professional basketball player but of a small boy playing alone in his parents' driveway. It missed, but that didn't matter. What mattered was all said in announcer Johnny Most's famous gravel-voiced call: "Havlicek stole the ball! Havlicek stole the ball!"

The 1965 Boston-Philadelphia playoff series was the finest that Russell and Chamberlain ever played against each other. Chamberlain scored 30 or more points in all but one of the games, and he grabbed more than 30 rebounds in five of the games. Russell scored only about half as many points and totaled significantly fewer rebounds. But it was what happened at the 0:05 mark in the last game that said the most about their careers. Russell did not trust anyone else with the ball. And Chamberlain did not want it.

15

Beantown, 1986

Raymond Arsenault

Nineteen eighty-six was arguably the greatest year in the long history of Boston sports, with the Super Bowl and World Series victories of 2004 providing more triumph, perhaps, but less drama and meaning. In January the New England Patriots made it all the way to the Super Bowl by upsetting the New York Jets, the Oakland Raiders, and the Miami Dolphins in the American Football Conference (AFC) playoffs. In June the Boston Celtics defeated the Houston Rockets in the National Basketball Association (NBA) finals, garnering their fifth championship in eleven years. And in October the Boston Red Sox came within one pitch of winning the World Series. In a span of nine months, the city had very nearly accomplished the unprecedented feat of winning three of the four major professional sports championships. No city—not even New York, Boston's perennial nemesis and archrival—has ever won three major championships in a single year. But in 1986 Boston almost did it. The city *almost* become the city of champions. After decades of disappointment on the diamond and the gridiron, in a city where modern championship banners hung from the rafters of the Boston Garden but nowhere else, Boston's teams *almost* ran the table.

The upstart Patriots eventually lost to the mighty Chicago Bears by the lopsided score of 46–10, and the Red Sox, having last won the World Series in 1918, succumbed to the New York Mets in seven games. But as several local and regional boosters pointed out, finishing second at the highest level of competition was nothing to be ashamed of. Despite the Super Bowl and World Series losses, there was great cause for celebration, and even the most cynical observers—even the hated sports pundits of New York—were obliged to acknowledge that the land of the bean and the cod had nearly pulled off the unthinkable. Inscribed in the record books for all to see, Boston and New England's brush with greatness was indelible and undeniable. As Casey Stengel once advised, "you could look it up."[1]

Unfortunately for the region's long-suffering fans, the real world beyond the record books was less sanguine than the results printed in box scores and statistical abstracts. What you could not look up—at least not in the record books—was the psychological cost of rising but unmet expectations, the cruelty of deferred dreams and dashed hopes. In the hypercompetitive calculus of modern American sports, coming close does not count for much, and few cities know the truth of this maxim better than Boston. Despite protestations to the contrary, many of the city's most loyal sports fans suffer from a noticeable inferiority complex, especially when they are in the presence of New Yorkers. It is not that Boston teams haven't done well: the Celtics rival the New York Yankees as the most successful franchise in sports history, and three of Boston's four professional teams have winning records overall, with only the Patriots coming up short.[2] So why did so many New Englanders find it almost impossible to set aside their disappointment and savor the victories of 1986? Why did Boston's high-flying year devolve into a tailspin of collective depression and self-pity?

One suspects that the psychological trough of 1986 had a lot to do with outsized expectations born of historical circumstances. Long ago Boston, along with a handful of other cities, invested its heart and soul in the world of professional sports. Inextricably bound to municipal and regional identity, this investment has placed the city's teams in an unofficial "super league" that transcends the American League, National Football League, National Hockey League, and National Basketball Association. Whether they like it or not, all Boston teams must compete at the highest level, a requirement that means taking on the behemoths of New York, Philadelphia, Chicago, San Francisco, and Los Angeles. At any given time, in one sport or another, competition with other cities such as Baltimore, Cleveland, Pittsburgh, St. Louis, Atlanta, and Montreal may be more immediate and compelling. But in the long run keeping up with the nation's most prominent cities is paramount. In the superleague coming in second is not good enough. Here bragging rights are everything, and only national or world championships really matter. Each superleague city wields considerable economic clout and boasts world-class cultural and educational institutions, all of which are subject to formal and informal ranking. But no element of this ongoing competition is more intense than the annual struggles for professional sports championships. In the context of mass culture, athletic competition is frequently the index of choice, a marker of position more accessible than the relative rankings of MIT and Cal Tech or the dueling reputations of the Boston Symphony and the Los Angeles Philharmonic.

All the superleague cities feel the pressure of championship competition. But in Boston the need to win is exacerbated by the city's demographic shortcomings. Unlike its rivals (with the exception of San Francisco), Boston is no longer one of the nation's largest cities. With a population of less than 600,000 inside the city limits, it currently ranks twentieth among American cities, and even its sprawling metropolitan area of nearly six million inhabitants ranks seventh.[3] What Boston has to offer is not demographic mass but rather cultural and historical reach. Boston represents all of New England, a fact that makes it one of the nation's most expansive communities. As the only large city in the region, Boston is the de facto cultural and sports capital of six states, a status that no other American city can claim. Perhaps more to the point, these are not just any six states. Notwithstanding a measure of parochialism and state chauvinism, Boston presides over a distinctive regional culture rooted in a distant but resonant colonial past. In myth, if not always in socioeconomic reality, New England remains a land of village greens, white steeples, town meetings, and stone walls. Somehow its acute sense of history—its quaint but telling notion of particularistic origins and enthusiasms—has survived two centuries of multicultural migration and industrial intrusion, leaving today's citizens and fans with enough cohesion to inspire a passionate, even frenzied, attachment to the region's chosen heroes. Except for a few perverse, New York–tinged stretches along the Connecticut Turnpike, New England is Boston's faithful hinterland, where self-esteem and sometimes even sanity hinge on the fortunes and misfortunes of the Red Sox, Celtics, Bruins, and Patriots.[4]

The identification of city and region with these teams has produced moments of pure joy and exhilaration. But far too often the proverbial thrill of victory ultimately gave way to feelings of victimization, depression, and even martyrdom. For many disappointed fans, it is not just that for so many years their teams failed to win "the big one"; it is how they failed. In Boston, perhaps more than in any other city, a pattern of bad luck, poor judgment, and physical breakdown led to repeated catastrophes in clutch situations. Until 2004, Red Sox stalwarts often blamed the dark legacy of the 1919 Babe Ruth trade—the so-called Curse of the Bambino—but the problem extended well beyond the confines of Fenway Park.[5] The amazing history of the Celtics is, of course, the great exception to this sad tale. But in recent years the leprechauns of the parquet have fallen on hard times. Their last championship was in 1986, a year which deserves to be remembered for both triumph and tragedy, but which most Boston fans remember as the year that broke their hearts.[6] Why this is so can only be comprehended through a retelling of the saga, fumble by fumble, error by error, sob by sob. The devil, as we shall see, is in the details.

Patriotic Gore

The story begins on the gridiron. Established in 1959 as part of the new American Football League (AFL), the Boston Patriots franchise was a family enterprise run (some say overrun) by the Sullivan clan. Majority owner and team president Billy Sullivan, an enterprising Boston businessman, led the team through a difficult first decade, compiling an overall record of 65–80. After eleven years of playing its home games at a variety of sites, from Boston University to Fenway Park, the team finally moved into a permanent home, Schaefer Stadium in suburban Foxboro, in 1971, the year Sullivan changed the team's name to the New England Patriots. By then the team was part of the postmerger National Football League, but Sullivan's hard-luck franchise continued to languish, making the playoffs only twice during the 1970s. Although Sullivan lavished money and attention on the team, attracting considerable talent on both offense and defense, the Patriots earned a reputation as an overpaid, underachieving organization. In 1981 the team hit rock bottom with the worst record in the NFL, 2–14, but bounced back to make the playoffs in the strike-shortened year of 1982. Some critics attributed this momentary success to the shortness of a season that did not allow the Patriots an opportunity for a late-season collapse. But the always-optimistic Sullivan carried on, naming his son Patrick general manager in February 1983 and renaming Schaefer Stadium as Sullivan Stadium three months later. Despite this show of faith, the Sullivans soon found themselves in financial difficulty, largely because of an ill-fated investment in pop star Michael Jackson's world tour and licensing rights. By 1985 New England was one of only four NFL franchises losing money, and the Sullivans reluctantly put the team up for sale. With a dubious product and an asking price of $100 million, there was little initial interest in the Sullivans' declining empire. But many Patriot fans remained hopeful that a new era was now at least a possibility.[7]

Fans who longed for a change had grown accustomed to disappointment and distractions on and off the field. But the tumultuous 1984–85 season was a fiasco even by New England standards. Blessed with a talent-laden lineup that included rookie wide receiver Irving Fryar, the number-one pick in the 1984 NFL draft, the team started strong. However, the situation began to unravel in October, when Coach Ron Meyer summarily fired defensive coordinator Rod Rust following a 44–24 loss to the Miami Dolphins. The fact that Meyer fired Rust without consulting the Sullivans proved to be his undoing, and on October 25 Billy Sullivan fired Meyer and rehired Rust. The Patriots' record was 5–3 at the time, but the new coach, Raymond Berry, a heralded wide-receiver who had played for the Baltimore Colts in the 1950s and 1960s, took over a team in turmoil. Soft-spoken and methodical, Berry presented a sharp contrast to the hard-driving Meyer, and during his first month as coach the players responded favorably to his understated style of leadership. After winning three of four games in November, Berry's Patriots were in a strong position to make the playoffs. But, as had happened so many times in the past, the team folded in December, suffering three straight losses. Despite a winning record of 9–7, the Patriots failed to make the playoffs for the twenty-first time in their inglorious twenty-five-year history.[8]

During the spring and summer of 1985 Berry insisted that his talented team was poised to shed its reputation for lackluster underachievement.

But most of the preseason polls predicted that the team would once again finish in the middle of the pack, well behind the AFC East's expected powerhouses, the Miami Dolphins and the New York Jets. Even the Patriots' strongest supporters recognized that the team faced an uphill struggle to make the playoffs, a projection seemingly confirmed by an early-September trouncing by the Chicago Bears. After five weeks the team had compiled a record of two wins and three losses and appeared to be going nowhere.

To this point, starting quarterback Tony Eason had shown only flashes of the brilliance that had made him one of the top picks in the 1982 draft, and the team's other offensive stars, Irving Fryar and running back Craig James, had been less than stellar. Fans and sportswriters hoping for a turnaround looked to Eason's strong young arm for salvation, but during an October 13 game against the Buffalo Bills he suffered a disabling shoulder separation. His replacement, Steve Grogan, was an experienced ten-year veteran who had lost his starting job the previous fall after Eason had come off the bench to engineer a remarkable comeback victory over the Seattle Seahawks. This time it was Grogan's turn to save the day, and he did so in convincing fashion, rallying the team to a 14–3 victory. Over the next five weeks, as Eason's shoulder healed, Grogan led the Patriots to five more victories, playing the best football of his career. Once known for his running ability, Grogan was now playing on wobbly knees that had endured countless hits and four operations. But somehow he got the job done, standing immobile and "tall in the pocket," as one admiring sportswriter put it. One of only two NFL quarterbacks to call his own plays, Grogan made a habit of handing the ball off to Craig James, the Patriots' talented but previously underused running back. Throughout November, as the Grogan-James combination spearheaded the Patriots' offense, boos turned to cheers as more and more fans came to believe that the team's 8–3 record was no fluke.[9]

Cynics and hardcore realists countered that the Patriots' unexpected winning streak was too good to be true—a teaser that would only leave the fans frustrated and disillusioned when the inevitable late-season collapse ensued. Even if Grogan was playing like an All-Pro quarterback now, many insisted, his knees would never make it to the end of the season. Sadly for Grogan and his growing coterie of admirers, the prediction that his body could not hold up proved true. In late November, during the first quarter of a crucial game at the Meadowlands, the New York Jets' towering defensive end Ben Rudolph fell on Grogan's left knee, putting the veteran quarterback out of action for the remainder of the regular season. Eason, well rested and fully recovered from his shoulder separation, played well in relief, leading the team to 10 fourth-quarter points that forced a sudden-death overtime. Nevertheless, coupled with Grogan's injury, the Patriots' heartbreaking 16–13 loss in overtime seemed to signal the beginning of the end for a team that had been bucking the odds for most of the season. The Jets, not the Patriots, now seemed to be the AFC's Cinderella team, the only challenger with any chance of derailing the title-bound Dolphins. For the umpteenth time since the treacherous 1919 Babe Ruth trade, it appeared, a group of New York bullies was about to relegate a promising Boston club to the ranks of the also-rans. As *Sports Illustrated* columnist Paul Zimmerman reminded his readers, the Jets had their own tradition of late-season collapses. The Jets, he observed, were "a slumbering monster that frightened you with its personnel but stumbled over its own feet when things got serious. For years the fans have watched the Jets' dazzling cast of characters and asked: When? When will they get it together and stop messing up? When will the underachievers finally achieve something?" Such questions haunt all cities and regions from time to time, but New England football fans had good reason to claim a special connection with underachievement. Even the most optimistic among them knew the script and braced themselves for the worst.[10]

This time, however, the expected fall from grace did not happen. Over the next two weeks both Eason and James, protected by a rock-solid offensive line, played inspired and winning football, as did a rejuvenated defense led by cornerback Raymond Clayborn and the All-Pro blitzing linebacker Andre Tippett. None of the early-December victories was especially pretty or statistically impressive, but after the fourteenth week of the season the injury-plagued and unheralded Patriots found themselves in a three-way tie with the Dolphins and the Jets. With two games to go, the Patriots' record was 10–4, and for the first time in years New Englanders began to believe that their team might still be playing in January. Since one of the two games was in Miami, where the Patriots had lost eighteen straight, few observers held out much hope that the team from Foxboro would win the Eastern Division championship. But if the Patriots could manage to win one of the two remaining games, and if the Jets cooperated by losing at least once, the Patriots would be in the playoffs as a wild-card team.

As expected, the Patriots lost to the Dolphins, but not before Eason engineered two fourth-quarter touchdowns that tied the score at 27. Unable to overcome the Orange Bowl jinx, the Patriots gave up a last-minute field goal, although pushing the heavily favored Dolphins to the limit allowed Eason and his teammates to leave the field with the confidence that they could play with the NFL's best. This feeling carried over to the final game of the regular season; the Patriots defeated the Cincinnati Bengals, 34–23. With this victory and a Jets loss, the Patriots and the Jets ended the season with identical 11–5 records, both earning wild-card berths in the AFC playoffs.[11]

Making the 1985–86 playoffs was a major accomplishment and cause for considerable celebration all across New England. But in truth no one expected the euphoria to last for very long. To reach the Super Bowl, the Patriots would have to win three games against heavily favored opponents, all on the road. To be specific, if the match-ups proceeded according to plan, the Patriots would have to beat the Jets at the Meadowlands, the Raiders at the Los Angeles Coliseum, and the Dolphins at the Orange Bowl. No team had ever overcome such long odds, and the Patriots, led by an inexperienced and untested coach and two banged-up quarterbacks, seemed an unlikely choice to make a historic underdog run for the title. Patriots fans had better celebrate now, some commentators bluntly suggested, because there would not be much to cheer about once the playoffs actually began.

The mood in Boston was somewhat subdued during the week before the Jets game, at least in terms of media hype. Boston and other New England sportswriters touted the Patriots' strengths and lampooned the Jets' weaknesses. But, with few exceptions, they seemed wary of overselling the Patriots' chances. By contrast, the New York sports scene was abuzz with excitement and anticipation. For the first time in NFL history, two playoff games would be played in the same stadium on consecutive days: the Jets versus the Patriots on Saturday, followed by the Giants versus the defending champion San Francisco Forty-niners on Sunday. Since both the Jets and the Giants were favored, the New York faithful fully expected to have two teams safely into the second round by the close of the weekend. In a year when none of greater New York's other teams—the Yankees, the Knicks, the

Nets, the Rangers, and the Islanders—was expected to do much, football fever had gripped the city, and there was already talk of the Jets and the Giants squaring off in the Super Bowl. In Boston the New Yorkers' speculation made the thought of an upset even sweeter, but all but the most optimistic Patriot boosters were afraid to hope for too much. Spoiling the New Yorkers' party seemed almost too much to ask from a franchise that had won only one playoff game in its twenty-five years of existence.[12]

The only ones who seemed to think otherwise were the Patriots themselves, who played "a near-perfect game," according to an astonished Paul Zimmerman. Capitalizing on four turnovers, the Patriots won handily, 26–14. Executing Berry's conservative game plan with precision and poise, Eason completed twelve of sixteen passes, including one for a touchdown. But it was the team's "vicious defense" that had tongues wagging in the postgame commentary. Linebacker Andre Tippett and defensive end Garin Veris, in particular, delivered hit after hit, including one that put Jets quarterback Ken O'Brien out of the game with a slight concussion. Predictably, some members of the New York press (which was partially consoled by a 17–3 Giants victory on Sunday) heaped scorn upon the Jets, paying little attention to the Patriots' performance. But other observers, especially in New England, began to take the team from Foxboro more seriously. Perhaps the Patriots were for real, after all.[13]

The team had little time to savor its upset victory at the Meadowlands. The next stop was the Los Angeles Coliseum, where owner Al Davis's legendary Raiders were lying in wait. Once again the Patriots would be heavy underdogs, and this time they would have to play more than 3,000 miles from home. The winner of three Super Bowls (1977, 1981, and 1984) in the last eight years, the Raiders were the antithesis of the Patriots: a franchise that always managed to win the big games. Indeed, in the winter of 1985–86 the Raiders seemed poised for a fourth visit to the Super Bowl, having won the AFC Western Division title with a 12–4 record, which tied the Dolphins for the best record in the conference. With All-Pro veterans and future Hall of Famers at several positions, including running back Marcus Allen, the NFL rushing king with 1,759 yards, the Raiders figured to make short work of the Patriots. Only another near-perfect game by the visitors, it seemed, would prevent the Raiders from advancing to the next round.

For much of the game the Patriots were anything but perfect, trailing 17–

7 midway through the second quarter. But just when the Raiders seemed to be moving toward a rout, the Patriots fought their way back into the game with an extraordinary 80-yard touchdown drive keyed by four Craig James runs and a controversial offside penalty on Howie Long, the Raiders' All-Pro defensive end. After that the Raiders' defense reasserted itself, and there were no more Patriot drives. However, to the amazement and consternation of most of the crowd, a series of Raiders turnovers kept the game close. In the third quarter a field goal by Patriots kicker Tony Franklin tied the game at 20–20, and on the ensuing kickoff the Raiders' normally sure-handed returner Sam Seale fumbled the ball in the end zone, where Patriots safety Jim Bowman fell on it. Although there was still a full quarter to go, the Raiders' final three possessions came up empty, and the Patriots walked off the field with a stunning 27–20 upset. The final stat sheet—one of the strangest in NFL playoff history—showed that the Raiders' six turnovers almost equaled the number of passes (seven) completed by Eason, the winning quarterback, and that the losing Raiders outgained the Patriots on the ground and in the air. Indeed, this time it was the Patriots, not the Raiders, who lived up to Al Davis's famous maxim: "Just win, baby."

In the postgame wrap-ups, television and radio commentators strained to make sense of what they had just witnessed, including a bizarre scuffle between the Patriots' general manager Patrick Sullivan and two of the Raiders, Howie Long and Matt Millen. Following his critical third-quarter miscue, Long—who reportedly had made several disparaging comments about the Patriots before the game—was subjected to a steady barrage of taunts from the Patriots' bench, primarily from Sullivan. "Where are you, Howie? We're coming to get you," Sullivan screamed again and again. Later, as Long and the dejected Raiders walked off the field, Sullivan could not resist one last taunt, a foolhardy indulgence that earned him a black eye administered by Millen. Afterward a defiant Long insisted that the loud-mouthed Sullivan ought to consider himself lucky. "I'm not going to let a classless, silver-spooned, non-working s.o.b. like that tell me anything," Long told reporters; Sullivan "doesn't sign my checks. He's the jellyfish of Foxboro. Anytime he wants to lock it up in a closet and waive all legal rules, he can give me a call. I'm listed."[14]

Sullivan's bravado produced plenty of ink on the nation's sports pages. But the big story was the Patriots' improbable victory on the field. While the sports establishment was not quite ready to tout the Patriots as a team of destiny, the victories over the Jets and the Raiders set the stage for a dramatic confrontation in Miami. Despite nineteen consecutive losses at the Orange Bowl, the Patriots had given the Dolphins all they could handle back in December. Moreover, Raymond Berry's low-key style of coaching, which called for fewer practices than almost any other NFL team, brought the Patriots into the championship game with fresh legs and relatively few injuries. The team seemed to be peaking at just the right time and had already demonstrated that it was quirky enough to foil conventional wisdom. All of this made for interesting banter and speculation in the days leading up to the AFC Championship game on Sunday, January 12. But aside from a few true believers, no one actually expected the Patriots to win, especially after January 8, when Fryar was sidelined with a severed tendon in his right hand, an injury incurred during a knife-wielding domestic squabble. As the Raiders' veteran cornerback Lester Hayes pointed out even before Fryar's injury, the Dolphins had both Dan Marino, the best young quarterback in football, and "the greatest home-field advantage in the NFL." "I give the Patriots two chances," he declared. "Slim and none."

Such disdain undoubtedly steeled the Patriots' resolve to prove Hayes and the oddsmakers wrong. But a collective motivation fueled by underappreciation and lack of respect was only part of the story as the Patriots routed the Dolphins 31–14. By dominating the Dolphins from start to finish, the Patriots finally proved, to themselves and to many others, that they were also a very good football team. For the third week in a row, the defense forced turnover after turnover; this time the fumbles and interceptions converted into 24 points, more than enough to offset the team's conservative offense. Throwing only twelve passes but handling the ball off to James and others fifty-nine times, Eason once again defied the unwritten laws of offensive balance. With only 71 yards of passing, Eason lagged far behind Marino's 234. But as Eason and his teammates explained after the game, the only statistic that mattered was the final score. Against all odds, the Patriots were going to the Super Bowl for the first time.[15]

The NFC champions, the Chicago Bears, were also making their first Super Bowl appearance. But their road to the big game bore little resemblance to the steep uphill climb of the Patriots. Compiling a 15–1 record during the regular season, the Bears had run off twelve straight victories before losing to Miami in late November. Two of their victories, back-to-back shutouts of Dallas and Atlanta, yielded a combined score of 80–0, and the team's overall scoring differential of 456 to 198 was one of the most lopsided in NFL history. Overpowering on both offense and defense, the "Monsters of the Midway" invited comparison with the greatest teams of all time. Leading the offense were Jim McMahon, the NFC's second-ranked passer, and the incomparable Walter Payton, a future Hall of Famer whose career rushing total was approaching 15,000 yards in 1986. On defense there was an entire lineup of stars, including All-Pro linebackers Richard Dent and Mike Singletary, and a 325-pound rookie defensive end, William "The Refrigerator" Perry, who sometimes lined up as a running back when a goal-line plunge was needed. After scoring a touchdown against Green Bay during an early-season Monday-night football broadcast, Perry became a national celebrity, joining McMahon, professional football's best-known hipster, and Coach Mike Ditka as media darlings. Soon to be parodied on NBC's *Saturday Night Live* comedy show, the fearsome but sometimes lovable Ditka had helped lead the Bears as a player to the 1963 NFC championship, Chicago's first football championship since 1946. And most observers had every expectation that, with the help of defensive coordinator Buddy Ryan, he would do the same as coach, returning Chicago to the top of the football world. Indeed, whatever doubts anyone harbored about the greatness of Ditka's (and Ryan's) Bears all but disappeared after the team shut out both the New York Giants (21–0) and the Los Angeles Rams (24–0) on successive Sundays, something no NFL playoff contender had ever done before.[16]

On the eve of the Super Bowl, the mighty Bears were ten-and-a-half-point favorites over the Patriots, though many sports insiders suspected that, as with previous Super Bowl mismatches, the actual margin would exceed the point spread by several touchdowns. Among the sportswriters who descended upon the Superdome in New Orleans, the site of the game, the most common speculation was not who would win but rather whether the Bears could administer a third straight shutout. Such talk infuriated Ditka, who, like all experienced coaches, feared the debilitating effects of overconfidence and complacency. Yet not even he could hide the expectation of an easy victory. Having crushed the Patriots in their season opener, he and the Bears were supremely confident that they could do it again. The Patriots themselves knew that they were a much better team than the one that had been pushed all over Soldiers' Field in September. But they also knew that they would have to play the game of their lives to have any chance against one of the best teams of the modern era. In Boston and all across New England, the faithful prayed for a fourth week of miracles, hoping against hope that the unexpected weeks of glory had not been just a cruel setup for a season-ending massacre. The only other time the Patriots had played for a championship, in the pre–Super Bowl American Football League days of 1963, the team had been humiliated by the San Diego Chargers, 51–10. But surely the fates would not allow something like that to happen twice, not to a noble land that had given the world Jonathan Edwards, William Lloyd Garrison, Unitarianism, and all-you-can-eat clambakes.[17]

A second 41-point loss was clearly out of the question. But unfortunately for the Patriots and their fans, a mere 36-point loss was not. The game began well enough with a Walter Payton fumble that led to a 36-yard field goal and a 3–0 Patriots lead. After that, however, it was all Bears, as Ditka's monsters lived up to their reputation for ferocious efficiency on "both sides of the line of scrimmage." By halftime the score was 23–3, but the Bears' dominance was greater than even a three-touchdown lead would suggest. With thirteen first downs to the Patriots' one, and with 236 total yards to the Patriots' −19, the Bears went into the locker room with the greatest statistical differential in Super Bowl history. Though not given to emotional outbursts, Berry did his best during the halftime break to convince his shell-shocked players that the contest was not over. But the second half was nearly as bad as the first. On the Bears' first possession of the third quarter, McMahon lofted a 60-yard pass to speedster Willie Gault that set up a fourth unanswered touchdown, and three plays later cornerback Reggie Phillips intercepted a Grogan pass for a fifth, advancing the score to 37–3. Two plays later, Chicago linebacker Wilber Marshall recovered a New England fumble and ran it back to the Patriots' 31-yard line, setting up a short drive and a one-yard touchdown plunge by "The Refrigerator." Trailing 44–3, the Patriots opened the fourth quarter with its only touchdown drive of the day. But the only other scoring in the final quarter came when Henry Wachter, a seldom-used reserve tackle, sacked Grogan in the end zone for a safety. The final score was 46–10, the most resounding victory in Super Bowl history, easily eclipsing the Raiders' 38–9 thrashing of the Redskins two years earlier.

After the game the Patriots' only consolation was having foiled the Bears' bid for a third straight shutout. But that was cold comfort for players who had come to believe in themselves, who had fully expected to give the Bears a serious challenge. Mercifully, most of the postgame commentary focused on Chicago's greatness rather than on New England's ineptitude. Indeed, Paul Zimmerman of *Sports Illustrated* counseled his readers: "Don't laugh at the Patriots for their futility. You would have to laugh at too many other good teams, the Giants and Rams and Cowboys, who went down 44–0." Yet nothing could hide the fact the Patriots had embarrassed themselves on the world's grandest sports stage. Sitting dejectedly in the losing locker room, New England right guard Ron Wooten undoubtedly spoke for many of his teammates when he told reporters: "I'm not embarrassed, I'm humiliated." Even the compassionate Zimmerman could not resist pointing out the historic nature of the Patriots' defeat. "It will be many years before we see anything approaching the vision of hell inflicted on the poor New England Patriots in Super Bowl XX," predicted Zimmerman, adding: "The game wasn't exciting . . . It wasn't competitive . . . Don't feel cheated. Louis-Schmeling II wasn't very competitive either. Nor was the British cavalry charge at Balaklava, but Tennyson wrote a poem about it. This game transcended the ordinary standards we use in judging football. It was historic."[18]

Under normal circumstances, New Englanders relish their association with history. Plymouth Rock, Bunker Hill, Concord and Lexington, Carlton Fisk's home run—these are all part of the region's proud heritage and identity. Super Bowl XX, by contrast, was destined to go down as a best-forgotten catastrophe, a historic misstep in the tradition of the Salem witch trials and the Babe Ruth trade. Borrowing a page from Chicago's history, one journalist dubbed it "the St. Ditka's Day Massacre." The experience left the Patriots and their fans in various states of shock and depression, and New Englanders brave enough to read the sports section on the proverbial morning after were subjected to a litany of woe. But for many the worst was yet to come. On Monday afternoon, with the Patriots still in New Orleans, Coach Berry convened a team meeting to discuss something even more troubling than the poor performance in the Super Bowl. Since taking over as coach in October 1984, Berry had been quietly battling what he considered to be a serious drug problem among his players. Long known as a "straight arrow," he had been an uncompromising opponent of drug use since his close friend and Baltimore Colts teammate Big Daddy Lipscomb had died of a heroin overdose in 1963. During the spring and summer of 1985, Berry reportedly "made a point of visiting virtually every Patriot player to talk about the evils of drug use," and he was a firm advocate of mandatory random drug testing, a policy rejected by the NFL players' union as an unwarranted invasion of privacy. Under a collective-bargaining agreement signed in 1983, all players were given preseason drug tests, but during the season all tests had to be based on "reasonable cause," that is, a strong suspicion that a particular player was using illegal drugs.

Despite the implementation of the agreement, nearly everyone involved with the NFL realized that drug use remained a serious issue, and some, including Berry, were determined to find a better means of dealing with the situation. In the meeting in New Orleans, Berry urged his players, in effect, to defy the collective-bargaining agreement and adopt a mandatory drug-testing program. Before taking a vote, he informed the players that an investigative reporter armed with "names and facts" was ready to expose the team's drug problem. What he did not tell them was that he was one of the reporter's chief sources. When approached by *Boston Globe* sportswriter Ron Borges in early January, Berry had admitted that the rumors of widespread drug use were true. "There are at least five players we know who have a serious problem," he told Borges, "and five to seven more whom we suspect very strongly." Although Berry later denied it, according to Borges the coach also provided the names of several of the players in question, a clear violation of the NFL's privacy policy. In return for Berry's cooperation, Borges agreed to withhold the story until after the playoffs were over. But, as Berry told his players at the team meeting, now that the season was over nothing could prevent the story from appearing in print. Their only viable option, he insisted, was to mitigate some of the potential damage by endorsing mandatory testing, which they promptly did by an overwhelming vote.[19]

On Tuesday morning, less than twenty-four hours later, the *Globe* ran Borges's story, a straightforward account that described a general pattern of abuse without mentioning specific offenders. On Wednesday, however, a second, more sensational installment named names, identifying Fryar and five other Patriots as chronic drug users. As shock waves spread across the region, Patriots officials confirmed that all six, plus one additional player, had "admitted drug use and agreed to counseling sessions and regular urine tests." Only one of the seven, Raymond Clayborn, denied using drugs, but all felt betrayed by team officials, who had promised not to give their names to the press or the public. On Thursday a team doctor disclosed that none of the seven had tested positive since early January and that several had been "clean" since the beginning of the season. But no amount of clarification could stem the rising tide of scandal and recrimination that engulfed the team by the end of the week. Players pointed fingers at management, and management pointed back; Berry accused Borges of misrepresenting their agreement, and the reporter countered with evidence to the contrary. Billy Sullivan blamed the NFL players' association for failing to take the drug problem seriously, and Gene Upshaw, the head of the association, shot back: "I can't think of anything that the Sullivans haven't screwed up yet." Among the Patriots themselves the rumor that several players had acted as informants spread distrust throughout the ranks, damaging some relationships beyond repair. As even loyal fans withdrew in disgust, the Sullivans wisely canceled a scheduled parade honoring the team. While some observers tried to keep the situation in perspective, pointing out that the Patriots' drug problem was probably no worse than that of most other NFL teams, for many the feeling that New England had sustained a self-inflicted "black eye" was inescapable. "Everything we did for this organization this year is shot," lamented Fryar. "This is our one time to the Super Bowl, and now we're right back in the basement. We might never get out." At the time that he made this statement, Fryar probably believed that the situation couldn't get any worse. Yet three months later he found himself under investigation for gambling on NFL games, including the Super Bowl. After a vehement denial, he took and passed a polygraph test. But suspicions lingered. It was a dark and bloody time in Patriots land.[20]

Celtics Pride

In the days and weeks following the Super Bowl, New England sports fans searched for solace in the one place where they were likely to find it, the Boston Garden. Home to the Bruins and the Celtics, the Garden, for all its dinginess, was a magical place inhabited by the ghosts of past champions. Twenty championship banners—fifteen from the NBA and five from the NHL—hung from the rafters. Hockey fans with long memories were well aware that the Bruins had played in fifteen Stanley Cup finals, losing ten times—seven times to the Montreal Canadiens alone. But somehow this record of near-misses didn't threaten the team's longstanding mystique. The Bruins have always been the one Boston team that local fans seem to love no matter what, perhaps because they always seem to be in the hunt. Although the Bruins had last won the Cup in 1972, during Bobby Orr's heyday, the team had finished first or second in its division every year but one (1985) since 1969. Unfortunately, in 1986, a year in which Boston fans could have benefited from a bit of magic on the ice, the Bruins continued the slide begun the year before. On Super Bowl Sunday they were in third place in the Adams Division, only four points behind Montreal. But they would never get any closer to the division lead, finishing well back of the eventual winner, Quebec, and losing 0–3 to Montreal in the first round of the playoffs.[21]

Mercifully, the situation was altogether different on the hardwood. Led by perhaps the greatest front line in the history of the NBA, the 1985–86 Celtics were lighting up the Garden scoreboard night after night. Having lost to their archrivals, the Los Angeles Lakers, in the 1985 finals, the Celtics were on a mission to bring the title back to Boston, where it belonged. Eight times before 1985 the Celtics had faced the Lakers in the finals, and each time Boston had prevailed, four times in a decisive seventh game. The latest assertion of Celtics Pride had come in 1984, when the team had bounced back from a 2–1 deficit, defeating the Lakers in three of the last four games, including the clincher in Los Angeles. But since then the Lakers had seemed to gain the upper hand. Blessed with two of the game's greatest stars, Kareem Abdul-Jabbar and Earvin "Magic" Johnson, the Lakers entered the 1985–86 season with almost unlimited potential, and some observers even suggested that they might be the best team in NBA history.[22]

Such talk was anathema to Celtics fans, but when the Lakers came to the Boston Garden on January 22, 1986, for the first Celtics-Laker game of the season, their record was 32–7, better than the Celtics' 30–8. Since the Celtics had the home-court advantage, few observers were surprised when Boston came out on top, 110–95. But the Celtics win was more than a mere victory. It was the way the Celtics won that caught everyone's eye. Even with power forward Kevin McHale hobbling on a severely strained heel, the

Celtics dominated the Lakers in every phase of the game. Dennis Johnson, the team's gritty point guard, held Magic Johnson in check and led the scoring with 22 points; Larry Bird, the most widely acclaimed Celtic since Bill Russell, chipped in 21 points and twelve rebounds; and center Robert "The Chief" Parish added 16 points, along with eleven rebounds. But the unexpected star of the game was Bill Walton, the eccentric former UCLA and Portland Trailblazers great who had joined the team six months earlier as a backup center. As one reporter exclaimed, "in 16 marvelous minutes, the thirty-three-year-old redheaded Dead Head made his first contribution to Boston lore with 11 points, eight rebounds, seven blocked shots and at least three college-style fist-wavings." Normally it was the Lakers who benefited from a strong bench, but this time it was the Celtics who demonstrated that they were not only good but deep. Earlier in the season some critics had wondered out loud if an aging Walton playing on wobbly knees was a good investment for a team that already featured three starters—Johnson, Bird, and Parish—who either had passed or were pushing thirty. But Walton's Russell-like performance on January 22 laid such speculation to rest. He was now part of the Celtics Mystique, the magical, indefinable force that set the team apart from all others.[23]

Backed by fifteen championship banners and the looming presence of the legendary coach-turned-general-manager Arnold "Red" Auerbach, the Celtics Mystique was a matter of both style and substance, an attitude buttressed by years of triumph and tradition. There was nothing else like it in the annals of Boston sports; indeed, with the possible exceptions of the New York Yankees' dominance and the Montreal Canadiens' reign, there was nothing else like it in all of professional sports. As Lakers coach Pat Riley conceded after the January 22 loss, knowledge of the Celtics' glorious past "can immobilize and debilitate" an opponent, providing an advantage that few teams can counter. Although he believed that his Lakers had developed a powerful mystique of their own, he was clearly concerned that the rejuvenated Celtics appeared to be "much different than they were at the end of last season." "They took it to us," he admitted, "and then away from us— early."

This was only one game, and it was unlikely that Walton would be able to repeat his heroics on a regular basis. But Riley had good reason to be concerned. Not only were the Celtics playing well as a team, but Bird was back. In the 1985 finals Bird had been hampered by severe back spasms that limited his effectiveness and playing time. And some observers had even whispered that at twenty-eight he was prematurely over the hill. They were wrong. During an extraordinary run of games in mid and late January, he exhibited the same dazzling skills that had earned him Most Valuable Player trophies in 1984 and 1985. On Super Bowl Sunday, just hours before the Patriots took the field in New Orleans, Bird led the Celtics to a comeback win over the talented Philadelphia 76ers, 105–103. It was their twelfth victory in thirteen games, a stretch in which Bird averaged 26.2 points per game and shot 53 percent from the field. Many of his points came from towering three-pointers, but he also mixed it up under the boards at both ends of the court. Whatever the team needed—an unselfish assist, an offensive rebound, an opportune steal, a clutch free throw—Bird provided, erasing, as one veteran sportswriter insisted, "any doubt about who is the best player in the league."[24]

Bird's ability to do whatever it took to win was on full display at the 1986 NBA All-Star game in Dallas, both in the game itself and in the preliminary three-point shot competition, which he won handily. Having lost to the Western Conference All-Stars in 1985 for the first time in six years, Bird and the Eastern Conference All-Stars were determined to restore their dominance. Late in the fourth quarter the West was leading 126–121, but in the final four minutes Bird, McHale, and their Eastern teammates put on an offensive and defensive clinic, outscoring their taller and younger opponents 18–6. Although Detroit point guard Isiah Thomas led the East in scoring with 30 points, earning MVP honors, many observers credited Bird with setting "the tempo and style of the East's winning burst." The ultimate team player, Bird could turn the tide even on the rare nights when his shooting touch was off. Indeed, when surrounded by talented teammates, as he was in Dallas or on almost any night during the 1985–86 season, Bird was almost unbeatable.[25]

In the weeks following the All-Star game, the Celtics demonstrated just how good they were. With Bird playing some of the best basketball of his career, the team lost only four games in February and March. On April 1, with two weeks left in the regular season, the Celtics' record was 61–13, a full thirteen games ahead of the 76ers, who held second place in the Atlantic Division. Even the mighty Lakers had lost eighteen games, including a second loss to the Celtics in late February. By that time, sportswriters had begun to ratchet up the superlatives, comparing the 1985–86 Celtics with the greatest teams in NBA history, including the legendary Celtics of the 1960s, the 1970–71 Milwaukee Bucks, and the Julius Erving–led 1982–83 Philadelphia 76ers. With the playoffs yet to come, most appraisals remained tentative. But there was no such restraint when it came to Bird. When *Sports Illustrated* columnist Jack McCallum conducted an informal survey of NBA notables in late February, the verdict was unanimous: Bird was "the best player ever to play the game." "Before Bird I used to vacillate," Bob Cousy, the former Celtic great and current Boston broadcaster, told McCallum. "The question didn't seem relevant. But Bird came along with *all* the skills, *all* the things a basketball player has to do. I think he's the greatest." Cousy's longtime rival, Laker general manager Jerry West, was only slightly less effusive, describing Bird "as nearly perfect as you can get in almost every phase of basketball." Even John Wooden, the legendary UCLA coach known for his cautious judgment, placed Bird on a par with the best ever. "I've always considered Oscar Robertson to be the best player in the game," Wooden declared. "Now I'm not so sure Larry Bird isn't."

The case for Bird's supremacy rested, in part, on statistics, the extraordinary numbers that he put up night after night in every category, from points and rebounds to steals and assists. He was the complete player, a 6-foot 9-inch big man who always seemed to be in the right place at the right time, a bruising forward who could shoot and pass with the best guards in the league. But what really set Bird apart was his attitude toward the game, a combination of concentrated energy, determination, and raw spirit that was unique in the annals of professional basketball. As McCallum put it, "There has never been a basketball player quite like the Celtics' Larry Joe Bird, in whom talent and tenacity rage a daily wire-to-wire battle for supremacy." Fused with this tenacity was a force of character that made him a natural, almost unquestioned leader on the court. "It's his presence, the total way that he commands attention on the court that counts," Auerbach once insisted, and many other less partisan observers agreed. The sense of command also came from his almost-unparalleled knowledge of the game. From his boyhood in southern Indiana to his career as a Celtic, Bird applied every ounce of his intelligence and imagination to the art and science of team basketball, perfecting what one writer called "his natural bent for building plays and finding the open man." Despite his image as an unsophisticated country boy, "the hick from French Lick," as he sometimes called himself, was nobody's fool, on or off the court. In his early years in Boston, he sometimes seemed a bit overwhelmed by the media and the fast-paced tempo of metropolitan living. But the Larry Bird of 1986 was a poised and worldly twenty-nine-year-old, a man of substance with more than enough experience and mental acuity to handle just about anything that came his way.[26]

One telling sign of Bird's intelligence — and his character — was his steadfast refusal to accommodate the racial politics swirling around both the NBA and the city of Boston. From the moment he was drafted by the Celtics in 1978, some individuals, both inside and outside the media, tried to tout him as the "Great White Hope," as potentially the best white player in a black man's game. To some, Bird — the Indiana equivalent of a southern redneck — and Boston — an increasingly tense and racially divided city — were a perfect match. The logic of this connection would have been unclear to earlier generations, but in the early 1970s Boston's historic image as the breeding ground of abolitionists had been shaken by an ethnocentric and sometimes overtly racist campaign against court-ordered busing. Modern Boston, it seemed, harbored some of the same prejudices and phobias that had tormented the Deep South for centuries. Suddenly Bostonians, and by association New Englanders, were on the defensive when it came to matters of race and civil rights. Now, the fact that the Red Sox had been the last team in major-league baseball to desegregate was more than an embarrassing oversight; it was also quite possibly part of a regional pattern of racialist pathology. Defenders of the city's record could counter that the Celtics had been the first team in the NBA to recruit a black player, Chuck Cooper in 1950, and that Bill Russell, the NBA's first black star and first black coach, had been the key to the Celtics' "dynasty," the remarkable run of eleven championships in thirteen years (1957–1969). At a time when the NBA was still predominantly white, Russell, along with other black Celtics such as Sam Jones, K. C. Jones, and Tom "Satch" Sanders, attested to the wisdom of Celtics owner Walter Brown's color-blind philosophy. "I don't care if they're green, black, white, or yellow, so long as they can play," Brown told Auerbach, who took the words to heart.

By the time Bird joined the Celtics in 1979, the NBA was more than two-thirds black, and the dominance of black superstars was taken for granted. But not everyone was comfortable with this trend in racial demography. In some quarters there was heightened sensitivity to the racial makeup of individual teams and lineups, as some observers wondered out loud if white players were an endangered species. Predictably, a good part of this scrutiny focused on Boston and the league's most successful franchise, especially after the team's racial balance began to tip toward the white end of the scale in the early 1980s. In 1984–85 Boston was the only team in the league with three white stars: Bird, Kevin McHale, and Danny Ainge. And after Auerbach signed two more white players, Bill Walton and Jerry Sichting, during the 1985 off-season, the Celtics' twelve-man roster included eight whites. Although two of the team's stars, Dennis Johnson and Robert Parish, were black, the oddity of a 75 percent white team in a league that was 75 percent black did not go unnoticed. As the Celtics' acknowledged leader, Bird faced the special challenge of defusing this potentially divisive situation, which he did with grace and humor. "I never notice what colors there are on the floor or think very much about it," he confessed, adding, "The only difference between black players and white players is that they get their rebounds above the rim and we get ours below the net."[27]

Such statements helped to fend off the media, but when all else failed Bird and his teammates could point to Coach K. C. Jones. Once Russell's sidekick at the University of San Francisco, where they won two NCAA championships, Jones joined the Celtics in 1958 and went on to become the league's premier defensive guard. After retiring in 1967, he coached the San Diego Conquistadors of the American Basketball Association and later the Washington Bullets before returning to Boston in the early 1980s as an assistant to coach Bill Fitch. When Fitch was fired in the spring of 1983, Jones was elevated to head coach and promptly guided the Celtics to a 62–20 record and a fifteenth NBA championship. Known for his amiable, laid-back style, Jones was immensely popular in Boston, even after the disappointing loss to the Lakers in the 1985 finals. His calming presence complemented the sometimes ferocious enthusiasm of both players and fans, and his status as a black leader in a predominantly white town made an important statement about the potential for racial tolerance and amelioration. The Celtics were not "South Africa's team," as some sensationalist critics claimed; they were K. C.'s team, a comfortable blend of whites and blacks united in their determination to hang another championship flag from the rafters of the Garden. "If it weren't for Red Auerbach, I wouldn't be anything," Jones had told the crowd at a January 1985 dinner honoring his mentor's thirty-five years with the Celtics. But those who knew the Celtics coach well knew better. K. C. had always been a class act, and putting on a Celtics uniform had simply given him the opportunity to develop and display his talents in the best setting in professional basketball.[28]

That setting was never better than in the spring of 1986. At the close of the regular season, the Celtics' record was 67–15, a staggering .817 winning percentage, the second best in franchise history. Only the 1972–73 Celtics, with 68 wins and an .829 winning percentage, had fared better; and few doubted that the current team was at least as good as the spirited but undersized squad led by center Dave Cowens. As good as Cowens had been, neither his court presence nor his stats were in the same league with Bird's, and perhaps not even with McHale's. Bird ranked in the top ten in five categories, finishing first in free-throw percentage (.896), fourth in scoring (25.8 points per game), fourth in three-point field goal percentage (.423), seventh in rebounds (9.8 per game), and ninth in steals (2.02 per game). He also led all NBA forwards in assists. On any other team, McHale's 21.3 scoring average and .574 field goal percentage (fifth in the league) or Parish's 9.5 rebounds per game (ninth in the league) and .549 field goal percentage (tenth in the league) might have earned local MVP honors, but on Bird's Celtics the extraordinary was, paradoxically, almost routine. This team was special, and by the beginning of the playoffs many Boston fans fully expected their team to sweep the divisional and conference series leading up to the expected confrontation with the Lakers in the NBA finals. Amazingly, the Celtics almost matched these outrageous expectations, losing only one game of twelve in the successive series against the Chicago Bulls, the Atlanta Hawks, and the Milwaukee Bucks.[29]

In late May the Eastern Conference Champions were ready to take on the Lakers for the third straight year. But the rematch was foiled by a team of towering upstarts from Houston. Led by the "twin towers"—7-foot Hakeem "The Dream" Olajuwon and 7-foot 4-inch Ralph Sampson—and coached by the hard-driving ex-Celtic Bill Fitch, the Houston Rockets upset the Lakers in the Western Conference finals. With the Lakers' elimination, the Celtics' march to the championship became easier, though perhaps a bit less satisfying emotionally. The Rockets, as the vanquishing of the Lakers made clear, were a talented team not to be taken lightly. But in the end they were no match for Bird and the Celtics. Despite inspired play by Olajuwon, a twenty-three-year-old Nigerian who refused to be intimidated by the Celtics mystique, Boston won in six, losing two games on the road but otherwise dominating the series. Fittingly, Bird was magnificent throughout, achieving two triple-doubles (double figures in points, rebounds, and assists), including a dazzling 29 points, eleven rebounds, twelve assists, and three steals in the deciding game, which the Celtics won 114–97. Already honored with a third consecutive MVP award for his play during the regular season—a feat achieved by only two other players, Bill Russell and Wilt Chamberlain—Bird was the unanimous choice as series MVP. Even so, as Bird himself was quick to point out, the victory belonged to the entire team, a focused and cohesive group that had taken the concept of unselfish team play to a new level. Notwithstanding the ravages of age and a dearth of speed and leaping ability, the 1985–86 Celtics had set a standard of collective accomplishment that all basketball fans, regardless of affiliation, could appreciate and admire. "Hang another banner, sew a few more stitches of tradition into that big green quilt that drapes the NBA," Jack McCallum rhapsodized in late June. "And know that this Celtic team, which finished the season 49–1 at the Garden and 82–18 overall, can take its place along any that has gone before."[30]

McCallum's tribute to the Celtics captured the pride that many Boston fans felt in the immediate aftermath of the 1986 NBA Championship series. In the midst of the euphoria, the Celtics mystique seemed more secure than ever. Even though the advanced age of several key players was a cause for concern, there was a sense that the Celtics led a charmed existence and that somehow Red Auerbach would find a way to perpetuate the dynasty, as he done so many times in the past. Indeed, at the NBA draft in mid-June the team seemed to be well on the way to guaranteeing its future by drafting Len Bias, an enormously talented power forward from the University of Maryland. Almost everyone agreed that Bias would make a great team even better, and at a June 18 press conference in Boston team officials proudly introduced the newest Celtics hero. Well-spoken and clean-cut, Bias projected just the right image, a solid, dependable team player on and off the court. The prospect of his playing on the same team with Bird and McHale seemed almost too good to be true, which sadly it was. On the morning of June 20, after flying back to Baltimore to celebrate his good fortune with friends and family, Bias succumbed to a fatal overdose of cocaine. Both a promising career and the myth of Celtics invulnerability were shattered in one night. While it would take weeks for an investigation to uncover Bias's secret life of drug addiction, his death cast an immediate pall over what had been the most joyous of Celtics seasons. In 1986, it seemed, there was a surprise around every corner.[31]

BoSox Blues

For some New Englanders the Celtics' sixteenth championship—even with the accompanying tragedy of Bias's death—was enough to dull the pain inflicted by the Patriots earlier in the year. But for others true relief would require something more, something epochal, something triangular emblazoned with the words "World Series Champions." Having won the inaugural World Series in 1903 and four more in the next fifteen years, the team known variously as the Boston Americans, Somersets, Pilgrims, Puritans, and Red Sox was the most successful franchise in the major leagues before the 1920s. Unfortunately, in the seven decades since 1918 the team had not won a single championship. Near-misses in 1946, 1967, and 1975 sustained the hope that somehow, someday it might happen. And in 1977 and 1978 Boston fielded talented squads that gave the New York Yankees, the eventual American League and World Series champions, all they could handle. But during the early 1980s the Red Sox went into a downward spiral that did not bode well for the franchise's chances of winning or even playing in a World Series anytime soon. In 1983 the situation hit rock bottom when perennial all-star Carl Yastrzemski retired after twenty-three years; in Yaz's last season the Red Sox managed to win only 78 games, the first time since 1966 that the team finished with a losing record. The following year the Red Sox record improved to 86–76, but in 1985 it fell back to a disappointing 81–81 and a fifth-place finish in the American League's Eastern Division. In the winter of 1985–86, when *Street and Smith's Official Baseball Yearbook* picked the 1986 Red Sox to finish sixth in the division, just ahead of the last-place Milwaukee Brewers, few fans were inclined to dispute this dismal prediction. Since the 1986 season marked the team's seventy-fifth year in

Fenway Park, the odd-shaped green cathedral that had enchanted generations of baseball fans, there was some hope that the coming season would
be special, that somehow the anniversary would break the spell, initiating a
new and glorious chapter in the Red Sox saga. But most of the faithful were
realists who fully expected another long and lackluster season.[32]

In the early going such realism seemed justified. After a disappointing
spring in Florida, where the team went 13–15, the Sox blew two leads and
squandered twelve hits in an opening-day loss in Detroit. By the end of the
first week the team was 3–4 and already three games behind the division-
leading Yankees. Most disturbingly, in the home opener on April 14, the
Kansas City Royals spoiled the "Fenway Birthday Bash" with a six-run rally
in the eighth inning, driving pitcher Dennis "Oil Can" Boyd from the
mound and dispelling any expectation of a charmed anniversary year, at
least for the moment. It was early, but the pattern that Boston fans had seen
so many times before—the classic Red Sox syndrome of strong hitting undercut by weak pitching—seemed to be set. Then something strange happened. The pitching got better, much better, and the team began to win. By
May 1, after winning eight of twelve, the Sox were 11–8 and in second place
behind the Yankees. Strong pitching by Boyd, a fifteen-game winner in
1985 and the acknowledged ace of the staff, was part of the story. But the big
news was the emerging stardom of Roger Clemens, a promising but injury-
plagued twenty-three-year-old righthander in his third major-league season.
In his first two years Clemens had pitched well, winning sixteen of twenty-
five decisions, but off-season shoulder surgery in the fall of 1985 made his
status a question mark—until Tuesday, April 29, 1986. On that day Clemens
amazed the baseball world with one of the greatest pitching performances
in major-league history. Striking out twenty Seattle Mariners in nine innings, he shattered the record of nineteen strikeouts held jointly by Steve
Carlton, Nolan Ryan, and Tom Seaver. In one stretch he struck out eight
batters in a row, tying the American League record, and during the final
five innings his fastball averaged an amazing 97 miles per hour.

Known as "The Rocket" since his college days at the University of Texas,
Clemens propelled the Red Sox to the top of the nation's sports pages, at
least for a day. But could his strong right arm also propel a hard-luck franchise to the top of the standings? At the beginning of May few observers
were ready to entertain this possibility. It would take several more weeks of

winning to do that. By the end of May—one of the greatest months in Red Sox history—everything looked different. After winning 20 of their last 27 games, Boston was 31–15 and led the second-place Yankees by two games. Only the "amazing" Mets, at 31–11, had a better record. And even a casual look at team statistics—the Red Sox led the American League in both batting average (.275) and pitching (3.32 ERA)—indicated that something extraordinary was happening in Boston. Already leading the league with a .385 average, Red Sox third baseman Wade Boggs, the defending American League batting champion, went five for five on May 31, raising his average to a Ted Williams–like .402. But the most shocking numbers were coming from the pitching mound, where Clemens was 8–0 with a 2.69 ERA. Along with Boyd and lefthander Bruce Hurst (2.95 ERA), Clemens gave the team one of the strongest starting rotations in baseball, and the relief staff, led by Joe Sambito and Calvin Schiraldi, Clemens's former teammate at the University of Texas, seemed to be up to the challenge whenever the starters faltered.[33]

As impressive as all of this was, many skeptics refused to believe that the Clemens-led Red Sox were for real. In late May, for example, Bob Haskell, a sportswriter for the *Bangor Daily News*, promised to strip down to his underwear and eat a chicken dinner on the lawn in front of his office if the Red Sox were still in contention by Flag Day, June 14. Provoked by Haskell's lack of faith, the novelist Stephen King, a Maine resident and devoted Red Sox fan, promised that he would do the same if the team was *not* in contention on that day. King won the bet, and in early July he gleefully looked on as Haskell, clad only in Army-issue longjohns, ate a plate of chicken, if not crow. Undaunted, the Bangor sportswriter quipped that he still believed "that the New York Yankees are going to win," a not-altogether-foolish notion given the long history of "El Foldos," the traditional late-season fold that broke the hearts of Red Sox fans year after year. This year it would be different, starry-eyed optimists insisted. But even they had learned to maintain a vigilant watch for signs of impending collapse. In June the attention of New Englanders had been diverted by both the Celtics' triumph and the death of Len Bias. But as the mid-July All-Star break approached, the spotlight returned to Fenway.

Amazingly, with the season nearly half over, there were no signs of collapse. On July 1 Boston was 48–25, seven and a half games ahead of the second-place Yankees, who had lost a team-record ten in a row at Yankee Stadium before edging the Tigers 3–2 on June 30. Boggs was still leading the league in hitting, and Clemens was still undefeated at 14–0, one win away from tying the American League record of 15–0 shared by Johnny Allen (1937) and Dave McNally (1969). In contrast to previous seasons, the pitching staff was holding up well, but just to make sure that the team had what it needed during the second half of the season general manager Lou Gorman acquired Tom Seaver from the White Sox on June 29. In the twilight of his career, the former Met great had been struggling in Chicago, but with 306 wins, a no-hitter, and three Cy Young Awards to his credit he had the experience and poise to help anchor a young pitching staff, or so Gorman hoped. In his first start, on July 1, Seaver pitched well, and the Sox defeated the Blue Jays to extend the team's winning streak to six. On the following day Clemens gave up only three hits in seven and a third innings, but the Blue Jays won the game 4–2, ending his remarkable run of victories.[34]

Clemens was human after all, though not as obviously as his talented but high-strung teammate Dennis Boyd. Known as "Oil Can" since his boyhood in Meridian, Mississippi, Boyd became a fan favorite after joining the Sox as a rookie in 1983. Like other black athletes before him, he had some difficulty adjusting to life in Boston, especially in the realm of personal finances. But for the most part he was able to keep his money problems private and his emotions in check until midway through the 1986 season. In 1985 Boyd had been disappointed when manager Sparky Anderson had failed to put him on the American League All-Star team. But with an 11–6 record in early July, he had every reason to believe that things would be different in 1986. With a $25,000 All-Star selection bonus hanging in the balance—a financial boost that he sorely needed—Boyd reported to Fenway Park on selection day, July 10, fully expecting to be named an All-Star.

However, after finishing his afternoon workout, he learned that manager Dick Howser had left him off the squad. Enraged, Boyd tore off his uniform and screamed obscenities at everyone from Red Sox manager John McNamara to his close friend and fellow pitcher Al Nipper, whom he called a "redneck." Storming out of the clubhouse, he jumped into his car and raced home to his condominium in Chelsea. An hour and a half later he returned to Fenway to apologize, but security guards refused to allow him to enter the clubhouse. The next day, when he failed to report for practice, the team issued a three-day suspension. After apologizing to McNamara and his teammates, he was reinstated on July 15, the day of the All-Star game (in which Clemens was the winning pitcher and MVP). But the following morning he was suspended again after team officials learned that he had scuffled with the police the night before. Stopped by two Chelsea detectives who searched his clothes and car for drugs, Boyd allegedly became abusive and violent, striking one of the detectives. Though no drugs were discovered, Boyd now faced assault-and-battery and disorderly-conduct charges. During the next week he underwent a series of psychological and pharmacological tests at a Worcester hospital, and after he regained his composure the team doctor gave him clearance to play on July 24.

After a few days of rehabilitation in Pawtucket, Boyd returned to the mound on August 5. But by that time the Red Sox were in a steep decline, having gone 3–10 on a recent road trip. Panicky fans had high hopes that the distraction was over and that Oil Can could reverse the team's declining fortunes, but Boyd's return was spoiled by, of all things, a two-run homer by White Sox catcher Carlton Fisk, the hero of the fabled sixth game in the 1975 World Series. The Red Sox had lost Fisk to the White Sox in 1981, and now he had come back to haunt his old team. Chicago won the game 3–1, and suddenly the Red Sox were only two and a half games ahead of the surging Baltimore Orioles. The Sox were still in first place, Boggs was still leading the league in hitting, and Clemens was 17–4, but many fans began to brace themselves for the inevitable collapse. As a front-page story in the *Boston Globe* put it, "a fatalistic gloom hangs over Boston."[35]

Fortunately, over the next three weeks the Orioles faded, and the Sox won more than they lost. On September 1, with one month of the regular season to go, Boston was 76–54, three and a half games ahead of its latest challenger, Toronto. Unlike the Mets, who had opened up a whopping 19-game lead over the second-place Philadelphia Phillies in the National League East, the Red Sox could hardly relax. But as Labor Day approached there was a growing sense that Oil Can, Clemens, Boggs, and company might be the long-awaited team of destiny after all. With a good balance of strong pitching and hitting, as well as a congenial mix of veterans and up-and-coming stars, the 1986 squad seemed less vulnerable and more poised than the ill-fated teams of the past. In March the team had acquired veteran slugger Don Baylor from the Yankees, and in June Seaver had come over from the White Sox, adding two respected leaders to a roster that already included fourteen-year veteran Dwight Evans, twelve-year veteran Jim Rice, and thirty-six-year-old first baseman Bill Buckner, a former National League batting champion. On the more youthful side, the team made a late-season trade in mid-August, acquiring shortstop Spike Owen, who had played with Clemens at the University of Texas, and outfielder Dave "Hendu" Henderson from the Seattle Mariners. Armed with good players and even better nicknames, the Red Sox entered the home stretch with a realistic chance of winning the division for the first time in eleven years.[36]

In Boston, September is often the cruelest month, the time when the Red Sox find yet another way to dash the hopes of their long-suffering fans. But in September 1986 there was no cruelty and no loss of hope, at least not at Fenway. As pennant fever gripped the city of Boston and much of New England, the Sox went on a torrid streak, winning eleven games in a row. In nine of the eleven victories, the Sox came from behind to win, convincing even the toughest of Beantown cynics that something strange was going on in their city. On September 28 Oil Can clinched the division championship with an eight-hit, complete-game victory against the Blue Jays, and Boston fans poured into the streets to celebrate. "They can't call us the Boston Stranglers anymore," quipped the Can. The team was still a pennant away from the World Series and would have to beat the Western Division champion California Angels to have a chance of actually ending Boston's sixty-eight years of frustration. But with the home field advantage, with the best pitcher in baseball in Clemens, who ended the year with a Cy Young and MVP award–winning 24–4 record, and with a three-time batting champion in Boggs, the Red Sox seemed well positioned to take the American League pennant. By the time the series against the Angels opened at Fenway on Tuesday, October 7, the oddsmakers had established the Red Sox as the clear favorite.[37]

With a well-rested Clemens on the mound, Boston expected to have little trouble in the opener. But to the shock and dismay of the home crowd, Clemens was outpitched by Mike Witt, who allowed only five hits in an 8–1 Angels rout. In the second game the Sox evened the series with a 9–2 win, but disaster struck again on Friday night in Anaheim when Boyd gave up two home runs in the eighth inning of what had been a 1–1 pitchers' duel. The Angels went on to win 5–3. On Saturday Clemens pitched for the second time in five days and was cruising along with a 3–0 shutout until the Angels tied the score with three runs in the bottom of the ninth. Two innings later Angel infielder Bobby Grich drove in the winning run with a clutch single, giving the Angels a commanding 3–1 lead in the series. Suddenly it appeared that, like so many other Red Sox contenders, this team didn't have what it took. With the fifth game in Anaheim and with Witt back on the mound, the chances of even making it back to Fenway for a sixth game looked slim. After eight innings the Angels were ahead 5–2, thanks in part to a Grich home run that ricocheted off Henderson's glove. By this time many Boston fans had turned away from their television screens in disgust, but amazingly the Sox scored four runs in the top of the ninth, the final run coming on a two-out, two-strike, two-run homer by Henderson. The Angels came back to tie the score with a run in the bottom of the ninth, forcing the Sox to win the game in the eleventh with a Henderson sacrifice fly.

Still needing two more victories to win the series, the unlikely hero Henderson and his teammates returned to Boston for the sixth game. But the fact that no team had ever come back from a 3–1 deficit in the seventeen years since the annual American League Championship series had been established did not make for an especially happy homecoming. The Sox might lose in six, or they might lose in seven. But few fans held out much hope for a miracle comeback. It all seemed too cruel, coming so close without getting a chance to go to the big show. Some fans, of course, took Henderson's heroics as a sure sign that nothing could stop their team, and for a time it appeared that they might be right. In the sixth game the Sox won handily 10–4, and in the seventh and deciding game Clemens scattered six hits, and Jim Rice hit a three-run homer in a delirious 8–1 victory. Against all odds, the Sox were going to the World Series.[38]

Their opponents were the New York Mets, a powerful team that had started the year with a 13–3 streak and had never looked back. Led by their ace righthander Dwight "Doc" Gooden, the Mets finished the regular season with a staggering 108 wins, tying the 1975 Cincinnati Reds—the most recent team to beat the Sox in the World Series—for the third most wins in National League history. Despite Boston's remarkable comeback against the Angels, the Mets held the home-field advantage and were favored to win the Series. By this time, fans who had followed the crazy ups and downs of the Angels–Red Sox series had come to expect the unexpected. But no one was fully prepared for the surprises in the first two games at Shea Stadium. In the opener, Boston's Bruce Hurst outdueled New York's Ron Darling 1–0, with the only run coming on a walk, a wild pitch, and an error by the Mets' normally sure-handed second baseman Tim Tuefel. In the second game there were more surprises as "the dream matchup" between Clemens and Gooden fizzled. Neither ace made it through the fifth inning, and the Sox pounded out eighteen hits to win 9–3.

The Mets' home-field edge was now gone, and all the Sox had to do was win two of the next three games at Fenway to take the Series. The Mets won game three behind the strong pitching of ex–Red Sox lefthander Bobby Ojeda, the first southpaw to beat the Sox in a Series game at Fenway since 1918. And the visitors went on to win game four, thanks to two towering home runs by catcher Gary Carter. This made winning game five a must for the Red Sox, who did not want go back to New York a game down. To avoid this fate, they would have to beat Gooden for the second time in five days. And with Hurst turning in another sterling performance, that is exactly what they did, chasing Gooden to the showers in the fifth inning and going on to win 4–2.[39]

The Red Sox victory in game five set the stage for one of the most dramatic confrontations in World Series history. The mighty Mets were back at Shea, where they had been almost unbeatable during the regular season. But to stay alive they would have to beat Clemens and Boston's growing sense that the elusive title, as Dwight Evans put it, was "at hand." Baseball fans of all persuasions anticipated a classic struggle for survival, full of grit and emotion, and they were not disappointed. Boston scored first with single runs in the first and second, but the Mets came back to tie the score with two runs in the fifth, erasing four innings of no-hit pitching by Clemens. In the seventh the Sox went ahead briefly 3–2, but after Clemens retired the Mets in the bottom of the inning a blister on his throwing hand forced McNamara to bring in reliever Calvin Schiraldi. In the eighth, Schiraldi yielded the tying run, and after a scoreless ninth the two teams took their quest for glory into extra innings.

In the top of the tenth, a leadoff home run by Henderson and a run-scor-

ing single by second baseman Marty Barrett put the Sox ahead 5–3, bringing the team of destiny within three outs of a world championship. In the
bottom of the tenth, Schiraldi retired the first two hitters, leaving Gary
Carter, who had gone hitless in his last seven trips to the plate, as the last
obstacle between the Red Sox and the sweetest victory since 1918. When
Carter singled, there was some cause for concern but no panic. And even
when Kevin Mitchell and Ray Knight followed with two more singles, the
title was still well within Boston's grasp. As the hearts and minds of Boston
fans raced with anxiety, McNamara strode to the mound and replaced
Schiraldi with veteran reliever Bob Stanley. One more out, McNamara told
Stanley; that's all we need. Despite the screaming crowd at Shea, "The
Steamer" quickly got a two-two count on the Mets' last hope, the fleet-
footed outfielder Mookie Wilson. After Wilson fouled off several pitches,
Boston fans everywhere were on their feet anticipating a season-ending
strikeout. And then it happened: Stanley's seventh pitch, a tailing inside
fastball, whizzed by catcher Rich Gedman's outstretched glove, hit the turf
with a thud, and rolled all the way to the backstop. As Gedman scrambled
to retrieve the ball, Mitchell trotted in with the tying run. Though never an
overpowering pitcher, Stanley was known for his good control and had
walked only one batter in six innings of relief in the first five Series games.
So no one really expected him to throw a wild pitch to Wilson—no one,
that is, but the closest students of Red Sox history, those who had incorporated a sense of dread into their very being.

Stanley's wild pitch was a jolting reminder of past disappointments,
enough to take one's breath away or to tie a stomach into knots. But what
happened next was a near-death experience. With Ray Knight now on third
representing the go-ahead run, Wilson fouled off a 3–2 pitch before hitting
a ground ball to the right side of the infield. It was, as tortured Red Sox fans
later insisted, a routine ground ball headed straight for first baseman Bill
Buckner. A thirty-six-year-old veteran, Buckner had fielded hundreds of
balls just like it during his long career in the major leagues. But on this
day the ball slid under his glove and through his legs into right field. As
Buckner and his teammates looked on in horror, Knight danced home with
the winning run. Game six was over, and miraculously the Mets were still
alive. The Red Sox had been one pitch away from the title that had eluded
them for so many years, but now they would have to come back to Shea one

more time and win game seven. Somehow they would have to find a way to forget about what had just happened and regroup. Many interested observers—in Boston, New York, and elsewhere—were convinced that the momentum had now shifted toward the Mets, but when a heavy rainstorm postponed the final game, giving the Red Sox an extra twenty-four hours to regain their composure, some speculated that 1986 might still be Boston's year.[40]

On the day of reckoning, Sunday, October 27, the dream was tattered but intact, at least for the first five and a half innings. In the second inning, back-to-back home runs by Evans and Gedman gave the Red Sox a 3–0 lead; but in the bottom of the sixth Bruce Hurst, who was trying to win his third game in nine days, tired and gave up three runs. A surprise starter, Hurst had got the nod over Boyd, who pleaded with McNamara that he was ready to go after six days' rest. Many fans would later question McNamara's decision to start Hurst, just as they would question the decision to leave a gimpy-legged Buckner out on the field in the tenth inning of the sixth game. But the real crisis came in the seventh, when the Mets scored three runs off Schiraldi, making the score 6–3. In the top of the eighth Evans' two-run homer brought the Sox within one run, but in the bottom of the inning the Mets countered with two runs of their own. When the Sox went down in order in the ninth, the numbers 8–5 on the Shea scoreboard told the tale, or at least part of it.

Once again the Red Sox had lost the Series, but for many faithful Boston fans what mattered most was how their team had lost. The Buckner error, in particular, was almost too much to bear. As Peter Gammons later wrote, "When the ball went through Bill Buckner's legs, 41 years of Red Sox baseball flashed in front of my eyes. In that one moment Johnny Pesky held the ball, Joe McCarthy lifted Ellis Kinder in Yankee Stadium, and . . . Bucky (Bleeping) Dent hit the home run." Even today, with the Curse broken, every Red Sox fan over the age of thirty can recall exactly where he or she was when the ball and the title slipped away through Buckner's legs. It is a moment frozen in time, like a political assassination or a death in the family. As a catastrophe "it's somewhere between the death of my father and the death of my mother," one fan confessed a few hours after the Buckner miscue. As another put it in a 1991 interview, "I still follow them, and I still go to games, but because of Game Six in '86, a part of me has been killed."[41]

Such melodrama may seem a bit forced, but in Boston professional sports is serious business worthy of historical memory and literary exposition. Charles Dickens was born a century too early to see the Green Monster at Fenway, to climb to the top of the Garden, or to visit Sullivan Stadium in Foxboro. But every seasoned Boston fan knows that the English wordsmith got it right. Anyone who experienced the highs and lows of 1986 cannot help hearing the ring of truth in the opening line of A Tale of Two Cities. "It was the best of times, it was the worst of times," Dickens wrote, coining what would become a cliché. In the Boston of Bird, Buckner, and Billy Sullivan, it was, paradoxically, both the best and the worst of times, though in the post-Dickensian world of professional sports the saga often appeared to be a tale of only one city. Over the years Boston fans have cheered and cried and even mourned together. Yet through it all they have endured, proving that individual hearts can be broken again and again without destroying the collective spirit of placebound culture. Life in the superleague is tough, but there is always next year, even in Beantown.[42]

C O D A

It started as soon as the game ended, shortly after midnight on October 17, 2003. Only seconds after New York Yankee pinch-hitter Aaron Boone Conaned the eleventh-inning home run that defeated the Boston Red Sox in the seventh game of the American League Championship series, the talk commenced. Talk of the star-crossed franchise. Talk of the most famous curse in sports history. All ending with a cry to the heavens: "When will it end! When will it end!"

The day after the day after, *Boston Globe* writer Bob Ryan still hurt. Every member of the Red Sox Nation realized, as the game slipped away, that what lay ahead was something much worse than a forty-eight-hour flu. No pills and no shots (save the obvious ones) would dull the pain or speed the recovery. Even the Yankees' loss to the Florida Marlins did not provide much solace. And the traditional "Wait till next year" rang hollow. It was, after all, well into October, and winter was close at hand, a winter, contrary to Harvard's finest poet, that would not keep us warm.

Loving something as vague and fickle as a team is inevitably a frustrating and agonizing pastime. It is also rewarding and exhilarating. Pretty much the same as life. Considering the range of emotions that come into play and the wild mood swings, it is a wonder that some ancient Greek did not invent baseball as a better form of drama. Its demands and promises are so great that it keeps us coming back year after year, hoping for some sort of grand spiritual fulfillment.

The fulfillment arrived in 2004. It began with the Patriots' victory in the Super Bowl, and continued in waves of emotions. There were the troughs of the Alex Rodriquez trade fiasco, the first half of the Red Sox season, and the first three American League Championship games against the Yankees. But then there were the heights—the second half of the season, the virtually unbelievable comeback against the Yankees, and the World Series sweep of the St. Louis Cardinals. It all ended with a sharply hit ball to closing pitcher Keith Foulke. Foulke fielded the ball cleanly, then proceeded to walk the ball over to first with the solemnity of a father escorting his daughter down the aisle. Stopping after a few steps, he carefully removed the ball from his glove and delicately tossed it underhanded to first baseman Doug Mientkiewicz. It looked like two boys using a Fabrege egg in an egg-tossing contest. Mientkiewicz, his foot on first base, received the priceless gift. And then it was all over. The inning was over. The game was over. The Series was over. The curse was over. Joy washed over the players and Red Sox Nation like grace.

After the game, a locker room reporter asked pitcher Tim Wakefield, "What does 1918 mean now?" Without a moment of hesitation or thought, Wakefield answered, "Nothing." And perhaps far too much talk and ink have been wasted on speculating about the curse. What member of the Red Sox Nation would trade something as fleeting as a World Series championship for the years that Ted or Yaz or Pedro played in Fenway? Or, for that matter, how many championships is Fenway itself worth? The oldest major-league ballpark in the nation, a reminder of a time when teams played baseball in parks and fields and not stadiums, Fenway is an artifact of another time. Someday it will die, or be reborn with luxury boxes for corporate guests. It will be a far sadder day than October 17, 2003. Because then there will not be a next year.

More than a century of Boston sports has led to one undeniable conclusion: in celebrating the athletes and places we ultimately are celebrating Boston itself—its physical presence, its emotional bonds, its history. Just as the course of the Marathon snakes through a patch of the American past, so Boston sports have formed a chain connecting one generation to the next. The chain has its separate links. A curse here, a dynasty there. Class arrogance and racism linked to ethnic and racial pride and an odd sort of democratic openness. Some bad, some good, some great. All memorable. Something for all seasons.

NOTES

1. All Gods Dead

1. *Boston Herald and Journal*, September 3, May 15, July 1, and July 13, 1918; *Boston Globe*, May 18, June 6, June 12, and July 9, 1918; *Boston Record*, June 9, 1918; *Sporting News*, May 23, July 18, and October 24, 1918; F. C. Lane, "The Clean Up Hitters," *Baseball*, August 1918; R. W. Hoefer, "Unwritten Letters," *Baseball*, September 1918.

2. *Boston Herald and Journal*, September 3, 1918; *Boston Post*, September 6 and 10, 1918; *Boston Evening Transcript*, September 10, 1918; *Boston Globe*, September 3, 10, and 12, 1918; *Sporting News*, September 12, 1918.

3. *Boston Post, Boston Globe, Boston Herald and Journal*, and *Boston American*, September 12, 1918; F. C. Lane, "The Hero of the Series," *Baseball*, November 1918; Max Flack, "The Muff That Lost the Series," ibid.

4. *Boston Herald and Journal, Sporting News*, and *Boston Globe*, September 12, 1918. On the 1918 season and World Series, see Allan Wood, *1918: Babe Ruth and the World Champion Boston Red Sox* (San Jose, Calif.: Writers Club Press, 2000); and Glenn Stout and Richard A. Johnson, *Red Sox Century: One Hundred Years of Red Sox Baseball* (Boston: Houghton Mifflin, 2000), 123–134. For primary-source accounts, see Ty Waterman and Mel Springer, *The Year the Red Sox Won the Series: A Chronicle of the 1918 Championship Season* (Boston: Northeastern University Press, 1999).

5. *Boston Herald and Journal*, September 6, 1918; *Boston Globe*, September 12, 1918.

6. *Boston Evening Transcript* and *Boston Post*, September 11, 1918; *Boston Herald and Journal*, September 13 and 15, 1918; *Boston Globe*, September 12, 1918; W. A. Phelon, "How the World's Championship Was Lost and Won," *Baseball*, November 1918; Charles Hollocher, "Behind the Scenes," ibid.; *Sporting News*, November 19, 1918.

7. *Boston Herald and Journal* and *Boston Globe*, September 12, 1918; Wood, *1918*, 338–339.

8. *Boston Herald and Journal*, September 13, 1918.

9. John Keegan, *The First World War* (New York: Vintage, 2000), 309–414.

10. David M. Kennedy, *Over Here: The First World War and American Society* (New York: Oxford University Press, 1980), 1–167.

11. Harold Seymour, *Baseball: The Golden Age* (New York: Oxford University Press, 1971), 244–254; *Boston Post*, July 20, 1918; *Boston Globe*, July 21, 1918; "Letters from Major Leaguers in the Service," *Baseball*, July 1918; F. C. Lane, "A Rising Menace to the National Game," ibid., August 1918; idem, "Baseball's Future," ibid., September 1918; *Sporting News*, July 11, July 25, August 8, August 22, and August 29, 1918.

12. *Boston Globe*, September 6, 9, and 10, 1918; *Boston Evening Transcript*, September 9, 1918.

13. Thomas O'Connor, *Bibles, Brahmins, and Bosses: A Short History of Boston*, 3d ed. (Boston: Trustees of the Boston Public Library, 1991), 187–188; *Boston Evening Transcript*, September 3, September 7, September 12, and October 19, 1918; *Boston Post*, September 1, 8, and 13, 1918.

14. Jeremy Brecher, *Strike!* rev. ed. (Boston: South End Press, 1997), 102–104; *Boston Evening Transcript*, September 4 and 5, 1918.

15. *Boston Herald and Journal*, September 9 and 11, 1918; *Boston Globe*, September 11 and 13, 1918; *Sporting News*, September 19, 1918.

16. Wood, *1918*, 317–326; *Boston Evening Transcript*, September 11, 1918.

17. *Boston Evening Transcript*, September 10, 1918; *Boston Herald and Journal*, September 11, 1918; *Boston Globe*, September 10 and 11, 1918; Waterman and Springer, *The Year the Red Sox Won the Series*, 250.

18. On flu in Boston, see Alfred W. Crosby, *America's Forgotten Pandemic: The Influenza of 1918* (New York: Cambridge University Press, 1989), 5–40; Pete Davies, *The Devil's Flu: The World's Deadliest Influenza Epidemic and the Scientific Hunt for the Virus That Caused It* (New York: Ovid Books, 2000), 41–62; Gina Kolata, *Flu: The Story of the Great Influenza Pandemic of 1918 and the Search for the Virus That Caused It* (New York: Farrar, Straus and Giroux, 1999), 12–18.

19. *Boston Evening Transcript*, September 14–21, September 24–27, October 1–4, October 7–10, and October 15, 1918.

20. Davies, *The Devil's Flu*, 60; Crosby, *America's Forgotten Pandemic*, 48; Kolata, *Flu*, 55–58; *Boston Evening Transcript*, October 14, 1918.

21. *Boston Post*, November 1, 1918; F. C. Lane, "The Fire Brand of the American League," *Baseball*, March 1919; Stout and Johnson, *Red Sox Century*, 116–120; Wood, *1918*, 4–17.

22. Stout and Johnson, *Red Sox Century*, 134; *Boston Herald and Journal*, September 12 and 14, 1918; *Boston Globe*, September 1, 12, and 13, 1918; *Boston Post*, September 11, September 15, September 16, September 21, September 23, September 27, and October 2, 1918; F. C. Lane, "Baseball's Future," *Baseball*, September 1918; Wood, *1918*, 344.

23. *Boston Post*, October 5, 1918; *Sporting News*, November 14, 1918; Waterman and Springer, *The Year the Red Sox Won the Series*, 273.

24. Frederick E. Parmly, "Baseball Will Win the War," *Baseball*, December 1918; Charles W. Murphy, "Baseball as a National Tonic," ibid., January 1919; Robin Baily, "Making Things Pleasant for Our Soldiers and Sailors," ibid., November 1918; Charles W. Murphy, "Why I Believe Baseball Should Continue during the War," ibid.; W. A. Phelon, "Shall Baseball Cease?" ibid., December 1918; Leslie Mann, "What the Soldiers Think of Major League Baseball," ibid.; W. A. Phelon, "Big League Players in Army and Navy," ibid., January 1919; *Sporting News*, October 10, 1918, November 7, 1918, March 13, 1919; *Boston Evening Transcript*, September 30, 1918; *Boston Post*, October 13 and November 11, 1918.

25. *Boston Evening Transcript*, November 11 and 12, 1918; *Boston Globe*, November 11 and 12, 1918.

26. *Boston Post*, October 28, November 19, November 25, November 26, and December 3, 1918; *Boston Evening Transcript*, November 25, 1918; *Boston Globe*, November 27, 1918; *Sporting News*, December 5 and 12, 1918.

27. *Boston Post*, December 5 and 12–14, 1918; *Boston Globe*, December 13 and 17, 1918; *Boston Evening Transcript*, December 13, 1918.

28. *Boston Post*, December 14, 1918; *Boston Globe*, December 19, 1918, December 23, 1918, January 10, 1919, January 15, 1919, January 19, 1919; *Boston Evening Transcript*, December 19, 1918, January 17, 1919; *Sporting News*, December 26, 1918, January 2, 1919.

29. *Boston Globe*, January 21, February 22, February 26, March 13, and March 19, 1919; *Sporting News*, February 20 and March 13, 1919.

30. On Ruth in Boston, see Kerry Keene, Raymond Sinibaldi, and David Hickey, *The Babe in Red Stockings: An In-Depth Chronicle of Babe Ruth with the Boston Red Sox, 1914–1919* (Champaign, Ill.: Sagamore, 1997); Robert W. Creamer,

Babe: The Legend Comes to Life (New York: Fireside Books, 1974), 84–213; Marshall Smelser, *The Life That Ruth Built: A Biography* (Lincoln: University of Nebraska Press, 1975), 68–122.

31. *Boston Post*, January 26, 1919; *Sporting News*, January 30, 1919; *Boston Herald*, February 4–25, 1919.

32. *Boston Globe*, January 22, January 28, February 10, February 18, February 20, February 22, February 26, March 6, and March 15, 1919; *Boston Herald*, February 13, February 15, March 5–9, March 11–13, March 15, and March 21, 1919; *Boston Post*, January 19, January 22, January 25, February 19, February 27, and March 2, 1919; *Sporting News*, January 30 and March 6, 1919.

33. *Boston Post*, March 16, 1919; *Boston Herald*, March 17–22, 1919; *Boston Evening Transcript*, March 16 and 22, 1919; *Boston Globe*, March 18–21, 1919.

34. *Boston Evening Transcript*, January 20, February 4, February 6, February 11, February 18, April 7, April 14–18, and April 21, 1919; Brecher, *Strike!* 114–116.

35. *Boston Evening Transcript*, April 10 and 15, 1919.

36. Jack Tager, *Boston Riots: Three Centuries of Social Violence* (Boston: Northeastern University Press, 2001), 144–146; *Boston Evening Transcript*, March 26, 1919; *Boston Herald*, February 18, 1919.

37. *Boston Evening Transcript*, February 24, 1919; *Boston Globe*, February 25, 1919; Thomas J. Knock, *To End All Wars: Woodrow Wilson and the Quest for a New World Order* (New York: Oxford University Press, 1992), 230–231.

38. Knock, *To End All Wars*, 231–270; Eliot Asinof, *1919: America's Loss of Innocence* (New York: Donald I. Fine, 1990), 17–125.

39. *Boston Globe*, March 24, March 25, and April 1–5, 1919; *Boston Herald*, March 22–25 and 30, 1919; *Boston Post*, April 5, 1919.

40. *Boston Post*, April 15–19, 1919; *Boston Globe*, April 22–24, 1919; Creamer, *Babe*, 189–191; *Sporting News*, April 3, April 10, April 17, and May 1, 1919.

41. *Boston Evening Transcript*, April 25, 1919.

42. *Boston Globe*, May 1 and 2, 1919; Tager, *Boston Riots*, 152–153.

43. *Boston Evening Transcript*, March 27 and April 30, 1919; *Boston Globe*, May 2, 1919. On baseball and American culture, see Gunther Barth, *City People: The Rise of Modern City Culture in Nineteenth-Century America* (New York: Oxford University Press, 1980), 148–191; Steven A. Riess, *City Games: The Evolution of American Urban Society and the Rise of Sports* (Urbana: University of Illinois Press, 1989), 61–68, 219–222; idem, *Touching Base: Professional Baseball and American Culture in the Progressive Era*, rev. ed. (Urbana: University of Illinois Press, 1999), 3–9, 19–30; G. Edward White, *Creating the National Pastime: Baseball Transforms Itself, 1903–1953* (Princeton: Princeton University Press, 1996), 3–83.

44. *Boston Globe*, May 1, 1919; *Boston Evening Transcript*, May 1, 1919; Babe Ruth as

told to Bob Considine, *The Babe Ruth Story* (New York: E. P. Dutton, 1949), 74–77; Smelser, *The Life That Ruth Built*, 95–96; Creamer, *Babe*, 192–195.

45. *Boston Post*, May 5, 1919; *Boston Globe*, May 15, 20, and 28, 1919; *Boston Herald*, May 4, 22, and 23, 1919; *Boston Evening Transcript*, June 5, 1919; *Sporting News*, May 8, May 22, May 29, and June 5, 1919.

46. *Boston Post*, May 21 and 22, 1919; *Boston Globe*, May 21, June 9, June 12, June 21, June 24, 1919; *Boston Herald*, June 18, 25, and 26, 1919; *Sporting News*, June 19, 1919.

47. *Sporting News*, May 22 and 29, 1919; *Boston Globe*, June 24 and 26, 1919; *Boston Herald*, June 26, 1919; Keene, Sinibaldi, and Hickey, *The Babe in Red Stockings*, 241.

48. *Evening Transcript*, July 15, 1919; *Sporting News*, July 10 and 31, 1919; Creamer, *Babe*, 196–200.

49. *Boston Herald*, July 31, 1919; *Boston Globe*, August 12, September 5, and September 18, 1919; *Boston Post*, August 15, 1919; *Sporting News*, August 7, August 14, and September 25, 1919.

50. *Boston Globe*, July 3, 18, and 19, 1919; *Boston Evening Transcript*, July 24, 1919.

51. *Boston Evening Transcript*, July 1 and 22, 1919; *Boston Herald*, June 25, July 1, July 6, July 13, July 19, July 22, July 25, August 15, August 18, August 24, and August 25, 1919; *Boston Globe*, July 22, July 25, August 25, August 26, and September 1, 1919; *Boston Post*, August 15 and September 9, 1919.

52. *Sporting News*, September 1, 1919; *Boston Herald*, July 19, July 20, July 25, July 26, August 6, and August 23, 1919; *Boston Globe*, July 10, July 26, July 30, August 21, and August 22, 1919; Smelser, *The House That Ruth Built*, 114.

53. Kal Wagenheim, *Babe Ruth: His Life and Legend* (New York: Praeger, 1974), 47; *Boston Herald*, July 6 and August 3, 1919; *Boston Globe*, July 14, 1919; *Boston Evening Transcript*, July 31, 1919.

54. Leverett T. Smith, *The American Dream and the National Game* (Bowling Green, Ohio: Bowling Green Popular Press, 1975), 110–120; Lary May, *Screening Out the Past: The Birth of Mass Culture and the Motion Picture Industry* (New York: Oxford University Press, 1980), 96–146.

55. Morris Cohen, "Baseball," *The Dial*, July 1919.

56. *Boston Evening Transcript*, July 17, July 20, August 9, September 2, and September 4, 1919; *Boston Globe*, July 18, 1919.

57. Brecher, *Strike!* 104–139; Kennedy, *Over Here*, 231–295; *Boston Evening Transcript*, June 26, 1919.

58. Asinof, *1919*, 225–290; *Boston Evening Transcript*, July 1, 1919; *Boston Globe*, July 8, 1919.

59. Tager, *Boston Riots*, 153–158; Jack Beatty, *The Rascal King: The Life and Times of James Michael Curley, 1874–1958* (Reading, Mass.: Addison-Wesley, 1992), 149–

211; James J. Connolly, *The Triumph of Ethnic Progressivism: Urban Political Culture in Boston, 1900–1925* (Cambridge, Mass.: Harvard University Press, 1998), 1–160; Doris Kearns Goodwin, *The Fitzgeralds and the Kennedys: An American Saga* (New York: Simon and Schuster, 1987), 110–129, 190–197; Thomas H. O'Connor, *The Boston Irish: A Political History* (Boston: Northeastern University Press, 1995), 95–208.

60. Francis Russell, *A City in Terror: The Boston Police Strike* (New York: Viking, 1975), 24–121; William Allen White, *A Puritan in Babylon: The Story of Calvin Coolidge* (1938; reprint, Gloucester, Mass.: Peter Smith, 1973), 151–153.

61. Russell, *A City in Terror*, 131–139; *Boston Globe*, September 10, 1919; *Boston Evening Transcript*, September 10, 1919.

62. *The Boston Police Strike: Two Reports* (New York: Arno Press and the New York Times, 1971); Russell, *A City in Terror*, 139–167; *Boston Globe*, September 11 and 12, 1919; *Boston Evening Transcript*, September 10–12, 1919.

63. *Boston Evening Transcript*, September 13–16, 1919; "No Bolshevism for Boston," *The Outlook*, September 24, 1919, 124–125; Robert Sobel, *Coolidge: An American Enigma* (Washington, D.C.: Regnery, 1998), 133–148.

64. *Boston Evening Transcript*, September 8, 1919; *Boston Herald*, September 9, 1919; *Boston Globe*, September 11, 1919; *Sporting News*, September 18, 1919.

65. *Boston Globe*, September 2, 1919; *Boston Herald*, September 2, 1919; *Sporting News*, September 11, 1919.

66. *Boston Post*, September 3 and 6, 1919; *Boston Globe*, September 4–8, 1919; *Boston Herald*, September 4–8, 1919.

67. *Boston Globe*, September 9, 1919; *Boston Herald*, September 10 and 11, 1919; Keene, Sinibaldi, and Hickey, *The Babe in Red Stockings*, 257; *Boston Post*, September 9, 1919.

68. Russell, *A City in Terror*, 168; *Boston Globe*, September 16–18, 1919.

69. *Boston Evening Transcript*, September 19, 1919; *Boston Globe*, September 20, September 21, and October 6, 1919; *Boston Herald*, September 21, 1919; *Sporting News*, October 2, 1919.

70. *Boston Herald*, September 21, 1919; *Sporting News*, October 2, 1919; *Boston Globe*, September 21 and 22, 1919.

71. *Boston Globe*, September 24 and 25, 1919; *Boston Herald*, September 25 and 28, 1919; *Sporting News*, October 2, 1919.

72. *Boston Herald*, September 29, 1919.

73. "Runs Scored By 'Babe' Ruth," *Literary Digest*, February 14, 1920; "The Greatest Sluggers of the Past Ten Years," *Baseball*, April 1920; Keene, Sinibaldi, and Hickey, *The Babe in Red Stockings*, 260–261; *Sporting News*, October 2, 1919; *Boston Globe*, December 23 and 27, 1919.

74. White, *Creating the National Pastime*, 117–118; "Why Freak Deliveries Must Go," *Baseball*, August 1919; *Sporting News*, November 6, 1919; *Boston Herald*, September 10, 1919.

75. *Boston Globe*, September 18, December 11, and December 21, 1919; *Sporting News*, November 18, 1919; Creamer, *Babe*, 200.

76. Keene, Sinibaldi, and Hickey, *The Babe in Red Stockings*, 258; Eliot Asinof, *Eight Men Out: The Black Sox and the 1919 World Series* (New York: Henry Holt, 1987).

77. Warren I. Susman, *Culture as History: The Transformation of American Society in the Twentieth Century* (New York: Pantheon, 1984), 122–149; Lynn Dumenil, *The Modern Temper: American Culture and Society in the 1920s* (New York: Hill and Wang, 1995), 56–97; Ann Douglas, *Terrible Honesty: Mongrel Manhattan in the 1920s* (New York: Farrar, Straus and Giroux, 1995), 3–107.

78. Smelser, *The Life That Ruth Built*, 126; *Boston Herald*, October 25 and 28, 1919; *Sporting News*, October 30, November 20, and November 27, 1919.

79. *Boston Globe*, October 23, October 25, October 30, and November 4, 1919; *Boston Post*, December 31, 1919; *Sporting News*, November 13, 1919.

80. *Boston Globe*, December 16 and 30, 1919; *Boston Post*, December 21, 1919; *Sporting News*, December 25, 1919, January 1, 1920, January 8, 1920.

81. Asinof, *1919*, 114–125, 204–223; *Boston Evening Transcript*, January 3, 1920; *Boston Herald*, July 6, 1920.

82. *Boston Globe*, *Boston Post*, and *Boston Herald*, January 6, 1919; Keene, Sinibaldi, and Hickey, *The Babe in Red Stockings*, 265–286.

83. *Boston Globe*, *Boston Post*, and *Boston Herald*, January 6–8, 1919. See also *Baseball*, April 1920.

84. *Boston Globe*, January 6, 1919; *Boston Post*, January 7 and 9, 1919; *Boston Herald*, January 6–8, 1919.

85. F. Scott Fitzgerald, *This Side of Paradise* (1920; reprint, New York: Scribner, 1998), 260.

86. Paul J. Zingg, *Harry Hooper: An American Baseball Life* (Urbana: University of Illinois Press, 1993), 190–191; Dan Shaughnessy, *The Curse of the Bambino* (New York: Dutton, 1990); Peter Golenbock, *Fenway: An Unexpurgated History of the Boston Red Sox* (New York: G. P. Putnam's Sons, 1992), 64.

2. The Boston Red Sox, 1901–1946

There is a huge literature on the Boston Red Sox, not surprisingly in a city with a tradition of good writing. Among the more readable overviews are John Boswell and David Fisher, *Fenway Park: Legendary Home of the Boston Red Sox* (Boston: Little, Brown, 1992); Peter Golenbeck, *Fenway: An Unexpurgated History of the Boston Red Sox* (New York: G. P. Putnam's Sons, 1992); Donald Honig, *The Boston Red Sox: An Illustrated History* (New York: Prentice-Hall, 1990); Fred Lieb, *The Boston Red Sox* (New York: G. P. Putnam's Sons, 1947); Dan Shaughnessy, *The Curse of the Bambino* (New York: Penguin, 1991); Dan Shaughnessy and Stan Grossfeld, *Fenway: A Biography in Words and Pictures* (Boston: Houghton Mifflin, 1999); Glenn Stout and Richard A. Johnson, *Red Sox Century: One Hundred Years of Red Sox Baseball* (Boston: Houghton Mifflin, 2000); and Stout, ed., *Impossible Dreams: A Red Sox Collection* (Boston: Houghton Mifflin, 2003). Charles H. Trout, *Boston, the Great Depression, and the New Deal* (New York: Oxford University Press, 1977), is excellent on the city in the age of Roosevelt. Edward Linn, *The Great Rivalry: The Yankees and the Red Sox, 1901–1990* (New York: Ticknor and Fields, 1991); David Halberstam, *The Teammates: A Portrait of a Friendship* (New York: Hyperion, 2003); and Ty Waterman and Mel Springer, *The Year the Red Sox Won the Series: A Chronicle of the 1918 Championship Season* (Boston: Northeastern University Press, 1999), do justice to those subjects.

Biographers sometimes do more than justice to their heroes, but there are good accounts of individual players in W. Harrison Daniel, *Jimmie Foxx: Baseball Hall of Famer, 1907–1967* (Jefferson, N.C.: McFarland, 1966); Jim Kaplan, *Lefty Grove: American Original* (Cleveland: Society for American Baseball Research, 2000); Edward Linn, *Hitter: The Life and Turmoils of Ted Williams* (New York: Harcourt Brace, 1993); and Bill Werber and C. Paul Rogers III, *Memories of a Ballplayer: Bill Werber and Baseball in the 1930s* (Cleveland: Society for American Baseball Research, 2001). Nicholas Dawidoff's *The Catcher Was a Spy: The Mysterious Life of Moe Berg* (New York: Pantheon, 1994) is so engaging that it can be enjoyed even by people who do not follow baseball, though I cannot imagine why they would want to deny themselves that pleasure.

By far the best source for historical articles, such as Bill Nowlin's on "The Frostbite League," is *Diehard,* a publication on the Red Sox available by subscription. Broun's droll recollection, "Carver to Speaker to Broun," was anthologized in Heywood Hale Broun, ed., *Collected Edition of Heywood Broun* (New York: Harcourt, Brace, 1941). John Updike, who has written about Ted Williams more than once, reveals his admiration for this athlete with a "dangerous rage to excel" in "The Batter Who Mattered," *New York Times Magazine,* December 29, 2002. John Demos's beguiling essay, "A Fan's Homage to Fenway (Or Why We Love It When They Always Break Our Hearts)" appeared in William E. Leuchtenberg, ed., *American Places: Encounters with History* (New York: Oxford University Press, 2000).

3. Ted Williams

I am grateful to Aaron Sachs for suggestions about this essay and, most especially, to Jeremiah Quinlan for his quite invaluable work as my research assistant.

1. Bryce E. Nelson, personal communication.
2. Details can be found in any of several first-rate biographies. See, for example, Ed Linn, *Hitter: The Life and Turmoils of Ted Williams* (New York: Harcourt Brace, 1993); and Michael Seidel, *Ted Williams: A Baseball Life* (Chicago: Contemporary Books, 1991). See also Ted Williams with John Underwood, *My Turn at Bat: The Story of My Life* (New York: Simon and Schuster, 1988).
3. Slightly different versions of this comment appear in virtually everything written by or about Ted Williams. See, for example, his own *My Turn at Bat*, 7.
4. See Robert W. Creamer, *Baseball and Other Matters in 1941* (Lincoln: University of Nebraska Press, 1991).
5. Ibid., chap. 36. For the quotation, see 269. For a day-by-day record of Ted Williams's 1941 season, see Linn, *Hitter*, 382–387.
6. Linn, *Hitter*, 223–225.
7. See Seidel, *Ted Williams*, 153.
8. These pivotal moments are described in detail in Linn, *Hitter*; and Seidel, *Ted Williams*.
9. John Updike, "Hub Fans Bid Kid Adieu," *New Yorker*, October 22, 1960, 111–131.
10. Most of these statistics are taken from Linn, *Hitter*, 422–423.
11. Williams, *My Turn at Bat*, 16.
12. Quoted in Linn, *Hitter*, 65.
13. On this point see ibid., 189–190.
14. Quoted in ibid., 82.
15. He spoke of his childhood struggles only with reluctance—and with obvious sorrow. Perhaps his fullest comment is found in Williams, *My Turn at Bat*, 28–33, where the word "embarrassment" appears again and again.
16. See ibid., 33.
17. The complete list is in Linn, *Hitter*, 401–404.
18. Quoted in *Sports Illustrated*, July 1, 1968, 45.
19. Quoted in ibid., June 17, 1968, 34.
20. Updike, "Hub Fans Bid Kid Adieu," 131; Williams, *My Turn at Bat*, 215–216.
21. For Shaughnessy's account of this, see his column, "Memories Are Unforgettable," in the *Boston Globe*, July 6, 2002, F1.
22. For these comments, see Williams, *My Turn at Bat*.
23. See Linn, *Hitter*, 15.

24. Ibid., 62–68, 301, 303.

25. Quoted in ibid., 286.

26. Updike, "Hub Fans Bid Kid Adieu," 127.

4. The Year of the Yaz

1. Peter Gammons, "Living and Dying with the Woe Sox," in *The Red Sox Reader: 30 Years of Musings on Baseball's Most Amusing Team*, ed. Dan Riley (Thousand Oaks, Calif.: Ventura Arts, 1987), 217.

2. George Herring, *America's Longest War: The United States and Vietnam, 1950–1975* (New York: Wiley, 2002), 182, 212; James S. Olson and Randy Roberts, *Where the Domino Fell: America in Vietnam, 1945–1990* (St. James, N.Y.: Brandywine, 1999), 157–158.

3. George Donaldson Moss, *Vietnam: An American Ordeal* (New York: Prentice-Hall, 2001), 241, 252; Terry Anderson, *The Sixties* (New York: Longman, 1999), 88; Allan J. Matusow, *The Unraveling of America: A History of Liberalism in the 1960s* (New York: HarperCollins, 1985), 362; David W. Zang, *Sports Wars* (Fayetteville: University of Arkansas Press, 2001), 102–103.

4. Donald Honig, *The Red Sox: An Illustrated History* (New York: Prentice-Hall, 1990), 46.

5. Bill McSweeney, *The Impossible Dream: The Story of the Miracle Boston Red Sox* (New York: Coward-McCann, 1968), 98.

6. Dan Shaughnessy, *At Fenway: Dispatches from Red Sox Nation* (New York: Crown, 1996), 5–7.

7. Carl Yastrzemski with Gerald Eskenazi, *Yaz: Baseball, the Wall, and Me* (New York: Doubleday, 1990), 86–88, 99–100; McSweeney, *Impossible Dream*, 117; Zang, *Sports Wars*, 23.

8. Dick Williams and Bill Plaschke, *No More Mr. Nice Guy: A Life of Hardball* (New York: Harcourt Brace Jovanovich, 1990), 72; Anthony J. Connor, *Voices from Cooperstown: Baseball's Hall of Famers Tell It like It Was* (New York: Collier, 1982), 267–268.

9. Bill Reynolds, *Lost Summer: The '67 Red Sox and the Impossible Dream* (New York: Warner, 1992), 26–29; Williams and Plaschke, *No More Mr. Nice Guy*, 82–83.

10. Williams and Plaschke, *No More Mr. Nice Guy*, 47–49; Jules Tygiel, *Baseball's Great Experiment: Jackie Robinson and His Legacy* (New York: Oxford, 1997), 43–45, 290–291, 330; Shaughnessy, *At Fenway*, 67.

11. Shaughnessy, *At Fenway*, 78; Reynolds, *Lost Summer*, 166. For Williams's views

on racism in baseball, see Williams and Plaschke, *No More Mr. Nice Guy*, 218, 222–223, 234–235.

12. Williams and Plaschke, *No More Mr. Nice Guy*, 83; Ken Coleman and Dan Valenti, *The Impossible Dream Remembered: The 1967 Red Sox* (Lexington, Mass.: Stephen Greene, 1987), 11–12.

13. Williams and Plaschke, *No More Mr. Nice Guy*, 83.

14. Reynolds, *Lost Summer*, 18–21; Yastrzemski, *Yaz*, 38–39, 55, 115.

15. Yastrzemski, *Yaz*, 108–110, 112; Reynolds, *Lost Summer*, 60.

16. Williams and Plaschke, *No More Mr. Nice Guy*, 73, 85–86; Coleman and Valenti, *Impossible Dream Remembered*, 25.

17. Coleman and Valenti, *Impossible Dream Remembered*, 41; David Halberstam, "The Fan Divided: He Gets to Follow Two Teams," in Riley, *Red Sox Reader*, 196–197; Yastrzemski, *Yaz*, 120. Al Gionfriddo of the Brooklyn Dodgers made a famous catch on a drive by Joe DiMaggio of the Yankees in the 1947 World Series.

18. Charles DeBenedetti with Charles Chatfield, *An American Ordeal: The Antiwar Movement of the Vietnam Era* (Syracuse: Syracuse University Press, 1990), 175; Anderson, *The Sixties*, 78, 91; Matusow, *Unraveling of America*, 225; Herring, *America's Longest War*, 209.

19. Zang, *Sports Wars*, 18–19; Reynolds, *Lost Summer*, 62–63.

20. Coleman and Valenti, *Impossible Dream Remembered*, 49, 74, 76; Williams and Plaschke, *No More Mr. Nice Guy*, 91, 93; Yastrzemski, *Yaz*, 121; Leonard Schecter, "Baseball: Great American Myth," in Riley, *Red Sox Reader*, 79.

21. David Cantaneo, *Tony C.: The Triumph and Tragedy of Tony Conigliaro* (Nashville: Rutledge Hill, 1997), 94; Richard Norton Smith, *The Harvard Century: The Making of a University to a Nation* (New York: Simon and Schuster, 1986), 244, 246.

22. Yastrzemski, *Yaz*, 122; Williams and Plaschke, *No More Mr. Nice Guy*, 91.

23. Williams and Plaschke, *No More Mr. Nice Guy*, 90; Schecter, "Baseball," 76.

24. Reynolds, *Lost Summer*, 78–79; Matusow, *Unraveling of America*, 362–363.

25. Thomas H. O'Connor, *Building a New Boston: Politics and Urban Renewal, 1950–1970* (Boston: Northeastern University Press, 1993), 56–57, 60–61, 226; Shaughnessy, *At Fenway*, 66–67.

26. Coleman and Valenti, *Impossible Dream Remembered*, 68.

27. Yastrzemski, *Yaz*, 115–117, 123.

28. Williams and Plaschke, *No More Mr. Nice Guy*, 89–90.

29. Anderson, *The Sixties*, 95–96, 98; Coleman and Valenti, *Impossible Dream Remembered*, 124; Williams and Plaschke, *No More Mr. Nice Guy*, 92; Reynolds, *Lost Summer*, 114.

30. Reynolds, *Lost Summer*, 125; Cantaneo, *Tony C.*, 99; Halberstam, "The Fan Divided," 97.

31. Williams and Plaschke, *No More Mr. Nice Guy*, 92.

32. Yastrzemski, *Yaz*, 139, 145.

33. Coleman and Valenti, *Impossible Dream Remembered*, 156–159, 168–169.

34. Yastrzemski, *Yaz*, 172–174; Williams and Plaschke, *No More Mr. Nice Guy*, 99.

35. Williams and Plaschke, *No More Mr. Nice Guy*, 99.

36. Reynolds, *Lost Summer*, 227.

37. Coleman and Valenti, *Impossible Dream Remembered*, 216; Ellery H. Clark Jr., *Red Sox Forever* (New York: Exposition, 1977), 112; McSweeney, *Impossible Dream*, 209.

38. Williams and Plaschke, *No More Mr. Nice Guy*, 102; McSweeney, *Impossible Dream*, 210; Coleman and Valenti, *Impossible Dream Remembered*, 221.

39. Williams and Plaschke, *No More Mr. Nice Guy*, 93; Bob Ryan, "Dream Team of '67 a Blast from the Past," *Boston Globe*, August 24, 2002.

5. The Boston Marathon

1. Claire Kowalchik, "Landmarks: Heartbreak Hill," http://www.runnersworld.com/events/boston02/hartbrak.html.

2. Joe Falls, *The Boston Marathon* (New York: Macmillan, 1977), 22.

3. Tom Derderian, *The Boston Marathon: The First Century of the World's Premier Running Event* (Champaign, Ill.: Human Kinetics, 1994), xxi–xxii.

4. Falls, *Boston Marathon*, 8.

5. Derderian, *Boston Marathon*, 4.

6. Ibid., 8–10.

7. Curt Garfield, *Middlesex News*, in *Boston Marathon Scrapbook*, townonline.com/marathon/history, 1995–2000.

8. On Clarence DeMar, see his autobiography, *Marathon: The Clarence DeMar Story* (Medway, Ohio: Cedarwinds, 1998). DeMar is ranked number 70 on the *Boston Globe*'s list of "New England's Top 100 Athletes." See Barbara Matson, "Boston's First Marathon Man," http://www.boston.com/sports/top100players/70/htm; also, Falls, *Boston Marathon*, 72–73.

9. Derderian, *Boston Marathon*, 77–79.

10. Frederick Lewis and Dick Johnson, *Young at Heart: The Story of Johnny Kelley, Boston's Marathon Man* (Waco: WRS, 1992), 19. See also "John Adelbert Kelley (The Elder)," http://www.runningpast.com/johna/html.

11. Falls, *Boston Marathon*, 40.

12. Derderian, *Boston Marathon*, 151.

13. Lewis and Johnson, *Young at Heart,* 29.

14. Jerry Nason, "Kelley at Work 7:30 Morning after Triumph," *Boston Globe,* April 21, 1935.

15. Art Walsh, "Brown Proves Red Man Can Laugh at Impromptu Hotel Room Reception," *Boston Herald,* April 21, 1936; Falls, *Boston Marathon,* 41; Derderian, *Boston Marathon,* 155.

16. "John Adelbert Kelley (The Elder)."

17. Garfield, *Boston Marathon Scrapbook,* 5; Bill Rodriguez, "The Best Racer of All," *Providence Journal-Bulletin, Sunday Journal Magazine,* April 19, 1981; Falls, *Boston Marathon,* 80; Derderian, *Boston Marathon,* 195–200.

18. Will Cloney, "Cote Outdistances Vogel for Fourth Marathon Win," *Boston Herald,* April 20, 1936; idem, "Kyriakides Beats Kelley in Sprint," ibid., April 21, 1946.

19. Falls, *Boston Marathon,* 186.

20. Leigh Montville, "Marathon's Man: Semple," *Boston Globe,* March 10, 1988.

21. Jim Garfield, "Finn's Final Spurt Wins," *Boston Herald,* April 21, 1959.

22. Derderian, *Boston Marathon,* 259, 303–305.

23. John Mehaffey, "Prejudice Clouds Women's Marathon History," www.rediff .com/sports/2001/pct/03/mara.html.

24. Jack McCarthy, "Japanese Beat All but Womanhood," *Boston Herald,* April 20, 1966; also Falls, *Boston Marathon,* 94.

25. Jack Clary, "Kay Steals Scene from Marathon," *Boston Herald,* April 20, 1967.

26. Derderian, *Boston Marathon,* 305; "2 Girls in Marathon Don't Have Lovely Leg to Stand On," *New York Times,* April 20, 1967.

27. See "The History of the Women's Marathon," www.realrunner.com/ukand europe/women/marathonhistory.html.

28. Jason Kehoe, "The Breakthrough," www.billrodgers.com/aboutus/breakthrough .html; also Rodgers's autobiography, *Marathoning,* written with Joe Concannon (Simon and Schuster, 1980); Rodgers is ranked number 20 on the *Boston Globe's* list of "New England's Top 100 Athletes." See Barbara Matson, "Boston's Road Warrior," www.boston.com/sports/top100players/20.htm.

29. Ernie Roberts, "He Couldn't Believe His Record Marathon," *Boston Globe,* April 22, 1975.

30. Merrell Noden, "Jim Fixx," *Sports Illustrated,* September 19, 1994, 131.

31. Derderian, *Boston Marathon,* 418–428.

32. Kevin Dupont, "Rosie Ruiz: From Kenmore Square to West Palm Beach, Fla.," *Boston Globe,* April 14, 1996; Malcolm Moran, "Doubts Rise on Woman's Feat," *New York Times,* April 22, 1980.

33. Bill Griffith, "Will Cloney, Was Race Director of the Boston Marathon," *Boston Globe,* January 18, 2003.

34. Leigh Montville, "Patriot's Day Is Now Payday," *Boston Globe*, April 22, 1986; "Boston Marathon," www.sportsfacts.net/history/athletics/marathons/boston_marathon.html.

35. Leigh Montville, "Switzer Fondly Recalls the Farewell Meeting," *Boston Globe*, March 10, 1988.

6. Rowing on Troubled Waters

1. Interview with David Higgins, August 27, 2002.
2. Former Penn sports information director Herb Hartnett once used this description in trying to explain the distance between Harvard and the other Ivy League schools.
3. Stephen Hardy, *How Boston Played: Sport, Recreation, and Community, 1865–1915* (Boston: Northeastern University Press, 1982), 5.
4. Ibid.; Harry Parker to author, September 3, 2002.
5. Hardy, *How Boston Played*, 6.
6. *New York Times*, December 7, 1906, 12.
7. Jeremiah Ford II, "Not Just Entertaining Sideshows," *Pennsylvania Gazette* 65 (October 1966), 30.
8. Hugh Whall, "Never Before—At Harvard or in History," *Sports Illustrated*, June 28, 1965, 41.
9. Ibid., 36.
10. John Seabrook, "Feel No Pain," *New Yorker*, July 22, 1996, 34.
11. Whall, "Never Before," 37; Roger Angell, "0:00.05," *New Yorker*, August 10, 1968, 72.
12. Whall, "Never Before," 37.
13. Hardy, *How Boston Played*, 5.
14. Interview with Harry Parker, August 12, 2002.
15. Ibid.
16. Ibid.
17. Ibid.
18. Ibid.; interview, Higgins.
19. Interview, Higgins; interview with Andrew Larkin, August 29, 2002; interview with Paul Hoffman, September 5, 2002; interview with Franklin Hobbs, September 11, 2002.
20. Interview with Ian Gardiner, September 3, 2002.
21. Interview, Hobbs.
22. Angell, "0:00.05," 79.
23. Interview, Larkin.

24. Interview, Higgins.
25. "Crimson Oarsmen Win Olympic Berth," *News & Views of Harvard Sports*, July 31, 1968, 1–4.
26. Ibid., 1.
27. Interview, Higgins.
28. Interview, Parker.
29. Interview, Higgins.
30. Angell, "0:00.05," 75.
31. Interview, Parker.
32. Ibid.
33. Interview, Hoffman.
34. Ibid.
35. Harry Edwards, *The Revolt of the Black Athlete* (New York: Free Press, 1969), 128–129.
36. Curt Canning to author, December 7, 2002; interview, Hoffman.
37. Interview, Hoffman; Canning communication; interview, Higgins.
38. Edwards, *Revolt of the Black Athlete*, 108–110; *News & Views of Harvard Sports*, July 31, 1968, 2.
39. Interview, Parker.
40. Interview, Hobbs; interview, Higgins; interview, Parker.
41. Interview, Hoffman.
42. George G. Daniels, *The Olympic Century: The XIX Olympiad, Mexico City 1968, Sapporo 1972*, vol. 17 (Los Angeles: World Sport Research and Publications, 1996), 53.
43. Interview, Higgins; interview, Hobbs; interview, Larkin; interview, Hoffman; interview with Curt Canning, September 7, 2002.
44. Interview, Hobbs.
45. Interview, Gardiner; *Newsweek*, October 28, 1968, 74; interview, Hoffman; interview, Hobbs.
46. Daniels, *The Olympic Century*, 17: 26; interview, Hoffman.
47. Interview, Hoffman.
48. Daniels, *The Olympic Century*, 17: 68, 88.
49. Interview, Parker; interview, Hobbs.
50. Harry L. Parker, "Olympic Report" to the Friends of Harvard Rowing, April 1969, in author's possession.
51. Interview, Hoffman.
52. Ibid.
53. Parker, "Olympic Report"; interview, Higgins.
54. Daniels, *The Olympic Century*, 17: 89.

55. Joseph M. Sheehan, "Promise . . . and Failure," in *1968 United States Olympic Book* (New York: U.S. Olympic Committee, 1969), 93.
56. Douglas F. Roby to Harry Parker, November 5, 1968.
57. Parker, "Olympic Report."

7. Francis Ouimet at The Country Club

1. On Shippen, see Calvin H. Sinnette, *Forbidden Fairways: African Americans and the Game of Golf* (Chelsea, Mich.: Sleeping Bear, 1998), 15–25. See also Peter McDaniel et al., *Uneven Lies: The Heroic Story of African Americans in Golf* (New York: American Golfer, 2000).
2. The best account of the club's founding remains Frederic H. Curtiss and John Heard, *The Country Club, 1882–1932* (Brookline, Mass.: The Country Club, 1932). The 1860 petition, from which the quotations are taken, appears on 7–8.
3. See Robert H. Wiebe, *The Search for Order, 1877–1920* (New York: Hill and Wang, 1967). On Forbes see John Lauritz Larson, *Bonds of Enterprise: John Murray Forbes and Western Development in America's Railway Age* (Iowa City: University of Iowa Press, 2001).
4. Curtiss and Heard, *The Country Club*, 17–25, 139–140.
5. This paragraph (and much of what follows) draws heavily on Richard J. Moss, *Golf and the American Country Club* (Urbana: University of Illinois Press, 2001).
6. Curtiss and Heard, *The Country Club*, 100–116; quotation on 102.
7. For the debate on golf's American origins, see Robert Browning, *A History of Golf* (London: J. M. Dent and Sons, 1955), 113–115; and Herbert Warren Wind, *The Story of American Golf: Its Champions and Its Championships* (New York: Farrar, Straus, 1948), 18–21.
8. Wind, *The Story of American Golf*, 5–15; Moss, *Golf and the American Country Club*, 18–23.
9. Wind, *The Story of American Golf*, 14–24; Moss, *Golf and the American Country Club*, 25–28.
10. Moss, *Golf and the American Country Club*, 27–31, 35, 43.
11. Curtiss and Heard, *The Country Club*, 64–67.
12. Changes in the layout are detailed in ibid., 67–80.
13. Ibid., 25–43, 54–61, 159–160.
14. On the history of discrimination against women at private and public golf courses, see Jerri Richardson, *Unplayable Lies* (Seattle: Northwest, 1996).
15. Moss, *Golf and the American Country Club*, 32, 39–45. The clubhouse at Inverness includes a grandfather clock given to the club in 1920 by grateful professionals; see Herbert Warren Wind, *Following Through* (New York: Ticknor and Fields, 1985), 212.

16. All quotations are from Moss, *Golf and the American Country Club*, 45–50.

17. Ibid., 90–91.

18. Ibid., 24–31.

19. On Sarazen and Trevino, see Wind, *Following Through*, 221–240, 247–272; on Hogan, see Curt Sampson, *Hogan* (New York: Rutledge Hill Press, 1997).

20. See Mark Frost, *The Greatest Game Ever Played: Harry Vardon, Francis Ouimet, and the Birth of Modern Golf* (New York: Hyperion, 2002.) See also Ouimet's own *A Game of Golf: A Book of Reminiscence* (New York: Houghton Mifflin, 1932).

21. Ouimet, *A Game of Golf*, 1–5.

22. Ibid., 6–10.

23. Ibid., 8–18.

24. Ibid., 23–37; Mary Ouimet's comment is on 24.

25. Ibid, 38–43. See also Frost, *The Greatest Game Ever Played*, 127–147; Darwin's comments are quoted on 137, 147. On Darwin, see Wind, *Following Through*, 153–167. For an introduction to his writing see Peter Ryde, *Mostly Golf: A Bernard Darwin Anthology* (New York: Classics of Golf, 1989).

26. Frost, *The Greatest Game Ever Played*, 37–51.

27. Ouimet, *A Game of Golf*, 44–45.

28. See Frost, *The Greatest Game Ever Played*, 160–162, 185, 208–209, 216, 222–223, 329.

29. This account is drawn from several sources, including the contemporary reports of Bernard Darwin, Ouimet's 1932 autobiography, and a host of subsequent histories, including Wind, *The Story of American Golf*; Browning, *A History of Golf*; Henry Cotton, *Golf: A Pictorial History* (Glasgow: William Collier and Son, 1975); George Peper, ed., *Golf in America: The First Hundred Years* (New York: Harry N. Abrams, 1988); and Robert T. Sommers, *The U.S. Open: Golf's Ultimate Challenge*, 2d ed. (New York: Oxford University Press, 1996). Surely the definitive recounting is Frost's *The Greatest Game Ever Played*, which devotes nearly 300 pages to the tournament.

30. Ouimet, *A Game of Golf*, 45.

31. Ibid., 48.

32. Ouimet, quoted in James Diaz, *Hallowed Ground: Golf's Greatest Places* (Shelton, Conn.: Greenwich Workshop, 1999), 30. Darwin's comment is quoted in Moss, *Golf and the American Country Club*, 108.

33. Wind, *The Story of American Golf*, 117. See also Frost, *The Greatest Game Ever Played*, 435–439.

34. Ouimet, *A Game of Golf*, 57–76.

35. Curtiss and Heard, *The Country Club*, 165–166.

36. I am grateful to the archivists at the U.S.G.A. for providing me with details of

Ouimet's suspension, including the text of the 1916 regulation. The comment by Travis is quoted in Cotton, *Golf*, 68–69.

37. See Wind, *Following Through*, 46, 209–220.

38. Ouimet wryly titled the 1920s chapter of his autobiography "Bobby Jones—and Others—Beat Me."

39. Quoted in Moss, *Golf and the American Country Club*, 132.

40. Ouimet, *A Game of Golf*, 266; Frost, *The Greatest Game Ever Played*, 472–474.

41. Curtiss and Heard, *The Country Club*, 35–37, 52–53.

42. Ibid., 71–72, 78–83, 109.

43. Wind, *Following Through*, 213. On the Ryder Cup, see Shirley Dusinberre Durham, *Mr. Ryder's Trophy* (Chelsea, Mich.: Sleeping Bear, 2002); and Bob Bubka, *The Ryder Cup: Golf's Greatest Event* (New York: Crown, 1999).

44. Quoted in Diaz, *Hallowed Ground*, 30.

8. The Lost Battle for Gentlemanly Sport, 1869–1909

Epigraph: Charles W. Eliot, "President Eliot's Report," *Harvard Graduates' Magazine* 3 (March 1894), 376.

1. Charles W. Eliot, "Inaugural Address," October 19, 1869, 22, Harvard University Archives (hereafter HUA).

2. Yale professor Thatcher in Harvard Athletic Committee Minutes, December 10, 1883, HUA.

3. Hugh Hawkins, *Between Harvard and America: The Educational Leadership of Charles W. Eliot* (New York: Oxford University Press, 1972), 3; Morton Keller and Phyllis Keller, *Making Harvard Modern: The Rise of America's University* (New York: Oxford University Press, 2001), 13; Bernard Bailyn, Donald Fleming, Oscar Handlin, and Stephan Thernstrom, *Glimpses of the Harvard Past* (Cambridge, Mass.: Harvard University Press, 1986), 64; and Henry James, *Charles W. Eliot*, 2 vols. (Boston: Houghton Mifflin, 1930), 1: 36.

4. Robert F. Herrick, *Red Top: Reminiscences of Harvard Rowing* (Cambridge, Mass.: Harvard University Press, 1948), 9.

5. James M. Whiton, "The First Harvard-Yale Regatta (1852)," *Outlook* 68 (1901), 286–289; and Charles F. Livermore, "The First Harvard-Yale Boat Race," *Harvard Graduates' Magazine* 2 (December 1893), 226.

6. B. W. Crowninshield, "Boating," in F. O. Vaille and H. A. Clark, *The Harvard Book*, vol. 2 (Cambridge, Mass.: Welch, Bigelow, 1875), 253.

7. James, *Charles W. Eliot*, 2: 80–81.

8. See Ronald A. Smith, *Sports and Freedom: The Rise of Big-Time College Athletics* (New York: Oxford University Press, 1988), 38–42. Harvard brought its own boat

builder and cook to London and purchased food and drink in secret as part of its effort to beat Oxford.

9. Henry D. Sheldon, *Student Life and Customs* (New York: D. Appleton, 1901), 53; T. Cook, "Some Tendencies of Modern Sport," *Quarterly Review* 99 (January 1904), 141, 151; and James F. Muirhead, *The Land of Contrasts: A Briton's View of His American Kin* (Boston: Lamson, Wolffe, 1898), 117.

10. Endicott Peabody, "The Ideals of Sport in England and America," *American Physical Education Review* 19 (1914), 277–282.

11. Alexis de Tocqueville, *Democracy in America*, vol. 2 (1840; reprint, New York: Vintage, 1945), 108.

12. Louis Hartz, *The Liberal Tradition in America* (New York: Harcourt, Brace and World, 1955).

13. Keller and Keller, *Making Harvard Modern*, 13.

14. Guy Lewis, "America's First Intercollegiate Sport: The Regattas from 1852–1876," *Research Quarterly* 38 (December 1967), 642.

15. *A History of American College Regattas* (Boston: Wilson, 1875), 642.

16. John W. White, W. S. Chaplin, and Albert Bushnell Hart, "Harvard College Report of the Committee Appointed to Consider the Subject of College Athletics, and to Report Thereon to the Faculty," June 12, 1888, 10, HUD 8388.3B, HUA; and John A. Blanchard, ed., *The H Book of Harvard Athletics, 1852–1922* (Cambridge, Mass.: Harvard Varsity Club, 1923), 182, 196, 297–298, 300.

17. White, Chaplin, and Hart, "Harvard College Report," 10–11.

18. Ibid., 12–14.

19. J. W. White, W. E. Byerly, and D. A. Sargent (Athletic Committee) to the faculty of Harvard College, December 2, 1884, attached to Athletic Committee Minutes, November 25, 1884, 55, HUA.

20. "Overseers Athletic Abuses Committee Report," ca. April 1888, 10, HUD 8388.5, HUA.

21. White, Chaplin, and Hart, "Harvard College Report," 24–27; and *Report of the President of Harvard College, 1888–1889* (Cambridge, Mass.: Harvard University, 1889), 12–13.

22. John W. White, Chair, Athletic Committee, "Annual Report, 1889–1890," to Charles W. Eliot, ca. March 1891, box 262, folder "1891, Jan.–Mar.," Eliot Papers, HUA. For the dual league controversy, see Ronald A. Smith, "The Harvard-Yale Dual League Plan of the 1890s: A Failure of Elitism," *New England Quarterly* 41 (June 1988), 201–213.

23. M. H. Morgan, Acting Secretary of the Harvard Faculty of Arts and Sciences, to J. B. Ames, Chair, Athletic Committee, March 20, 1895, box 264, folder "1895, Jan.–Mar.," Eliot Papers, HUA; Ames to Harvard Faculty of Arts and Sciences, February 25, 1895, ibid.

24. Charles W. Eliot, "President Eliot's Report," *Harvard Graduates' Magazine* 9 (March 1901), 452; "Report of the Brown University Conference on Intercollegiate Sports," February 18, 1898, HUD 8398.75, HUA.

25. William James Jr., "Sport or Business?" *Harvard Graduates' Magazine* 11 (December 1903), 225.

26. John Richardson to Charles W. Eliot, July 16, 1908, box 202, folder "Athletics," Eliot Papers, HUA.

27. Blanchard, *H Book of Harvard Athletics*, 141, 296, 456.

28. Telegram contained in Ira N. Hollis to Charles W. Eliot, January 23, 1902, box 143, Eliot Papers, HUA.

29. Arthur T. Hadley, Yale president, to Charles W. Eliot, December 18, 1901, box 117, folder 260, Eliot Papers, HUA.

30. Athletic Committee Minutes, January 10, 1902, 417; Hollis to Charles W. Eliot, January 23, 1902.

31. Karl F. Brill, "Football Revelation Period," newspaper clipping, November 1905, HUD 10905, HUA.

32. Richard Henry Dana to Charles W. Eliot, December 18, 1905, box 209, folder "Dana," Eliot Papers, HUA.

33. L. B. R. Briggs to Charles W. Eliot, December 4, 1905, box 204, folder "Briggs," Eliot Papers, HUA.

34. "Report of the Overseers Committee," *Harvard Graduates' Magazine* 14 (March 1906), 497.

35. Theodore Roosevelt to Edward Deshon Brandegee, March 7, 1906, in *The Letters of Theodore Roosevelt*, ed. Elting E. Morison, vol. 5 (Cambridge, Mass.: Harvard University Press, 1952), 46.

36. "From a Graduate's Window," *Harvard Graduates' Magazine* 14 (December 1905), 216–223.

37. R. G. Watson to Charles W. Eliot, July 26, 1895, box 138, folder 1283, Eliot Papers, HUA.

38. William R. Thayer to Charles W. Eliot, December 31, 1905, box 252, folder "William R. Thayer," Eliot Papers, HUA.

39. L. B. R. Briggs, "Athletic Sports," *Harvard Graduates' Magazine* 17 (June 1909), 697.

40. "Athletic Committee Minutes," *Harvard Graduates' Magazine* 16 (September 1907), 128–129.

41. Joseph H. Beale, Chair, Athletic Committee, to Charles W. Eliot, July 8, 1896, box 128, folder 615, Eliot Papers, HUA; Eliot, "President Eliot's Report," 452.

42. Ira N. Hollis to Charles W. Eliot, January 16, 1903, box 110, folder 143, Eliot Papers, HUA.

43. For scholarship holders see box 170, folder "Nov. 1902"; box 274, folder "Nov. 1903"; box 276, folder "Dec. 1905"; and box 278, folder "Dec. 1907," all Eliot Papers, HUA.

44. Archibald C. Coolidge, "Professional Coaches," *Harvard Graduates' Magazine* 114 (March 1906), 392–395.

45. Athletic Committee Minutes, December 12, 1888, November 11, 1889, June 16, 1890, December 15 and 18, 1890, and January 26, 1892, HUA.

46. H. A. Bellows, "Athletics," *Harvard Graduates' Magazine* 13 (March 1905), 473.

47. William Blaikie to Charles W. Eliot, March 4, 1904, box 203, folder "Blaikie," Eliot Papers, HUA.

48. Athletic Committee Minutes, January 10, 1901, January 6, 1904, February 7, 1905, HUA; Coolidge, "Professional Coaches," 394. For a fuller account of Reid's hiring as Harvard football coach, see Ronald A. Smith, "Introduction," in *Big-Time Football at Harvard, 1905: The Diary of Coach Bill Reid*, ed. Smith (Urbana: University of Illinois Press, 1994), xiii–xxxviii.

49. Athletic Committee Minutes, December 6, 1907, HUA.

50. L. B. R. Briggs to Charles W. Eliot, January 27, 1902, box 102, folder "Briggs," Eliot Papers, HUA.

51. Charles W. Eliot to Dr. William Everett, December 8, 1908, box 202, folder "Athletics," Eliot Papers, HUA.

9. Sports, Politics, and Revenge

1. Leigh Montville, "The Patsies," *Sports Illustrated*, November 2, 1992, 33–34; Bob Ryan, "Boston," *Sport*, July 1989, 56.

2. Larry Fox, *The New England Patriots* (New York: Atheneum, 1979), 10.

3. Ibid., 12 37.

4. Ibid., 44–49.

5. Ibid., 59, 77, 87; Robert H. Boyle, "There's No Need to Pity the Pats," *Sports Illustrated*, October 18, 1971, 31.

6. Fox, *The New England Patriots*, 141–143; *Boston Globe*, August 11, 1971.

7. *Newsweek*, April 26, 1965, 77–78; Thomas H. O'Connor, *Bibles, Brahmins, and Bosses: A Short History of Boston*, 3d ed. (Boston: Boston Public Library, 1991), 205–208.

8. Fox, *The New England Patriots*, 142–143; Mark Mulvoy, "Slow Death by Committee in Boston," *Sports Illustrated*, June 12, 1967, 81; *New York Times*, February 20 and 26, 1966, March 26, 1967; Thomas H. O'Connor, *The Boston Irish: A Political History* (Boston: Northeastern University Press, 1995), 236–237.

9. Boyle, "No Need to Pity the Pats," 31; David Harris, *The League: The Rise and*

Decline of the NFL (New York: Bantam, 1986), 124; Mulvoy, "Slow Death by Committee in Boston," 79; *Boston Globe*, February 8, 1970.

10. Fox, *The New England Patriots*, 140–141; *Boston Globe*, January 27, 1970.

11. *Boston Globe*, January 27, 29, and 31, and February 2, 1970; *Boston Evening Globe*, January 27 and 28, 1970.

12. *Boston Evening Globe*, January 27 and February 13, 1970; *Boston Globe*, February 7, 1970.

13. *Boston Globe*, January 27 and February 4, 1970; *New York Times*, February 4, 1970; *Newsweek*, February 16, 1970, 58.

14. *Boston Globe*, February 12, 7, and 13, 1970.

15. Ibid., February 8, 1970; *Boston Evening Globe*, February 11, 1970.

16. *Boston Globe*, March 8, 9, 13, 4, 8, and 10, 1970; *Boston Evening Globe*, March 13 and 16, 1970.

17. *Boston Globe*, March 19, 23, and 24, 1970; Fox, *The New England Patriots*, 143–144.

18. *Boston Globe*, April 14, 1970, June 7, 1970, August 11, 1971.

19. Ibid., May 27, 1970; Fox, *The New England Patriots*, 144.

20. Steven A. Reiss, *City Games: The Evolution of American Urban Society and the Rise of Sports* (Urbana: University of Illinois Press, 1989), 24; *Boston Globe*, August 11 and 16, 1971; Boyle, "No Need to Pity the Pats," 31, 35; Fox, *The New England Patriots*, 144, 146.

21. *Boston Evening Globe*, August 16, 1971; *Boston Globe*, August 15, 1971.

22. *Boston Globe*, August 15, 16, and 17, 1971; Fox, *The New England Patriots*, 143; Boyle, "No Need to Pity the Pats," 32; *Boston Evening Globe*, August 16, 1971.

23. Montville, "The Patsies," 37; *Sports Illustrated*, October 13, 1980, 29.

24. Fox, *The New England Patriots*, 164–173; Harris, *The League*, 127.

25. Harris, *The League*, 512; *Business Week*, January 25, 1988, 40; John Steinbreder, "The $126 Million Fumble," *Sports Illustrated*, March 14, 1988, 65.

26. Harris, *The League*, 629–632; *Business Week*, November 18, 1985, 96; Steinbreder, "The $126 Million Fumble," 69.

27. Steinbreder, "The $126 Million Fumble," 65, 64; *New York Times*, October 29, 1987.

28. *New York Times*, January 19, 1986, and February 17, March 18, and April 1, 1988; Steinbreder, "The $126 Million Fumble," 64–66.

29. Montville, "The Patsies," 37; *New York Times*, November 11, 1991; *Business Week*, February 25, 1991, 46.

30. Montville, "The Patsies," 34; Norm Alster, "Orthwein's Dilemma," *Forbes*, March 15, 1993, 48–49.

31. *New York Times*, July 1, 1993, January 13, 1994, and September 4, 25, and 28, 1993.

32. Leigh Montville, "A Surge of Patriotism," *Sports Illustrated*, January 17, 1994, 74.

33. *New York Times*, November 29, 1998, January 20, 1997; *Boston Globe*, December 16, 1998; Wilbur C. Rich, "Who Lost the Megaplex?" *Policy Studies Review* 15 (spring 1998), 107.

34. Rich, "Who Lost the Megaplex?" 105–111; *Boston Globe*, December 16, 1998.

35. Rich, "Who Lost the Megaplex?" 111–113; *Boston Globe*, December 16, 1998; *New York Times*, January 22, 18, and 12, 1997.

36. *Boston Globe*, December 16, 1998, September 29 and 19, 1997; Stephen Sawicki, "Hartford's Long Bomb," *U.S. News & World Report*, December 7, 1998, 33.

37. *Providence Sunday Journal*, September 28, 1997; *Providence Journal-Bulletin*, September 24, 4, 20, and 16, 1997.

38. *Business Week*, October 6, 1997, 52; *Boston Globe*, September 22, 19, and 21, 1997.

39. *Providence Journal-Bulletin*, September 25, 8, 22, and 21, 1997.

40. *New York Times*, January 12, 1997; *Boston Globe*, September 21, 1997; *Providence Journal-Bulletin*, September 18, 1997.

41. *Boston Globe*, September 19, 20, and 26, 1997.

42. *Providence Journal-Bulletin*, September 26, 1997; *Boston Globe*, September 27, 28, and 21, 1997.

43. *New York Times*, October 2, 1997, November 20, 1998; *Boston Globe*, October 2, 1997, November 18, 1998, November 14, 1997.

44. *Boston Globe*, December 16 and November 22, 18, and 20, 1998; *Hartford Courant*, November 19 and 20, 1998; *New York Times*, November 22, 1998.

45. *Boston Globe*, November 20 and 19, 1998; *New York Times*, November 20 and 21, 1998.

46. William C. Symonds, "Hartford's 'Hail Mary' Pass," *Business Week*, December 7, 1998, 38; *Hartford Courant*, November 29, 26, and 22 and December 2, 1998.

47. *Hartford Courant*, December 10, 13, 3, 29, 1, and 9 and November 27, 1998.

48. Ibid., December 10, 6, and 9, 1998.

49. Ibid., December 14, 15, and 16, 1998; *Boston Globe*, December 13 and 15, 1998.

50. *Hartford Courant*, January 13, 1999, February 13 and 12, 1999; *New York Times*, February 15, 1999.

51. *Hartford Courant*, February 25, 11, 23, 24, 25, and 4, 1999, April 2, 1999; *New York Times*, February 12, 1999.

52. *Hartford Courant*, February 28 and April 17 and 27, 1999.

53. Dean Chadwin, "Block That Stadium!" *The Nation*, June 7, 1999, 25–26; *Hartford Courant*, January 31, February 26, and March 26 and 31, 1999.

54. *Boston Globe*, January 30 and 29, 1999, March 16, 1999; *Hartford Courant*, April 25 and March 17, 1999; Chadwin, "Block That Stadium!" 26; *New York Times*, March 6, 1999.

55. *Boston Globe*, May 19 and April 16, 1999.
56. *New York Times*, April 23, 1999; *Boston Globe*, March 25 and 26, 1999, April 18, 25, 27, and 28, 1999.
57. *New York Times*, May 3, 1999; *Boston Globe*, May 2, 1999.
58. *Boston Globe*, May 1, 1999; *Hartford Courant*, May 1, 1999.
59. *Boston Globe*, May 3, 8, 14, 18, and 19, 1999; *New York Times*, November 12, 1999, December 3 and March 3, 2000.
60. *New York Times*, May 19, 1999, August 24, 2000; *Boston Globe*, August 6, 2002.

10. The Champion of All Champions

1. I have written more extensively on Sullivan in *The Manly Art: Bare-Knuckle Prize Fighting in America* (Ithaca: Cornell University Press, 1986), chap. 7, from which this piece is adapted. The classic study on the Irish of Boston is Oscar Handlin, *Boston's Immigrants, 1790–1880: A Study in Acculturation* (Cambridge, Mass.: Harvard University Press, 1991). Perhaps the best work on the Irish is Kerby Miller, *Emigrants and Exiles: Ireland and the Irish Exodus to North America* (New York, 1985). More recent studies of the Irish focus on the intersection of race and class, on how, in Noel Ignatiev's words, "the Irish became white." The best of that literature remains David Roediger, *The Wages of Whiteness: Race and the Making of the American Working Class* (New York, 1991). See also Noel Ignatiev, *How the Irish Became White* (New York, 1996).
2. The best and most complete work on Sullivan is Michael T. Isenberg, *John L. Sullivan and His America* (Urbana, 1988).
3. Ibid., chap. 1; John L. Sullivan, *The Life and Reminiscences of a Nineteenth Century Gladiator* (Boston, 1892), 23–25. On sport in New York, see Melvin Adelman, *Sporting Time: New York City and the Rise of Modern Athletics, 1820–1870* (Urbana, 1990). For Boston, see Stephen Hall Hardy, *How Boston Played: Sport, Recreation, and Community, 1865–1915* (Boston, 1982).
4. Isenberg, *John L. Sullivan and His America*, chaps. 1, 2; Sullivan, *Life and Reminiscences*, 23–25.
5. On early baseball, see Warren Goldstein's excellent *Playing for Keeps: A History of Early Baseball* (Ithaca, 1991); for late nineteenth-century sports, try Elliott Gorn and Warren Goldstein, *A Brief History of American Sports* (New York, 1993), chap. 3.
6. The great chronicler of the ring was Pierce Egan, whose *Boxiana, or Sketches of Ancient and Modern Pugilism* (London, 1812), remains unsurpassed. On the early ring, also see Gorn, "Prologue," in *The Manly Art*; and John Ford, *Prize Fighting: The Age of Regency Boximania* (South Brunswick, U.K., 1971).

7. William Hazlitt, "The Fight," in *The Complete Works of William Hazlitt*, vol. 17 (London, 1933), 79–86.

8. Egan, *Boxiana*, 360–420; idem, "Memoirs of Tom Molineaux," *The Fancy* 1 (1822), 492. Also see Gorn, *The Manly Art*, 19–22.

9. Gorn, *The Manly Art*, 34–36.

10. On New York City street life, see Sean Wilentz, *Chants Democratic: New York City and the Rise of the American Working Class, 1788–1850* (New York, 1984); and Tyler Anbinder, *Five Points: The Nineteenth Century New York City Neighborhood That Invented Tap Dance, Stole Elections, and Became the World's Most Notorious Slum* (New York, 2002). The Hyer-Sullivan match was covered in local sporting newspapers, and some of these stories were then excerpted in cheap compilations such as the anonymous *The Life and Battles of Yankee Sullivan* (New York, 1854); Ed James, *The Life and Battles of Tom Hyer* (New York, 1879); and the anonymous *American Fistiana* (New York, 1849, 1860, 1873). For a general discussion of these early years see Gorn, *The Manly Art*, chaps. 2 and 3.

11. Gorn, *The Manly Art*, 81–97.

12. There is a growing body of work on masculinity. For examples, see E. Anthony Rotundo, *American Manhood: Transformations in Masculinity from the Revolution to the Modern Era* (New York, 1993); Michael Kimmel, *Manhood in America: A Cultural History* (New York, 1996); Mark Carnes and Clyde Griffen, eds., *Meanings for Manhood: Constructions of Masculinity in Victorian America* (Chicago, 1990); and Gail Bederman, *Manliness and Civilization: A Cultural History of Gender and Race in the United States* (Chicago, 1996). On boxing's first golden age in the 1850s, see Gorn, *The Manly Art*, chaps. 3 and 4.

13. Gorn, *The Manly Art*, chap. 5.

14. On the sports revival of the late nineteenth century, see Steven Pope, *Patriotic Games: Sporting Traditions in the American Imagination, 1876–1926* (New York, 1997); Donald Mrozek, *Sport and American Mentality, 1880–1910* (Knoxville, 1983); Hardy, *How Boston Played*, chaps. 3 and 4; and Gorn and Goldstein, *Brief History of American Sports*, chap. 3.

15. See Theodore Roosevelt, "Professionalism in Sports," *North American Review* 15 (August 1890), 187–191.

16. G. Stanley Hall, *Life and Confessions of a Psychologist* (New York, 1923), 578–579; Roosevelt, "Professionalism in Sports," 191; Michael Donovan, *The Roosevelt That I Know* (New York, 1909), chap. 1; Carl S. Smith, "The Boxing Paintings of Thomas Eakins," *Prospects* 4 (1979), 403–420; Duffield Osborn, "A Defense of Pugilism," *North American Review* 46 (April, 1888), 434–435.

17. John Boyle O'Reilly, *The Ethics of Boxing and Manly Sports* (Boston, 1888), 75, 79; Sullivan, *Life and Reminiscences*, appendix.

18. Isenberg covers this ground well; *John L. Sullivan and His America*, 32–36.

19. Sullivan, *Life and Reminiscences*, 40–46; Isenberg, *John L. Sullivan and His America*, 82–101.

20. José Martí, *The America of José Martí*, trans. Juan de Onis (New York, 1953), 117–120.

21. The Ryan fight was thoroughly covered in the *Police Gazette*. Also see Sullivan, *Life and Reminiscences*, 70–76; and Isenberg, *John L. Sullivan and His America*, 102–113.

22. Isenberg, *John L. Sullivan and His America*, 109.

23. William Edgar Harding, *Life and Battles of John L. Sullivan*, pp. 13, 25; Isenberg, *John L. Sullivan and His America*, 113.

24. Sullivan, *Life and Reminiscences*, 97–156.

25. Ibid., 241–244.

26. The importance of cleaning up the ring—but not too much—to attract a new clientele is a main theme of Gorn, *The Manly Art*, chap. 7.

27. Sullivan, *Life and Reminiscences*, chaps. 9, 10.

28. William Edgar Harding, *The Life and Battles of Jake Kilrain* (New York, 1888), 5–19, 29; idem, *Life of Sullivan*, 74–92; Sullivan, *Life and Reminiscences*, chaps. 9, 10.

29. Harding, *Life of Sullivan*, 80–92; Sullivan, *Life and Reminiscences*, 207–212; Anon., *The Modern Gladiator* (St. Louis, 1892), 139–160.

30. *Modern Gladiator*, 196–197, 356; Sullivan, *Life and Reminiscences*, 213–219.

31. William Edgar Harding, *Life and Battles of James J. Corbett* (New York, 1892), 25–56; Sullivan, *Life and Reminiscences*, chaps. 11, 12. On Sullivan's tour, see Isenberg, *John L. Sullivan and His America*, chap. 11.

32. Isenberg, *John L. Sullivan and His America*, 290–293.

33. William H. Adams, "New Orleans as the National Center of Boxing," *Louisiana Historical Quarterly* 39 (1956), 96–100; Dale Somers, *The Rise of Sports in New Orleans, 1850–1900* (Baton Rouge, 1972), 174–191.

34. John Rickard Betts, *America's Sporting Heritage, 1850–1900* (Reading, Mass., 1974), 63–68; "State of Louisiana vs. The Olympic Club," 46, pt. 2, 1894, in Henry Demis, *Reports of Cases Argued and Determined in the Supreme Court of Louisiana* (New Orleans, 1895), 952–957.

35. Sullivan's legacy is the subject of Gorn, *Manly Art*, chap. 7.

36. Somers, *Rise of Sports in New Orleans*, 79–83; Adams, "New Orleans as Center of Boxing," 101–105.

37. Harding, *Life and Battles of Corbett*, chap. 7; idem, *Life of Sullivan*, 92–102; James Connors, *Illustrated History of the Great Corbett-Sullivan Ring Battle* (Buffalo, 1892).

38. William Lyon Phelps, *Autobiography with Letters* (New York, 1939), 356.

39. Theodore Dreiser, *A Book about Myself* (New York, 1942), 150–151.

40. Vachel Lindsay, "John L. Sullivan, the Strong Boy of Boston," in *Selected Poems of Vachel Lindsay*, ed. Mark Harris (New York, 1963), 13.

11. Rocky Marciano and the Curse of Al Weill

1. For a fuller discussion of Marciano's image in the cultural context of the early 1950s, see Russell Sullivan, *Rocky Marciano: The Rock of His Times* (Urbana: University of Illinois Press, 2002), 139–163. See also Eric Foner, *The Story of American Freedom* (New York: W. W. Norton, 1998), 249–273 (examining the anticommunist crusade of the era in juxtaposition with the ideal of freedom). For more on the racial and ethnic symbolism surrounding Marciano and affecting his image, see Sullivan, *Rocky Marciano*, 69–94 and 233–253.

2. *Boston Herald Traveler*, September 3, 1969, 35.

3. Ibid.

4. McKenney quoted in *Boston Post*, March 25, 1950, 1, 13; Egan in *Boston Daily Record*, March 27, 1950, 57.

5. *Boston Evening American*, July 8, 1950, 20.

6. Gillooly quoted in *Boston Evening American*, July 11, 1950, 40; Marciano in *Boston Sunday Globe*, July 27, 1952, 53.

7. Hamilton quoted in *Boston Herald*, July 11, 1950, 12; Siegel in *Boston Traveler*, July 11, 1950, 34.

8. Egan quoted in *Boston Daily Record*, March 27, 1950, 57; Almy in *Boston Sunday Post*, July 8, 1951, 29, 33.

9. *Boston Traveler*, July 12, 1951, 16.

10. *Boston Post*, August 28, 1951, 1, 17.

11. *Boston Traveler*, August 29, 1951, 29.

12. *Boston Post*, October 27, 1951, 1, 8.

13. Hern quoted in *Boston Post*, February 15, 1952, 21; Keane in *Boston Globe*, February 14, 1952, 1, 12.

14. Kaese quoted in *Boston Evening Globe*, September 24, 1952, 15; *Boston Globe*, September 25, 1952, 1, 16; and *Boston Evening Globe*, September 22, 1955, 20; Hern in *Boston Post*, May 20, 1955, 23.

15. The Marciano-Liston exchange quoted in *Boston Sunday Post*, May 8, 1955, 33, 35; Marciano in *Washington Post*, September 27, 1953, 1C, 4C.

16. *Boston Post*, July 13, 1951, 1, 13; *Boston Sunday Post*, July 15, 1951, 23, 25.

17. Kaese quoted in *Boston Globe*, September 20, 1952, 7; Hern in *Boston Post*, September 26, 1952, 26; priest in *Boston Post*, September 26, 1952, 27.

18. *Boston Evening Globe*, July 28, 1952, 8.
19. *Boston Evening Globe*, May 14, 1953, 1, 26.
20. Hurwitz quoted in *Boston Evening Globe*, September 25, 1952, 18; Nason in *Boston Evening Globe*, September 19, 1955, 1, 10.
21. *Boston Post*, September 26, 1953, 7; *Boston Post*, June 13, 1954, 49; *Boston Post*, September 20, 1955, 20.
22. *Boston Globe*, November 10, 1951, 5.
23. Kaese quoted in *Boston Globe*, May 16, 1955, 1, 7; Silverman in *Boston Globe*, June 19, 1954, 10.
24. Weill quoted in *Boston Evening Globe*, May 15, 1953, 14; Silverman in *Boston Globe*, June 19, 1954, 10; IBC source in *Boston Evening Globe*, May 15, 1953, 14; Silverman in *Boston Globe*, June 19, 1954, 10.
25. *Boston Sunday Globe*, July 10, 1977, 77, 95.
26. Goodman quoted in *Boston Globe*, May 18, 1953, 7; IBC source and Nason in *Boston Evening Globe*, May 15, 1953, 14.
27. Silverman and Valenti quoted in *Boston Globe*, June 19, 1954, 10; Kaese in *Boston Globe*, May 16, 1955, 1, 7.
28. *Boston Record-American*, September 2, 1969, 66.
29. Benjamin G. Rader, *American Sports: From the Age of Folk Games to the Age of Spectators* (Englewood Cliffs, N.J.: Prentice-Hall, 1983), 198, 360.
30. *Boston Globe*, June 19, 1954, 10.
31. For more on the life, career, and significance of Rocky Marciano, *see* Sullivan, *Rocky Marciano*; and Everett M. Skehan, *Rocky Marciano: The Biography of a First Son* (1977; reprint, London: Robson, 1998).

12. Long before Orr

I thank the following for their help in my research: Tom Burke, Tom and Rosalie Brown; Rich Johnson at the Sports Museum of New England; Jack Grinold at Northeastern University; Dave Kelly at the Library of Congress; Aaron Schmidt at the Boston Public Library; Jeff Mifflin at the MIT Archives; Bruce Kidd, Phyllis Berck, Rick Gruneau, John Wong, Bill Fitsell, Howard Shubert, Bill Cleary, Joe Bertagna, Sean Pickett, Paul DeLoca, Andy Holman; Phil Pritchard and his staff at the Hockey Hall of Fame; and Randy Roberts.

1. For a splendid argument against an "inevitable or predetermined" Canadian tradition, see Richard Gruneau and David Whitson, *Hockey Night in Canada: Sport, Identities, and Cultural Politics* (Toronto: Garamond, 1993), 6.
2. Jacob Abbot, *Caleb in Town: A Story for Children* (Boston: Crocker and Brewster, 1839), 38. Abbot was the author of the famous "Rollo" series. For a description of

a standard game, see Walter P. Eaton, "Shinny," *Outing* 63 (December 1913), 288–289.

3. For diffusion histories, see Allen Guttmann, *Games and Empires* (New York: Columbia University Press, 1994); George Kirsch, *The Creation of American Team Sports: Baseball and Cricket, 1838–72* (Urbana: University of Illinois Press, 1989); Melvin Adelman, *A Sporting Time: New York City and the Rise of Modern Athletics, 1820–70* (Urbana: University of Illinois Press, 1986); Maarten van Bottenburg, *Global Games* (Urbana: University of Illinois Press, 2001); Andrei Markovits and Steven Hellerman, *Offside: Soccer and American Exceptionalism* (Princeton: Princeton University Press, 2001).

4. *Polo on Skates: American Skaters' Polo Rules*, pamphlet, 1884, Library of Congress; *Boston Herald*, January 9 and 10, 1885; J. W. Fitsell, "The Rise and Fall of Ice Polo," in *Total Hockey*, ed. Don Diamond, 2d ed. (Kingston, N.Y.: Total Sports Publishing, 2000); Mark Pollak, *Sports Leagues and Teams: An Encyclopedia, 1876–1996* (Jefferson, N.C.: McFarland, 1998), 359–420; *Boston Herald*, January 4, 1885; Bob Cubie, "Slap Shot on Wheels," *Brockton Enterprise*, May 23, 1993, 25, 29; Dwight Hoover, "Roller-skating toward Industrialism," in *Hard at Play: Leisure in America, 1840–1940*, ed. Kathryn Grover (Rochester, N.Y.: University of Massachusetts Press and Strong Museum, 1992), 61–76; Robert Weir, "Take Me Out to the Brawl Game: Sports and Workers in Gilded Age Massachusetts," in *Sports in Massachusetts: Historical Essays*, ed. Ronald Story (Westfield: Institute for Massachusetts Studies, 1991), 16–36.

5. Kip Farrington Jr., *Skates, Sticks, and Men: The Story of Amateur Hockey in the United States* (New York: David McKay, 1972), 64; J. A. Tuthill, *Spalding Ice Hockey and Ice Polo Guide, 1898* (New York: American Sports Publishing, 1897), 75. The game varied from five to seven players.

6. *Boston Herald*, December 15, 1894; January 5, 1895; January 8, 9, 15, and 17, 1896; December 23, 1897; Alfred Winsor, "Hockey," in *The H Book of Harvard Athletics*, ed. John A. Blanchard (Cambridge, Mass.: Harvard Varsity Club, 1923), 555; Nathaniel Hasenfus, *Athletics at Boston College: Football and Hockey*, vol. 1 (Worcester, Mass.: Heffernan, 1943), 282; Fred Hoey, "Hockey through the Years," *Boston Garden Sports News* 18, no. 5 (winter 1945–46), 4 (hereafter cited as Hoey I). For more on the rise of school sports, including hockey, see Stephen Hardy, "Performance, Memory, and History: The Making of American Ice Hockey at St. Paul's School, 1860–1915," *International Journal of History of Sport* 14 (April 1997), 97–115; idem, *How Boston Played: Sport Recreation and Community* (Knoxville: University of Tennessee Press, 2003), chap. 6.

7. *Boston Herald*, January 6, 1898; Tuthill, *Spalding Ice Hockey and Ice Polo Guide*, 33, 35.

8. *Boston Herald*, January 20, 1908; Tuthill, *Spalding Ice Hockey and Ice Polo Guide,* 9–13; Hoey I, 4.

9. *Boston Herald*, January 6, 1896; Jas. A. T. Bird, *The Diagram: Containing Plans of Theaters and Other Places of Amusement in Boston* (Boston: Harper, 1869), 37; *Clipper*, February 19, 1870, 363. My thanks to Paul DeLoca for the last two references.

10. Winsor, "Hockey," 555–556; Kate S. Bingham, "Boston's Outdoor Winter Sports," *New England Magazine* 53 (February 1911), 600–606; *Boston Sunday Herald,* February 10, 1907.

11. "The Story of the Boston Arena" (n.p., n.d), 5, 7; Henry R. Ilsley, "Boston's New Ice Rink Will Boom Skating," *Baseball*, January 1910, 33–35. I thank Jack Grinold of Northeastern for copies of the above; Fred Hoey, "Fans Hope Arena Will be Rebuilt," *Boston Herald*, December 19, 1918.

12. Edwin Teale, "Science Turns Ice Hockey into Big Business," *Popular Science Monthly*, February 1935, 109; "The Story of the Boston Arena," 7, 9, 11, 13; Ilsley, "Boston's New Ice Rink Will Boom Skating." Funk personal data in e-mail correspondence from Jeffrey Mifflin, assistant archivist, MIT, February 11, 2003.

13. Fred Hoey, "Hockey through the Years," *Boston Garden Sports News* 18, no. 6 (1945–46), 1 (hereafter cited as Hoey II); *Boston Post*, December 6, 7, 9, and 16, 1910.

14. Hoey II, 5.

15. On the rise of product branding, see Susan Strasser, *Satisfaction Guaranteed: The Making of the American Mass Market* (New York: Pantheon, 1989). For more on sports branding, see Bernard Mullin, Stephen Hardy, and William Sutton, *Sport Marketing*, 2d ed. (Champaign, Ill.: Human Kinetics, 2000), 136–137. For the seminal work on hockey branding, see Bruce Kidd, *The Struggle for Canadian Sport* (Toronto: University of Toronto Press, 1994), 184–231, 254–261.

16. *Boston Post*, December 30, 1910; cartoon on Hockey Fever, ibid., December 31, 1910; Hoey II, 5.

17. *Boston Herald*, March 20, 22, and 23, 1911; *Boston Post*, March 19, 25, and 26, 1911; Hoey II, 2.

18. For early football, see Ronald Smith, ed., *Big-Time Football at Harvard, 1905: The Diary of Coach Bill Reid* (Urbana: University of Illinois Press, 1994); idem, *Sports and Freedom: The Rise of Big-Time College Athletics* (New York: Oxford University Press, 1988); Michael Oriard, *Reading Football: How the Popular Press Created an American Spectacle* (Chapel Hill: University of North Carolina Press, 1993).

19. "All Stars," *Boston Herald*, February 26, 1912; Hoey I, 5–6; a young Baker in *Boston Herald*, February 12, 1908.

20. Frazier's column in *Boston Herald*, March 9, 1962; Hoey in *Boston Journal*, February 5, 1913; *Boston Herald* on Baker, February 26, 1912, and December 27, 1918. See also John Davies, *The Legend of Hobey Baker* (Boston: Little, Brown, 1966); Ron Fimrite, "A Flame That Burned Too Brightly," *Sports Illustrated*, March 18, 1991, 70–90.

21. Winsor, "Hockey," 566.

22. *Boston Herald*, January 25, 1914, and April 2, 1916; *New York Times*, February 15 and 22, 1914; Harvard records in Blanchard, *H Book*, 588–589.

23. *Boston Post*, March 4, 1911; *Boston Herald*, December 16, 1911; Winsor, "Hockey," 565; *Boston Herald*, December 22, 1911.

24. *Boston Herald*, December 10, 1911, and February 27 and March 2, 1912; *Boston Traveler*, January 18 and 19, 1912; Hoey II, 6.

25. *Boston Herald*, March 23, 1917. For early women's hockey, see Joanna Avery and Julie Stevens, *Too Many Men on the Ice: Women's Hockey in North America* (Victoria, B.C.: Polestar, 1997), 83–85; Gai Berlage, "The Development of Intercollegiate Women's Ice Hockey in the United States," *Colby Quarterly* 32 (March 1996), 58–71.

26. "Hockey and Ice Polo Guide"; Winsor, "Hockey," 562–563; *Boston Herald*, December 20, 1918.

27. *Boston Herald*, December 15 and 18, 1918.

28. *Boston Herald*, December 19 and 29, 1918.

29. Hoey II, 21; Victor O. Jones, "George V. Brown's Chair Is Vacant," *Boston Garden-Arena Sports News*, 1937–38 (Boston, 1937), 8; Lapham obituary in *New York Times*, December 17, 1939, 49; *The Country Club: Constitution, By-Laws, and List of Members* (Boston: J. L. Fairbanks, 1929), 72.

30. Interviews with Thomas Brown, son of George V. Brown, July 14 and September 29, 2002. On the BAA, see Hardy, *How Boston Played*, 134. For the amateur movement, see David Young, "How the Amateurs Won the Olympics," in *The Archeology of the Olympics*, ed. Wendy Raschke (Madison, Wisc., 1988); Ted Vincent, *Mudville's Revenge: The Rise and Fall of American Sport* (New York, 1981); Steven Pope, *Patriotic Games: Sporting Traditions in the American Imagination* (New York: Oxford, 1997). For a look at three other members of this new professional class, see my "Entrepreneurs, Structures, and the Sportgeist: Old Tensions in a Modern Industry," in *Essays on Sport History and Sport Mythology*, ed. Donald Kyle and Gary Stark (College Station: Texas A&M Press, 1990), 45–82.

31. Tom Burke, typescript outline of Brown family history in Charles Holt Archives of American Hockey, Dimond Library, University of New Hampshire; Brown obituary, *New York Times*, October 19, 1937; arena announcements in *Boston Herald*, June 8, 1920, and January 2, 1921.

32. *Boston Globe*, January 1 and 2, 1921; *Boston Sunday Herald*, January 2 and 9, 1921.

33. *Boston Herald*, January 2, 1925. On work and consumption in the 1920s, see Lynn Dumenil, *The Modern Temper: American Culture and Society in the 1920s* (New York: Hill and Wang, 1995), 77.

34. *Boston Herald*, December 4, 1924.

35. *Official Arena Program*, 1923–24 (n.p., n.d.); my thanks to Jack Grinold for this source. Newton noted in *Boston Traveler*, January 23, 1924; *Official Ice Hockey Guide*, 1924 (New York: American Sports Publishing, 1924), 78.

36. *Boston Evening Globe*, February 13, 1929.

37. Hasenfus, *Athletics at Boston College*, 1: 304; BU information obtained in correspondence from hockey historian Sean Pickett.

38. *Boston Herald*, March 8, 1923; Richard Johnson, *A Century of Boston Sports* (Boston: Northeastern University Press, 2000), 48–50; James Hutchinson and John Chase, "Hockey," in *The Second H Book of Harvard Athletics*, ed. Geoffrey Movius (Cambridge, Mass.: Harvard Varsity Club, 1964), 268–270; Brown and USAHA in *Hockey Guide*, 1924, 77.

39. Eric Zweig, "Pittsburgh Pirates," in *Total Hockey*, 238; Mullins in *Boston Herald*, March 31, 1924; Bob Dunbar in ibid., January 19, 1925.

40. *Boston Herald*, April 7, 1924; January 5, 18, and 22, 1925.

41. Stanley Woodward had worked as a publicist for the Arena; interview with Thomas Brown, July 14, 2002; *Boston Herald*, February 14, March 7, and December 7, 1924; January 22, 1925; *Official Arena program*, 1923–24.

42. *Boston Traveler*, January 7 and 22, 1924; *Boston Globe*, February 1, 1924; Fred Hoey, "Ice Hockey in New England," in *Official Ice Hockey Guide*, 1924, 17.

43. On pro franchise speculation, see *Boston Herald*, December 19, 1911; *New York Times*, January 27, 1912. On the politics and expansion of the NHL at this time, see John Wong, "The Development of Professional Hockey and the Making of the National Hockey League" (Ph.D. diss., University of Maryland, 2001); Kidd, *Struggle for Canadian Sport*, 184–231; Morey Holtzman and Joseph Nieforth, *How the NHL Conquered Hockey* (Toronto: Dundurn Group, 2002).

44. Adams obituary in *New York Times*, October 3, 1947.

45. The Duggan-Adams partnership was later contended in court. See *Boston Globe*, March 6, 7, and 9, 1929. Duggan's role is overlooked in most histories such as Clark Booth, *Boston Bruins: Celebrating 75 Years* (Del Mar, Calif.: Tehabi Books, 1998), 51–52; Brian McFarlane, *The Bruins* (Toronto: Stoddart, 1999), 3–4; Aidan O'Hara, "Common Ice: The Culture of Hockey in Greater Boston," in *Total Hockey*, 30–31. For Adams's maneuvers, see *Boston Herald*, February 11, March 26, April 6, April 8, April 29, and November 15, 1924; Wong, "Development of Professional Hockey," 228.

46. *Boston Herald*, November 15, 27, and 28, 1924.

47. *Boston Herald*, December 2, 1924; Charles Coleman, *The Trail of the Stanley Cup*, 2 vols. (Sherbrooke, Quebec: National Hockey League, 1964, 1969), 1: 465–472; Fred Hoey, "Hockey through the Years," *Boston Garden Sports News* 18, no. 7 (1945–46), 7 (hereafter cited as Hoey III).

48. Jones, "George V. Brown's Chair," 23; Hoey III, 9; Coleman, *Trail of the Stanley Cup*, 1: 494; radio columns, *Boston Herald*, January 12, 1926. On NIIL radio broadcasts in Canada, see Kidd, *Struggle for Canadian Sport*, 254–261.

49. *Boston Herald*, November 17, 1926; Coleman, *Trail of the Stanley Cup*, 2: 11–12, 26; Bruins souvenir program, 1926–27, 2, 13, Sports Museum of New England Archives, Boston.

50. *Boston Globe*, November 7, 1927; *New York Times*, November 6, 1926; *Chicago Daily News*, April 17, 1926.

51. *Boston Globe*, November 29, 1927.

52. "B&M Opens First Unit of New Passenger Station at Boston," *Railway Age*, August 25, 1928, 337–341; W. E. Belcher, "Old North Station at Boston Replaced by a Modern Structure Including a Coliseum," *Engineering News Record*, February 28, 1929, 339–344; *Boston Globe*, November 18, 1928; *Boston Herald*, November 21, 1928.

53. For tickets see *Boston Evening Globe*, January 19, 1929.

54. *Boston Post*, January 8, 1929; *Boston Daily Globe*, January 9, 1929; *Boston Evening Globe*, January 9, 1929; Johnson, *Century of Boston Sports*, 50.

55. Charles H. Trout, *Boston, the Great Depression, and the New Deal* (New York: Oxford University Press, 1977), 26.

56. On Sunday sports, see *Boston Globe*, January 22, 1929.

57. Jack and Bill Riley, Bill Cleary Jr., and Bob Cleary are in the U.S. Hockey Hall of Fame, Evelyth, Minn. See their biographies at http://www.ushockeyhall.com/inductees.htm. For Bill Cleary Sr., see *Boston Evening Globe*, January 30, 1929; *Boston Daily Globe*, February 23, 1929.

58. Boston Tigers in *Boston Daily Globe*, March 9, 1929. By 1934 Lapham and his Arena investor had taken over control of the Garden. See Jones, "George V. Brown's Chair," 7–8, 23–24; interview with Thomas Brown (son of George V. Brown), July 14, 2002, Charles Holt Archives of American Hockey, Dimond Library, University of New Hampshire; "Boston Garden, Arena Merged," undated news clipping, Brown Family file, Holt Archives; Victor O. Jones, "Young Lapham-Brown Combination Carries On," *Garden-Arena Sport News* 12 (1939–40), 3, 28.

59. Michael Hollerin, *Boston's "Changeful Times": Origins of Preservation and Planning in America* (Baltimore: Johns Hopkins University Press, 1998), 8. For

more on the role of place in sports, see John Bale, *Sport, Space, and the City* (London: Routledge, 1993); idem, *Landscapes of Modern Sport* (New York: Leicester University Press, 1994); Bruce Kuklick, *To Everything a Season: Shibe Park and Urban Philadelphia, 1909–1976* (Princeton: Princeton University Press, 1991).

60. James Ullyot, "Basketball," in Movius, *Second H Book of Harvard Athletics*, 196. For a valuable argument about finite space on the "sports calendar," see Markovits and Hellerman, *Offside*.

61. Hockey fights in "Thrills and Spills in the Hockey Rink," *Literary Digest*, January 12, 1929, 56. For contemporary thoughts on the science of hockey, see "Thrills That Rock the Hockey Fan Benches," ibid., February 25, 1928, 52–56; Dumenil, *Modern Temper*, 58–59. For similar interpretations of sports and popular culture in the 1920s, see John W. Ward, "The Meaning of Lindbergh's Flight," in *Studies in American Culture*, ed. Joseph Kwait and Mary Turpie (Minneapolis: University of Minnesota Press, 1960); Elliott Gorn, "The Manassa Mauler and the Fighting Marine: An Interpretation of the Dempsey-Tunney Fights," *Journal of American Studies* 19 (1985), 27–47; Ben Rader, *American Sports* (Englewood Cliffs, N.J.: Prentice-Hall, 1990), 131–150; Jeffrey Sammons, *Beyond the Ring: The Role of Boxing in American Society* (Urbana: University of Illinois Press, 1988), 235.

62. Lewis Erenberg, *Steppin' Out: New York Nightlife and the Transformation of American Culture, 1890–1930* (Chicago: University of Chicago Press, 1981), xiii; Mack cartoon in *Boston Globe*, March 21, 1929. On the importance of interactivity to popular culture, see Michael Kammen, *American Culture, American Tastes: Social Change and the Twentieth Century* (New York: Knopf, 1999). Fan taunts in *Daily Globe*, March 6, 1929.

63. Woodward quoted in "Bruins and Senators," *Boston Herald*, April 12, 1927. My view of hockey's popularity has benefited from Mel Adelman's theory of early baseball in *A Sporting Time*, 114–116.

13. Number 4 Is the One

1. Herbert Warren Wind, "Orr Country," *New Yorker*, March 27, 1971, 107.

2. John R. McDermott, "The Goalie Is the Goat," *Life*, March 4, 1966, 33.

3. Frank Deford, "A High Price for Fresh Northern Ice," *Sports Illustrated*, October 17, 1966, 62; Wind, "Orr Country," 107.

4. Deford, "A High Price for Fresh Northern Ice," 61; Bobby Orr with Mark Mulvoy, *Bobby Orr: My Game* (Boston: Little, Brown, 1974), 13.

5. Orr, *Bobby Orr*, 13–19.

6. Ibid., 16–21.

7. Ibid., 24.

8. Tom Dowling, "The Orr Effect," *Atlantic Monthly*, April 1971, 64; Orr, *Bobby Orr*, 24–28, covers the courting and signing period.

9. "Boston's Orr: Fire on Ice," *Newsweek*, March 24, 1969, 64.

10. Ibid., 63; Downing, "The Orr Effect," 63.

11. Deford, "A High Price for Fresh Northern Ice," 61.

12. On Orr's contract negotiations see Orr, *Bobby Orr*, 31–33; Russ Conway, *Game Misconduct: Alan Eagleson and the Corruption of Hockey* (Toronto: Macfarlane Walter and Ross, 1997), 136; and "Bobby's Boston," *Newsweek*, November 21, 1966, 77. As is often the case, there is not complete agreement in the various accounts of the exact amounts.

13. George Plimpton, *Open Net* (Guilford, Conn.: Lyons Press, 2003), 196.

14. Orr, *Bobby Orr*, 43–44.

15. Ibid., 44; Jack Olsen, "Sportsman of the Year: Bobby Orr," *Sports Illustrated*, December 21, 1970, 39.

16. Stan Fischler et al., *Hockey Chronicle: Year-by-Year History of the National Hockey League* (Lincolnwood, Ill.: Publications International, 2002), 292.

17. Mark Mulvoy, "Bobby Skates and Orr Claim for Everyone," *Sports Illustrated*, September 2, 1968, 41.

18. Phil Esposito and Peter Golenbock, *Thunder and Lightning: A No-B.S. Hockey Memoir* (Chicago: Triumph Books, 2003), 70.

19. Ibid., 71.

20. "Boston's Orr: Fire on Ice," *Newsweek*, March 24, 1969, 64–67.

21. Mark Mulvoy, "It's Bobby Orr and The Animals," *Sports Illustrated*, February 3, 1969, 18.

22. Ibid.

23. Gary Ronberg, "Tea Party for Bobby's Bruins," *Sports Illustrated*, May 4, 1970, 21.

24. Ibid., 18, 21.

25. Ibid., 21.

26. Leo Monahan, "Got Those St. Louis Blues," *Sports Illustrated*, May 18, 1970, 59; "The Phenomenal Mr. Orr," *Newsweek*, May 18, 1970, 94.

27. Wind, "Orr Country," 112.

28. Orr, *Bobby Orr*, 44.

29. Olsen, "Sportsman of the Year," 36–42; "The Phenomenal Mr. Orr," 94.

30. Olsen, "Sportsman of the Year," 40; Conway, *Game Misconduct*, 129–131.

31. Olsen, "Sportsman of the Year," 42.

32. Ibid., 36.

33. Conway, *Game Misconduct*, 129–150.

34. Plimpton, *Open Net*, 67.
35. Ibid.

14. The Battle of the Beards

1. *Boston Globe*, April 5, 1965.
2. Wilt Chamberlain and David Shaw, *Wilt: Just like Any Other 7-Foot Black Millionaire Who Lives Next Door* (New York: Macmillan, 1973), 20–40.
3. Ibid., 41–48.
4. Nelson George, *Elevating the Game: The History and Aesthetics of Black Men in Basketball* (New York: Simon and Schuster, 1992), 95–102.
5. Ibid., 97, 100–101.
6. Bob Cousy with Ed Linn, *The Last Loud Roar* (Englewood Cliffs, N.J.: Prentice-Hall, 1964), 49–50.
7. *Boston Globe*, April 6, 1965.
8. *Philadelphia Inquirer* and *Boston Globe*, April 7, 1965.
9. *Boston Globe*, April 7, 1965.
10. Bill Russell as told to William McSweeny, *Go Up for Glory* (New York: Coward-McCann, 1966), 7.
11. Ibid., 9–15.
12. Ibid., 19–21.
13. Ibid., 21–23.
14. Chet Walker with Chris Messenger, *Long Time Coming: A Black Athlete's Coming-of-Age in America* (New York: Grove, 1995), 64.
15. Ibid., 77–83.
16. Charles Rosen, *The Wizard of Odds: How Jack Molinas Almost Destroyed the Game of Basketball* (New York: Seven Stories, 2001), 210–214.
17. Walker, *Long Time Coming*, 86–97.
18. Ibid., 163.
19. *Boston Globe*, April 9 and 8, 1965.
20. Wilt Chamberlain with Bob Ottum, "My Life in a Bush League," *Sports Illustrated*, April 12, 1965, 32–43; April 19, 1965, 39–41, 116–118.
21. *Philadelphia Inquirer* and *Boston Globe*, April 9, 1965.
22. *Boston Globe*, April 9, 1965.
23. Chamberlain, "My Life in a Bush League," 32.
24. Chamberlain and Shaw, *Wilt*, 67–68.
25. *Boston Globe* and *Philadelphia Inquirer*, April 10, 1965.
26. *Philadelphia Inquirer*, April 12, 1965.
27. *Boston Globe*, April 12, 1965.

28. *Boston Globe* and *Philadelphia Inquirer,* April 13, 1965.
29. Bill Russell and Taylor Branch, *Second Wind: The Memoirs of an Opinionated Man* (New York: Random House, 1979), 123–124.
30. Ibid., 126.
31. Edward Linn, "I Owe the Public Nothing," *Saturday Evening Post,* January 18, 1964, 62.
32. *Philadelphia Inquirer* and *Boston Globe,* April 14, 1965.
33. *Boston Globe,* April 15, 1965.
34. *Philadelphia Inquirer* and *Boston Globe,* April 16, 1965.
35. *Bill Russell: My Life, My Way,* HBO Studio HSP Productions.
36. Russell, *Go Up for Glory,* 114–117; *Boston Globe,* April 19, 1965.
37. Walker, *Long Time Coming,* 164–165.
38. Russell, *Go Up for Glory,* 116; Leigh Montville, "Green Ghosts," *Sports Illustrated,* April 17, 1995, 62.

15. Beantown, 1986

1. *The 2003 ESPN Information Please Sports Almanac* (New York: Hyperion, 2003); Dan Riley, ed., *The Red Sox Reader* (Boston: Houghton Mifflin, 1991), 273–279, 283–286; Maury Allen, *You Could Look It Up: The Life of Casey Stengel* (New York: Times Books, 1979); Robert W. Creamer, *Stengel: His Life and Times* (New York: Simon and Schuster, 1984).
2. The overall (1901–2003) record of the Red Sox is 8,155 wins and 7,753 losses. The Celtics' record (1947–2002) is 2,612 wins and 1,735 losses. The Bruins' record (1925–2002) is 2,847 wins, 1,947 losses, and 755 ties. The Patriots' record (1960–2002) is 310 wins, 345 losses, and 9 ties. See www.boston.redsox.mlb.com; www.nba.com/celtics; www.bostonbruins.com; and www.patriots.com. See also *2003 ESPN Information Please Sports Almanac; The Baseball Encyclopedia: The Complete and Definitive Record of Major League Baseball,* 10th ed. (New York: Macmillan, 1996); Jan Hubbard, ed., *The Official NBA Encyclopedia,* 3d ed. (New York: Doubleday, 2000); Dan Diamond, ed., *Total Hockey: The Official Encyclopedia of the National Hockey League* (New York: Total Sports, 2001); and Bob Carroll and David S. Neff, eds., *Total Football II: The Official Encyclopedia of the National Football League* (New York: Harperinformation, 1999).
3. *The 2003 World Almanac and Book of Facts* (New York: World Almanac Books, 2003), 402–403. On the connection between sports and local/regional/national/ group identity and pride, see Jay Coakley, *Sport in Society: Issues and Controversies,* 7th ed. (New York: McGraw-Hill, 2001), 389–390; Randy Roberts and James Olson, *Winning Is the Only Thing: Sports in America since 1945* (Balti-

more: Johns Hopkins University Press, 1989), 214–217; and Joseph A. Maguire, *Global Sport: Identities, Societies, Civilizations* (Cambridge: Polity, 1999).

4. On the origins and evolution of New England's distinctive culture, see David Hackett Fischer, *Albion's Seed: Four British Folkways in America* (New York: Oxford University Press, 1989), 3–205, 783–898; Joel Garreau, *The Nine Nations of North America* (Boston: Houghton Mifflin, 1981), 14–48; Raymond D. Gastil, *Cultural Regions of the United States* (Seattle: University of Washington Press, 1975), 138–156; James Truslow Adams, *The History of New England*, 3 vols. (Boston: Little, Brown, 1927); Charles F. Haywood, *Minutemen and Mariners: True Tales of New England* (New York: Dodd, Mead, 1967); Edwin Valentine Mitchell, *Yankee Folk* (New York: Vanguard, 1948); Christina Tree, *How New England Happened: A History and Guide to New England's Cultural Landscape* (Woodstock: Countryman, 2001); and Charles M. Webster, *Town Meeting Country* (Westport, Conn.: Greenwood, 1970). On Boston's historic primacy in New England, see Caleb H. Snow, *A History of Boston* (Boston: A. Bowen, 1825); Isaac Smith Homans, *History of Boston, from 1630 to 1856* (Boston: F. C. Moore, 1856); Edward Everett Hale, *A History of Boston and Its Neighborhood* (New York: D. Appleton, 1898); and Mark Antony DeWolfe Howe, *Boston: The Place and the People* (New York: Macmillan, 1924); Herbert Warren Wind, "Bird and Boston," *New Yorker*, March 24, 1986, 44, 67; Bob Ryan, *The Four Seasons* (Indianapolis: Masters, 1997).

5. Dan Shaughnessy, *The Curse of the Bambino* (New York: Dutton, 1990). See also the HBO documentary film *The Curse of the Bambino* (New York: HBO Films, 2003); the website www.bambinocurse.com; the essays in Riley, *The Red Sox Reader*; and the interviews in Rick Wolff with Rhonda Sonnenberg, ed., *For Red Sox Fans Only!* (n.p.: Lone Wolf, 2003). The team's crushing seventh-game collapse in the 2003 American League Championship series inspired a new round of commentary on the curse and the dark side of Red Sox history. See especially Mark Shields, "Puritans' Aversion to Pleasure Carried On by Their Descendants, Red Sox Fans," *St. Petersburg Times*, October 18, 2003; and *Boston Globe*, October 16–19, 2003.

6. In the seventeen years since 1986, the Celtics have had eight losing seasons and have made it to the NBA finals only once, in 1987. See www.nba.com/celtics/history; and Hubbard, *Official NBA Encyclopedia*.

7. Beau Riffenburgh, ed., *The Official NFL Encyclopedia* (New York: New American Library, 1986), 140–142; Lois Therrien, "Losses, Lawsuits, and Michael Jackson Have the Patriots Punting," *Business Week*, November 18, 1985, 96. See also Larry Fox, *The New England Patriots* (New York: Atheneum, 1979); George McGuane, *The New England Patriots* (Virginia Beach, Va.: JCP, 1980); Joe Fitz-

gerald, *New England's Patriots: Minutemen of the Gridiron* (Englewood Cliffs, N.J.: Prentice-Hall, 1974); Alan Ives, *New England Patriots Trivia* (Boston: Quinlan, 1988); Julie Nelson, *New England Patriots* (Mankato, Minn.: Creative Education, 2001); and www.patriots.com/history.

8. Riffenburgh, *Official NFL Encyclopedia*, 137, 142; *Boston Globe*, October 21–December 18, 1985. Meyer, a successful coach at Southern Methodist University in Dallas, replaced New England's head coach Ron Erhart after the 1981 season. In his two and a half seasons with the Patriots, Meyer compiled a record of 18 wins and 16 losses. On Berry, who played from 1955 to 1967, and who was inducted into the Hall of Fame in 1973, see Riffenburgh, *Official NFL Encyclopedia*, 412; *Baltimore Sun*, July 27 and 28, 1973; *Boston Globe*, October 26 and 27, 1984; and Tom Callahan, "A Sudden Flash of Patriotism," *Time*, January 27, 1986, 50.

9. *Boston Globe*, August 15–September 10, October 14–December 1, 1985; Ralph Wiley, "Cool Head, Hot Hand for the Pats," *Sports Illustrated*, November 18, 1985, 60–61 (quotation); E. M. Swift, "He's a One-Man James Gang," *Sports Illustrated*, January 27, 1986, 50–52.

10. Paul Zimmerman, "A Tower of Power," *Sports Illustrated*, December 2, 1985, 22–26.

11. *Boston Globe*, December 2–24, 1985; Riffenburgh, *Official NFL Encyclopedia*, 142.

12. *Boston Globe*, December 26–29, 1985; *New York Times* and *New York Post*, December 27–29, 1985; Paul Zimmerman, "Up and Over, Down and Out," *Sports Illustrated*, January 6, 1986, 10–17; Callahan, "A Sudden Flash of Patriotism."

13. Zimmerman, "Up and Over, Down and Out," 12–14, 15 (quotations), 16–17.

14. Ralph Wiley, "A Corker at the Coliseum," *Sports Illustrated*, January 13, 1986, 12–16 (quotations); Callahan, "A Sudden Flash of Patriotism"; *Boston Globe* and *Los Angeles Times*, January 2–6, 1986; Riffenburgh, *Official NFL Encyclopedia*, 128–129, 340. On Al Davis and the Raiders, see Glenn Dickey, *Just Win, Baby: Al Davis and His Raiders* (New York: Harcourt Brace Jovanovich, 1991); Mark Ribowsky, *Slick: The Silver and Black Life of Al Davis* (New York: Macmillan, 1991); and Ira Simmons, *Black Knight: Al Davis and His Raiders* (Rocklin, Calif.: Prima, 1990).

15. Paul Zimmerman, "A Wild Ride for the Wild Cards," *Sports Illustrated*, January 20, 1986, 20–24, 29–31; Callahan, "A Sudden Flash of Patriotism"; *Boston Globe*, January 13, 1986; Riffenburgh, *Official NFL Encyclopedia*, 312; Wiley, "A Corker at the Coliseum," 16 (quotation). On Marino and the Dolphins, see John Holmstrom, *Dan Marino, Joe Montana* (New York: Avon, 1985); Dan Marino with Steve Delsohn, *Marino* (Chicago: Contemporary Books, 1986); Dan Marino, *Marino: On the Record* (San Francisco: Collins, 1996); Barry Wilner, *Dan*

Marino (New York: Chelsea House, 1996); and *Dan Marino: The Making of a Legend* (Dallas: Beckett, 1999).

16. Steve Axthelm, "It's the Bears–In a Crunch," *Newsweek*, January 27, 1986, 54–55; Paul Zimmerman, "Up Against It," *Sports Illustrated*, January 27, 1986, 26–28, 33–37; Swift, "He's a One-Man James Gang"; Callahan, "A Sudden Flash of Patriotism"; idem, "'Sweetness' and Might," *Time*, January 27, 1986, 46–49; Riffenburgh, *Official NFL Encyclopedia*, 94–98, 312. On the Bears mystique, see Scott Simon, *Home and Away: Memoir of a Fan* (New York: Hyperion, 2000); Richard Whittingham, *Bears in Their Own Words* (Chicago: Contemporary Books, 1991); and idem, *The Chicago Bears, From George Halas to Super Bowl XX: An Illustrated History* (New York: Simon and Schuster, 1986). On Payton, see Walter Payton with Jerry B. Jenkins, *Sweetness* (Chicago: Contemporary Books, 1978); and Walter Payton with Don Yaeger, *Never Die Easy: The Autobiography of Walter Payton* (New York: Villard, 2000). On Ditka, see Mike Ditka with Don Pierson, *Ditka: An Autobiography* (Chicago: Bonus Books, 1986); and Armen Keteyian, *DITKA: Monster of the Midway* (New York: Pocket Books, 1992).

17. Zimmerman, "Up Against It"; Callahan, "A Sudden Flash of Patriotism"; Axthelm, "It's the Bears–In a Crunch"; *Boston Globe*, January 24–26, 1986; *New York Times*, January 25 and 26, 1986; *Chicago Tribune*, January 24–26, 1986; *St. Petersburg Times*, January 24–27, 1986. A survey compiled from wire reports and printed in the *St. Petersburg Times* on January 25 revealed that thirty-three of forty-eight sports editors around the nation picked the Bears to win. Five — Bernie Lincicome of the *Chicago Tribune*, Howard Balzer of *The Sporting News*, Brian Hewitt of the *Chicago Sun-Times*, Joe Gergen of *Newsday*, and Jim Huber of *CNN* — predicted a Bears shutout. Four of the fifteen picking the Patriots were New England–based journalists.

18. Riffenburgh, *Official NFL Encyclopedia*, 283; *Boston Globe* and *St. Petersburg Times*, January 27, 1986; Paul Zimmerman, "A Brilliant Case for the Defense," *Sports Illustrated*, February 3, 1986, 28–36 (quotations on 28, 33, 36); N. O. Unger, "Bears Give Super Shuffle to Boston in 'Thunderdome' Tiff," *Jet*, February 10, 1986, 51–52. See also P. Fichtenbaum and J. Rolfe, "That Was Then, This Is Now," *Sport Magazine* 77 (February 1986), 31–35, for an intriguing comparison of Super Bowl I and Super Bowl XX.

19. *St. Petersburg Times*, January 27, 1986 (first quotation); *Boston Globe* and *Boston Herald*, January 28, 1986; Craig Neff and Robert Sullivan, "The NFL and Drugs: Fumbling for a Game Plan," *Sports Illustrated*, February 10, 1986, 82–89 (second, third, and fourth quotations); Tom Callahan, "After the Game, the News," *Time*, February 10, 1986, 83 (fifth quotation).

20. Neff and Sullivan, "The NFL and Drugs," 84, 89 (quotations); Callahan, "After

the Game, the News"; "Pats' Super Loss Worse after Drug Users Named," *Jet*, February 17, 1986, 46; Douglas S. Looney, "The Pats Are Trying to Patch Things Up," *Sports Illustrated*, July 28, 1986, 28–30.

21. On the Boston Garden, see Richard A. Johnson, *The Boston Garden* (Charleston, S.C.: Arcadia, 2002). On the Bruins, see www.bostonbruins.com; Clark Booth, *The Boston Bruins: Celebrating 75 Years* (Del Mar, Calif.: Tehabi, 1998); Harry Sinden, *The Picture History of the Boston Bruins* (Indianapolis: Bobbs-Merrill, 1976); Stan Fischler, *Bobby Orr and the Big, Bad Bruins* (New York: Dodd, Mead, 1969); Bobby Orr with Mark Mulvoy, *Bobby Orr: My Game* (Boston: Little, Brown, 1974); Al Hirshberg, *Bobby Orr: Fire on Ice* (New York: Putnam, 1975); and Ryan, *The Four Seasons*. Diamond, *Total Hockey*; *1998 ESPN Information Please Almanac* (New York: Hyperion, 1997), 405–406, 411; *Boston Globe*, January 26 and June 1–30, 1986; Wind, "Bird and Boston," 44–46.

22. On the Celtics of the early and mid-1980s, see James A. Peterson and Susan L. Peterson, *The 1984 Celtics: Soar like a Bird* (New York: New American Library, 1984); Bob Schron and Kevin Stevens, *The Bird Era: A History of the Boston Celtics, 1978–1988* (Boston: Quinlan, 1988); and Peter May, *The Last Banner: The Story of the 1985–86 Celtics, the NBA's Greatest Team of All Time* (New York: Simon and Schuster, 1996). On the 1984–85 Lakers, see Alexander Wolff, "The 'Movie Stars' Changed Their Act," *Sports Illustrated*, June 10, 1985, 36–38, 42, 45; idem, "Finally, a Happy Laker Landing," *Sports Illustrated*, June 17, 1985, 22–27; and K. Moore, "Not Just a Pretty Face," *Sports Illustrated*, October 28, 1985, 82–86. *1998 ESPN Information Please Sports Almanac*, 360; Jack McCallum and Bruce Newman, "Journey of Discovery," *Sports Illustrated*, February 3, 1986, 77–79.

23. McCallum and Newman, "Journey of Discovery," 78–90; *Boston Globe*, January 22–23, 1986; Wind, "Bird and Boston," 77–78. On Walton, see ibid., 62, 67; and Bill Walton with Gene Wojciechowski, *Nothing but Net: Just Give Me the Ball and Get Out of the Way* (New York: Hyperion, 1994).

24. On the Celtics Mystique, see Bob Cousy and Bob Ryan, *Cousy on the Celtics Mystique* (New York: McGraw-Hill, 1988); Joe Fitzgerald, *That Championship Feeling: The Story of the Boston Celtics* (New York: Scribner, 1975); Bob Ryan, *The Boston Celtics: The History, Legends, and Images of America's Most Celebrated Team* (Reading, Mass.: Addison-Wesley, 1989); Dan Shaughnessy, *Ever Green: The Boston Celtics* (New York: St. Martin's, 1990); and Tom Callahan, "The Sharing of the Green," *Time*, June 10, 1985, 72. On Auerbach, see Frank Deford, "No. 2 in the Rafters, No. 1 in Their Hearts," *Sports Illustrated*, January 14, 1985, 40–42, 44, 79, 81; Red Auerbach with Joe Fitzgerald, *On and Off the Court* (New York: Macmillan, 1985); and Dan Shaughnessy, *Seeing Red: The Red*

Auerbach Story (New York: Crown 1994); McCallum and Newman, "Journey of Discovery," 81, 88, 90 (quotations); *Boston Globe*, January 10–31, 1986.

25. *Boston Globe*, February 8–10, 1986; Wind, "Bird and Boston," 80, 83 (quotation).

26. *Boston Globe*, February 1–April 1, 1986; Jack McCallum, "Boston Socks It to the Champs," *Sports Illustrated*, February 24, 1986, 16–19; idem, "'As Nearly Perfect as You Can Get,'" *Sports Illustrated*, March 3, 1986, 13–14 (quotations); Wind, "Bird and Boston," 54–60, 61 (quotation), 62, 67–70 (quotation), 71–84; Tom Callahan, "Masters of Their Own Game," *Time*, March 18, 1985, 52–57, 60; Larry Bird with Bob Ryan, *Drive: The Story of My Life* (New York: Doubleday, 1989). See also Cousy and Ryan, *Cousy on the Celtics Mystique*, 163–191.

27. On the racial crisis in Boston in the 1970s, see J. Anthony Lukas, *Common Ground: A Turbulent Decade in the Lives of Three American Families* (New York: Knopf, 1985); Ronald P. Formisano, *Boston against Busing* (Chapel Hill: University of North Carolina Press, 1991); and Susan E. Eaton, *The Other Boston Busing Story: What's Won and Lost across the Boundary Line* (New Haven: Yale University Press, 2001). On race and Boston sports, see Howard Bryant, *Shut Out: A Story of Race and Baseball in Boston* (New York: Routledge, 2002); Bill Russell and William McSweeny, *Go Up for Glory* (New York: Coward-McCann, 1966); Bill Russell and Taylor Branch, *Second Wind: The Memoirs of an Opinionated Man* (New York: Random House, 1979); M. L. Carr, *Don't Be Denied* (Boston: Quinlan, 1987); Nelson George, *Elevating the Game: Black Men and Basketball* (New York: HarperCollins, 1992), 95–102, 105–115, 139–141, 148–155, 207–208; Cousy and Ryan, *Cousy on the Celtics Mystique*, 31–61; Tom Callahan, "Impressions in Black and White," *Time*, December 23, 1985, 60 (quotations); Wind, "Bird and Boston," 60–61; Alexander Wolff, "D. J. Spins a Happy Tune," *Sports Illustrated*, May 26, 1986, 32–38; Tom Callahan, "A 16th Flag in Sight," *Time*, June 9, 1986, 68.

28. Callahan, "Impressions in Black and White" (first quotation); Deford, "No. 2 in the Rafters, No. 1 in Their Hearts," 44 (second quotation); Thad Martin, "K. C. Jones: Continuing the Celtics' Winning Tradition," *Ebony* 40 (April 1985), 59–60, 62, 64; "Coach K. C. Jones Makes Celtics Job Look So Easy," *Jet*, June 23, 1986, 51; Cousy and Ryan, *Cousy on the Celtics Mystique*, 55–56, 64, 67, 85–87; George, *Elevating the Game*, 108, 151–152, 188; Wind, "Bird and Boston," 72. For an intriguing but highly questionable interpretation of the racial and political orientation of the Celtics franchise, see Chuck Klosterman, "If You Root for the Celtics, You Probably Vote Republican," *Gentleman's Quarterly*, December 2002, 220, 222, 225, 227.

29. *Boston Globe*, April 12–May 25, 1986; www.nba.com/celtics/history; Sam Goldaper, "Celtics Thriving on New Balance," *New York Times*, reprinted in *St. Petersburg Times*, April 15, 1986; Alexander Wolff, "The Celtics Await in Their

Victory Garden," *Sports Illustrated,* May 26, 1986, 22–23; Callahan, "A 16th Flag in Sight." On the 1972–73 Celtics, see Fitzgerald, *That Championship Feeling.*

30. Callahan, "A 16th Flag in Sight"; Jack McCallum, "The High and the Mighty," *Sports Illustrated,* June 9, 1986, 14–19; idem, "No Stopping 'Em," *Sports Illustrated,* June 30, 1986, 14 (quotation), 15–17; *1998 ESPN Information Please Sports Almanac,* 372. See also May, *The Last Banner.* On the Rockets, see Jack McCallum, "Towering Dream in Rocket Country," *Sports Illustrated,* February 10, 1986, 80–81.

31. *Boston Globe,* June 17–21, 1986; *New York Times,* June 20, 1986; Lewis Cole, *Never Too Young To Die: The Death of Len Bias* (New York: Pantheon, 1989); C. Fraser Smith, *Lenny, Lefty, and the Chancellor: The Len Bias Tragedy and the Search for Reform in Big Time College Basketball* (Baltimore: Bancroft, 1992).

32. The best sources for Red Sox statistics are www.boston.redsox.mlb.com; and *2003 Boston Red Sox Media Guide* (Boston: Red Sox Publications and Archives Department, 2003). On the history of the Red Sox, see Glenn Stout and Richard A. Johnson, *Red Sox Century: One Hundred Years of Red Sox Baseball* (Boston: Houghton Mifflin, 2000); Peter Golenbock, *Fenway: An Unexpurgated History of the Boston Red Sox* (North Attleborough, Mass.: Covered Bridge, 1997); Henry Berry, *Boston Red Sox* (New York: Collier, 1975); Albert Hirshberg, *The Red Sox, the Bean and the Cod* (Boston: Waverly House, 1947); Fred Lieb, *The Boston Red Sox* (New York: G. P. Putnam's, 1947); Peter Gammons, *Beyond the Sixth Game* (Boston: Houghton Mifflin, 1985); Jack Lautier, *Fenway Voices* (Camden, Maine: Yankee Books, 1990); George V. Higgins, *The Progress of the Seasons: Forty Years of Baseball in Our Town* (New York: Prentice-Hall, 1989); Riley, *The Red Sox Reader;* and *Street and Smith's Official Baseball Yearbook, 1986* (New York: Conde Nast, 1986), 30–39.

33. *St. Petersburg Times,* April 3–May 1 and June 1, 1986; *Boston Globe,* April 8–June 1, 1986; *Street and Smith's Official Baseball Yearbook, 1986,* 142, 159. On Boyd, see Peter Gammons, "A New Yarn for the Sox," *Sports Illustrated,* June 24, 1985, 30–31; idem, "One Woe after Another," *Sports Illustrated,* August 4, 1986, 29–33; and Michael Martinez, "Out of His Era," *New York Times,* October 21, 1986. On Clemens, see Peter Gammons, "Striking Out toward Cooperstown," *Sports Illustrated,* May 12, 1986, 26–29; idem, "Word from the Sox: No Clemensy," *Sports Illustrated,* June 30, 1986, 12–15; and Stout and Johnson, *Red Sox Century,* 398–399.

34. *Boston Globe,* June 1–July 4, 1986; *St. Petersburg Times,* July 4, 1986 (quotation); Peter Gammons, "Poised for Another El Foldo," *Sports Illustrated,* August 4, 1986, 33; idem, "Word from the Sox: No Clemensy," 13–15. On Seaver, see Gene Schoor, *Seaver: A Biography* (Chicago: Contemporary Books, 1986).

35. *Boston Globe,* July 10–August 6, 1986; Gammons, "One Woe after Another," 28–

33; idem, "Poised for Another El Foldo," 33; Golenbock, *Fenway*, 417 (quotation); Alexander Wolff, "Whole Lotta Shakin' Goin' On," *Sports Illustrated*, August 18, 1986, 22–29; Stout and Johnson, *Red Sox Century*, 397, 400.

36. *Boston Globe*, August 7–September 1, 1986; Golenbock, *Fenway*, 414, 416–418. On Baylor, see Craig Neff, "His Honor, Don Baylor," *Sports Illustrated*, June 16, 1986, 58–72. While playing for the Chicago Cubs in 1980, Buckner led the National League with a .324 batting average. He retired in 1990 after twenty-two seasons in the major leagues with a .289 lifetime batting average; *Baseball Encyclopedia*, 838.

37. *Boston Globe*, September 2–October 6, 1986; Peter Gammons, "A Dream Series in the Works?" *Sports Illustrated*, October 6, 1986, 28–35; Tom Callahan, "Four Long-Suffering Souls," *Time*, October 13, 1986, 78–79; *St. Petersburg Times*, September 29, 1986 (quotation).

38. *Boston Globe*, October 7–17, 1986; *New York Times*, October 13–17, 1986; Golenbock, *Fenway*, 418–420; Riley, *Red Sox Reader*, 230–233; Stout and Johnson, *Red Sox Century*, 402–406; Peter Gammons, "Bosox vs. Angels: A Pair of Heart-stoppers," *Sports Illustrated*, October 20, 1986, 22–25.

39. On the 1986 Mets, see Peter Golenbock, *Amazin': The Miraculous History of New York's Most Beloved Baseball Team* (New York: St. Martin's, 2002), 445–495; *Boston Globe* and *New York Times*, October 18–25, 1986; *1998 ESPN Information Please Sports Almanac*, 106–107; Ron Fimrite, "It Went Thataway," *Sports Illustrated*, October 27, 1986, 18–27 (quotation), 28–33.

40. *Boston Globe* and *New York Times*, October 26 and 27, 1986; Stout and Johnson, *Red Sox Century*, 407–412; Wolff, *For Red Sox Fans Only!* 194–204; Golenbock, *Fenway*, 420 (quotation), 421–426; Ron Fimrite, "Good to the Very Last Out," *Sports Illustrated*, November 3, 1986, 21–22; Peter Gammons, "Living and Dying with the Woe Sox," *Sports Illustrated*, November 3, 1986, 22–28, 33; Riley, *Red Sox Reader*, 289. See also Dan Shaughnessy, *One Strike Away: The Story of the 1986 Red Sox* (New York: Beaufort, 1987).

41. *Boston Globe*, *Boston Herald*, and *New York Times*, October 28, 1986; Fimrite, "Good to the Very Last Out," 16–22; Gammons, "Living and Dying with the Woe Sox," 22–23 (quotation); Golenbock, *Fenway*, 423–424 (second and third quotations). Such sentiments resurfaced in the wake of the 2003 American League Championship series, in which the Yankees defeated the Red Sox four games to three. In the seventh and deciding game, the Red Sox held a three-run lead in the eighth inning but ultimately lost in extra innings. See *Boston Globe*, October 8–26, 2003; *New York Times*, October 15–19, 2003.

42. Charles Dickens, *A Tale of Two Cities* (New York: New American Library, 1980), 13. On the endurance of Red Sox fans in particular, see Riley, *Red Sox Reader*, 235, 243–289.

ACKNOWLEDGMENTS

This book has been a labor of love for me, but probably just a plain labor for the many people I have asked for help over the years. I would like to single out a few, perhaps if only to represent the many. I owe each author a profound debt, and thank them all. It has been a joy working with Joyce Seltzer again after a few decades. She distributes her wisdom, humor, and friendship at just the right time and in just the right doses. Joyce's assistant Rachel Weinstein has also been helpful with more problems than I care to remember. Ann Hawthorne, the copy editor, did a wonderful job, and Kate Brick, the production editor, managed the entire book. Watching my daughters Kelly and Alison play sports constantly reminded me that the final score is always less important than the players, and I tried to remember this insight watching Boston's teams. My wife Marjorie has provided the ideal example of priorities in place. I apologize for being a slow learner.

CONTRIBUTORS

Raymond Arsenault is the John Hope Franklin Professor of Southern History and director of the University Honors Program at University of South Florida, St. Petersburg. He is the author of *The Wild Ass of the Ozarks: Jeff Davis and the Social Bases of Southern Politics* (1984), *St. Petersburg and the Florida Dream, 1888–1950* (1988), and the co-editor of *The Changing South of Gene Patterson: Journalism and Civil Rights, 1960–1968* (2002).

James Campbell teaches at Brown University, plays golf internationally, and is the author of *Songs of Zion: The African Methodist Episcopal Church in the United States and South Africa* (1995).

John M. Carroll, a native of Red Sox country, teaches at Lamar University. His books include *Fritz Pollard: Pioneer in Racial Advancement* (1992) and *Red Grange and the Rise of Modern Football* (1999).

John Demos, a native of Cambridge, Massachusetts, is the Samuel Knight Professor of American History at Yale University. Among his books are *A Little Commonwealth: Family Life in Plymouth Colony* (1970), *Entertaining Satan: Witch-*

craft and the Culture of Early New England (1982), and *The Unredeemed Captive: A Family Story from Early America* (1994), which was a National Book Award finalist.

Elliott J. Gorn, professor of history at Brown University, specializes on Americans at work and play. His books include *The Manly Art: Bare-Knuckle Prize Fighting in America* (1986) and *Mother Jones: The Most Dangerous Woman in America* (2001).

Aram Goudsouzian, a native of Boston, teaches history at the University of Memphis and is the author of *Sidney Poitier: Man, Actor, Icon* (2004) and *The Hurricane of 1938* (2004).

Stephen Hardy, a native of Boston and professor at the University of New Hampshire, has written widely on the history of sports, including the book *How Boston Played: Sport, Recreation, and Community, 1865–1915* (1982). He is currently writing a history of hockey.

William E. Leuchtenburg, Professor Emeritus at the University of North Carolina, is the author of many books, including *Franklin D. Roosevelt and the New Deal, 1932–1940* (1963), *The Perils of Prosperity, 1914–1932* (2nd ed., 1993), and *In the Shadow of FDR: From Harry Truman to George W. Bush* (2001). He served as a consultant to Ken Burns for his documentary, *Baseball* (1994).

Matthew Oshinsky and **David M. Oshinsky** are a father-and-son team. David is the George Littlefield Professor of American History at the University of Texas. His books include *A Conspiracy So Immense: The World of Joe McCarthy* (1985) and *Worse than Slavery: Parchman Farm and the Ordeal of Jim Crow Justice* (1997). Matthew, an independent journalist, is a graduate of the New York University School of Journalism.

Randy Roberts, professor of history at Purdue University, writes on sports, film, and war. His books include *Jack Dempsey: The Manassa Mauler* (1979), *Papa Jack: Jack Johnson and the Era of White Hopes* (1983), *"But They Can't Beat Us": Oscar Robertson and the Crispus Attucks Tigers* (1999), and, with James S. Olson, *John Wayne: American* (1995) and *A Line in the Sand: The Alamo in Blood and Memory* (2000).

Ronald A. Smith, Professor Emeritus at Pennsylvania State University, specializes in the history of college sports. Among his books are *Sports and Freedom: The Rise of Big-Time College Athletics* (1988), *Big-Time Football at Harvard, 1905: The Diary of Coach Bill Reid* (1994), and *Play-by-Play: Radio, Television, and Big-Time College Sport* (2001).

Russell Sullivan, a graduate of Yale University and Harvard Law School and a resident of the Boston area, is the Senior Vice President and General Counsel of Linkage, Inc. He is also author of *Rocky Marciano: The Rock of His Times* (2002).

David Welky teaches at the University of Central Arkansas and has written on sports, film, and the Great Depression. He is the co-editor of *The Steelers Reader* (2001) and *Charles A. Lindbergh: The Power and Peril of Celebrity, 1927–1941* (2003).

David W. Zang, a sports historian and director of sport studies at Towson University, is the author of *Fleet Walker's Divided Heart: The Life of Baseball's First Black Major Leaguer* (1995) and *SportsWars: Athletes in the Age of Aquarius* (2001).

INDEX